Gender, Religion, and Migration

Gender, Religion, and Migration

Pathways of Integration

Edited by Glenda Tibe Bonifacio
and Vivienne S. M. Angeles

LEXINGTON BOOKS
A division of
ROWMAN & LITTLEFIELD PUBLISHERS, INC.
Lanham • Boulder • New York • Toronto • Plymouth, UK

Published by Lexington Books
A division of Rowman & Littlefield Publishers, Inc.
A wholly owned subsidiary of The Rowman & Littlefield Publishing Group, Inc.
4501 Forbes Boulevard, Suite 200, Lanham, Maryland 20706
http://www.lexingtonbooks.com

Estover Road, Plymouth PL6 7PY, United Kingdom

British Library Cataloguing in Publication Information Available

Library of Congress Cataloging-in-Publication Data

Gender, religion, and migration : pathways of integration / edited by Glenda Tibe
    Bonifacio and Vivienne S.M. Angeles.
       p. cm.
    Includes bibliographical references and index.
    ISBN 978-0-7391-3313-2 (cloth : alk. paper) -- ISBN 978-0-7391-3315-6 (electronic)
    1. Freedom of religion. 2. Religious tolerance. 3. Religious pluralism. 4. Emigration
and immigration--Religious aspects. 5. Sex role--Religious aspects. I. Bonifacio, Glenda
Tibe, 1963- II. Angeles, Vivienne S. M., 1944-
BL640.G46 2010
200.86'912--dc22   2009032211

Printed in the United States of America

Table of Contents

Latin America

North America

Preface

Ideas travel across boundaries. We were in Melbourne, Australia in October 2007 as part of the workshop panel on Religion and Migration: Pathways of Integration. The panel was organized by Glenda Tibe Bonifacio for the 12th International Metropolis Conference. Inspired by the interest on the topic by scholars, practitioners, and representatives of non-government organizations and different government agencies from many countries, we decided to put together a collection of papers that will represent the diversity and complexity of gender and religion in migration. Gender, religion, and migration represent three of the most controversial topics in modern society. Discourses on gender emanate from the feminist social revolution that has contributed to reducing discriminatory policies affecting women mainly in liberal democratic states. Religion is an essential part of human expression and identity and lies at the crux of how people relate with one another. However, differences in religious beliefs have sparked continued conflicts in many parts of the world. Migration, particularly international migration, has become more visible and rapid in the last century and continues to intensify with the wheels of globalization and civil strife, among others. Because of the breadth and scope in treating these three interrelated topics in one project, we opted to focus on the issue of integration of immigrants and migrants into the host societies as this issue has preoccupied the media, governments, and civic organizations of late. Since migration interweaves with social, political and economic forces, we have engaged scholars from diverse disciplines to examine the notion of integration from their perspectives. In some academic disciplines, like psychology, integration is referred to as an aspect of acculturation. We believe that this is the first attempt of a multi-disciplinary perspective on the intersections of religion, gender, and migration in the integration process that span the regions of Asia-Pacific, Europe, Latin America and North America.

Acknowledgements

We express our profound gratitude to all contributors for sharing their work without which this project would not have come to fruition; for their professionalism and utmost patience throughout a year of incessant queries and never-ending emails; and their resilience as we face many facets of human emotions, from joy of birth to pain of losing a loved one, in the course of completing the book project.

We are equally grateful to Bev Garnett who provided much time and patience in preparing the manuscript. As we share the moments through spring and summer months in Alberta, Bev is a source of comfort, raising our hopes that we can deliver our first "bookchild." The best times are not those spent eyes-hooked to the computer screen but the brief moments of laughter of many personal stories we shared. Bev is a sure gem.

We also acknowledge Gretchen Barnhill for reviewing the chapters; our colleagues for their encouragement; the University of Lethbridge and La Salle University for their continuing support in our research activities; and Dr. Josefa Saniel who continues to cheer us on our academic work from across the miles.

And, more importantly, to the unfailing support and understanding of our families who made everything possible for us. Vivienne wishes to express her sincere appreciation to her husband, Quy Nguyen, and their children, Michael, Robert and Jamie. Glenda warmly extends her zillion thanks to her husband, Ike, and their five daughters, Charmaine, Czarina, Charelle, Czyna and Charithe; as well as Nanay Lourdes for showing her the meaning of spirituality.

Chapter One
Introduction
Glenda Tibe Bonifacio and Vivienne SM. Angeles

Migration and religion are dynamic forces in human lives. Men and women who migrate to nearby communities or travel to distant lands have different motivations and access to resources that would allow them to leave their homelands in search of better opportunities. Their departures are either voluntary or forced as in cases of war, civil strife, and even as a result of environmental degradation. In varying scales the waves of migration within and across nations are but a continuing saga of human existence. Migration, however, does not simply involve the act of moving to another place or being confined to certain moments of sojourn. It is a continuing process that intersects with the ways in which we view the world as shaped by our belief systems and our place in it. Often when immigrants are faced with a hostile environment and myriad challenges of settlement, religion fosters the building of social networks and sense of community belonging (Baumann and Salentin 2006) that in some ways ease the difficulty of adjustment in the host country. Although migration is a fixture of human civilization (Cohen 1995; Manning 2005), and has continuously increased over time, our understanding of the role of religion and faith-based beliefs in the integration of diverse groups of immigrant and migrant men, women and youth in a globalized yet security-braced world seems a bare scratch on the surface of scholarly discourse.

In this collection, we interrogate religion as a pathway of integration based on the gendered migration experiences of peoples across geographic regions: Asia-Pacific, Europe, Latin America and North America. We present multidisciplinary perspectives on the role of religion in the integration process, from Anthropology, Geography, International Studies, Religious Studies, Psychology, Social Work, and Sociology to Theology and Women's Studies. The rich exposition of religion as a social practice in western and non-western societies from different disciplinary frameworks offers a comprehensive presentation on the often missed connection between gender, migration, and integration.

From the moment we are born, our lives have been shaped by social constructs that define the role and behavior of women and men in society. Gender not only shapes identities but also expectations and perceptions on how we interpret meanings within prescribed norms. As an analytic category, gender is

fluidly conceived not only in the context of roles but as "relational and situ-
ational" (Mahler and Pessar 2006: 28) embedded in social structures such as the
family and religion. This volume highlights the intricate relations and tensions
between religion and integration in migration discourse from a gendered perspective. These themes continue to remain peripheral in mainstream discussion
on migration (Chen 2005; Goździak 2008) with gender as a relatively new dimension in analyzing the dynamics of migration (Kofman 1999; Hondagneu-
Sotelo 2000). Studies on migration generally tend to focus on macro level analysis of immigration policies, economic institutions and state systems (Chant
1992; Mahler and Pessar 2006). Pierrette Hondagneu-Sotelo contends that "gender is one of the fundamental social relations anchoring and shaping immigration patterns, and immigration is one of the most powerful forces disrupting and
realigning everyday life" (2003: 3). Traditional roles of women and men may
shift or be reinforced upon migration. Since the 1980s there has been a burgeon-
ing scholarship that includes gender which, according to Nicola Piper, demonstrates that "gender is relevant to most, if not all, aspects of migration" (2008:
1). This recognition is made cogent by the feminization of migration in the second half of the twentieth century as record numbers of women migrate to work
as domestic workers, caregivers, nannies, and nurses, or pursue other service-
related occupations. By 2005, half of the world's migrant population, or about
95 million, are women (Morrison, Schiff and Sjoblom 2008: 2). Not only are
they classified by gender, but most profess a set of beliefs that shape the ways in
which they engage host societies. This is, however, not to preclude the array of
other categories such as race and class in their experiences of migration and settlement.

We argue that the intersection of gender and religion in migration and integration is a compelling area of study in the post 9/11 era. Since the Al-Qaeda
attack on American soil on September 11, 2001 (referred to as 9/11) and the
ensuing war on terror against Muslim extremists launched by the United States
during the term of President George W. Bush, there has been a heightened
awareness of the role of religion in the perceived social integration of immigrants whose religious beliefs differ from that of the majority population in host
societies. For example, the continuous adherence to Islam while living in predominantly Christian countries in Europe and the United States remains controversial and politically volatile in popular discourse after 9/11 (Brown 2002; Appollonia and Reich 2008). Immigrants with different religious orientation than
the rest of society are sometimes viewed as incapable of being socially integrated or worse, a threat to society (Lucassen 2005). Religion is, therefore, seen
as anathema to social integration. But is it?

We echo the position raised by many scholars (Herberg 1960; Handlin
1973; Foley and Hoge 2007; Hirschman 2007) that religion is as an important
aspect in the lives of immigrants then as it is today. Under the aegis of globalization, we examine the intersections of migration, religion, integration, and gender
that are often treated independently from each other. In doing so, we place emphasis on the global flows of people and culture, particularly the impact of relig-

ion in the migration and integration discourse affecting the lives of diverse groups of immigrant population in western and non-western societies. This is, so far, the first collection of works focusing on gender, religion and integration in migration across different geographic areas.

Globalization, Migration and Religion

Globalization has increased migration flows not only to traditional immigrant receiving countries such as Australia, Canada and the United States, but also to many industrialized countries and regional centers around the world. The intersection of globalization, migration and religion has a long history predicated since ancient times by such situations as the spread of Greek culture in the Mediterranean world, the travels of Arab traders who brought Islam to Asia, and the more organized voyages of discoveries launched by Western Europe bringing Christianity to Asia, Africa and South America. Religion, at the time of initial contacts with the Europeans in many indigenous communities, was the "privileged strategy of power" (da Silva 2001: 427) to transform these communities.

Global movements continue through time, and people's motivations to cross international borders have not really changed. In particular, economic globalization, which is indicative of the entrenchment of national economies to the global market system, facilitates international labor migration. The demand for labor among developed countries coupled with increasing poverty in many developing states funnel the desire to seek improved social and economic conditions and fulfillment of other human aspirations. While the economic impetus for migration is still there, the changes, however, come in the form of speed, direction and extent of movement of peoples facilitated by new technology in the twentieth century to what is now referred to as the "age of migration" (Castles and Miller 2009).

Migration is intertwined with globalization which is a multidimensional phenomenon involving diverse domains of activity and interaction, including economic, political, military, legal, cultural and environmental realms (Held 1998:13). Arjun Appadurai (1996) looks at globalization in terms of cultural flows of which religion is part. It is transported, transplanted and recreated or reshaped in another environment but it seems inadequate to merely subsume it under *ethnoscapes*, the "landscapes of persons who constitute the shifting world in which we live" (e.g., immigrants, refugees, exiles, and guest workers), or *ideoscapes*, the ideas, terms and images, including ideologies and counter-ideologies (Appadurai 1996: 33). This needs a clarification of the term religion and its dynamics in globalizing processes like migration.

Religion is a complex concept whose definition has been debated through time. The issues have to do with the applicability or limitation of the definition, especially since religion is not just a matter of believing in a sacred reality and acting on that belief. Mircia Eliade and Clifford Geertz are among those whose explanations of the term religion have dominated the field of religious studies for decades. To Eliade, religion is an "experience *sui generis* incited by man's encounter with the sacred"—an experience in a class by itself (1969: 25). Geertz saw religion as a system of symbols acting to establish powerful, pervasive and long-lasting moods of motivations in men (1973: 90), ignoring women's separate experiences. In the attempt to resolve the definition conundrum, Lawrence Cunningham and John Kelsay proposed a broad definition which states that:

> religion signifies those ways of viewing the world which refer to a notion of sacred reality, made manifest in human experience in such a way to produce long lasting ways of thinking, acting and feeling with respect to problems of ordering and understanding existence (2006: 22).

Cunningham and Kelsay's definition merge the substance and function of religion and, at the same time, hint at the multiple dimensions of religion such as thoughts, feelings, actions, ethics, and social existence discussed further in their work. Although the above samplings of definitions are helpful and useful in understanding religious experiences, Talal Asad reminds us that the symbols Geertz wrote about need to be understood in connection with their historical relations with non-religious symbols or of their articulation in and of social life in which their work and power are crucial (Asad 2006: 129). The above definitions do not seem to suffice when we speak of religion in a global society where transnational migration is an increasing occurrence. What seems to be lacking in these earlier conceptions of religion is the dynamism, the transformative quality of religion—not so much in terms of spiritual transformation of the individual but the way religion is understood, shaped and utilized as transnational migration takes place within the globalization process.

In the more global twenty-first century where religion has become much more varied and highly multifunctional, Asad's position is particularly relevant and necessary. The requirements of the present are contextualized understandings of religion that views how it is manifested, used and acted out in particular situations rather than a universal understanding of religion that zeroes in on human encounter with the sacred or ultimate reality without consideration of the social, historical, political and other contexts in which these responses are manifested. Also worthy of consideration here is the subjective element of globalization, which R. Dean Peterson, Delores Wunder and Harlan Mueller describe as "the social redefinition of identities and worldviews that emerge from the human confrontation and dialogue caused by objective globalization" or the visibly marked aspects such as multinational corporations, international organizations, imports, exports and others (1999: 16). People respond to the globalization process in ways that may not be as quantifiable as the number of imports and exports or the number of migrants crossing transnational borders. Such responses are linked to notions of identity creation and its redefinition and maintenance, and to issues of displacement and emplacement as a migrant settles in the receiving country. Identity is of critical importance since migration affects the way a person views himself or herself, or how he or she relates to others and the world (Richter et al. 2005: 21). Religion forms part of this identity and can come into play as immigrants negotiate their way in the new society and, in turn, in how this society responds.

In this age of heightened transnational migration, an understanding of religion in terms of its relevance and applicability assumes greater significance. Returning now to Appadurai's view of globalization as flows, religion is part of these flows and yet, as noted earlier, cannot be simply lumped with *ideoscapes* or *ethnoscapes*. Religion flows with the people crossing borders and yet, at the same time, it becomes part of the means through which humans cope with the process of migration or transnational journeys that becomes more visible with globalization. Religion needs to be understood within the context of these new realities.

Thomas Tweed concedes to the dynamism of religion and adds *sacroscapes* to Appadurai's five cultural flows (i.e., *ethnoscapes*, *mediascapes*, *technoscapes*, *financescapes*, and *ideoscapes*). Tweed, who studied Cuban religious experiences in Miami, defines religion as "confluences of organic-cultural flows that intensify joy and comfort suffering by drawing on human and suprahuman forces to make homes and cross boundaries" (2006: 54). These confluences merge, interact and create "institutional networks that in turn prescribe, transmit and transform tropes, beliefs, values, emotions artifacts and rituals" (69). Using spatial metaphors of crossing and dwelling, Tweed views religion as about finding a place and moving across space. These spatial and aquatic metaphors suggest movement, interaction, and transformations and recognize the intersections of religion, economy, society and politics. Religions are not viewed in isolation or completely distinct from other aspects of life. In the situation of the migrant, the mere fact of migration is all at once linked to the economy (response to labor demand overseas), politics (migration policies as political instruments), society (as the migrant adjusts to the host countries and establishes social relations) and religion (the migrant draws upon human and suprahuman forces in negotiating with the new social environment). Religions also involve emotions and "intensify joy and comfort suffering" as they provide the "lexicon, rules and expression for many different sorts of emotions, including those framed as most positive and most negative, most cherished and most condemned" (70). Tweed's view of religion as both dwelling and crossing provide us with a theoretical orientation on the intersections of religion, migration, and to which we add gender.

Robert Wuthnow and Conrad Hackett (2003) view religion as a form of social capital which provides opportunities both to cross social boundaries and forge ties with the people, thus enabling linkage with the host society and providing a form of identity for the newcomer. The question is, to what extent does religion help in integrating immigrants in society? Religion can function both negatively and positively. Religion can isolate its adherents from the larger society especially if they are from a minority religion. At the same time, religion fosters social networking among members of the same religious tradition which provides the spaces of engagement with the host society. Since many immigrants are culturally different from the host society, they often face negative public reception and discrimination. As newcomers, immigrants have limited access to resources and may lack the knowledge of existing programs available to them. They are, therefore, put in a situation where they need to rely on their own resources to survive. As observed in many societies, immigrants tend to participate in socio-cultural and religious activities of people with the same ethnicity or background (Hirschman 2007). While this may be beneficial to the well being of the immigrant, these tendencies raise the issue of whether minority religions promote or inhibit their integration into host communities. As immigrants continue to organize their own churches or places of worship, they contribute to the growing religious pluralism of host societies.

Studies on immigration and religion have increased since the 1990s and continue to attract new debates and various approaches (Alba, Raboteau and DeWind 2008; Baumann and Salentin 2006; Guest 2003; Haddad, Smith and Esposito 2003; van der Veer and Vertovec 1991). This book expands on these studies by using religion and gender as variables for immigrant integration. So far, it is safe to say that "little is known on both individual and contextual determinants of immigrants' religion" (van Tubergen 2006: 168) in society.

Religion and Integration in the Twenty-First Century

Central to the issue of immigration is integration, and the question of religion often becomes a salient feature in its public discourse. The entry of immigrants with different cultural practices from host societies, particularly in the West, has intensified concerns on their successful integration. For example, there are about five million Muslims in France alone and Islam is the second largest religious community and the fastest growing religion in Europe (Killian 2006: 3). Social scientists and policy makers have "a deep concern" on how the foreign-born population integrates into society (van Tubergen 2006: 1). Embracing a different religious orientation than the mainstream beliefs of the receiving society is popularly perceived as anathema to integration that further creates social dissonance. Models of integration are currently debated and policymakers and social scientists have yet to agree on which of these really works.

Integration is broadly defined as a general sociological mechanism that describes the way in which all people, immigrants as well as non-immigrants, find their place in society (Lucassen 2005: 18). Integration is often interchanged with *acculturation* and *adaptation* and there is no consensus on what it constitutes (George 2006: 3). Other scholars prefer to use the term *incorporation* (Baumann and Salentin 2006; Hagan 2006; Iosifides et al. 2007; Koenig 2005; Naples 2007) and *social inclusion* in many ways that deal with integration (Colic-Peisker 2005; Omidvar and Richmond 2003; Radtke 2003; Zufiaurre 2006).

Integration is primarily viewed in Europe as the "inclusion of new populations into the existing social structures of the immigration country with a consequent reduction of difference in their positions and relations" comprising four dimensions: structural integration, cultural integration, social integration, and identificational integration (Heckmann 2005: 15). Structural integration refers to the attainment of rights and access to citizenship, education, employment, housing, and other institutions in the host society. Cultural integration connotes a process of change on immigrants' behavior, culture and attitudes in the host society that is also transformed by their participation. Social integration is reflected by change in forging relationships, both private and collective, such as general social involvement, friendship, marriage, and membership in organizations. Identificational integration suggests a sense of belonging and identity toward the nation-state. In essence, integration is, as James Frideres points out, a "process best conceived as multidimensional—social, cultural, political, identity, and economic" (2008: 79). These dimensions of integration, as conventionally understood by receiving states, require newcomers to imbibe certain expected concessions in their personal and public lives. It may seem that integration is a more politically correct term than the much criticized notion of assimilation.

A survey of literature shows that the extent of social integration of immigrants follows the so-called three "integration pathways": "straight-line assimilation," "segmented assimilation," and the "deliberate non-integration pathway" (Haan 2007 cited in Frideres 2008: 82-83). Under the "straight-line" integration pathway, immigrants tend to become more like the rest of the native-born population over time. "Segmented assimilation" suggests that structural impediments in the host society like racism or discrimination results in the immigrants' participation in counter-cultures or use of their social capital to engage in limiting spheres of participation. A "deliberate non-integration pathway" purports to the "voluntary efforts on the part of the ethnic group to remain outside the mainstream society" whose success depends on their institutions, size, and collective social capital as is observed among the Chinese in Canada or the Cubans in Miami (Frideres 2008: 83).

In the twenty-first century, an era of heightened security, complicated by and the global economic meltdown in 2009, religion is a controversial subject in framing integration in immigration. This is largely due to the rise of populist anti-immigration groups and restrictive policies in many industrialized Western countries (Bookman 2002: 185-207). The contributors in this collection offer an alternative discourse of religion as a pathway of integration not from a policy perspective but from the lived experiences of immigrants and practitioners themselves. Most recent studies on immigration and integration hinge on nationalist policy frameworks and other variables such as education, language, and employment and largely deny the facilitative agency and perspective of the religiously-inclined immigrant practitioner (Biles, Burstein and Frideres 2008; Engbersen 2003; Mueller 2006). Frank van Tubergen (2006: 5) argues that immigrant integration should be analyzed at the macro level incorporating the determinants of origin and destination countries as well as the immigrant community to include religious participation rather than the limiting micro level approach of assimilation.

Consistent with the identified dimensions of integration, many governments in the West have instituted policies of integration and, consequently, established different mechanisms to measure the degree and level of immigrants' integration in their respective societies (Biles, Burstein and Frideres 2008; Heckmann and Schnapper 2003; Ireland 2004; Lahav 2004; Messina 2002). In France, for example, the assimilation strategy of integration is implicit in the expectation that immigrants conform to the French republican model of citizenship. The United Kingdom works on equal opportunities, cultural tolerance, and antidiscrimination legislation, to mention a few, in its efforts to integrate ethnic minorities. Canada's program of integration is enshrined in the policy of multiculturalism since 1971 which "'recognizes the potential of all Canadians, encouraging them to integrate into their society and take an active part in its social, cultural, economic and political affairs" (Citizenship and Immigration Canada). By and large, our understanding of these measurements purport to the continuing marginalization of the immigrant population more pronounced by their religious identity and other social markers. Since 9/11 most countries in the west publicly rage on the compatibility of Islam with democratic values and question the political integration of Muslim immigrants (Tillie and Slijper 2007).

The different national paradigms of integration for the immigrant population provide a statist perspective on how they should belong and in what areas their contribution is recognized and valued by the host society. Religion is mainly perceived as "less indicative of integration" (van Tubergen 2006: 168) compared to other measurements like language ability. In this book, we turn to religion as a pathway of integration and include seemingly unexplored themes in the value of religion and faith-based practices in migration. Religion manifests in different realms and spaces in the lives of men and women, be it social, cultural, and economic (Kurien 2002). This even extends to the political as religion becomes the core mechanism to resist oppression, struggle for social justice, and advocate for migrant welfare. We situate the statist view of integration with grounded perspectives of religion in the gendered lives of immigrants and migrants both in western and non-western states.

Gendered Pathways of Integration

Migration is, basically, gendered (Hondagneu-Sotelo 2003; Oishi 2005; Willis and Yeoh 2000). People leave and enter "gendered and stratified societies" (Piper 2008: 1) which impact on the ways in which immigrants integrate in receiving states. However, initial scholarly attention relied heavily on the perspective of the male immigrant or the ungendered migrant consistent with the trend in migration studies. Since the 1980s a number of significant contributions about the lives of immigrant women or what Donna Gabaccia (1994) calls "from the other side" have come to light including expressions of religiosity in diaspora

(Joseph 2001; Griffith and Savage 2006). Still, Eleanore Hofstetter in her multidisciplinary bibliography on women in migration from 1945 to 2000 underscores the "little attention" on immigrant women and religion, and, in most cases, the visible manifestations of religiosity like the use of *hijab* among Muslim women seems to be the primary focus of discourse in the West (2001: 361). This has resulted in the stereotypical representation of Muslim women in the West as traditionalists (Read 2003) and has been bolstered by popular media images as well. In doing so, religion and the embodied woman, often visibly marked by dress and other accoutrements, seems fixed in time unchanged by the process of migration and settlement.

However, the gendered nature of beliefs and practices and access to institutional resources also impact on the ways in which religion finds meaning in the lives of women and men upon migration. Recent studies on religion, gender and migration present the diversity of experiences among adherents. For example, Helen Rose Ebaugh and Janet Saltzman Chafetz's study (1999) shows thirteen immigrant religious institutions in Houston, Texas in which participants of Chinese, Greek, Indo-Pakistani, Korean, Mexican, and Vietnamese women demonstrate their increasing involvement in formal functions unlike those practiced in their own countries of origin, and that while religious institutions provide support in their adaptation, they are instrumental in reproducing traditional gender roles as well. Carolyn Chen (2005) shows how religion is used in the lives of Taiwanese immigrant women in southern California to empower themselves outside of the family. Line Nyhagen Predelli (2004) focuses on immigrant Muslim women in Norway and points at religion as a primary influence on their views and practices at home and their participation in the labor market. A more recent work of Caitlin Killian (2006) on the North African Muslim women in France provides a nuanced view on how immigrant women construct their identities and resist oppressive representation of Islam. These studies remind us that migration is a complex process that intersects with the social structures that defines or shapes our roles within it. We argue that these structures are imbued with gendered practices in patriarchal societies, both western and non-western. And, that a highly gendered social institution like religion and its tradition of defining male and female roles necessarily impact on the migration and integration of newcomers.

Notes on Chapters

Women and men have differing experiences in migration and integration. In this collection, we illustrate how gender manifests in the use of religion and faith-based beliefs and practices in the integration of immigrants, migrant workers, overseas students, and the youth in host societies as well as how religion is utilized to respond to challenges in immigration. The essays present a broad perspective of how religion functions in the lives of newcomers in Asia-Pacific, Europe, Latin America, and North America. These include religion as expression of identity; religion as community formation; and religion as refuge from oppression and site of resistance and activism.

In the Asia-Pacific region, the cases of Christian Filipina domestic workers in Hong Kong, the Japanese-descent Catholic Brazilians in Japan, the Indian overseas students and recently-arrived Muslim men in Australia describe the important role of religion in negotiating for inclusion in seemingly hostile environments. Gemma Cruz writes about Filipina domestic helpers in Hong Kong and puts into context the gendered migration, transitions, and violence in their lives. She explains how they turn to religious leaders, institutions, symbols and activities in negotiating and resisting their multifaceted oppression from a feminist theological perspective. Reinterpreting Biblical passages to make sense of and exalt their work as servants is a case of religion providing comfort to suffering. Hugo Córdova Quero examines the dynamics of migration and adaptation of Japanese-descent Catholic Brazilians in the Kanto region in Japan. Using different analytic framework including queer liberation theory, Quero explores how gender intersects with religious experience of Japanese Brazilians and the ways in which heteronormativty are reproduced in faith-based communities. In Australia, Wafa Chafic presents an empirical analysis on the role of Islamic values in the integration of Muslim men in Sydney and offers a nuanced understanding of the transformative potential of these values into notions of citizenship. Michiel Baas' narrative essay shows how religious institutions particularly the *gurdwara* and Hare Krishna mission centers are frequented by Indian overseas students intending to become permanent residents in Australia. Worship is not the main thing that draws the students but rather commensality and social activities. Religious places of worship help alleviate their economic deprivation by providing free meals, and, at the same time, enabling these students to define their place in Australian society.

The studies on Europe touch on multiple issues linked to religion. This section highlights the Muslim immigrants in Germany, Denmark and France as well as the Vietnamese Pentecostal migrant workers in Germany. Synnøve K.N. Bendixsen writes on the issue of identity and authenticity among young Muslims in Germany. In this chapter, Bendixsen introduces the generational differences in the approach to Islam focusing on self-reflection, increase of religious knowledge, use of the German language, and a search for a "pure" Islam among young female Muslims in Berlin. She discusses how these children of Muslim immigrants from Egypt, Turkey and Palestine relate to an ethnic identification based on religion and suggests the increasing individualization of religious belonging shaping the Muslim social field in Germany. Gertrude Hüwelmeier examines the dynamics of gender and power relations among Vietnamese Pentecostals in Berlin mainly composed of male pastors and female believers. Based on ethnographic materials of an all-female group who split from one congregation, Hüwelmeier pursues the question of whether religion is a liberating factor for women in charismatic Pentecostal churches or a means to reproduce male authority. Helene Pristed Nielsen analyzes faith-based community organizations and the participation of immigrant Muslim women in Denmark. Nielsen poses the question, "why is faith-based mobilization not a preferred strategy for facilitating the integrative ways of belonging among immigrant women in Denmark?" Jamel Stambouli and Sonia Ben Soltane explore the connections between the pilgrimage ritual and business activities of French Muslims. Although men are visibly involved in the pilgrimage market, women are actively engaged in making negotiations and arrangements for the *hajj* and hints at a changing but definitely empowering roles for migrant Muslim women in diasporic communities.

In Latin America, we present the role of Islam in the integration of immigrant Muslim women in Brazil by Cristina Maria de Castro. Being a Muslim in a predominantly Catholic society brings positive and negative impact on the integration process of women of Lebanese origin. De Castro looks at recognizing varied ways of negotiating the minority status of Muslims in the secular state through the maintenance of religious identity in the public sphere, self-esteem, and strategies of resisting discrimination in the labor market.

North America is one of the favored destination regions of immigrants and migrants, both documented and undocumented. Canada and the United States are traditional countries of immigration that shape their historical and social milieu. In this section, the cases of Polish, Kenyan, Mexican, Yoruba, and Filipino immigrants in the United States and Canada are examined as well as faith-based activism directed at undocumented migrants from Central America. Krystyna Błeszyńska and Marek Szopski focus on the role of religion and the parochial community in the acculturation and integration process of Polish immigrants based on a longitudinal study. Their work highlights the problems encountered by Polish immigrants, the role of religion and Catholic institutions in maintaining Polish identity in a foreign setting, and activities among parochial communities in the United States. Lilian Odera investigates the impact of religious service attendance, transnational ties, and demographic factors related to the acculturation of Kenyan immigrants in the United States. Using regression analysis, Odera aims to determine the gender differences in cultural adjustment of Kenyan immigrants. Abolade Ezekiel Olagoke examines the ethno-religious power of Yoruba immigrant women in the United States. Originally from southwestern Nigeria, Yoruba women play a central role in maintaining cultural continuity, in mediating local and community participation, and in providing counsel in economic, spiritual or other affairs affecting members of the community. Yoruba immigrant women provide key leadership authority in women's organizations, cell groups, homes, and fellowship in trans-Atlantic mode. Patricia Ruiz-Navarro presents the religious practices, identities, and affiliation of Mexican Catholic immigrants in the United States. Using ethnographic data from participants of a pilgrimage crossing the Mexico-U.S. border, Ruiz-Navarro demonstrates the reshaping of the American Catholic church. Glenda Tibe Bonifacio and Vivienne SM. Angeles illustrate two groups of Filipinos in the United States and Canada, the immigrants in Philadelphia and the migrant workers in Alberta. Since Filipino migration is highly gendered, Bonifacio and Angeles presuppose that the pathway of integration through religion and shared beliefs is necessarily gendered. By looking at the roles and spaces of religious engagement, they showcase the centrality of Catholic-based spirituality in the lives of Filipinos. The last chapter in this section cements the function of religion as a source of activism in humanitarian efforts directed toward undocumented migrants from Central America. Connie Oxford urges us to recognize how faith-based ideology informs activists in today's transnational societies. Using a feminist analysis of border crossers, activists, and institutions, as well as her own personal involvement with different humanitarian organizations, Oxford shows us that faith inspires people to make a difference even to those who are unwanted.

We envision that these cases where religion and gender intersects provide insights into the complex human capacity of endurance, survival and hope in the process of migration, settlement, and integration in the centuries to come.

Bibliography

Alba, Richard, Albert J. Raboteau, and Josh DeWind, eds. *Immigration and Religion in America: Comparative and Historical Perspectives*. New York: New York University Press, 2008.

Appadurai, Arjun. *Modernity at Large: Cultural Dimension of Globalization*. Minneapolis: University of Minnesota Press, 1996.

Appollonia, Ariane Chebel d' and Simon Reich, eds. *Immigration, Integration and Security: America and Europe in Comparative Perspective*. Chicago, IL: University of Chicago Press, 2008.

Asad, Talal. "The Construction of Religion as an Anthropological Category." Pp. 114-132 in *Reader in the Anthropology of Religion*, edited by Michael Lambek. Massachusetts: Blackwell, 2006.

Baumann, Martin and Kurt Salentin. "Migrant Religiousness and Social Incorporation: Tamil Hindus from Sri Lanka in Germany." *Journal of Contemporary Religion* 21, no. 3 (October 2006): 297-323.

Biles, John, Meyer Burstein, and James Frideres, eds. *Immigration and Integration in Canada in the Twenty-first Century*. Montreal and Kingston: Queen's University and McGill-Queen's University Press, 2008.

Bookman, Milica Z. *Ethnic Groups in Motion: Economic Competition and Migration in Multiethnic States*. London: Frank Cass, 2002.

Brown, Chris. "Narratives of Religion, Civilization and Modernity." Pp. 293-302 in *Worlds in Collision: Terror and the Future of the Global Order*, edited by Ken Booth and Tim Dunne. New York: Palgrave MacMillan, 2002.

Castles, Stephen and Mark Miller. *The Age of Migration: International Movements in the Modern World*, 4th ed. Basingstoke: Palgrave MacMillan, 2009.

Chant, Sylvia, ed. *Gender and Migration in Developing Countries*. London: Belhaven Press, 1992.

Chen, Carolyn. "A Self of One's Own: Taiwanese Immigrant Women and Religious Conversion." *Gender and Society* 19, no. 3 (2005): 336-357.

Citizenship and Immigration Canada. *Canadian Multiculturalism: An Inclusive Citizenship.* http://www.cic.gc.ca/multi/inclusv-eng.asp (accessed March 27, 2009).

Cohen, Robin, ed. *The Cambridge Survey of World Migration.* New York: Cambridge University Press, 1995.

Colic-Peisker, Val. "At Least You're the Right Color: Identity and Social Inclusion of Bosnian Refugees in Australia." *Journal of Ethnic and Migration Studies* 31, no. 4 (2005): 615-638.

Cunningham, Lawrence and John Kelsay. *The Sacred Quest: An Invitation to the Study of Religion.* New Jersey: Prentice Hall, 2006.

Da Silva, Denise Ferreira. "Voicing 'Resistance': Race and Nation in the Global Space." Pp. 427-440 in *Identity, Culture and Globalization,* edited by Eliezer Ben-Rafael with Yitzhak Sternberg. The Netherlands: International Institute of Sociology, 2001.

Ebaugh, Helen Rose and Janet Saltzman Chafetz. "Agents for Cultural Reproduction and Structural Change: The Ironic Role of Women in Immigrant Religious Institutions." *Social Forces* 78, no. 2 (December 1999): 585-613.

Eliade, Mircia. *The Quest: History and Meaning in Religion.* Chicago: University of Chicago Press, 1969.

Engbersen, Godfried. "Spheres of Integration: Towards a Differentiated and Reflexive Ethnic Minority Policy." Pp. 59-76 in *Identity and Integration: Migrants in Western Europe,* edited by Rosemarie Sackmann, Bernhard Peters, and Thomas Faist. Aldershot, England: Ashgate, 2003.

Frideres, James. "Creating an Inclusive Society: Promoting Social Integration in Canada." Pp. 77-101 in *Immigration and Integration in Canada in the Twenty-first Century,* edited by John Biles, Meyer Burstein, and James Frideres. Montreal and Kingston: Mc-Gill-Queen's University Press, 2008.

Foley, Michael W. and Dean R. Hoge. *Religion and the New Immigrants: How Faith Communities Form Our Newest Citizens.* New York: Oxford University Press, 2007.

Gabbacia, Donna. *From the Other Side: Women, Gender, and Immigrant Life in the U.S., 1820-1990.* Bloomington and Indianapolis: Indiana University Press, 1994.

Geertz, Clifford. *The Interpretation of Cultures.* New York: Basic Books, 1973.

George, Usha. "Immigrant Integration: Simple Questions, Complex Answers." *Canadian Diversity* 5, no. 1 (Winter 2006): 3-6.

Goździak, Elżbieta M. "Pray God and Keep Walking: Religion, Gender, Identity, and Refugee Women." Pp. 180-195 in *Not Born a Refugee Woman: Contesting Identities, Rethinking Practices,* edited by Maroussia Hajdukowski-Ahmed, Nazilla Khanlou and Helene Moussa. Oxford, UK: Berghahn Books, 2008.

Griffith, R. Marie and Barbara Diane Savage, eds. *Women and Religion in the African Diaspora: Knowledge, Power, and Performance.* Baltimore: The Johns Hopkins University Press, 2006.

Guest, Kenneth J. *God in Chinatown: Religion and Survival in New York's Evolving Immigrant Community.* New York and London: New York University Press, 2003.

Haan, Michael. "The Homeownership Hierarchies of Canada and the United States: The Housing Patterns of White and Non-White Immigrants of the Past Thirty Years." *International Migration Review* 41, no. 2 (Summer 2007): 433-65.

Haddad, Yvonne Yazbeck, Jane I. Smith, John L. Esposito, eds. *Religion and Immigration: Christian, Jewish, and Muslim Experiences in the United States.* Walnut Creek, CA: Alta Mira Press, 2003.

Hagan, Jacqueline. "Negotiating Social Membership in the Contemporary World." *Social Forces* 85, no. 2 (December 2006): 631-642.

Handlin, Oscar. *The Uprooted*, 2nd ed. Boston: Little, Brown and Company, 1973.

Heckmann, Friedrich. "The Integration of Immigrants in European Societies." Pp. 14-23 in *Migrations in Society, Culture, and the Library*, edited by Tom Kilton and Ceres Birkhead. Atlanta, GA: American Library Association, 2005.

Heckmann, Friedrich and Dominique Schnapper, eds. *The Integration of Immigrants in European Societies: National Differences and Trends of Convergence.* Stuttgart, DE: Lucius & Lucius, 2003.

Held, David. "Democracy and Globalization." Pp. 11-27 in *Re-imagining Political Community: Studies in Cosmopolitan Democracy*, edited by Daniele Archibugi, David Held and Martin Kohler. Palo Alto, CA: Stanford University Press, 1998.

Herberg, Will. *Protestant-Catholic-Jew: An Essay in American Religious Sociology.* Revised ed. Garden City, New York: Anchor Books, 1960.

Hirschmann, Charles. "The Role of Religion in the Origins and Adaptation of Immigrant Groups in the United States." Pp. 391-418 in *Rethinking Migration: New Theoretical and Empirical Perspectives*, edited by Alejandro Portes and Josh Dewind. New York: Berghahn Books, 2007.

Hofstetter, Eleanore O. *Women in Global Migration, 1945-2000: A Comprehensive Multidisciplinary Bibliography.* Westport, CT: Greenwood Press, 2001.

Hondagneu-Sotelo, Pierrette. "Gender and Immigration." Pp. 3-19 in *Gender and U.S. Immigration: Contemporary Trends*, edited by Pierrette Hondagneu-Sotelo. Berkeley and Los Angeles: University of California Press, 2003.

———. "Feminism and Migration." *The Annals of the American Academy of Political and Social Science* 571, no. 1 (2000):107-120.

Iosifides, Theodoros, Mari Lavrentiadou, Electra Petracou and Antonios Kontis. "Forms of Social Capital and the Incorporation of Albanian Immigrants in Greece." *Journal of Ethnic and Migration Studies* 33, no. 8 (November 2007): 1343-1361.

Ireland, Patrick Richard. *Becoming Europe: Immigration, Integration, and the Welfare State.* Pittsburgh, PA: University of Pittsburgh Press, 2004.

Joseph, Norma Baumel. "Jewish Women in Canada: An Evolving Role." Pp. 182-195 in *From Immigration to Integration: The Canadian Jewish Experience*, edited by Ruth Klein and Frank Dimant. Toronto: Institute for International Affairs, B'nai Brith Canada, 2001.

Killian, Caitlin. *North African Women in France: Gender, Culture, and Identity.* California: Stanford University Press, 2006.

Koenig, Matthias. "Incorporating Muslim Immigrants in Western Nation States—A Comparison of the United Kingdom, France, and Germany." *Journal of International Migration and Integration* 6, no. 2 (Spring 2005): 219-234.

Kofman, Eleonore. "Female 'Birds of Passage' a Decade Later: Gender and Immigration in the European Union." *International Migration Review* 33, no. 2 (Summer 1999): 269-299.

Kurien, Prema A. *Kaleidoscopic Ethnicity: International Migration and the Reconstruction of Community Identities in India.* New Brunswick, New Jersey: Rutgers University Press, 2002.

Lahav, Gallya. *Immigration and Politics in the New Europe: Reinventing Borders.* New York: Cambridge University Press, 2004.

Lucassen, Leo. *The Immigrant Threat: The Integration of Old and New Migrants in Western Europe since 1850.* Chicago: University of Illinois Press, 2005.

Mahler, Sarah J. and Patricia Pessar. "Gender Matters: Ethnographers Bring Gender from the Periphery toward the Core of Migration Studies." *International Migration Review* 40, no. 1 (February 2006): 27-63.

Manning, Patrick. *Migration in World History.* New York and London: Routledge, 2005.

Menjivar, Cecilia. "Religion and Immigration in Comparative Perspective: Catholic and Evangelical Salvadorans in San Francisco, Washington, D.C. and Phoenix." *Sociology of Religion* 64, no. 1(Spring 2003): 21-45.

Messina, Anthony M. *West European Immigration and Immigrant Policy in the New Century.* Santa Barbara, CA: Greenwood Publishing Group, 2002.

Morrison, Andrew, Maurice Schiff and Mirja Sjoblom, eds. *The International Migration of Women.* Washington, DC: The International Bank for Reconstruction and Development/The World Bank, 2008.

Mueller, Claus. "Integrating Turkish Communities: a German Dilemma." *Population Research and Policy Review* 25 (December 2006): 419-441.

Naples, Nancy. "The Social Regulation of Community: An Intersectional Analysis of Migration and Incorporation in the Heartland." *The Journal of Latino-Latin American Studies* 2, no. 3 (Spring 2007): 16-23.

Oishi, Nana. *Women in Motion: Globalization, State Policies, and Labor Migration in Asia.* California: Stanford University Press, 2005.

Omidvar, Ratna and Ted Richmond. "Immigrant Settlement and Social Inclusion." Working Paper Series. Toronto: Laidlaw Foundation, 2003. http://maytree.com/PDF_Files/SummaryImmigrantSettlementAndSocialInclusion2003.pdf (accessed January 15, 2009).

Peterson, R. Dean, Delores F. Wunder and Harlan L. Mueller. *Social Problems: Globalization in the Twenty-first Century.* New Jersey: Prentice Hall, 1999.

Piper, Nicola, ed. *New Perspectives on Gender and Migration: Livelihood, Rights and Entitlements.* New York and London: Routledge, 2008.

———. "International Migration and Gendered Axes of Stratification." Pp. 1-18 in *New Perspectives on Gender and Migration: Livelihood, Rights and Entitlements,* edited by Nicola Piper. New York and London: Routledge, 2008.

Predelli, Line Nyhagen. 2004. "Interpreting Gender in Islam: A Case Study of Immigrant Muslim Women in Oslo, Norway." *Gender and Society* 18, no. 4 (2004): 473-493.

Radtke, Frank-Olaf. "Multiculturalism in Germany: Local Management of Immigrants' Social Inclusion." *International Journal on Multicultural Societies* 5, no. 1 (September 2003): 55-76.

Read, Jen'nan Ghazal. "The Sources of Gender Role Attitudes among Christian and Muslim Arab-American Women." *Sociology of Religion* 64, no. 2 (Summer 2003): 207-222.

Richter, Kent E., Eva M. Rapple, John C. Modschiedler and R. Dean Peterson. *Understanding Religion in a Global Society*. Belmont, Ca: Thomson/Wadsworth, 2005.

Tillie, Jean and Boris Slijper. "Immigrant Political Integration and Ethnic Civic Communities in Amsterdam." Pp. 206-225 in *Identities, Affiliations, and Allegiances*, edited by Seyla Benhabib, Ian Shapiro, and Danilo Petranovic. Cambridge, UK: Cambridge University Press, 2007.

Tweed, Thomas A. *Crossing and Dwelling: A Theory of Religion*. Cambridge, MA and London: Harvard University Press, 2006.

———. *Our Lady of the Exile: Diasporic Religion at a Cuban Catholic Shrine in Miami*. New York: Oxford University Press, 1997.

Van der Veer, Peter and Steven Vertovec. "Brahmanism Abroad: Caribbean Hinduism as an Ethnic Religion." *Ethnology* 30, no. 2 (1991): 149-166.

Van Tubergen, Frank. *Immigrant Integration: A Cross-National Study*. New York: LFB Scholarly Publishing LLC, 2006.

Willis, Katie and Brenda Yeoh, eds. *Gender and Migration*. Cheltenham: Edward Elgar, 2000.

Wuthnow, Robert and Conrad Hackett. "The Social Integration of Practitioners of Non-Western Religions in the United States." *Journal for the Scientific Study of Religion* 42, no. 4 (December 2003): 651-667.

Zufiaurre, Benjamin. "Social Inclusion and Multicultural Perspectives in Spain: Three Case Studies in Northern Spain." *Race, Ethnicity and Education* 9, no. 4 (December 2006): 409-424.

Chapter Two
It Cuts Both Ways: Religion and Filipina Domestic Workers in Hong Kong
Gemma Tulud Cruz

The presence of Filipino domestic workers in Hong Kong, more popularly known as DHs, is part of a larger phenomenon of massive Filipino labor migration. Understanding their migration to Hong Kong entails getting a grasp of the origins or, at the very least, the place of their migration within the landscape of Filipino labor migration. Labor migration is not a strange phenomenon among Filipinos. As a matter of fact, the distinct pattern of movements of this historical and continued outflow of Filipino migrant workers is enshrined in what is called the four waves of Filipino labor migration (Catholic Institute for International Relations 1987). The first wave, in the 1900s, saw Filipino men migrating for cheap labor in sugar and pineapple plantations in Hawaii and later to the United States mainland as apple pickers (Kanlungan Center Foundation 1997: 8). This first group of Filipino migrants originated mostly from Northern Luzon and parts of Visayas which have a history of migration to other parts of the country due to land problems (Mission for Filipino Migrant Workers, MFMW 1983).

The second wave (1940-1960) brought the movement of thousands of Filipinos to the United States, Canada, and Europe as war brides, professionals, and highly-skilled workers as a result of more open immigration policies. This new group, however, has a distinct characteristic. Most of them were better-educated and skilled, marking these years as the "brain drain" period of Filipino migration. The second wave included a variety of professionals from doctors, accountants, and nutritionists to physical therapists and others. This group included women who worked mostly as nurses and/or hospital staff.

Labor migration as a state policy, in the meantime, was the most powerful driving factor for the third wave of Filipino labor migration in the 1980s. Seeing a significant source of national income in the remittances of the OFWs (Overseas Filipino Workers) then President Marcos institutionalized labor migration in the mid 1970s through the Labor Export Program (LEP).[1] The "trade" then covered almost all occupational groups from doctors, engineers, teachers and nurses, to seamen, band singers, domestic helpers, chambermaids, and construction workers. This period saw the expansion of sea-based work from the shipping industry to the fishing industry. If the second wave is marked by "brain drain" or the migration of the skilled and the intellectuals of the Philippines, the third wave went a little further by exporting both the "brains" and the "brawns" of Filipino society.[2]

Globalization, however, ushered in not only new areas or shifts in destination, i.e., from Europe and America to the tiger economies in Asia (Singapore, Malaysia, Taiwan, Hong Kong). With its concomitant international division of labor and the expansion of the service sector, globalization also created areas of job concentration and Filipino migration. This resulted in an unprecedented out-migration of Filipino women, also known as *Filipinas*, mainly as nurses, entertainers, and domestic workers which led to the fourth wave in the 1990s characterized by the feminization of Philippine labor migration (Beltran and Javate de Dios 1992: vii). With domestic work being the most prominent face of this movement of workers, the migration of Filipinas to Hong Kong as domestic workers reached high proportions.

Based on records of the Immigration Department in Hong Kong, the earliest documented migration of Filipinas as domestic workers was in 1973. Driven by the economic instability in the Philippines many of them left the country to work as maids for expatriates in the former British colony. Most of the early migrants have a high level of education. They were young, single, educated women, mostly in their twenties to thirties, and with rural origin or background (French 1986: 7-15; Lane 1992: 24-32).

When the British government liberalized the entry of female foreign domestic workers mainly from the Philippines, their number rose significantly and steadily. From the early 1970s to the 1990s Hong Kong was the consistent destination of Filipina DHs in the same way as Filipina DHs have been the consistent favorite because of their relatively better facility with the English language. Today, although their numbers are dropping, the Filipina DHs make up the majority of Hong Kong foreign house help.[3] Life for the Filipina domestic workers in Hong Kong, however, is a constant (re)negotiation of the gamut of problematic situations they go through as foreign workers. In any case, religion plays a central role in this everyday struggle. Using existing studies on the Filipina domestic workers in Hong Kong as presented in books, journals, magazines, newspapers, case files, dissertations, conference proceedings, and other sources, together with my research and informal interviews in centers and shelters for domestic workers in Hong Kong, this essay then explores the double-edged role and significance of religion in the faith-informed struggle of the Filipina domestic workers in Hong Kong from a feminist theological perspective.

Mapping Gendered Oppression

Filipina migration to Hong Kong started when Hong Kong was experiencing an economic boom while the Philippine economy was beginning to decline. Because Hong Kong housewives had more opportunities to work—or were forced to work to meet increasing economic demands—and local domestic workers were expensive, the demand for cheap migrant domestic workers arose. Hong Kong's further industrialization attracted local workers, including local women workers, to jobs that paid higher than the expanding service sector. This intensified the demand for the English-speaking Filipinas who then came in droves. While they compose the majority of Hong Kong's foreign house help and its largest ethnic migrant group, life for the Filipina DHs is a saga riddled with drama. It is a complex tale of struggle born in the constricting mold of gendered migration, intensified by gendered transitions, and sealed in their experience of gendered violence (Asian Migrant Center 2000; Boase 1991).

Gendered Migration

In many ways, the migration of the Filipina DHs in Hong Kong is gendered. Firstly, the global job market is a gendered market where poor and poorer women of color, continue to be segregated in jobs associated with the service sector or care work. Secondly, the Filipina DHs' decision to migrate, which is often a family strategy for upward social mobility, reflects the sexual division of labor, rooted in gender stereotypes, which plays a major role in singling out the womenfolk to be the ones to leave and work abroad. Filipino families think it is but "natural" for the daughter, sister, or wife to apply for the job because domestic work is a woman's work. For single women, families often capitalize on the language of care among women as nurturance in all aspects for the women to agree to leave to work as DH. Parents especially tap into the highly ingrained sense of responsibility among daughters in choosing them to be the one to migrate. Elsa's account of her last conversation with her father reflects the dynamics, not only of the expectation for and socialization of Filipino women for care work, but also the reality of patriarchy that is operative within the Filipino family:

> "Elsa" he told me, "can you help your sisters in their schooling? Because they like to study and you know that I don't have any capability to send them to college." He said, "Elsa can you help me? Your sisters, they like to go to school.". . . and so I said, "OK. No problem. This is my opportunity to help . . . Don't worry, *Tay* [father], I will try my best to help you" (cited in Constable 1997: 18).

Hope Antone, a Filipina feminist theologian based in Hong Kong, affirms this patriarchy-rooted ideology of domesticity:

> Women have been socialized early in life to do multiple responsibilities in the home—for their siblings, their parents, the elderly, and sometimes even others in the community. This ideology of domesticity is so ingrained that many Asian women feel it is their fate or destiny to sacrifice in order that those who depend on them can have a better life. Migration then becomes an option not only for mere economic reasons but also for the ideological-cultural factor of

gender socialization into the ideology of domesticity and multiple responsibilities (Antone 2003: 102).

Gendered Transitions

The Filipina DHs also undergo gendered transitions when they work and live in Hong Kong. For married DHs guilt for being "absentee mothers" is a source of much oppression. At the root of their guilt is what they perceive as a transgression of a "good" Christian woman's proper place and role which is at home with her husband and children. This personal and even societal perception of their sojourn in Hong Kong as a betrayal of their primary duty and responsibility then becomes like a millstone hanging around their necks. This perception is such that some of them do not even say goodbye to their children nor immediately tell the truth as to where they are going.

To ease their guilt, DHs find a *tagasalo* (surrogate) whereby they pass on their direct nurturing responsibility to another woman such as mother, sister, niece, eldest daughter, or the hired services of a poorer Filipina to be their own domestic helper (Mulong 2000: 4-5; Mulong 2001: 9). These DH mothers, however, still try to make up for their absence by resorting to transnational mothering. They are often known as "cell phone mothers" because they try to fulfill their responsibilities as mothers via the cell phone, which includes helping their children do their homework.

Unmarried, single, or unattached DHs, in the meantime, find difficulties in having a relationship with the opposite sex or, in their own words, "finding a good man to be a husband." According to a study by Marilen Abesamis, single DHs prioritize the "white, middle-class male" thinking that marrying a white, middle-class male would mean higher social class, and more "freedom" and rights (cited in Doyo 2002: 39-43). But this does not usually happen because of cultural differences exacerbated by the low social regard for them. For others who do get involved with foreigners, particularly Chinese, not being taken seriously remains a problem. As a result, many unmarried DHs end up preferring Filipino men. But since there are also very few Filipino men in Hong Kong, and class boundaries within the Filipino migrant community are very much in place,[4] the "field" of "available" men for the single DHs becomes all the more limited.

The limited possibilities among unmarried Filipina DHs to marry in Hong Kong often becomes a problem, especially since Filipino women are socialized in the Philippines that marriage and children is the be-all and end-all of a woman's existence. This is especially so because most of them are in the marrying age and some quite beyond the marrying age.[5] That is why some who are always asked why they are not married yet get annoyed (Gonzalez 1999: 13-14). The prevalence of this mentality among the DHs and in the Filipino community at home and in Hong Kong explains why marriages are primary occasions for celebration for the DHs. Wedding pictures even land on the cover page of magazines that have mostly DHs as contributors and readers. Not surprisingly, conflicts or fights about men or boyfriends, especially about boyfriend-grabbing, also occur within their peer groups.

Gendered Violence

Gendered violence also plagues the Filipina DHs economically, physically, and sexually. Economically, foreign DHs are victimized a number of times to solve or alleviate Hong Kong's economic woes. Wage cuts which targeted only the domestic workers—an occupation the Hong Kong government knows is dominated by women—was meant to ease Hong Kong's economic slowdown. Domestic workers are already the lowest paid worker in Hong Kong and singling them out for further reduction of wages is tantamount to "making the poor even poorer."[6]

The Hong Kong government further institutionalized gendered violence in 1999 with the proposal to remove maternity protection for foreign domestic helpers. Concocted as a means to offer flexibility to employers to terminate their foreign DHs on the basis of mutual agreement, the proposal, according to the Asian Migrant Coordinating Body (AMCB), is not only discriminatory as it is applicable only to those in the category of foreign domestic helpers, but also racist and sexist as it seeks to exclude workers of certain nationalities from enjoying a right available to local workers and those of other nationalities. Moreover, it targets women by considering pregnancy and maternity as a "hindrance" to effective and productive labor. The proposal, the AMCB argues, brings back the age of slavery where the right to bear children was considered a threat to productivity[7] —a violation of the DHs' reproductive rights which is a hard-won right of women workers around the world.

The scourge of the Filipina DHs as women comes not only from the Hong Kong government, but also from their employers and recruiters. For instance, the popular perception in Hong Kong is that foreign domestic workers will go to great lengths to snag rich men like their male employers so the DH's physical appearance is usually controlled by women employers. Dress codes are imposed through the maid's uniform, jeans, T-shirts or other unattractive and gender-neutral clothes. Body control and discipline are important adjustments the DH has to make right from the start (Constable 1997). Recruiters, upon the desires of prospective employers, "transform" the DH's body and appearance by dictating her body weight, length of hair, facial appearance (no make-up), type of footwear, and so forth. When the external fits the prescribed ideal DH's body appearance, the internal is the next one the recruiters tinker with. Aside from being subjected to the X-ray machine and the weighing scale, the DH's body is exposed to numerous tests as part of the application process. These include tests for hepatitis, syphilis, herpes, and even a pregnancy test. When the DH passes the "body quality control" she is photographed twice—a close-up of the face and a "full body" shot—with her "signature" clothes: the pastel pink or blue-striped maid's uniform. The "perfect maid" look dictates she must be neat and tidy but not so attractive.

Employers, especially women, allegedly do not hire pretty domestic workers. If the prospective DH is Chinese looking and has "physical imperfections" like acne, scars, birthmarks, and a bit [but not too] dark complexion, the more likely she will be employed.[8] As a result, there is quite a number of what DHs call, "from airport to airport." These are those who were terminated the moment their employer laid eyes on them at the airport and saw "how beautiful" or "how dark" they were.

Various forms of physical abuse, in the meantime, plague many DHs who actually get to work. These include slapping on the face, hands, or any part of the body, spitting, kicking, being hit with or thrown objects at, beating, and so forth by their employers. Others, like the case of Lilia Dangco get treated more atrociously:

> Six days later (after arriving in Hong Kong), her employer burned her left forearm with a flat iron after she failed to follow her employer's instruction to put a handkerchief on top of a black long skirt that she was ironing. She was confined at the Queen Mary Hospital. She said her employer warned her not to tell the incident to anybody or her face would be the next target (MRV Case Files).

In terms of sexual violence, unwanted kissing, touching, and sexual advances are the most common forms of abuse experienced by Filipina DHs. This is closely followed by the employer displaying himself naked or asking the DH to touch him. Other complaints include being peeped at by employers when taking a bath or getting changed, being videotaped while in the bathroom or bedroom, and being touched while sleeping.[9] Male employers also tend to regard their DH as in-house masseuse who is available for twenty-four hours. Some make "substitute wives" out of their DH, especially if the wife seems not able to provide adequate "sexual services." Some DHs are allegedly even turned into virtual sex slaves.

Religion and Migration

Religion as a Source of Oppression

To survive their multi-faceted and gendered oppression, Filipina DHs turn to a pervasive influence in their lives, that is, religion. But religion also exists as a double-edged sword in the struggle of the DHs. This section explores how religion contributes to their oppression.

At the outset, religion becomes a problem for the DHs as Hong Kong is not a predominantly Christian country like the Philippines. Moreover, the majority of the DHs' employers nowadays are non-Christian Chinese who may not be tolerant when it comes to Christian religious practices or holidays. Also, within the Filipino Christian and even the Catholic community there is a wide array of charismatic groups that peddle a "prosperity gospel."

Class issues also make other Filipina migrant Christian communities and the local Christian community dissociate from Filipina DHs. On the part of the local Christian community, this is affirmed by the following excerpt from the national report on Hong Kong presented at the Symposium on Filipino Migrant Workers in Asia:

> As we appreciate the contribution of our Filipino brethren to the Church of Hong Kong, we also recognize the difficulties in establishing a Church that is both Filipino and Chinese. We are aware that we still need to inculcate among our Chinese people that the Church is universal and that two cultures can proclaim the same faith in the same Church, in different ways and languages. The Diocese of Hong Kong would like to see the Chinese and the Filipinos join one another at Mass and gatherings, as equals and as friends. We may still be a long way from the reality of our dream but we hold this reality as our best dream and with the cooperation of the jolly and forgiving Filipinos, this will surely come true in God's own time.[10]

As Filipinos who come from the first Christian country in Asia known for its religiosity (Ileto 1988: 194), DHs immediately find the nearest church and join a religious group as soon as they can. Eliseo Tellez Jr, a social worker, alleges that the strong reliance on religion for comfort also opens another problem with the local people who frown at the crowds created in church grounds and consider their presence as "nuisance." Tellez maintains that

> the church is a sanctuary to them . . . Anyone who utters the name of Jesus is their friend. This makes them easy prey for charismatic groups which do not ordinarily concern themselves with things mundane like the migrants' almost slave-like conditions. The growing number of commercialized charismatic groups is one of the current challenges to the churches in Hong Kong (Tellez 1991: 82).

Fr. Pidgeon, a Redemptorist priest, says the indifference of the local church at the grassroots level leads to the proliferation of myriad and assorted religious groups, many of whom do their members more damage than good. He also points out how the migrants' hunger for religion or deep desire to experience the comfort of religion are taken advantage of by religious groups, which do not have sound leadership and are un-Catholic in their teaching (Pidgeon 1999). The Tracer study reports one case where the Philippine consulate in Hong Kong traced the insanity of a few migrant workers to their membership in a church group. Although the group's name was not revealed, the consulate said that "allegedly, the group placed too much pressure on their members causing the unfortunate events" (Vasquez, Tumbaga and Cruz-Soriano 1995: 68).

The oppressive experiences associated with Christian, especially Catholic religion, is not only external but also internal. A Filipino religious minister in Hong Kong comments that their oppression is rooted in a situation of "centuries of the misuse of religion . . . [which] has created a people that are susceptible to blackmail." "Filipino Christianity," he says, is "a brand of Christianity that is more enslaving rather than liberating."[11] Many DHs also become captive victims of charismatic groups that emphasize non-liberating concepts of the divine.

Strong association with religion has been heavily woven in gendered oppression since the Spanish colonization of the Philippines. Sr. Mary John Mananzan (1989) states:

> Her [Filipina] freedom of choice in important aspects of her life was curtailed by the imposition of new laws and mores. Confined in her area of action, the woman poured all her innate sensibility and energy into the activities allowed her, developing a religious fervor which would verge on fanaticism. She was constantly reminded of her innate danger to men as the seductive Eve and was relentlessly exhorted to follow an impossible model — the Virgin Mother. She could venerate her but her efforts to emulate her brought her into scrupulous frustrated efforts which ended up giving her an abiding guilt complex which added to her timidity and lack of self-confidence and, in many cases, reducing her to frigidity . . . patriarchal society succeeded in alienating her [Filipina] from public life, public decisions and public significance. She should henceforth be a delicate ornament of the home or the victim soul of the convent (cited in Brock 1996: 66).

Today this preoccupation with religion persists especially among Filipina migrant workers. To them religion is a cogent and authoritative tool in demonstrating appropriate behavior in light of their oppression. Whether superficial or deep, exploitative or responsive, religion is *a* and oftentimes *the* norm to view and confront personal and social oppression. Religion is used, at best, to cushion the impact and, at worst, rationalizes or justifies their multifarious oppression. Religion is often invoked as a source of life orientation as evident in their writings in the print media. DH writers in *Tinig Filipino* (Filipino Voice), for instance, often couch their advice to fellow DHs in religious language. Lanie Jose, in an article titled "Because of Love," encourages her fellow DHs to learn to love their employers no matter how bad their employers may be.

> If you only came here to work and you're just after money and never winning your employer's trust and confidence, then, there's something wrong with you . . . They may be the meanest boss, very inconsiderate, too meticulous, fault-finder, and strict but then, we have to learn to dance with them . . . My secret in winning their confidence? Simple! I always have a ready smile . . . I maintain my patience and above all, I always seek the Lord's guidance (cited in Constable 1997: 190).

DHs also rationalize their oppression by seeing it from the perspective of religious-based notions of dependence on God and suffering. They become even more submissive when the latter is linked with sacrifice and becomes "redemptive suffering" or the notion that it is acceptable, even good, to suffer if it will mean redeeming someone. Like Jesus, the dutiful Son, they consider their submission to the oppressive situation as an act of a dutiful daughter, wife, mother, or a Filipino citizen.

Positive or romanticized religious notions of sacrifice as a means of viewing and enduring their oppression are common among Filipina DHs. Melanie Romero, in a letter entitled "Rewarding Sacrifice," shares how "strong faith," "grace of perseverance," and "prayer" are keys to finishing a troublesome contract and rationalizes that one has to bear the difficulties because blessings will come afterwards (Romero 1999: 22). Tina Bautista, however, puts it succinctly: "Central to every Christian's respect for life is the hope that sadness will always give way to joy. As we reach the end of our journey, climbing ever nearer the summit of Calvary, we are assured that death gives way to resurrection and everlasting life" (Bautista 1999: 27).

Most make sense of, accept, and even embrace their oppression by viewing it from a religious perspective, especially in terms of "the sufferings and death of Jesus" which "remain at the very heart of their spirituality" (Pidgeon 1996: 30). This spiritualization and valorization of suffering is evident in many DHs' reflections on their experiences of injustice like the following:

> We find ourselves wondering about these unpleasant situations and often bow our heads in despair. There are times when we shed tears and question God for abandoning us . . . Instead of becoming bitter, why not thank the Lord for the troubles that helps us recognize our spiritual needs. When we take these burdens a challenge for us, we come to . . . understand clearly that it brings us humility, contentment, and spiritual health. These difficulties we face supply us with spiritual growth if we accept them as a test of our faith in God (Becasen 1999: 14).

The Bible is also used to justify suffering and as a ticket to heaven. Erlinda Layosa, for example, quotes a biblical passage which says, "You servants must submit to your masters and show them complete respect . . . If you endure suffering even when you have done right, God will bless you for it" (cited in Constable 1997: 192). All publications catering to the DHs have columns or articles on religion, especially on the Bible. *TNT*, for example, has a "*Pag-aralan ang Biblia*" (Bible Study) column. Others, like *Tinig Filipino*, have columns on religion which significantly uses the Bible in relation to the DHs' situation. Mommie Jingco, a regular columnist on religion, utilizes and even quotes from the Bible to make her fellow DHs feel good and accept their role as "servants" as well as make them understand why it is alright for them to be submissive to their "masters." She writes:

> What is wrong with being a domestic helper anyway, or shall I use the word servant or *muchacha*? From Christ's point of view these are the people who will become great because they humble themselves to serve others. It was [Christ who] promoted servanthood . . . Here are some tips to remember from the Scriptures: ". . . Servants be obedient

to those who are masters according to the flesh, with fear and trembling as to Christ; not with eye service, as men pleasers, but as bond servants of Christ doing the will of God from the heart, with goodwill doing service, as to the Lord, and not to men, and knowing that whatever anyone does, he will receive the same from the Lord, whether he is slave or free" (Ephesians 6:5-7) (cited in Constable 1997: 192).

Kimberly Chang and L. H. M. Ling's analyses based on their 1992-1997 field work on the Filipina DHs are, by far, the most comprehensive and perceptive on the DHs' utilization of faith to redefine service. Chang and Ling note that DHs "define themselves as servants of the Lord rather than the physical world of men" and "describe this service to God and Church as cleansing, filling them with a sense of "righteousness" and "completeness" (2003: 73-87). They cite here Erlinda Layosa's "Chosen People to be Helpers of the World," a "love letter" supposedly written by God to Filipina overseas workers. In the said letter God supposedly urges Filipina domestic workers to embrace their work as servants, bringing to it their "true Christian values, your resilient, cheerful, persevering, and helpful qualities and humble ways" (cited in Constable 1997: 39). These statements cleanse the notion of the Filipina DHs' service of its sexual overtones and turns it into "an almost sacred activity, giving the women a sense of moral identity and purpose" (Chang and Groves 2000: 73-87).

Religion as a Means in the Struggle for Survival and Liberation

Religion also helps the DHs constructively oppose oppression (Youngs 2003: 44-58). Noted Filipino sociologist Randy David, based mainly on his work on Filipina migrants in Hong Kong, Singapore, and Japan, asserts that in the midst of "the loneliness that grips [them] . . . the terror and insecurity that they must deal with on a day-to-day basis as unprotected guest workers in foreign lands . . . the resilience of *Pinoy* [Filipino] OCWs is legendary. Their joys and celebrations are louder than their distress. Only in rare instances do they crack; they gently bend with the wind."[12] This joyful resilience, according to David, is due to their religion.

Like other Filipino migrants who live up to the renowned Catholic image of the Philippines, the church is not just the principal site of celebration for Filipino identity and community among the DHs. It is their refuge in times of crisis and their home when they want to shout for joy. A Filipino priest said in a Mass I attended in Hong Kong: "The Filipinas have only one day a week of freedom so they maximize it by liberating the Filipino spirit. That spirit includes communing with God."

Sunday—the day of freedom and the most favored off-day—will not be complete without going to a religious service. In Hong Kong, it is common knowledge that it is the Filipinas who fill up the churches on Sundays. Saint

Joseph's Church, the most popular Catholic Church, has countless Filipinas flocking to it not only because a number of Masses are said in *Tagalog* but also because it has Mass almost every hour from morning till dusk on Sundays. And the sight at Saint Joseph's Church on a Sunday is, indeed, extraordinary. How often do you find a church where crowds fall in line, both from the front and the back, just to get inside? How often do you find a church that has to close its doors to people because it is already filled to capacity? Lastly, how often do you find a church that is truly a women-church? This is Saint Joseph's Church on a Sunday—a handful of men [including the priest] and a sea of women.

Sunday religious service is a non-negotiable weekly event or ritual among the DHs in their sojourn in Hong Kong. Amidst the confusion and isolation wrought by their marginalization, the service is a powerful means for defying their feelings of negation. For a number of them, it does not matter where and which church they go to. The important thing is they see a church building, a cross, or Filipinas in a religious gathering. That is enough to draw them. In fact, there are some who officially belong to one denomination but go for the service of another denomination. The young DH I met on the grounds of Saint John's Cathedral goes to the service there even if she is not a Catholic. What matters to her is she has been to a Christian Sunday ritual.

Even the lack of actual church buildings is not a problem for many DHs. If there is no church building available for them, Filipinas find places, create, and build their own "church" out of parks, gyms, and auditoriums. Eliseo Tellez Jr. says that Filipino NGOs in Hong Kong even establish and forge links with DHs by "visiting churches and hanging around church grounds" since the church is where the DHs meet. Even "the physical structure of a church is sometimes enough to assure them that things will improve" (Tellez 1991: 82). It is also where they socialize. Indeed, the establishment of literally "Filipina churches" provides what could be the single most important source of continuity in their world that has changed in so many ways. Religion is a basic institution among Filipinos and, for the DHs, their "church" represents the continuation of this most important institution in their lives. The church is both a religious and a social center—the place where they hold meaningful rituals and forge ties with their fellow DHs. Randy David describes one such experience of this power of religion in the DHs' life in Hong Kong:

> I recently sat through a Sunday service in one such gym in Hong Kong, and wondered what it was that drew in the participants. It could not have been the long high-pitched and thoroughly uninspiring lecture-sermon of the *pastora*, who certainly did not deserve her audience's reverential attentiveness. I am more certain now that it was the community, and the bonding and the comfort they derived from each other's sheer presence, that made them come . . . For when it was time to sing . . . the gym came alive. A band started to play a rousing tune, and costumed dancers with ribbons and tambourines took center court. I thought for a while it was a prelude to a basketball tournament. Three thousand Pinoys, almost all of them women, stood up. With eyes closed and arms raised, they swayed their bodies to the rhythm of a prayer. They cheered, they clapped

and they shouted God's name; and in that anonymous collective
drone, they cried out their individual pain (1998: 50-51).

Shu-Ju Ada Cheng, in her comparative study of migrant women domestic
workers in Hong Kong, Singapore, and Taiwan singles out this religious practice
of the DHs in Hong Kong as a factor that explains their ability to break the
isolation and engender visibility. Church attendance "provides an important
opportunity and space for Filipino women to establish their support system and
networking, which is essential for breaking the isolation of the household"
(Cheng 1996: 119). Many DHs admit to a feeling of "homecoming" whenever
they join other DHs for a religious service. Wherever it is held, "it's another
home" where they can "forget [the] misgivings induced by being a stranger in
another country" (Yeung in MFMW 1983: 66). They do not care whether they
have to stand instead of sit, kneel on a rough floor, or put up with the noise and
the stares of curious passers-by. For them, it is the spirit in which one attends the
Mass that counts.

The time spent in and for the church does not end with the Sunday service.
Many of them spend practically their one and only day-off in the parish. Some
even engage in pastoral work or outreach activities every Sunday by caring for
sick people, visiting the needy, and performing other charitable activities
(Federation of Asian Bishops Conference 1994: 15). In Saint Joseph's Church,
many DHs stay and eat in the church grounds with their friends. Most linger for
a chat on the latest stories or news in their friends' lives or for news about the
Philippines. Some peruse or buy books from the makeshift booth of religious
items set up by the Daughters of Saint Paul. Others return or borrow books from
the "Borrow a Book" program of the parish. Reading a book is one of the
Church-initiated activities that Filipina DHs take advantage of to resist *pagpurol
ng utak* (dulling of the mind because of lack of use). But even without the book-
lending program, most of them gravitate to the church primarily as a way of
resisting the loneliness and isolation of migration. Hence, the church also
becomes a focal point in their lives for social reasons. Isabel Escoda, in her
portrait of the *amah* (domestic servant) as Filipina, writes about how "she starts
to feel at home, especially after she has met some congenial fellow Filipinas at
the Catholic Church where she attends Mass each Sunday" (Escoda 1989: 49-
50).

But it is also in church, particularly during their activities like fellowships,
that many Filipina DHs who are at the forefront of the struggle for migrant
domestic workers' justice got their inspiration and started their "mission."
Connie Bragas–Regalado, a Filipina DH activist witnesses to this:

> When I first came to Hong Kong, my first Sunday's off was at the
> Church of All Nations in Repulse Bay. An old friend who was
> already involved with the Filipino Fellowship of the said church
> fetched me. It all started with Bible Studies and Choir service . . . I
> volunteered to be part of the Church Board of Social Ministry. Then
> the group decided to request a paralegal training, which was
> conducted by the Mission for Filipino Migrant Workers. Then I

learned about the Mission and UNIFIL . . . their work (MFMW 2000: 24-25).

Connie joined and served as a leader in UNIFIL (United Filipinos in Hong Kong) and other widely-respected Asian migrant worker associations while in Hong Kong. She is now back in the Philippines serving as an officer in *Migrante* (migrant), a political party by and for OFWs.

To further ease their feelings of loneliness and isolation, DHs turn to the church by forming or joining choir groups, fellowships, and participating in Bible study sessions. It is also in their churches where they hold their regular prayer meetings; come and informally share their troubles and so-called "adventures" with their friends; engage in their usual devotions and comply with their Christian obligations; and turn to "Pastor," "Father," or "Sister" who, in the Filipino Christian (especially Catholic) mentality, is not only a figure of authority, but also their "savior" in many ways. Religious leaders not only provide for their spiritual needs, but even for their temporal needs. The following excerpt from a letter to a priest by a DH illustrates their role:

> [I]f you have received my letter which I mailed last October 2 because until now I haven't receive any reply regarding the extension of my visa . . . I have no money at hand if only I knew that I'm going to pay I should have sacrifice to borrow . . . All this was done too late. Is there any remedy for this father? I cry for self-pity. I spend all my money, sacrifices and efforts just for this but I'm frustrated so I call again for your help father on what I will do to extend my visa (MFMW 1983: 98).

Aside from giving religious services, churches provide a well-organized and extensive system to help the DHs. Catholics, for example, have the Diocesan Pastoral Center for Filipinos (DPCF) while the Protestants have the Mission for Filipino Migrant Workers (MFMW). These two Church-based institutions have a variety of strategic activities designed to respond to the DHs' challenging situation. They organize the DHs into groups and create social activities. Both have hotlines and shelters for DHs in distress. They provide counseling services, help in pursuing legal cases, religious formation programs, retreats, leadership training and livelihood courses which many of the DHs take advantage of, especially those designed for reintegration. Some churches even set up special joint savings accounts in which DHs may place a portion of their earnings for later withdrawal to pay for education or travel expenses. This is the churches' way of making sure that DHs will be able to save even just a little for critical future needs since most DHs are not usually able to save money for themselves.

Prayer also plays a major role in negotiating their difficulties. Their resolute propensity for praying or calling on God is confirmed in the Tracer study (Vasquez, Tumbaga, and Cruz-Soriano 1995: 40, 54, 75-76). One interesting religious phenomenon among the DHs in their sojourn in Hong Kong is the emergence of the image of God as a foreigner, a host, or as God of strangers. These are not common God images in the Philippines, but DHs are discovering and embracing these in an apparent resistance to how their host society treats them as migrants. One of their songs in a Eucharistic celebration I attended in the Philippine consulate in Hong Kong illustrates this shift in imagery:

> The Lord is my shepherd, He is Lord
> And I'm His guest.
> Fresh and green are the pastures
> Where He leads me to my rest.
> Near peaceful waters He leads me
> To cheer up my cheerless heart
> He guides me on the safe path
> He will always do His part.

DHs' recourse to Christian-based resources is strongly facilitated by the desire to fight the difficulties and injustices born out of their status as Filipinos, as women, and migrant domestic workers in Hong Kong. But when their exposure to the multiple religious traditions in Hong Kong seeps in, and the stifling Filipino Christian traditions and norms weigh heavily on them, DHs take another religion-related means to resist their oppression. This is religious conversion. Most conversions occur within denominations or within the same religious tradition, particularly Christianity. The change is often from the established Catholic and Protestant denominations to the popular charismatic groups.

Across religious traditions, however, a significant number of conversions to Islam also occur. Sithi Hawwa in *Religious Conversion of Filipina Domestic Helpers in Hong Kong* reports that DHs make up 70 percent of the sixty to seventy annual average number of converts to Islam.[13] DHs are primarily brought and converted to Islam through their Pakistani boyfriends and Sr. Madiha: a DH convert whose similar background and good relationship with them has led to the conversion of 300 Filipinas in just a matter of five to six years.

Apparently, their formation of social networks to resist their discrimination is the primary means by which they come into close contact with Pakistani men. Many of these Pakistani men become their boyfriends and even husbands, thus contributing to their conversion to Islam. Aside from romantic involvement and inter-marriage with Pakistani men, other factors such as prior contact with Muslims, previous work experience in the Middle East, influence from converted family members, employers or co-workers, dissatisfaction with their former religion, mere curiosity, or a desire for enlightenment also account for DHs' conversion. Most conversions are fueled by a desire for "greater autonomy and liberation" especially from stifling marriage-related policies in the Philippines such as the ban on divorce and abortion.

Many Filipina DHs feel that Christianity, particularly Filipino Catholicism, is another source of their oppression and they perceive religious conversion as a means to mitigate the oppression. But a number of them revert back to their religion when Islam becomes repressive or less able to take the edge off their situation. Hawwa enumerates the reasons for the reversion: "inability of Mosque to fund sisters in terms of financial crises, the absence of a physical space for converts with terminated contracts, the unwillingness of fellow Muslims to employ them . . . and the dissatisfactory behavior of Muslim men" (Hawwa 1999: 10).

Conclusion: Migrant Religion and Women's Liberation

Religion has, arguably, never gone through so much significance, dynamism, expansion, transformation, and even revolution as in the context of contemporary migration (Beyer 1994). One can see this in how it features significantly in the lives of the Filipina DHs in Hong Kong. Away from their home country, and in search of company, pleasure, and intimacy, religion becomes a formidable anchor in their lives. Even historians and sociologists point out the salience of religion in the lives of migrants and contend that any study of migrants that ignores the role of religion will most likely be incomplete and skewed. In 1978, for instance, sociologist Timothy Smith went as far as to say that immigration itself is a "theologizing experience" since immigrants often make sense of the alienation that is inherent in migration in religious terms.[14] Hence, it would be a tragedy if Christian theology does not put this phenomenon under closer scrutiny.

For one, there is the gender issue. Traditionally, women are stereotyped as the "keepers" of religion and this is still in place among migrants. In fact, in their study of migrant congregations, Helen Rose Ebaugh and Janet Saltzman Chafetz (2000) point out that while there are conditions under which [migrant] religious congregation promotes an improvement in the status of women, situations that legitimate their traditional subordinated status persist. For instance, they often do traditional women's work in their churches like preparing food, teaching Sunday school classes, and performing music and social services. While this definitely needs some looking into, it is also noteworthy to look at how this somehow becomes a strategy for survival for migrant women.

The fellowships or meals that usually follow the DHs' religious gatherings also give us a glimpse of the rich possibilities that Filipino migrant women's faith expressions, in the context of migration, can offer for feminist-theological reflections. First of all, the women usually go to great lengths to procure the necessary ingredients for the ethnic viands which are usually the staple food whenever they gather. They exert much energy and creativity just to come up with the real or, at least, close to the real recipe.[15] Hence, one could imagine the joy of a migrant woman not only at seeing compatriots, especially fellow women, but also at seeing, smelling, and eating "home" food.

I, for one, remember how delighted and, at the same time, amazed I was at seeing and eating Philippine viands like *adobo* and native delicacies like *bibingka* on a table in a house in The Netherlands on the third Sunday of my first month in the country. The women-dominated Filipino migrant community in the Dutch city where I used to live does this once a month like all the other

Filipino-Dutch communities in the Netherlands, most of which are led and sustained by women. I have been to a number of gatherings of some of these women-run Filipino communities in The Netherlands and I am very much inclined to say that, like the DHs, the *salo-salo* (shared meal) after the service could actually be the real Eucharist. Seeing one is indeed like witnessing the Gospel at table. The spirit of joy, the atmosphere of warmth and affection, and the sense of community are such that the experience itself becomes a God-experience. It is like seeing "the substance of religion and more . . . the strength that comes from valuing the intangibles, the meanings that are continually created and understood, when human beings come together to share their lives and their fears, their meals and their memories" (David 1998: 52). It is the Eucharist in the flesh rooted in the resiliency, tenacity, and beauty of woman-spirit. It is a reminder of the times in the New Testament when religious communities, which we now know as churches, were based in households and women exerted considerable influence. Their fellowship also points to the fact that Christian life is not just about individual salvation but also about collective liberation. It teaches us that Christian spirituality must not just be about fasting, but also about celebrating; it must not just be about families but also about communities. Most of all, it reminds us that spirituality must never be confined to prayer or any other religious activity but to anything and everything that celebrates our humanity.

Truly, religion in the context of migration is a double-edged sword. In the context of the Filipina DHs in Hong Kong, life is not just about religious-based marginalization, but also about faith-informed strategies for survival which offer us windows into human liberation. The extent in which we are able to critically reflect on these faith-informed strategies will shape our articulation of contemporary forms of forging relationships with the sacred.

Notes

1. This continues to strongly motivate the Philippine government to promote labor migration. In 2006 alone OFWs sent $22 billion, even exceeding by 25 percent the country's national budget for the same year. See Manuel Amora, "A Closer Look at the Filipino Diaspora," http://www.globalnation.inquirer.net (accessed December 17, 2007).

2. The latter primarily has to do with the massive recruitment of men for construction work in the petro-dollar rich Middle East, particularly Saudi Arabia.

3. As of October 2007, about 123,000 of the 250,000 foreign domestic helpers working in Hong Kong were Filipinos. Indonesians comprised 115,000 while Thais, Nepalese, Sri Lankans and other nationalities made up the rest. See "Filipina Domestic Workers Losing Out to Indonesians in HK Job Market," http://traffickingproject.blogspot/2008/02/filipinos-domestic-workers-losing-out.html (accessed November 4, 2008).

4. See, for example, "Class Conscious," *TNT Hong Kong* 2, no. 11 (January-February 1997): 10-11.

5. The ideal marrying age is around twenty-five. In rural areas the usual marrying age even tends to be younger.

6. After failing to impose its proposed 20 percent wage cut (the employers wanted 35 percent) in 1998, the Hong Kong (HK) government reduced their minimum wage by 5 percent during the economic crisis in 1999. Because of growing budget deficit, the government implemented another (and higher) wage cut for contracts signed after April 1, 2003 bringing the HK$3,670 a month minimum wage of the already lowest-paid Hong Kong workers to HK$3,270. See James Tien, "Hong Kong is Suffering: Even the Foreign Maids Must be Willing to Sacrifice," *South China Morning Post*, November 22, 2002; Daffyd Roderick, "Making the Poor Even Poorer," *TIME Asia*, August 25, 2003; "RP Maids' Dilemma in HK," http://.archive.inq7.net/archive/2001-p/nat/2001/dec/24/nat_7-1-p.htm (accessed October 31, 2003).

7. See the related report in "Maternity Benefits for Maids Opposed," *Philippine Daily Inquirer*, July 4, 1997, 3. Constable cites a similar violation of the DHs' reproductive right whereby the DH was given an abortion without her knowledge when her employer brought her for physical exam and pregnancy test. See Nicole Constable, *Maid to Order in Hong Kong* (Ithaca: Cornell University Press, 1997), 72.

8. Chinese employers shun women with darker skin because they purportedly scare the children.

9. Roseanne Calamaan, for instance, was forced by her employers to watch them have sex and was also asked to watch the couple's "private videos." See "Maid 'Forced to Watch Sex,'" *Asia Migrant Bulletin* 11, nos. 3/4 (July-December 1994): 4.

10. For a discussion of this report see "Filipino Migrant Workers in Hong Kong," *Asian Migrant* 7, no. 1 (January-March 1994): 7.

11. See Profile # 6, "Ministry alongside Migrant Workers," *Migrant's Focus Magazine*, no. 1, http://www.migrants.net/resources/magazine/issue1/profiles6.htm (accessed February 12, 2003).

12. OCWs or Overseas Contract Workers is the former term for OFWs (Overseas Filipino Workers). See Randy David, *Public Lives: Essays on Selfhood and Social Solidarity* (Pasig City: Anvil Publishing, 1998), 50-52.

13. Hawwa also attributes the facilitation of the conversion to the "intensity of religious faith of Filipino women and their prior tendency to shift among different denominations within Christianity." See Sithi Hawwa, "Religious Conversion of Filipina Domestic Helpers in Hong Kong," *ISIM Newsletter* 4 (1999): 10.

14. As early as 1960 Will Herberg pointed out how the early immigrants in the United States would "sooner or later . . . give up virtually everything he had brought with him and the 'old country'—his language, his nationality, his manner of life—and will adopt the ways of his new home" except his religion for "it was largely in and through his religion that he, or rather his children and grandchildren, found an identifiable place in American life." See Will Herberg, *Protestant-Catholic-Jew: An Essay in American Religious Sociology* (Garden City, NY: Doubleday, 1960) as quoted in Helen Rose Ebaugh and Janet Saltzman Chafetz, "Introduction," in *Religion and the New Immigrants*, ed. Helen Rose Ebaugh and Janet Saltzman Chafetz (Walnut Creek, CA: Altamira Press, 2000), 7.

15. Ebaugh and Chafetz, *Religion and the New Immigrants*, 90-92 argues that the collective consumption of traditional foods, together with the use of native language, plays a central role in how migrant groups define cultural boundaries and reproduce ethnic identities and to the extent that women monopolize this role, they constitute a critical lynchpin in the reproduction of ethnicity within migrant congregations.

Bibliography

Amora, Manuel A. "A Closer Look at the Filipino Diaspora," *Inquirer*, December 12, 2007. http://www.globalnation.inquirer.net (accessed December 17, 2007).
Antone, Hope S. "Asian Women and the Globalization of Labor." *The Journal of Theologies and Cultures in Asia* 2 (2003): 97-111.
Asian Migrant Center. *Baseline Research on Racial and Gender Discrimination towards Filipino, Indonesian and Thai Domestic Helpers in Hong Kong.* Hong Kong: AMC, 2000.
Bautista, Tina. "Pro-Life Corner," *TNT Hong Kong* 5, no. 4 (April 1999): 27.
Becasen, Miriam C. "Are You Dealing with Agonizing Burdens?" *TNT Hong Kong* 5, no. 4 (April 1999): 14.
Beltran, Ruby and Aurora Javate de Dios. *Filipino Women OCW's... At What Cost.* Manila: Women in Development Foundation, 1992.
Beyer, Peter. *Religion and Globalization.* London: Sage Publications, 1994.
Boase, Melville. "The Two Weeks Rule in the Context of the Legal Position of Foreign Domestic Helpers (FDHs)." Pp. 85-94 in *Serving One Another: The Report of the Consultation on the Mission and Ministry to Filipino Migrant Workers in Hong Kong*, by the Christian Conference of Asia, April 28-May 1, 1991, Kowloon, Hong Kong. Hong Kong: CCA Urban Rural Mission, 1991.
Brock, Jane Corpuz. "Gospel, Cultures, and Filipina Migrant Workers." *International Review of Mission* 85, no. 36 (January 1996): 63-84.
Catholic Institute for International Relations. *The Labor Trade: Filipino Migrant Workers around the World.* London: CIIR, 1987.
Chang, Kimberly and Julian McAllister Groves. "Neither 'Saints' Nor 'Prostitutes': Sexual Discourse in the Filipina Domestic Worker Community in Hong Kong." *Women's Studies International Forum* 23, no. 1 (2000): 73-87.
Chang, Kimberly and L. H. M. Ling. "Globalization and its Intimate Other: Filipina Domestic Workers in Hong Kong." Pp. 27-43 in *Gender and Global Structuring: Sightings, Sites, and Resistances*, edited by Marianne H. Marchand and Anne Sisson Runyan. London: Routledge, 2003.
————."Romancing Resistance and Resisting Romance: Ethnography and the Construction of Power in the Filipina Domestic Worker Community in Hong Kong." Pp. 316-343 in *At Home in the World? Filipinos in Global Migrations*, edited by Filomeno V. Aguilar. Quezon City: Philippine Migration Research Network, 2002.
Cheng, Shu-Ju Ada. "Migrant Women Domestic Workers in Hong Kong, Singapore, and Taiwan: A Comparative Analysis." Pp. 109-121 in *Asian Women in Migration,* edited by Graziano Battistela and Anthony Paganoni. Quezon City: SMC, 1996.
"Class Conscious." *TNT Hong Kong* 2, no. 11 (January-February 1997): 10-11.
Constable, Nicole. *Maid to Order in Hong Kong: Stories of Filipina Workers.* Ithaca: Cornell University Press, 1997.
Daffyd, Roderick. "Making the Poor Even Poorer," *TIME Asia*, August 25, 2003. http://www.time.com/time/world/article/0.8599.189810.00.html (accessed December 23, 2005).
David, Randy. *Public Lives: Essays on Selfhood and Social Solidarity.* Pasig City: Anvil Publishing, 1998.
Doyo, Ma. Ceres P. "Tomboy Love." Pp. 39-43 in *Risks and Rewards: Stories from the Philippine Migration Trail*, by Inter Press Service. Bangkok: IPS Asia-Pacific, 2002.

Ebaugh, Helen Rose and Janet Saltzman Chafetz, eds. *Religion and the New Immigrants: Continuities and Adaptations in Immigrant Congregations.* Walnut Creek, CA: Altamira Press, 2000.

Escoda, Isabel Taylor. *Letters from Hong Kong: Viewing the Colony through Philippine Eyes.* Manila: Bookmark, 1989.

Federation of Asian Bishops Conference. *Pilgrims of Progress??? A Primer of Filipino Migrant Workers in Asia.* Manila: FABC-OHD, 1994.

"Filipina Domestic Workers Losing Out to Indonesians in HK Job Market." http://traffick ingproject.blogspot.com/2008/02/filipinos-domestic-workers-losing-out.html (accessed November 4, 2008).

"Filipino Migrant Workers in Hong Kong." *Asian Migrant* 7, no. 1 (January-March 1994): 7.

French, Carolyn. *Filipina Domestic Workers in Hong Kong: A Preliminary Survey.* Hong Kong: The Chinese University of Hong Kong, 1986.

Gonzalez, Ping. "Thirty-five and Still Single." *TNT Hong Kong* 5, no. 8 (August 1999): 13-14.

Hawwa, Sithi. "Religious Conversion of Filipina Domestic Helpers in Hong Kong." *ISIM Newsletter* 4 (1999): 10.

Herberg, Will. *Protestant-Catholic-Jew: An Essay in American Religious Sociology.* Garden City, NY: Doubleday, 1960.

Ileto, Reynaldo. "Toward a History from Below." Pp. 191-199 in *Southeast Asia: Sociology of Developing Societies,* edited by John G. Taylor. London: Macmillan, 1988.

Jingco, Mommie. "Lowly yet Fulfilling," *Tinig Filipino,* October 1991, 24.

Jose, Lanie Mathias. "Because of Love," *Tinig Filipino,* February 1992, 8.

Kanlungan Centre Foundation, Inc. *Destination: Middle East: A Handbook for Filipino Women Domestic Workers.* Quezon City: KCFI, 1997.

Lane, Barbara. "Filipino Domestic Workers in Hong Kong." *Asian Migrant* 5, no. 1 (January-March 1992): 24-32.

Layosa, Erlinda. "Into Thy Hands," *Tinig Filipino,* April 1994, 6.

———. "Don't Find Fault ... Find a Remedy," *Tinig Filipino,* July-August 1990, 15.

"Maid Forced to Watch Sex." *Asia Migrant Bulletin* 11, nos. 3-4 (July-December 1994): 4.

Mananzan, Mary John. "The Filipino Women: Before and After the Spanish Conquest of the Philippines." Pp. 6-38 in *Essays on Women,* edited by Mary John Mananzan. Manila: Institute of Women's Studies, 1989.

"Maternity Benefits for Maids Opposed," *Philippine Daily Inquirer,* July 4, 1997, 3.

"Ministry Alongside Migrant Workers." *Migrant's Focus Magazine* no. 1. http://www.m igrants.net/resources/magazine/issue1/profiles6.htm (accessed February 12, 2003).

Mission for Filipino Migrant Workers. "Talks with Connie Bragas-Regalado." *Migrant Focus Magazine* 1, no. 2 (October-December 2000): 24-25.

———. *The Filipino Maids in Hong Kong: MFMW Documentation Series No. 1.* Hong Kong: MFMW, March 1983.

"MRV Case Profiles: Lilia Bernardino Dangco." http://www.asianmigrants.org/mrvcases/ 999433070427.php (accessed February 2, 2003).

Mulong, E. "Mothers Once Again." *TNT Hong Kong* 6, no. 4 (June-July 2000): 4-5.

———. "When Children Become Parent Carers." *TNT Hong Kong* 7, no. 1 (February-March 2001): 9.

Pidgeon, Frank J. "Challenging the Christian Community." *TNT Hong Kong* 5, no. 4 (April 1999): 6-7.

————. "Pag-Aralan ang Biblia." *TNT Hong Kong* 2, no. 2 (February 1996): 30.

Romero, Melanie. "Up Close and Personal." *TNT Hong Kong* 5, no. 4 (April 1999): 22.

"RP Maids' Dilemma in HK: Take Pay Cut or be Jobless." http://.archive.inq7.net/archiv e/2001-p/nat/2001/dec/24/nat_7-1-p.htm (accessed October 31, 2003).

Tellez, Eliseo Jr. "An Overview of Filipino Migrant Workers in Hong Kong." Pp. 75-83 in *Serving One Another: The Report of the Consultation on the Mission and Ministry to Filipino Migrant Workers in Hong Kong,* by Christian Conference of Asia April 28-May 1, 1991 Kowloon, Hong Kong. Kowloon, H.K.: CCA Urban Rural Mission, 1991.

Vasquez, Noel, Letty C. Tumbaga and Minnette Cruz-Soriano. *Tracer Study on Filipina Domestic Helpers Abroad: The Socio-Economic Condition of Filipina Domestic Workers from Pre-Departure until the End of their First Two-Year Contract in Hong Kong.* Geneva: International Organization for Migration, 1995.

Yeung, Chris. "A Building that Serves both God and Mammon," *South China Morning Post,* June 27, 1983. Reprinted in *Filipino Migrant Workers: Off to Distant Shores by the Mission for Filipino Migrant Workers.* MFMW Documentation Series No. 2. Hong Kong: MFMW, 1983.

Youngs, Gillian. "Breaking Patriarchal Bonds: Demythologizing the Public/Private." Pp. 44-58 in *Gender and Global Structuring: Sightings, Sites, and Resistances,* edited by Marianne H. Marchand and Anne Sisson Runyan. London: Routledge, 2003.

Chapter Three
Faithing Japan:
Japanese Brazilian Migrants and the
Roman Catholic Church
Hugo Córdova Quero

Since the late 1970s and the so-called "bubble economy," Japan has received an increasing number of migrants. As a consequence of its economic growth, the need for the industrial sector to employ unskilled laborers peaked exponentially. The first wave of workers migrated from neighboring countries. In the 1970s the first migrants were Filipino women recruited for the entertainment and sex industry; later, in the mid-1980s, mostly men from Bangladesh, Pakistan and Malaysia followed. At the same time new waves from South Korea and China, arrived in Japan to work at small and medium size factories (Morita and Sassen 1994:156). [1] Soon after the arrival of these migrants, the number of undocumented workers grew larger as well. The Japanese authorities then sought to eradicate that situation by proposing a different approach: to open the possibility for descendants of Japanese in the Americas like Brazil to migrate to Japan. Since 1990 this option guaranteed that workers would fill the unskilled labor needs of small and medium size factories without disrupting the ethnic/racial homogeneity of Japan.

As the migratory path of Japanese Brazilians grew larger, academic research on the subject increased. Although it was primarily focused on issues related to work, a few scholars were approaching issues of religion or gender. My case study is based on fieldwork among Japanese Brazilian parishioners within seven Roman Catholic communities. It was conducted throughout the Kanto region of Japan between 2006 and 2008. [2] I interviewed fifty parishioners and church staff (clergy and lay people) of which twenty-three were males and twenty-seven were females.

This chapter seeks to unpack the role that gender and religion play in the daily lives of Japanese Brazilians attending the Roman Catholic Church in Japan. The first part focuses on the historical context of their migration to Japan, especially in relation to ethnic, labor, and legal issues. The second part of the chapter explores the intersection of gender and religious experience into their migration experiences; and the third section deconstructs those experiences, especially in relation to the situation of women and the second generation.

On Becoming a Migrant

On December 8, 1989, the Japanese Parliament enacted the reformed *Immigration Control and Refugee Recognition Law,* which took effect in 1990 (Sassen 1998: 60). The low degree of population growth, the tendency for young and educated Japanese to avoid low-skilled employment like factory work, and the increasingly aging population constitute important reasons in favoring the decision to accept foreign workers and solve the need of unskilled workers in the industrial sector.

The decision of the Japanese Government under Prime Minister Toshiki Kaifu to reform the immigration law coincided with social, economic, and political situations in Latin America and created a niche for migration. The increasing economic instability caused thousands of Japanese descendants, especially from Brazil, to migrate to Japan. The tremendous economic and social consequences of a military dictatorship in Brazil (1964-1985), the constant economic crisis, and the rise of unemployment due to failed economic plans were important *push* factors in the decision to migrate. In the midst of all these, many middle class Japanese Brazilians began to search for possible countries to migrate and find work.

Even prior to the passage of the immigration law reform in 1989-1990, some Japanese Brazilians were already in Japan, albeit in small numbers. From the mid-1980s until the beginning of the 1990s most of these migrants were composed of *issei* (first generation), who already possessed Japanese citizenship. Scholars usually locate the peak of their migration in the years between 1989 and 1991 (Higuchi and Tanno 2003: 34). In fact, the annual statistics of the Ministry of Justice of Japan (Yamanaka 2003a: 180) indicate that while in 1988 there were only 4,159 Brazilian nationals registered in Japan, by 1989 this number escalated to 14,528. In 1990 when the immigration law reform took effect that number sky-rocketed to 54,429. By 1991, Brazilian residents in Japan doubled to 119,333. Since then, the influx of migrants became steady. According to Japanese government statistics there are 316,979 Japanese Brazilians currently residing in Japan—with women constituting about 40 percent. This means that of the total population, 141,480 are women and 171,499 are men (Ministry of Justice of Japan 2007a).

Japanese Brazilian workers occupy jobs that are not much different from those of other foreign workers. These jobs are known as the "three K" jobs (Linger 2001: 22). This expression comes from the Japanese words *kiken* (dangerous), *kitanai* (dirty), and *kitsui* (tiring). Essentially, they take jobs despised by nationals, but are necessary to the development and functioning of the industrial market.

At the beginning of the migration wave, the majority of the Japanese Brazilian population was concentrated around industrial areas, mostly in prefectures such as Aichi, Shizuoka, Gunma and Nagano. Today, it is possible to find Japanese Brazilians in every city and rural area of the country, and a growing number of them are working and living in major cities like Tokyo and Osaka. According to recent statistics, of the total 390,321 foreigners who are registered and residents in Tokyo, 4,454 are Japanese Brazilians (Tobace 2008: 19).

Migration and Racial/Ethnic Relations

The increasing presence of foreign migrants in every city of Japan has produced some tensions within the larger society. While the Brazilian economic conditions constituted the *push* factor in the Japanese Brazilians' decision to migrate, it was the political and legal decision of the Japanese Government—by reforming its immigration law—that became the *pull* factor, thus, making the process of immigration possible. Descendants of Japanese born and raised abroad are known as *Nikkeijin* (literally, "individual of Japanese ancestry"). It is important to note that the decision to accept descendants of Japanese as temporary migrant workers was based on a racial/ethnic assumption:

> [T]he legal admission of *Nikkeijin* was a political compromise made by the Japanese government to accommodate labor-starved employers while at the same time maintaining social homogeneity in the face of accelerating transnationalization. By constructing the new category of *Nikkeijin*, the government could maintain the core principle of its nationality and immigration laws, *jus sanguinis* (law of blood), which gave the revision process the appearance of being technical rather than political (Yamanaka 2003a: 176).

Accordingly the category of "long-term resident" was established for Japanese Brazilians. While the second (*nisei*) and third generation (*sansei*), as well as their families, could access to this category, the fourth generation (*yonsei*) was not included in the reform of the Immigration Law. In the beginning, the majority of Japanese Brazilian migrants were men, but they were soon followed by women and entire families which consequently enlarged the migrants' flow. Not all of them are Japanese descendants, as some spouses are from other ethnic groups.

While the Immigration Law reform in 1990 sharply reduced the flow of migrants from Southeast Asia and the Middle-East, it also facilitated the rise of Japanese Brazilian immigration—and other South American *Nikkeijin* like the Peruvians—on the grounds of ethnicity. In the monthly magazine of the Liberal Democratic Party, an interesting perception of the issue of privileging *Nikkeijin* over other Asian migrants was presented:

> Admitting *Nikkeijin* legally will greatly help to ameliorate the present acute labor shortage. People who oppose the admission of the unskilled are afraid of racial discrimination against foreigners. Indeed, if Japan admitted many Asians with different cultures and customs than those of Japanese, Japan's homogeneous ethnic composition could collapse. However, if *Nikkeijin* were admitted, this would not be a problem . . . *Nikkeijin*, as relatives of the Japanese,

would be able to assimilate into Japanese society regardless of
nationality and language (Nojima 1989: 98-99).

This perception privileges Japanese Brazilians over other Asians who do not
possess Japanese ancestry, and certainly reflects the racial categorization at stake
in Japanese racial formation (Yoshino 1997: 199-211). It assumes that the
Japanese racial/ethnic component is stronger than the socialization within
Brazilian racial formation (Daniel 2006: 27-28; Adachi 2004: 49). Even when
Japanese Brazilians are offered low-wages in unskilled, temporary work, it is
their ancestry that constitutes a positive element toward their acceptance, thus,
guaranteeing the maintenance of Japanese society's ethnic homogeneity. Apichai
Shipper argues that, in Japan, foreign workers are "organized hierarchically,"
(2002: 41-42) with Japanese Brazilians below the Korean and Chinese *zainichi
gaikokujin* (Japan-born foreign residents) and above other non-Japanese
temporary workers such as Filipinos, Vietnamese or Iranians.
    Nevertheless, Japanese Brazilians suffer many forms of discrimination,
sometimes due to the lack of knowledge of Japanese language or because of
their perceived *brazilianness* (Tsuda 2003: 103-151). Many times their social
and cultural behavior differs from Japanese expectations such as non-public
display of physical expression or emotion, or following correctly the complex
trash recycling system (which in Japan differs from city to city). Matthews
Masayuki Hamabata (1990: 134) explains that a cultural expectation in Japanese
society is the balance between *tatemae* and *honne*. While *tatemae* refers to the
display of the public persona and social obligations, *honne* refers to the
expression of inner feelings. Japanese Brazilians in Japan seem to behave
differently because they act according to the expectations of Brazilian culture,
where such a separation between public persona, social obligations, and inner
feelings would hinder a society deeply marked by personal relations and display
of affection and emotions (Novinger 2003: 89). Japanese Brazilians, like many
South Americans in contemporary modern society, are not inhibited in
displaying their feelings in public to spouses, relatives or friends. For example,
couples may be seen walking hand-in-hand on the street, which is something
uncommon in Japan.
    Another form of discrimination faced by foreigners in Japan is access to
rental apartments (Roth 2002). Many Japanese owners would not rent
apartments to them, or, in case they would be open to consider this possibility,
they will make the requirements more difficult, like interviewing the same
person four times before making a decision. Lately, Japanese Brazilians are seen
along with all the foreigners residing in Japan under the social fear of
criminality or terrorism. However, police statistics reveal that the percentage of
criminality among foreigners is less than 2 percent of the total reported cases per
year in Japan (Solidarity Network with Migrants Japan 2007: 117).
    It seems that what sustains the difference between nationals and foreigners
is the discourse of Japanese uniqueness or *Nihonjinron,* which conveys the
message that Japanese society is mono-ethnic and mono-cultural, thus superior
to other cultures. Kosaku Yoshino describes *Nihonjinron* as follows:

The *nihonjinron*, which literally means "discussions of the Japanese" refer to a vast array of literature which thinking elites have produced to define the uniqueness of Japanese culture, society and national character. Publications on Japanese uniqueness reached their peak in the late 1970s but continued into the 1980s . . . [T]his is the decade that the effects of the *nihonjinron* were strongly felt among wider sections of the population, as it takes time for thinking elites' ideas to diffuse to other social groups (1992: 2).

The self-perception of *Japaneseness* is reinforced through education and mass media (Lie 1992: 38). Furthermore, John Lie argues that the homogeneity of Japan (inside) contrasts with the heterogeneity of foreigners (outside), resulting in a dichotomy where "inside denotes simplicity and purity, [and] outside represents complexity and pollution" (2003: 83). At the level of public opinion and mass media, discrimination toward migrants can be seen from the very beginning of the high intakes of migration flows. Yoshino further states:

The mass media have projected a vision of waves of darker-skinned "others" hitting the shores of Japan and threatening social cohesion and integrity. These views are ironic given that over 80 percent had entered Japan through the agency of Japanese recruiters and brokers, who had recruited them to work in jobs that most Japanese are unwilling to undertake (1992: 38).

After analyzing sixteen Japanese television shows, Takeyuki Tsuda surmises that the media presents a paradox; while attempting to eradicate some prejudices against descendants of Japanese who migrated from the Americas to Japan, it reinforces "traditional attitudes" and "prejudices" against migrants including Japanese Brazilians (2004: 4).

Consistent with immigration reforms in 2006 to tighten national security and the global campaign against terrorism, Japanese Brazilians who have obtained "long term residency" are meted with new requirements to obtain permanent residency.[3] Based on the website of the Immigration Bureau of Japan in the Portuguese language, Japanese Brazilians must certify "good behavior." This new requirement is justified as follows:

Individuals carrying status of Long-Term Residency have been responsible for considerable indices of criminality, entering Japan as descendants (*nikkei*) with such status. *Foreign residents in Japan have committed serious crimes, causing great concern for the security of Japanese citizens* and, for this reason, the requirement of [a certificate of] "good behavior" have been added for people with Japanese ancestry (*nikkei*) as well as the members of their family who attempt to obtain status of permanent resident (Ministry of Justice of Japan 2006. Translation and emphasis mine).

Interestingly enough, the English website does not list the same paragraph for English-speaking Japanese descendants, although the issues of illegality and criminality are, nonetheless, addressed:

> To revive the title 'Japan—The safest country in the world,' [the]
> Immigration Bureau aims to reduce the number of illegal stay
> foreigner[s] to the half the number [from] 2004 until 2008 and in
> order to achieve the goal we need your cooperation (Ministry of
> Justice of Japan 2007a).

In this sense, Japanese Brazilians, despite their ancestry, are considered by Japanese people as *gaikokujin* (foreigners) and, therefore, subject to the same treatment as other foreigners. This also explains why Japanese Brazilians are sometimes separated from social interactions in both workplaces and neighborhoods. Japanese and Japanese Brazilian workers eat at separate tables and wear uniforms of a different color in many factories. The interaction between both groups is not only minimal, but also socially discouraged (Tsuda 2003: 16).

Even though interactions between Japanese and Japanese Brazilians are different and varied, separation and minimal contact is the most common experience. Some participants in my study refer to the willingness of some Japanese nationals to interact and communicate with foreigners, but that the language barrier (on both sides) is the main obstacle to do so. There is a subtle negotiation of spaces for interaction in their daily lives. Japanese Brazilians are fostering alternative spaces, communities and activities to empower themselves, although the result may not improve contact and communication with the Japanese nationals.

Intersections: Migration, Gender and Religion

Gender and religion are of special interest in the daily life of Japanese Brazilians; however, in most of the existing scholarly literature concerning this group, gender is rarely mentioned. With the exception of a few scholars such as Keiko Yamanaka (1996, 1997, 2003a, 2003b) and Karen Tei Yamashita (2001), gender is an unusual topic. This is not the case with other migrant groups. For example, there is an extensive corpus of research conducted in relation to Filipino women in Japan on issues about prostitution and human trafficking (IOM 1997; Parreñas 2006), or about international marriage (Cahill 1990; Faier 2007; Ogena, Valencia, and Roma 2007).

The same is true about religion. The study of the interaction of Japanese Brazilians with the Roman Catholic Church is quasi absent, with a few exceptions such as the works of Regina Yoshie Matsue (2006a, 2006b) and Rafael Shoji (2008a, 2008b). Certainly, there are many scholars who study religions both in Brazil and in Japan, but there is a need to study more explicitly the role of religion among Japanese Brazilian migrants, especially the Christian branches such as Protestantism and Roman Catholicism.

The intersections of gender, religion and migration reveal the complex situation of Japanese Brazilians in Japan, particularly in regards to the performance of cultural and social expectations of the host society. It shows how religious practices become a source of strength in the daily lives of those potentially disempowered by the state.

Recovering the Gender Connection to Migration

Gender is often seen as a secondary variable of analysis rather than the main lens for analysis. It is a "key relational dimension" culturally informed and with "consequences for social or cultural positioning" of females and males (Indra 2004: 2). Gender has been "simplistically read as 'women' rather than as relations of power, privilege, and prestige informed by situated notions of maleness and femaleness" (Indra 2004: xiv). Based on Michel Foucault's relationality of power and new approaches to gender, Doreen Indra concludes that "there is increasing consensus that cultural, race, class, ethnic, national, and sexual orientation differences between women and men must be given more significance" (2004: 8). In other words, gender is critical in bringing these categories together and in order to analyze the daily lived experiences of Japanese Brazilian migrants amidst their incorporation into Japanese society.

Gender is central in understanding the distribution of jobs and mechanisms of the industrial market. At the peak of the Japanese Brazilians' migration, Naoto Higuchi (2003: 396) notes that women paid higher broker fees than men in order to obtain their ticket, visa and to find a job in Japan. For the same service, men were charged around US$2,800, while women were charged around US$3,750. The differential costs based on gender affected the possibilities for migration in many cases.

Japanese Brazilians are faced with a number of challenging situations related to prescribed gender roles and expectations, particularly involving the younger generations, whether they are born in Brazil or in Japan. One situation pertains to the formation of families. Another relates to the issue of cultural identity. Parents are not always prepared either to face or to negotiate the multiple issues arising in the midst of cultural conflict, especially when connected to gender performances. These concerns were raised by many Japanese Brazilian parents that I interviewed.

Intermarriage is also an issue related to the type of families formed among Japanese Brazilians. It implies intermixing of different cultural heritage (Japanese, Japanese Brazilian or other ethnicities), with its legal and social consequences, especially in Japan. According to Tsuda, "[t]he intermarriage rate is reported to be around 40 percent, and as a result, 6 percent of the *nisei* and 42 percent of the *sansei* are of mixed descent" (2000: 3). In the past, intermarriage was condemned socially among Japanese migrants, but it has become recently more tolerable (Butsugan 1980).

In Japan, the second generation faces some consequences depending on their parents nationality. Japan grants citizenship only through *jus sanguinis* (law of blood) and not through *jus soli* (law of land) like in Brazil. Therefore, children born in Japan from non-Japanese citizen parents will either get their parents' nationality or be stateless, as is the case for refugees and undocumented migrants (Ami 2002; Yasumoto 2008; Hongo 2008). Brazil enacted a reform of its citizenship law in 2007 that allows the registration of citizenship to children born in other countries to Brazilian citizens who have emigrated.[4] However, this may not solve the problem of incorporation of the new generation of Brazilian children in Japan. Children who bear Brazilian nationality, born in Japan, and who have never been to Brazil, are still discriminated against in Japanese society. Furthermore, as the educational system in Japan does not contemplate either multilingual or multicultural education, children are mainly socialized in the Japanese language, which renders them unable to keep the cultural and linguistic connection with their parents. In my observations at several churches, I heard many parents speaking in Portuguese to their children while the latter replied to their parents in Japanese. In worst cases, children are *semi-lingual* or unable to express abstract ideas neither in Japanese nor in Portuguese (Andrade 2008).

Other issues refer to domestic violence or sexual orientation, which are becoming more visible both in the ethnic media in Portuguese and in current research on Japanese Brazilians in Japan. In cases of domestic violence, the language barrier becomes a major issue when victims of violence are unable to seek help or counseling either from the police or nongovernmental organizations (NGOs). Both the police departments and NGOs hire translators to respond to this situation. However, according to existing regulations, the Japanese spouse will likely get custody of the children, which, in turn, may prevent the foreign spouse from initiating divorce due to the fear of losing the children. Besides, once a foreign spouse obtains divorce, he/she is likely to lose her/his visa status if that was obtained through her/his Japanese spouse. (Iritani 1996). On the contrary, many gays and lesbians, who were "out" in Brazil, are now "closeted" in Japan. This constraint is worsened when social exclusion inside the migrant's networks may result in the weakening of their possibilities to find information or obtain services. Furthermore, prejudice against foreigners is also high inside the Japanese gay community (Pinkerton and Abramson 1997: 80-81).

Recovering the Religious Connection to Migration

Religion continues to play an important role in modern societies. This is particularly visible when connected to migration. For example, in the process of adapting to the new society, the role of faith-based communities has been remarkable in offering support, facilitating varied integrative ways of belonging, and networking for the protection of migrants' rights. This is not exclusive to Japanese Brazilians in Japan, but one that is shared with migrants around the globe. Charles Hirschman (2003) points out that migrants tend to become more religious in the host society and states:

> Customary religious practices, such as attending weekly services, lighting candles, burning incense in front of a family altar, and

reciting prayers are examples of communal and family rituals, which were brought from the old country to the new. However, these activities often take on new meanings after migration. The normal feeling of loss experienced by immigrants means that familiar religious rituals learned in childhood, such as hearing prayers in one's native tongue, provide an emotional connection, especially when shared with others. These feelings are accentuated from time to time with the death of a family member or some other tragedy . . . [R]eligious beliefs and attachments have stronger roots after immigration than before (2003: 6-7).

Japanese Brazilians have a rich religious heritage rooted in Roman Catholicism. In Japan, they interact with a predominantly Buddhist and Shintoist society which affect the individual in different ways. While some participate in Buddhism or Shintoism, the religions of their ancestors, many keep the Roman Catholic faith they adopted in Brazil. Based on my fieldwork, a few hold double religious membership. But the contact between Japanese nationals and foreigners in religious organizations, as in the larger society, is almost minimal.

Constructing Faith—Constructing Gender

Religious discourses are intrinsically related to cultural and social analysis. The Roman Catholic Church presents both a support and a challenge in terms of gender relations. In other words, migrants not only have to negotiate gender expectations in Japanese society, but also have to conform to their religious beliefs. Although this is beneficial in many cases, in others, it results in the reification of hetero-patriarchal normativities. By intersecting religion, migration, ethnicity and gender, my analysis reveals spaces of resistance, (re)negotiation and (re)construction of faith experiences of transnational migrants like Japanese Brazilians.

In my analysis, I also benefit from the contribution of Queer Theory and Queer Liberation Theology. As in the case of gender, Queer Theory has been misread as equal to gay and lesbian constructions. Although those constructions are often included in the analysis of Queer Theory, its main purpose is to expose the multiple ways in which power and agency are performed through relatively fluid social constructions of (genderized/sexualized) identities (Butler 1997:12-16). Furthermore, it also reveals how those performances affect not only socio-economic status, but also more minute and coded play of bodies, desires, and other intersubjective patterns of interactions in daily life (Butler 1997: 138-139; 1993: 34-35). Queer Theory, in this case, is used to critically examine traditional constructions, assumptions, and power relationships in order to expose or open up new possibilities of analysis (Butler 1999: 185).

In the same way, Queer Liberation Theology analyzes the role of faith experiences in the lives of subaltern migrants within a religious organization, in my case study, the Roman Catholic Church. According to Marcella Althaus-Reid

(2000: 19) Queer Liberation Theology does not focus only on established institutional religion and accepted dogmas, but looks behind structures and beliefs in order to expose their gendered/sexualized assumptions. In addition, Queer Liberation Theology unpacks and encourages the multiple ways in which unconventional forms of those established beliefs and practices may provide religious experience and meaning in the daily lives of displaced migrants (Althaus-Reid 2003: 43-45). In other words, gender, Queer Theory and Queer Liberation Theology help us to establish analytical connections in order to uncover occluded performances of gender and religious beliefs in the daily lived experiences of Japanese Brazilian migrants.

Within Christian discourses, Queer Theology helps to explore hidden dynamics related to issues of ethnicity and gender performances within political and economic contexts. In other words, in analyzing sexualized and racialized individuals like Japanese Brazilians in different situations of migration, Queer Theology points out how belief systems and practices empower or hinder them. At the same time, by focusing on the religious aspects of societies, hetero-normativity is exposed since, in most cultures, body, gender and sexuality are policed and molded after religious beliefs. I have observed this especially at the homily (sermons) of many priests at several Roman Catholic Masses in Japan. Although well-intentioned, the sermons tend to reproduce the hetero-patriarchal sexual division of labor as "father" equals "bread-winner" and "mother" equals "raising the children and doing domestic activities," even when women also work in the production line of factories (Yamanaka 2003a: 169; Indra 2004: 5-6). It may be that the sermons and counseling from priests, nuns, and committed lay people such as those who, for example, carry the ministry of *Encontros de Casais* (Meetings of Married Couples) are helping some families to be together amidst many adversities. Sermons and counseling in Roman Catholic practices may also be reproducing the hetero-patriarchal system, which, in some cases, benefits neither women nor children, like for example, in cases of domestic violence.

Every year, the Roman Catholic Church hosts a Mass called *Missa da Sagrada Familia* (Mass of the Holy Family). Drawing from the family experience of Jesus and his parents, Mary and Joseph, the Mass usually evolves into contemplating the lives of families in the congregation. In every Mass that I attended, one of the songs chosen for closure was the *Oração Pela Familia* (Prayer for the Family), written by Brazilian Padre Zezinho (1997). The song reads in one of its stanzas:

> That the man would carry over his shoulder the grace of [being] a
> father; /that the woman would be a heaven of tenderness, embrace
> [*aconchego*] and affection [*calor*]. /And that the children would know
> the strength that emerges from love.

The hetero-patriarchal tone not only praises the sexual division of labor by framing everything into the nuclear family model, but also in how women and men are characterized: for example, relating men to force and toughness and women to emotions. This continues throughout the song, which, in another stanza reads:

> That husband and wife would have the strength to love without
> limits/ . . . That the children would learn in their lap the meaning of
> life. / That the family celebrates the sharing of hugs and bread.

For the non-religious reader this could be just another performativity of
hetero-patriarchal ideology, but it goes deep into Christian history. By listening
to this song and questioning the traditional/common constructions of bodies and
gender, we also encounter colonial performance, since particular or local
constructions from the Western world are universalized. Religion legitimizes
constructions of gender and race. Historically, it has been the case of Northern-
European and (North) American constructions passed along through different
devices, but especially through colonizing theological constructions, which
operated within the realm of *revelation* (Mignolo 2000: 21). In other words, a
local construction not only becomes universal but is also legitimized
transcendentally. At the end, these constructions cannot be questioned, as they
are taken as *natural* in a given society within the Western world. For example,
the experience of the modern nuclear family, a product of the European
industrial revolution in the middle of the eighteenth century, became *the* model
for families, and became universalized. Roman Catholicism shows this trend
worldwide.

In Asia, the Christian missions have tended to import Christian beliefs
contained in cultural devices, exogenous to the new context, sometimes
legitimizing or molding local practices after themselves. The nuclear family and
its subsequent characteristics of subordination of women to patriarchal power, as
well as hetero-normativity, policing and forbidding deviant gender performances
became *the* model through which Christian morality expanded. This was not
always carried out by religious organizations, but by secular Western powers
that had already been immersed within the Christian moral discourse. The
policing of the body and narrow visions of decency completed the process. For
example, one of the most striking performances of gender divisions of the
Roman Catholic Church in Japan is the practice of some women wearing veils
over their heads during the Mass. Of course, men are not required to cover
themselves. Devoted nuns and elder women also offer long scarves to young
women wearing short-blouses or t-shirts in order to cover their arms, while men
are allowed to enter the church without this requirement. Still, women's bodies
are policed and censored when it is not in compliance with given norms of
gender division and notions of *purity* and *decency*, while men enjoy—regardless
of their ethnicity—the privileges of their gender.

A consequence of colonial performativities is the erosion of the ways
different societies and cultures negotiate both orders of body construction and
gender performance, as well as the possibilities for mobility or subversion of
these orders. Colonial performativities and their discourses collide with
hegemonic religious performativities and discourses in (local) dominated places.
This is not to say that *original* (local) notions of body and gender performances

are necessarily *ideal* or *correct*. For example, Christianity in Japan, especially after the Edo period when missionaries were allowed to enter the country again, did not question the pre-existent hetero-patriarchal order, but rather conformed themselves to this order to better fit into Japanese society. While societies rapidly change within the processes of globalization, religious organizations like the Roman Catholic Church lag behind modernizing processes.

Finding Faith in Japan

The majority of Japanese Brazilian migrants in my study do not attend church services in Brazil. They are Roman Catholics because it is the social expectation in Brazil. Many Japanese Brazilians converted to Roman Catholicism after the Second World War. Their participation within the Roman Catholic Church in Brazil is important even today, although a large number remain as *nominal* or non-practicing Catholics. When consulted about their experience after migration, many respondents express that they have "found" their faith in Japan. Rosinha, one of my informants, narrates her experience as follows:

> In Japan I have found faith again [*reencontrado*]. I was born Catholic in Brazil, but did not have really faith. Now I have faith . . . I have knowledge of Jesus, and I am happy! If I have a problem, I have Jesus. Therefore, if I have problems, I know I will overcome them.

Rosinha, a woman in her early 40s, migrated to Japan along with her family. She married a Japanese man in Brazil with whom she had two children. She regularly attends one of the Roman Catholic parishes where I conducted fieldwork. However, in a conversation, she complains about the lack of commitment of some migrants to their Christian faith. She comments:

> Many Brazilians only think of earning more and more money in Japan . . . They do not think about religion. But I believe that almost 70 percent of the people sooner or later find again [*reencontram*] their faith while in Japan.

Rosinha seems to be an example of the many Japanese Brazilians in my study. Some of them even discovered a religious vocation. Two of my interviewees have decided to pursue religious training. Flavio, a man in his early 20s, will soon become a diocesan priest. Stella, a woman in her early 30s, has already begun her training as a nun within an international religious order. Both decided to follow their religious vocations after their arrival and committed participation within the Roman Catholic Church. Stella came from a family of eleven siblings, all residing in Japan. She migrated in order to earn the money to pay the loan she took in order to attend the university in Brazil, from which she finally graduated. After eight years of working, she entered a religious order to become a nun. She narrates her religious experience as follows:

After a year [beginning of the second year in Japan] I had a very strong and special encounter with Jesus, and that is why all my plans have changed, because they are not the same than before [coming to Japan]. It was something so strong that for approximately a year and a half I quit my job at the factory and I dedicated my time to serve the community, to serve the Lord. I visited people who were in prison, I visited people who were sick, and I also did social work. It was a moment that I have that authority to do such impossible things; yet, at the end it gave me a lot of experiences. I participated in that community [of the Roman Catholic Church] for about four years.

After that time, she prepared for another three years discerning her vocation. She finally took the necessary steps to enter the convent. Although not all Japanese Brazilian migrants that I interviewed took the decision to become a priest or a nun, many people express the same experience: from being a non-practicing Catholic in Brazil to being a committed one in Japan. Stella is a good example because she is also part of a strong number of women who actively dedicate their free time to serve the Roman Catholic Church in several social ministries, from visiting people who are in prison or are sick to counseling people. In the case of Stella, she even quit her job for nearly a year and half in order to serve others.

Stella, as well as many women within the Roman Catholic Church, is one nexus to the strong social networks already present among Japanese Brazilians. These networks are important in every aspect of their survival within the context of Japanese society. As soon as one walks into a church or social gathering of Japanese Brazilians, the (re)configuration of new networks is observed. These networks not only include friends and relatives, but also unknown people who meet for the first time inside the Roman Catholic Church. In Brazil, many of these individuals would not get together due to different reasons, such as ethnic or racial issues, social status or geographic locations. On the other hand, in Japan, the situation of migration allows for new contacts and new relationships necessary for the fostering of a better life. Nowadays, the reconfiguration of social interactions ease the process of immigration and settlement in Japan as a worker, and in supporting those left behind in Brazil.

The experiences of Rosinha and Stella, along with that of thousands of other women, reveal that faith occupies a strong part in their lives as migrants. While the Roman Catholic Church has a strong male leadership—for example, all the leaders are male, from the Pope to the parish priest—the daily activities of the Church, as well as the more *domestic* activities (e.g., cleaning, preparing the altar, flower arrangements or coffee hour after mass), are mainly done by women.

Although the first social networks arose in the peak of migration between 1989 and 1991 (Sasaki 2003: 427), in recent years the Roman Catholic Church has expanded its social role in order to focus in other areas for the adaptation of Japanese Brazilian migrants to Japanese society. This social role includes providing moral support, hope, ethical counseling and spiritual well-being. The role of women, especially Japanese Brazilian migrants, who distribute their time between factory work, families and church activities, is vital to this change. Despite the fact that their roles are continuously subordinated to hetero-patriarchalism, in daily life activities their actions keep the church alive. Nonetheless, both the Encyclical Letter of Pope John Paul II, *Redemptoris Mater* No. 46 (1997) and *Erga Migrantes Caritas Christi* No. 70 (2000), which contain teachings of the church about migration, recognize the importance of women for the life and mission of the Roman Catholic Church. Although these represent hetero-patriarchal ideologies migrant women find empowerment through their activities while their subordinated role is paralleled in broader Japanese society. Still, it is the time and dedication of migrant women like Japanese Brazilians that are revitalizing the Roman Catholic Church in Japan, fostering migrants' connections and community.

Conclusion

As globalization continues to operate in the world's economies, cultures and societies, it is likely that there will be more Japanese Brazilian men and women migrating to Japan. Their presence challenges the cultural homogeneity of Japan and contributes to perceived racial/ethnic tensions. The discourses on *Japaneseness* and *Brazilianness* demonstrate the negotiation of particular identities, as well as the (re)configuration of their cultural and social capital in Japanese society as an unavoidable correlate of the migration experience.

Japanese Brazilians are one of the most visible examples of ethnic groups from Latin America facing challenging situations in Japan, and certainly the main nexus between both regions (Asia and Latin America). Their interactions, especially the role of women, within the Roman Catholic Church in Japan constitute an important contribution to this branch of Christianity which attempts to be universal and to include different ethnic groups. The Roman Catholic churches in Japan play a role in how Japanese Brazilians negotiate spaces along gender, race/ethnic lines. However, this does not prevent migrant women from finding and living a faith-filled life. Many Japanese Brazilian women commit themselves to serve actively in the many activities of the Church. Notwithstanding the reproduction of hetero-patriarchal sexual division of labor, their lives and their actions are not only invigorating the Roman Catholic Church but also *faithing* the Japanese Brazilian community in Japan.

Notes

I owe thanks to Professors Keiko Yamanaka, Joshua Hotaka Roth, Raphael Shoji, and Diana Rocco Tedesco as well as Ms. Pauline Cherrier, Fr. Robert Zarate and Fr. Olmes Milani for their support while writing this chapter.

1. Japan received Korean and Chinese workers in the 1890s, the 1920s and the 1930s. See Keiko Yamawaki, "Foreign Workers in Japan," in *Japan and Global*

Migration, ed. Mike Douglas and Glenda Roberts (Honolulu: University of Hawaii Press, 2000), 40, 43-47.
   2. The Kanto region includes Tokyo City and Chiba, Ibaraki, Tochigi, Gunma, Saitama, and Kanagawa prefectures.
   3. Law 172, article 7, clause 1, item 2, Decree of the Ministry of Justice of Japan.
   4. Constitutional Amendment No. 54 was signed on September 20, 2007. See the Ministry of Foreign Affairs of Brazil, *Sobre a Nacionalidade Brasileira*, 2007, http://www.abe.mre.gov.br/mundo/asia/japao/toquio/servicos/nascimento-1 (accessed July 29, 2008).

Bibliography

Adachi, Nobuko. "*Japonês:* A Marker of Social Class or a Key Term in the Discourse of Race?" *Latin American Perspectives* 31, no. 3 (May 2004): 48-76.
Althaus-Reid, Marcella. *Indecent Theology: Theological Perversions in Sex, Gender and Politics*. London: Routledge, 2000.
———. *The Queer God*. London: Routledge, 2003.
Ami, Hiroko. "Despite Being Born in Japan, 7-year-old is Deemed Stateless," *The Japan Times*, February 2, 2002. http://japantimes.co.jp/cgi-bin/nn20020202b6.html (accessed December 7, 2007).
Andrade, Viviana Businger de. "Zainichi Burajirujin Jidou no Gengo Gakushu Mondai [Concerning the issues of language learning among Brazilian students at elementary schools]." Pp 120-125 in *Sociedade Japonesa e Migrantes Brasileiros: Novos Caminhos na Formacao de uma Rede de Pesquisadores*, edited by Chiyoko Mita, Hugo Córdova Quero, Aaron Litvin and Sumiko Haino. Tokyo: Center for Lusophone Studies, Sophia University, 2008.
Butler, Judith. *Bodies that Matter: On the Discursive Limits of Sex*. New York: Routledge, 1993.
———. *The Psychic Life of Power: Theories in Subjection*. Stanford, CA: Stanford University Press, 1997.
———. *Gender Trouble: Feminism and the Subversion of Identity*. New York, NY: Routledge, 1999.
Butsugan, Sumi. "Participação Social e Tendência de Casamentos Interétnicos." Pp. 101-112 in *A Presença Japonêsa no Brasil*, edited by Hiroshi Saito. São Paulo: Editôra da Universidade de São Paulo, 1980.
Cahill, Desmond. *Intermarriages in International Context: A Study of Filipino Women Married to Australian, Japanese and Swiss Men*. Quezon City: Scalabrini Migration Center, 1990.
Daniel, G. Reginald. *Race and Multiratiality in Brazil and the United States: Converging Paths?* University Park, PA: Pennsylvania State University Press, 2006.
Faier, Lieba. "Filipina Migrants in Rural Japan and their Professions of Love." *American Ethnologist* 34, no. 1 (2007): 148-62.
Hamabata, Matthews Masayuki. *Crested Kimono: Power and Love in the Japanese Business Family*. Ithaca, NY: Cornell University Press, 1990.
Higuchi, Naoto. "Migration Process of *Nikkei* Brazilians." Pp. 379-406 in *Emigración Latinoamericana: Comparación Interregional entre América del Norte, Europa y Japón* (JCAS Symposium Series no. 19), org. Yamada Mutsuo. Osaka: The Japan Center for Area Studies (JCAS), National Museum of Ethnology, 2003.

Higuchi, Naoto, and Kiyoto Tanrro. "What's Driving Brazil-Japan Migration? The Making and Remaking of the Brazilian Niche in Japan." *International Journal of Japanese Sociology* 12 (2003): 33-47.

Hirschman, Charles. "The Role of Religion in the Origins and Adaptation of Immigrant Groups in the United States." Paper presented at the conference on Conceptual and Methodological Developments in the Study of International Migration, Princeton University, May 23-25, 2003.

Hongo, Jun. "Bar to Kids' Citizenship Ruled Illegal: Supreme Court Opens Door to Unwed Foreign Moms' Children," *The Japan Times*, June 5, 2008. http://japantimes.co.jp/cgi-bin/nn20080605a1.html (accessed September 5, 2008).

Indra, Doreen. "Not a "Room of One's Own": Engendering Forced Migration Knowledge and Practice." Pp. 1-22 in *Engendering Forced Migration: Theory and Practice*, edited by Doreen Indra. New York: Berghahn Books, 2004.

International Organization for Migration. *Trafficking in Women to Japan for Sexual Exploitation: A Survey on the Case of Filipino Women.* Geneva, Switzerland: International Organization for Migration, 1997.

Iritani, Evelyn. "Lost in a Loophole: Foreigners Who Are on the Losing End of a Custody Battle in Japan Don't Have Much Recourse," *Los Angeles Times*, September 19, 1996, E1.

Lie, John. "Foreign Workers in Japan." *Monthly Review* 44, no.1 (May 1992): 35-42.

———."The Discourse of Japaneseness." Pp. 70-90 in *Japan and Global Migration: Foreign Workers and the Advent of a Multicultural Society*, edited by Mike Douglas and Glenda S. Roberts. Honolulu: University of Hawaii Press, 2003.

Linger, Daniel Touro. *No One Home: Brazilian Selves Remade in Japan.* Stanford, CA: Stanford University Press, 2001.

Matsue, Regina Yoshie. "Religious Activities among the Brazilian Diaspora in Japan: The Cases of the Catholic Church, Sekai Kyuseikyo and Soka Gakkai." Unpublished PhD dissertation, University of Tsukuba, 2006a.

———. "Religious Activities among the Japanese-Brazilians 'Dual Diaspora' in Japan." Pp. 121-146 in *Religious Pluralism in the Diaspora,* edited by P. Pratap Kumar. Leiden: Brill Academic Publishing, 2006b.

Mignolo, Walter. *Local Histories/Global Designs: Coloniality, Subaltern Knowledges, and Border Thinking.* Princeton, NJ: Princeton University Press, 2000.

Ministry of Foreign Affairs of Brazil. *Sobre a Nacionalidade Brasileira.* 2007 http://www.abe.mre.gov.br/mundo/asia/japao/toquio/servicos/nascimento-1 (accessed July 29, 2008).

Ministry of Justice of Japan. *Sobre a emenda Parcial do Decreto "Residente de Longo Período"* (Long Term Resident). 2006. http://www.immi-oj.go.jp/portuguese/keizib an/happyou/longterm_resident.html (accessed July 2, 2008).

———. *Reception of Report on Illegal Stay Foreigner at the Office on Closing Days (Notice).* 2007a. http://www.immi-oj.go.jp/english/keiziban/happyou/an%20informa nt_070921.html (accessed July 2, 2008).

———. *Statistics on the Foreigners Registered in Japan.* Tokyo: Ministry of Justice of Japan, 2007b.

Morita, Kikiro, and Saskia Sassen. "The New Illegal Immigration in Japan, 1980-1992." *International Migration Review* 28, no. 1 (1994): 153-63.

Nojima, Toshihiko. "Susumetai Nikkeijin no Tokubetsu Ukeire [Toward the Special Admission of the Nikkeijin]." *Gekkan Jiyu Minshu* (November 1989): 98-99. Translated and quoted by Keiko Yamanaka, "Return Migration of Japanese-Brazilians to Japan: The *Nikkeijin* as Ethnic Minority and Political Construct."

Diaspora 5, no. 1 (1996): 76.

Novinger, Tracy. *Communicating with Brazilians.* Austin, TX: University of Texas Press, 2003.

Ogena, Nimfa V., Minda Cabilao Valencia and Golda Myra R. Roma. "Filipina Marriage Migration Streams to Japan, Taiwan and South Korea." Paper presented at the Conference on International Marriage Migration in Asia, Seoul, South Korea, September 13-14, 2007.

Padre Zezinho. *Oração pela Familia.* CD 6848-9. Paulinas - COMEP. Audio CD, 1997.

Parreñas, Rhacel. "Trafficked? Migrant Filipina 'Entertainers' in Tokyo's Nightlife Industry." Paper presented at the annual meeting of the American Sociological Association, Montreal, Quebec, Canada, August 11, 2006. http://www.allacadcmic.com//meta/p_mla_apa_research_citation/0/9/5/2/4/pages95240/p95240-1.php (accessed October 28, 2008).

Pinkerton, Steven D. and Paul R. Abramson. "Japan." Pp. 67-86 in *Sociolegal Control of Homosexuality: A Multi-nation Comparison,* edited by Donald James West and Richard Green. Heidelberg: Springer, 1997.

Pope John Paul II. *Redemptoris Mater.* London: Catholic Truth Society, 1987.

———. *Erga Migrantes Caritas Christi* (The Love of Christ towards Migrants). Vatican City: Pontifical Council for the Pastoral Care of Migrants and Itinerant People, 2000.

Roth, Joshua Hotaka. *Brokered Homeland: Japanese Brazilian Migrants in Japan.* Ithaca: Cornell University Press, 2002.

Sasaki, Elisa Massae. "Redes Sociales de Migrantes Brasileños Descendientes de Japoneses de Maringá para Japón." Pp. 418-450 in *Emigración Latinoamericana: Comparación Interregional entre América del Norte, Europa y Japón* (JCAS Symposium Series no.19), org. Yamada Mutsuo. Osaka: The Japan Center for Area Studies, National Museum of Ethnology, 2003.

Sassen, Saskia. "Economic Internationalization: The New Migration in Japan and the United States." Pp. 55-76 in *Globalization and its Discontents: Essays on the New Mobility of People and Money,* edited by Saskia Sassen. New York: The New Press, 1998.

Shipper, Apichai W. "The Political Construction of Foreign Workers in Japan." *Critical Asian Studies* 34, no. 1 (2002): 41-68.

Shoji, Rafael. "The Failed Prophecy of Shinto Nationalism and the Rise of Japanese Brazilian Catholicism." *Japanese Journal of Religious Studies* 35, no. 1 (2008a): 13-38.

———."Religiões entre os brasileiros no Japão: Pentecostalismo Decasségui e Redefinição Étnica." *Rever* (Junho 2008b):46-85.

Solidarity Network with Migrants Japan (SMJ). *Living Together with Migrants and Ethnic Minorities in Japan: NGO Policy Proposals.* Tokyo: SMJ, 2007.

Tobace, Ewerthon. "Eles Moran na Capital," *Higashi Alternativa,* March 20, 2008, 18-29.

Tsuda, Takeyuki. "The Benefits of Being Minority: The Ethnic Status of the Japanese-Brazilians in Brazil." CCIS Working Paper 21. San Diego, CA: The Center for Comparative Immigration Studies /University of California at San Diego, 2000.

———. *Strangers in the Ethnic Homeland: Japanese Brazilians Return Migration in Transnational Perspective.* New York: Columbia University Press, 2003.

———. "Media Images, Immigrant Reality: Ethnic Prejudice and Tradition in Japanese Media Representations of Japanese-Brazilian Return Migrants." CCIS Working Paper 107. San Diego, CA: The Center for Comparative Immigration Studies/University of California at San Diego, 2004.

Yamanaka, Keiko. "Factory Workers and Convalescent Attendants: Japanese-Brazilian Migrants Women and their Families in Japan." Pp. 87-116 in *International Female Migration and Japan: Networking, Settlement and Human Rights*, edited by International Peace Research Institute, Meiji Gakuin University. Tokyo: PRIME, 1996.

————. "Return Migration of Japanese Brazilian Women: Household Strategies and Search for the 'Homeland.'" Pp. 11-34 in *Beyond Boundaries: Selected Papers of Refugees and Immigrants* (Series V), edited by Diane Baxter and Ruth Krulfeld. Arlington, VA: American Anthropological Association, 1997.

————."Feminization of Japanese Brazilian Labor Migration to Japan." Pp. 163-200 in *Searching for Home Abroad: Japanese Brazilians and Transnationalism*, edited by Jeffrey Lesser. Durham: Duke University Press, 2003a.

————."Feminized Migration, Community Activism and Grassroots Transnationalisation in Japan." *Asian and Pacific Migration Journal* 12, no. 1-2 (2003b): 155-88.

Yamashita, Karen Tei. *Circle K Cycle.* Minneapolis, MN: Coffee House Press, 2001.

Yamawaki, Keizo. "Foreign Workers in Japan: A Historical Perspective." Pp. 38-51 in *Japan and Global Migration: Foreign Workers and the Advent of a Multicultural Society,* edited by Mike Douglass and Glenda S. Roberts. Honolulu: University of Hawaii Press, 2000.

Yasumoto, Mariko. "Japanese-Filipino Kids Await Fate: Top Court to Rule on Nationality Law Tied to Paternal Recognition," *The Japan Times,* June 4, 2008. http://japantimes.co.jp/cgi-bin/nn20080604fl.html (accessed June 10, 2008).

Yoshino, Kosaku. *Cultural Nationalism in Contemporary Japan: A Sociological Enquiry.* London: Routledge, 1992.

————. "The Discourse on Blood and Racial Identity in Contemporary Japan." Pp. 199-211 in *The Construction of Racial Identities in China and Japan: Historical and Contemporary Perspectives,* edited by Frank Dikötter. Honolulu, HI: University of Hawaii Press, 1997.

Chapter Four
On Being Part of the Whole: Positioning the Values of Muslim Men in Sydney
Wafa Chafic

This chapter examines the role of religious or Islamic values in the settlement and integration process of immigrants. It attempts to fill some of the empirical void associated with theoretical debates about citizenship (Kabeer 2005), by exploring the settlement experiences and sense of belonging of recently arrived Muslim men in Australia. This study shows how the "risk" agenda post 9/11, based mainly on the negative attributions associated with being a Muslim, has shaped Muslim men's experience of belonging. I review the political campaign over Australian values and citizenship driven by former Prime Minister John Howard and key ministers. The values-citizenship debate posits Muslims in Australia as having a conditional and revocable citizenship, thus marking them off from other Australians. I compare this political narrative with the values, sense of belonging and experiences of incivility expressed by Muslim men. The last section reviews the solutions Muslim men offer for challenges they encounter while settling in a new society. Muslim men, usually the object of much public discourse characterized by negative stereotyping, are engaged as "experts" on their own settlement experience.

While there has been much more attention and interest given to the relationship of Muslim women and the interaction between religion, gender and place (Aitchinson, Hopkins and Kwan 2007: 4), this chapter brings to fore the experiences of Muslim men who arrived in the state of New South Wales, Australia. These men, mainly refugees and asylum seekers, came from Iraq, Afghanistan and a number of African countries (e.g., Sudan, Somalia, Sierra Leone, Liberia, and Burundi). This sample is reflective of settlement trends for the period 2002-2003 through to 2006-2007, which identifies the top three countries of birth for all humanitarian entrants into Australia as Sudan (18,633), Iraq (8,612), and Afghanistan (5,639) (Department of Immigration and Citizenship, DIAC 2007: 13). Approximately 12 percent of humanitarian entrants in New South Wales settle in the Auburn local government area (DIAC 2007: 24). Muslim men in this research were recruited as a result of their connection, mainly as clients, with the Auburn Migrant Resource Centre in Sydney's western suburbs.

Research was carried out over a two-year period (2006-2008) and involved the use of a combination of one-to-one interviews and group consultations. By way of context, information was also gathered from a survey questionnaire given to seventy Muslim men from a variety of ethnic and linguistic backgrounds who arrived in Australia before and after 2000, and are living in different parts of Sydney. This approach elicited information on Muslim men's experience of life in Australia, their concerns, challenges and positive encounters in the community; the type of information, support or services Muslim men regarded as useful in their settlement transition; existing linkages which serve to mitigate isolation within the wider community; and finally, their sense of connectedness and settlement in Australian society, and the key principles and/or values important to these men. It is the latter points, namely of integration, belonging and values that are the focal points of this chapter.

Risk, Values and Australian Citizenship

In 2006, the Australian government initiated a public discussion about citizenship that was mainly constructed around the acceptance of so-called "Australian values." It sought input from the wider community on the plan to implement a citizenship test for individuals wanting to become full members of Australian society. For several years in the lead up to this debate, members of the Howard Liberal Coalition government made comments about Muslim values and beliefs as being unacceptable within the mainstream Australian society. Australian values became central markers of belonging, formalized in the conferring or granting of citizenship. The erosion of multiculturalism and social justice policy frameworks during the Howard years saw a return to a more exclusionary and assimilationist approach to national identity, citizenship and immigration policy. The "nationalism of exclusion" and "nationalism of assimilation," which Mary Kalantzis (2000) identifies as distinct concepts, play out jointly in the contested narratives of the Australian citizenship debate of 2006.

Montserrat Guibernau argues that among the "main strategies generally employed by the state in its pursuit of a single national identity capable of uniting its citizens" is the creation and dissemination of a certain image of the nation, a set of symbols or rituals, a well defined set of civil, legal, political and socio-economic rights and duties, the creation of common enemies "be it imminent, potential or invented" and education and media systems which advance ideals of "good" citizenship (2007: 25). Using Guibernau's model, it may be argued that the Australian nation is sustained through the image of a "mainstream Australia," with a set of symbols known as Australian values at its core, with well defined citizenship and anti-terrorism legislation. Muslims are constructed as the potential, if not imminent threat to ideals of good citizenship.

In the Australian post 9/11 context, Michael Humphrey identifies the emergence of a social construction equating Muslims with "risk," as culturally abject, and subject to conditional citizenship (2005, 2007). This is, no doubt, exacerbated by tragic international events (e.g., London, Madrid and Bali attacks), as well as local occurrences related to the Gang Rapes in southwest Sydney (2000);[1] the Tampa incident (2001);[2] three well publicized speeches given in 2006 by high ranking religious representatives, namely Archbishop of Sydney Cardinal George Pell,[3] the Mufti of Australia Sheikh al-Hilali and Pope Benedict XVI;[4] the Cronulla Riot (2005);[5] and the extra-judicial detentions of Mamdouh Habib (2001-2005) and David Hicks *inter alia* (2001-2007)[6] in Guantanamo Bay, and of Mohamed Haneef in Brisbane (2007),[7] all on allegations of terrorism.

On the political front, negative social constructions are evident in several initiatives undertaken by the former Australian Prime Minister John Howard. They include the "alert but not alarmed" anti-terrorism advertising campaign (officially known as "Let's Look Out for Australia," 2002),[8] the various calls to curb Muslim immigration, and, more importantly, the question of who has the right to lead and represent the Australian Muslim community as characterized by Prime Minister Howard's personal interest in constituting his Muslim Reference Group (2005).[9]

The values and citizenship initiative led by the Howard government and its most senior ministers sustain these same adverse constructions, be it overt or tacit. This is illustrated with comments of the Prime Minister and two other key ministers, namely the Treasurer and the Minister of Education, in the period between August 2005 and February 2006. Comments relating to Muslims from members of the Liberal Coalition government are not limited to these examples.

As the nation's leader, John Howard was not hesitant in expressing a concern that there is a "small section of the Islamic population," which holds extremist views preventing effective integration of Muslims into Australian society. He stated:

> this is not a problem we have ever faced with other immigrant communities who become easily absorbed by Australia's mainstream . . . We want people, when they come to Australia, to adopt Australian ways . . . We don't ask them to forget the countries of their birth, we respect all religious points of views and people are entitled to practice them but there are certainly things that are not part of the Australian mainstream (ABC News 2006a).

The implications of being a "unique problem," that is not easily absorbed or assimilated into the Australian community, and difficult to integrate into the standard of the mainstream yardstick, evoke a concern with Muslims as inherent societal misfits with dubious religious belief and practices. This, coupled with the ominous claim that Australia has never faced such a problem with immigrants before, encapsulates the depth of risk Muslims present to the social cohesion of the Australian nation. Other concerns voiced by Howard revolve around Muslim extremists views on the rights of women and *jihad* (ABC News 2006b). In November 2005, during what became known as the "anti-Muslim raids" instigated for national security reasons, John Howard urged Muslims to support the fight against terrorism, imploring:

> I say to my fellow Australians who are Muslims—you are part of our
> community, we value you, we want you to fully participate in
> Australian life . . . but we also want you to understand that people
> who have anti-social attitudes, people who support terrorism, are
> your enemies as much as they are the enemies of the rest of the
> Australian community (ABC News 2005b).

In the past decade or so Muslim identity has been interrogated by many competing attribution theories and pseudo-theories that are influential within both the realm of state policy and popular culture. Theories which suggest the "clash of civilizations" to claims that "if you are not with us, you are against us," serve to amalgamate many negative and ambiguous attributions to Muslims that abound in the public arena. Howard's sermon-like plea to his fellow Australians infers the potentially subversive impact criminals can play among a gullible, possibly suspect Muslim population in the midst of the Australian community. National security rhetoric of risk serves to socially exclude, and together with the Australian governments' anti-terrorism laws has "the effect of intensifying surveillance . . . thereby producing new social categories of suspicion and undermining the equality of citizenship" (Humphrey 2005: 133).

The Treasurer, Peter Costello, who was accused by various sections of the Australian community of whipping up *Islamophobia*, highlights the threat of Islamic *Sharia* law as being outrightly incompatible with Australian law and values, and affirms that there can only be one law in the nation. He also claims that if the conduct of citizens does not meet the standards of the citizenship test, they could be invited "to forfeit their Australian citizenship" (ABC News 2006 c, d and e). This sets up in the public discourse the idea of "conditional citizenship," meaning citizenship once granted may be revoked by testing against certain measures. This leaves in the first instance a segment of the Australian community, namely those with dual citizenship and those of Muslim persuasion or attribution, open to ongoing scrutiny and surveillance. Consequently, conditional belonging in the wider Australian community relegates Muslims to an apriori second-class citizenship. Formal citizenship status may have been attained, but the question remains as to whether a full or substantive citizenship and belonging can be exercised under such constraints.

In 2005, Brendan Nelson, the Minister of Education for the Liberal government, called for Muslims to "clear off" (i.e., leave Australia) if they "don't want to support and accept and adopt and teach Australian values." He highlighted the importance of understanding "our history and our culture, the extent to which we believe in 'mateship' and giving another person a fair go" (ABC News 2005a). This earlier example of the notion of conditional citizenship is blatantly addressed to Muslims during this episode of the "values debate." The tone and imputations of such comments presume and assert to the wider public that Muslims are necessarily foreign to the sacred symbols of core Australian values such as mateship and fairness. Those being asked to leave may already be Australian citizens, born in Australia or naturalized. The legality of such a stance is highly contentious, but its impact elsewhere may be far reaching. Indeed, the "power of stereotypes derives from their persistence, regardless of evidence" (Kabeer 2005: 5).

Consistent, unequivocal, impassioned stances from the most senior of government members may be interpreted as state-led and endorsed harassment of the Muslim community. Much of the citizenship debate revolves around assertions of the incompatibility of Muslim values with Australian values, with members of the Muslim community needing to address, alter, adjust or reform their values in order to belong as respected members of the community. However, inclusion in such a citizenship is conditional, and therefore hierarchical by nature, with the real potential of exclusion at its heart.

Quest for Islamic or Australian Values

Muslim men who participated in focus group discussions had been refugees or asylum seekers who had endured many hardships in their quest to arrive in Australia. Many expressed relief and a genuine sense of gratitude for being in Australia. One person witnessed a variety of conditions in which Afghan refugees had lived in different places around the world and that he appreciated the high standard of living, the lack of rigid segregation, good infrastructure and support offered to them in Australia. High aspirations for the nation and responsibility to the new country also emerged as themes. In one interview with a man of Iraqi background about his hopes for Australia, he states:

> We hope good for our children, our community and not only for us,
> for everyone in this country to have an education, to have a nice job,
> to have good knowledge, and for us we hope that we have the
> opportunity to serve this community in good ways and good manners,
> to live in good ways . . . that is what I hope.

His reply reflects the sentiments aired by other men as well. This emphasis on "acting well" is also expressed by young Muslim men. They do not see any conflict in being a Muslim in a western society. They feel proud to be part of a community, and that they have a responsibility to act well, as good citizens and good Muslims.

A recurrent theme that emerged in the focus group consultations was the issue of what constitutes Islamic or Australian values. Muslim men reported that respecting Australian rules and values is an Islamic teaching and duty. Respect for their fellow Australians and members of other religious groups, or "all religions and all Prophets" is attributable to their Muslim beliefs. One man sums up these sentiments well:

> Because we are Muslims, we are living in an atmosphere of
> brotherhood with all people regardless of religion, race or language.

Loyalty to their new land and laws is also expressed in comments like:

> We respect Australian rules and values, that is what our religion says; one should not take any steps against the benefit of the people or nation. Our expectation is that you voice our voice.

Another man says:

> I don't know about other communities but I know for all Muslims they do as much as they can faithfully for the country because this is our country. We are not feeling separate from Australian. Since we arrived here, we want to show that this is our country and we want to do good for the country as much as we can.

Survey responses to the open ended question "What three values/principles are important to you?" were sought and collated from seventy men who arrived in Australia recently, i.e., after 2000, and those who may be classified as long term residents, i.e., arriving in Australia before 2000. The most frequently indicated principles of personal importance centered on several main themes. These are related to religion and faith; the importance of family; the importance of truthfulness while identifying honesty, sincerity, and integrity as key factors; and of civic values (see Table 4.1).

Table 4.1 Three Valued Principles of Personal Importance
(NB respondents gave more than 1 response)

Arrived ≥2000		*Arrived<2000*	
Religion and faith	23	Religion and faith	20
Family	20	Civic values – society/	
Culture	9	institutional/equality and	
Truthfulness – honesty/		justice	21
sincerity/integrity	7	Truthfulness – honesty/	
Civic values – society/		sincerity/integrity	13
institutional/equality		Family	8
and justice	6	Morality and ethics	6
Education	5	Friendship	4
Respect	3	Respect	3
Morality & ethics	2	Discipline	2
Employment	2	Education	2
Health	2	Culture	1
Elders	2	Employment	1
Friendship	1	Financial Security	1
Discipline	1	Health	1
Financial Security	1	Love	1
Sport	1	Sport	1
Love	0	Elders	0

It is interesting to note that the open-ended responses relating to civic values encompass three distinctions. The first distinction is related to the *society and community* at large citing such notions as services to society, neighborly help, contributing to humanity, community harmony, good citizenship, and multiculturalism. The second distinction relates to the *institutional basis of civic society* such as democracy, freedom, human rights, government honesty, and law and order. The third distinction related to values of *equality and justice* citing equality of people, respecting all difference, fair go for all, equity, peaceful society and justice.

The above values, while viewed by non-Muslims as somehow antithetical to Islamic belief in the public domain, are, in fact, reflective of an Islamic ethos which places great importance on family (*usra*), service (*khidma*), charity (*sadaqa*), peace and harmony (*salam*) and fairness and justice ('*adl*). Many of these values may well be regarded as generic Australian values. Indeed, this very factor of grounding in Islamic senses of morality may well serve to ease and facilitate integration in a new society where resonant values can also be found. The twin factors of truthfulness as characteristics of moral and ethical integrity, and of civic values as characteristics of civic mindedness are perhaps the most relevant to the discussion on social exclusion. The expectation of moral ineptitude as characterized by the assumption that Muslims have problematic, defective or abject values (Humphrey 2007) is confounded by such results. Quite possibly, then, settlement orientation frameworks (formal and informal) that draw from and/or cite Islamic values and narratives, could offer that transformative impetus toward the integration process, upon which social inclusion and belonging can securely be built.

Social Inclusion and Belonging

As indicators of social inclusion and belonging, Muslim men were asked about their own perception of how "connected" and "settled" they feel in Australian society. Most responses indicate a healthy sense of connectedness and "feeling settled" into Australian society. For both questions, however, approximately a quarter of respondents who arrived after 2000 indicate a low or non-existent feeling of connectedness to Australian society and a poor sense of feeling settled. Such results may be due to their having arrived recently which in turn reflect the possibility that connectedness and feelings of being settled improve as a function of time. These findings illustrate the importance of effective and concerted social inclusionary strategies for minority groups, especially for the recently arrived.

Muslim men were asked to define what "feeling settled" means to them. Responses were grouped into a number of categories. Newer arrivals (i.e., after 2000) gave responses, (in descending order) which indicate a preoccupation with having gainful employment; personal safety and security; social acceptance and a feeling of belonging; education; and positive personal states (i.e., feelings of independence, confidence, happiness, being relaxed and organized). These results are broadly consistent with what one might expect to be pressures and issues faced by new migrants in their new country. Respondents who arrived before 2000 rate social acceptance and a feeling of belonging as highest on the list followed by gainful employment, financial security, integrity of the family unit, and freedom of religious practice and/or identity. "Social acceptance and a feeling of belonging" and "gainful employment" are the two most frequently cited responses for both newer and older residents (see Table 4.2 and 4.3).

Table 4.2 Self-rating: Feeling "Connected" and "Settled" in Australia (>2000)

ARRIVED >2000

Rating	Connected		Settled	
5 (very)	(2)	6%	(4)	11%
4	(11)	31%	(8)	22%
3	(12)	33%	(14)	39%
2	(9)	25%	(9)	25%
1 (not)	(1)	3%	(0)	0%
Unstated	(1)	3%	(1)	3%
	36	100%	36	100%

Table 4.3 Self rating: Feeling "Connected" and "Settled" in Australia (<2000)

ARRIVED <2000

Rating	Connected		Settled	
5 (very)	(13)	38%	(15)	44%
4	(6)	18%	(10)	29%
3	(13)	38%	(8)	24%
2	(2)	6%	(1)	3%
1 (not)	(0)	0%	(0)	0%
Unstated	(0)	0%	(0)	0%
	34	100%	34	100%

Experiences of Incivility

During the focus group sessions, Muslim men expressed a variety of experiences. Many responses indicate that people feel accepted and relaxed in Australia. As earlier discussed men regarded that by virtue of their "Muslimness" they aspire to living in harmonious ways with their fellow Australians. However, many also indicated experiences of discrimination and harassment as forms of incivility, whether in trying to find work and accommodation, and or in public spaces. Scott Poynting and Greg Noble describe a "pervasive landscape of fear and incivility [which] fundamentally alters the social opportunities for Australian Arabs and Muslims to function as citizens" (2004: 19). Muslim men mention that the sweeping anti-terror legislation, and the "be alert not alarmed" campaign, make them feel intimidated or vulnerable to neighbors' scrutiny and surveillance, and fearful that neighbors' lack of cultural awareness could lead to suspicion. Thus, anything suspicious or uncertain could lead to inappropriate referrals and over-reporting. This, of course, is exacerbated by a background of negative portrayals in the media and political spheres leaving men with a feeling of "being singled out." The experience of fear may be a real consequence of the intertwining impact of negative media representation, of political agendas, and the resultant changes in the legal sphere, impacting on civil rights principles.

The media, in particular, is regarded as a major instigator of vilification and discrimination, with Muslims being open game, e.g., whipping up of ethnic-religious hatred and fury during the Cronulla Riots, the Gang Rapes, and the Wars in Iraq and Afghanistan.[10] In addition, the more ubiquitous and selective reporting of news and events coupled with the language of reporting and commentary, are other aspects of media complicity in vilification. That is, constant, repetitive, unfair, and imbalanced associations of Islam/Muslims to adverse events and extreme ideas and actions, convey a generalized but compelling suspicion, fear, or hatred toward Muslims at large. The selective attribution of religion as a major identifier for local or international events and people is seen to be peculiarly applied to Islam and Muslims. They note, on the other hand, that the actions of "non-Muslim others" were not as prone to attribution to their particular religious affiliation. Hence, Muslim men feel that their communities are specifically being targeted and unfairly treated.

Most experiences of discrimination is "ethno-religious" in nature—intertwining race and religion, and having a profound effect on the lives of Muslim men. Characterizations of who exactly is a "Muslim man" are often complex amalgamations of religious, racial and cultural attributions with stereotypical signifiers associated with being criminal or terrorist. The untangling of the racial or religious elements as the basis of discrimination in the case of Muslims can be tedious, if not unproductive. Kevin Dunn and colleagues address the idea of the social construction of specific cultural groups as problematic or "out-groups" and find that there is a "substantial degree of intolerance of Muslim and Arab-Australians" (2004: 426). They attribute this to "geopolitical events, international media and local moral panics" which serve to heighten levels of *Islamophobia* (Dunn et al. 2004: 426). Discrimination affects lives directly and on many levels. One man in this study tells:

> These things affect the family financially, socially, and mentally because the family doesn't feel financially secure, father or son can't find a job, because the hair is not blonde, the skin color, the color of your eyes, even if you change your name.

One experience that is worthy of mention is the situation encountered by a young man of Iraqi background, who spent many of his early years as a refugee prior to arriving in Australia. He responded to a question about whether he felt safer or happier in Australia:

> Not completely, I think because our features can easily identify us. I think some people here don't like us . . . One day I was going to a government office for a job. I was reading the floor directory in the building . . . a lady came out of one room and looked at me (in a nasty way) and asked me "are you here to kill someone?" [I said] "No I am looking for directions." She was on her way out, but I am still thinking about these words, why did she say that? Maybe I look dangerous, I don't know, but I am not [dangerous]. Why did this lady think that? Maybe, I don't know, is it an exaggerated idea about my face? Was it her personal idea? I don't know, but I ask myself why did the lady say that? . . . I am not usually an angry person. I am not a dangerous person. I am not looking for problems because I have enough of my own, so why did she say that? I can't find the right answer for that.

The distress as a residual of this uncivil encounter is evident in this young man's perplexed words. Here we can see the relationship between social incivility and the discomfort it causes, the diminished sense of psychological safety especially for refugees, and a precarious sense of belonging (Noble 2005; Dreher 2006a). This precariousness of belonging or of feeling at home is acutely more important for those of refugee background, and particularly those who experienced trauma. Indeed, in the consultations, Muslim men report a "layering of distress" by virtue of the nature of refugee and asylum seeking migration and settlement processes.

Muslim men who work in welfare services comment that all Muslim men are likely to face some sort of discrimination, observing that "black" Muslim men face it more severely. Congruent with other studies on North African refugees (Perrin and Dunn 2007), Somali and Sudanese Muslim men in this study report their concerns about facing difficulty with government services, and with the police, in attempting to have their skills recognized and in seeking employment.

Older Muslim men speak with deep concern about the younger generation; and they are genuinely worried about young people being insulted with the term "terrorist," labeled or bullied especially at school. They are particularly concerned that there might be a type of collective punishment or blame of community members for the actions of a minority they had no association with, and did not relate to. They want young people to experience opportunities to develop their full potential, to be able to give back to society, and "to be good citizens." Young Muslim men express pride in being part of a community, and that they have a responsibility to act well, as good citizens and good Muslims. Indeed, a consultation conducted with young Muslim men reveals that they are often, cast into the role of "accidental spokesmen," put into the spotlight, having to answer questions about Islam and the actions of other Muslims. They feel inadequately prepared for this, stating they do not have "all the necessary information" to deal with public inquiry.

Similar to the older men, young Muslim men suggest how they might approach such dilemmas, indicating their preparedness to deal with challenges proactively. Solutions to such problems of racism, discrimination and social exclusion include communications and leadership training, interfaith and intercultural opportunities, working with others, and exploring ways to overcome the poor public image of Muslims within the wider community, to name a few. It is important to note the Muslim men's desire to leverage their religious knowledge and community structures and to make constructive engagements with welfare services, government agencies, the legal system and the media. By the same token, they regard governments and media organizations as having a strong responsibility for creating and maintaining social harmony and for protecting vulnerable members of the community. Throughout the consultations Muslim men reflect a strong ethos of collaborative responsibility.

Substantial Citizenship and Honorability

The tendency for young people to "take seriously the question of their relationship to the wider society," display high levels of responsibility and find "it much easier to talk about responsibilities than rights" is evident in this group of young men (Lister et al. 2003: 250-251). They regard themselves as new spokesmen, and claim that they have limited resources by way of skills or social, religious and political knowledge to deal with this new role and responsibility. They indicate an interest in participating in mentoring programs; training in communication skills; learning about Islam; exploring cultures, values and self-identity; and how to best represent their communities. Indeed, this sense of responsibility and relationship with the wider society is evident in older men as well. Both younger and older men indicate that the Muslim community is not proactive enough in combating the poor public image of Muslims, particularly in terms of disassociating Islam from "terrorist." Older men also welcome the possibility of training in communication and leadership skills, in participating in interfaith and inter-community activities, working with government and community organizations, dealing with negative perceptions and generating acceptance within the wider community. Some of the suggestions they made aim at reducing community segregation and closing gaps between the Muslim and mainstream communities by "[building] respect and responsibility, brotherhood, and citizenship." This desire to participate more fully in the various segments of society, beyond the formalistic acquisition of citizenship reflects the tendency toward substantial citizenship. Stephen Castles defines substantial citizenship as having "equal chances for participation in various areas of society, such as politics, work and social security" (2000: 192).

Tanya Dreher (2006b) extends the implications of social inclusion to encompass the idea of responsibility between communities and government which is also echoed by Muslim men. She identifies three principles of anti-racism practices. The first emphasizes the importance of sustainable practice as opposed to the overload that the Arab and Muslim communities endure at times of crisis and can be seen in the response of young Muslim men taking on the new role of spokesmen with very few resources. The second principle recommends partnerships across communities and with government, and the third, community capacity building which builds skills and allows skills transfer. Similarly, Muslim men speak of working collaboratively with government, community organizations and the media to deal with issues of social inclusion and participation. Responsibility is not regarded as one sided since each party has a role to play.

Muslim men regard the media as having the responsibility to report and give fair commentary. They recognize the media as a major social and political driver within the Australian community, "contributing to experiences of fear and exclusion" (Dreher 2006a) and, as such, is accountable for its role in maintaining a harmonious and civil society. Muslim men also view the government as having a role in actively creating and maintaining conditions for social harmony as a way of protecting its citizens. As one Muslim man puts it, the government has a role in directing the media not to "negatively reflect, nor injure the sense of the people, in order to avoid disappointment and the point of frustration." Ghassan Hage poses the question "what value has a citizenship that confers rights but denies people's humanity?" (2002: 3). The concept of honorability as "an expression of a universal ethical valorization of dignity and autonomy in inter-personal and inter-cultural relations" (Hage 2002: 8) is clearly important to Muslim men and their sense of belonging in Australian society.

Conclusion

There is no doubt that experiences of discrimination and incivility faced by Muslim men are aggravated by the post 9/11 climate. As witnessed in the Howard years, it is also impacted by politically motivated imputations of unworthy citizenship and conditional belonging based on religious ascription. However, the industrious approach adopted by Muslim men geared toward collaborative social responsibility inverts the many stereotypes attached to their religious identity. Indeed, religious values are regarded as "common ground" within the wider society. This commonality of values is a positive indicator of belonging, and creates a currency and agility for functioning as contributing members of society. As we can see in the case of these Muslim men, religious values should be regarded as enabling factors that serve social inclusion rather than the contrary. It is, therefore, imperative that policy makers and political leaders give proper attention to concepts and practices of citizenship which honor and respect new residents and, at the same time, capitalize on genuine common ground, rather than exclude on the basis of religion, in the creation of spaces for meaningful citizenship and belonging.

Notes

1. The Gang Rape incidents refer to a series of gang rape attacks on women in the southwestern Sydney by a group of Australian men of Lebanese background. These crimes were portrayed in the media as being racially motivated. See "Skaf Brothers Appeal Against Rape Convictions," *ABC News* , June 20, 2008, http://www.abc.net.au/news/stories/2008/06/20/2280730.htm (accessed December 14, 2008); Kiran Grewal, "The 'Young Muslim Man' in Australian Public Discourse," *Transforming Cultures Journal,* 2, no. 1, (November 2007) http://epress.lib.uts.edu.au/ojs/index.php/TfC/article/view/599/546 (accessed December 15, 2008).

2. Tampa Incident (2001) refers to the rescue of 438 Afghan refugees by Captain Rinnan of the Norwegian cargo ship named "Tampa." The Australian government headed by Prime Minister Howard refused the entry of the Tampa into Australian waters as a way to evade applications for residence among asylum seekers, asserting that only the government had the right to decide who comes into the country and how. This incident created controversy as the Australian government pursued a path to limit the influx of refugees into the country by excising territory from Australia's migration zone. For a full discussion on "border protection issues" and the federal government's "Pacific Solution" see David Marr and Marian Wilkinson, *Dark Victory* (Crows Nest NSW: Allen and Unwin, 2004).

3. In a speech to the Legatus Summit in Naples, Florida, USA (February 4, 2006) Cardinal Pell, Catholic Archbishop of Sydney, refers to Islam as an intolerant religion, which advocates violence. See George Pell, "Islam and Western Democracies" (paper presented at the Legatus Summit, Naples, Florida., February 2006), http://www.sydney.catholic.org.au/Archbishop/Addresses/200627_681.shtml (accessed December 14, 2008).

4. Both the Mufti Sheikh al-Hilali and Pope Benedict XVI caused controversy with the comments they made and later apologized for. The Mufti apologized for comments linking women's dress to risk of sexual assault, while the Pope apologized for negative comments about Islam. See "Sheik Apologizes for Sexist Comments," *The Age*, October 26, 2006, http://www.theage.com.au/news/national/sheik-sorry-for-sexist-comment/2006/10/26/1161749243241.html (accessed December 14, 2008); "Pope Sorry for Offending Muslims," *BBC News*, September 17, 2006, http://news.bbc.co.uk/2/hi/europe/5353208.stm (accessed December 14, 2008).

5. For a comprehensive report on the Cronulla Riots see Liz Jackson, "Riot and Revenge," *Four Corners*, March 13, 2006, http://www.abc.net.au/4corners/ content/2006/s1590953.htm (accessed December 14, 2008).

6. For a detailed account of alleged terrorists, Habib and Hicks, see Nigel Brew et al., "Australians in Guantanamo Bay: A Chronology of the Detention of Mamdouh Habib and David Hicks," *Chronologies Online: Parliamentary Library of Australia*, May 29, 2007, http://www.aph.gov.au/library/pubs/online/Australians_GuantanamoBay.htm (accessed December 14, 2008).

7. Mohamed Haneef was detained in Brisbane in 2007 on allegations of supporting a terrorist organization involved in bomb plots in the United Kingdom. See "Gov't Confirms Haneef Inquiry," *ABC News*, March 13, 2008, http://www.abc.net.au/news/sto ries/2008/03/13/2188378.htm (accessed December 14, 2008).

8. The "Let's Look Out for Australia" was the first phase of the National Security Public Information Campaign. See Australian Government, "Australian National Security," September 26, 2008, http://www.ag.gov.au/agd/www/nationalsecurity.nsf/Pag e/Information_for_IndividualsNational_Security_Public_Information_Campaign (accessed December 14, 2008).

9. See Jason Dowling, "Howard Move on Muslim Dialogue," *The Age*, September 11, 2005, http://www.theage.com.au/news/war-on-terror/howard-move-on-muslim-dialog ue/2005/09/10/1125772732630.html (accessed December 14, 2008).

10. The Human Rights and Equal Opportunities Commission in at least two separate reports, documents the concerns and need for media fairness in coverage of issues related to Islam or Muslims. See Human Rights and Equal Opportunities Commission, *Racist Violence: Report of the National Inquiry into Racist Violence in Australia* (Canberra: AGPS, 1991) and *Isma-Listen: National Consultations on Eliminating Prejudice against Arab and Muslim Australians* (Sydney: HREOC, 2004).

Bibliography

ABC News. "Minister Tells Muslims: Accept Aussie Values or 'Clear Off'," August 24, 2005a. www.abc.net.au/news/stories/2005/08/24/1445181.htm (accessed 14 Dec. 2008).

———."PM Denies Raids Anti-Muslim," November 2, 2005b. http://www.abc.net.au/news/stories/2005/11/09/1500786.htm (accessed December 14, 2008).

———."PM Critical of 'Extremist' Muslims, February 20, 2006a, http://www.abc.nct.au/ncws/storics/2006/02/20/1573689.htm. (accessed December 14, 2008).

———. "Howard Reinforcing Negative Stereotypes, Muslims Say," February 20, 2006b. http://www.abc.net.au/news/stories/2006/02/20/1573972.htm (accessed December 14, 2008)

———."Costello Pushes Nationality 'Test,'" February 24, 2006c. http://www.abc.net.au /news/stories/2006/02/24/1577182.htm (accessed December 14, 2008).

———."Costello Defends Muslim Citizenship Comments," February 24, 2006d. http://www.abc.net.au/news/stories/2006/02/24/1577268.htm (accessed December 14, 2008).

———."Costello Accused of 'Islamophobia,'" February 24, 2006e. http://www.abc.net.au/news/stories/2006/02/24/1577530.htm (accessed December 14, 2008).

———."Gov't Confirms Haneef Inquiry," March 13, 2008a. http://www.abc.net.au/new s/stories/2008/03/13/2188378.htm (accessed December 14, 2008).

———."Skaf Brothers Appeal against Rape Convictions," June 20, 2008b. http://www.abc.net.au/news/stories/2008/06/20/2280730.htm (accessed December 14, 2008).

Aitchison, Cara, Peter Hopkins and Mei-Po Kwan, eds. *Geographies of Muslim Identities: Diaspora, Gender and Belonging.* Hampshire, England: Ashgate, 2007.

Australia Forum. "Australian Citizenship: Much More than a Ceremony, But Much More than Passing a Test, Far More about Principles than 'Values,' Far More about

Extending Mateship for Inclusion than Screening for Exclusion." A response and submission to the Citizenship Discussion Paper by Andrew Robb, MP and Parliamentary Secretary to the Minister of Immigration and Multicultural Affairs, Australia, September 2006.

Australian Government. *Australian National Security.* September 26, 2008. http://www.ag.gov.au/agd/www/nationalsecurity.nsf/Page/Information_forIndividua lsNational_Security_Public_Information_Campaign (accessed December 14, 2008).

BBC News. "Pope Sorry for Offending Muslims." September, 17, 2006. http://news.bbc.co.uk/2/hi/europe/5353208.stm (accessed December 14, 2008).

Brew, Nigel, Jan Miller, Roy Jordan and Sue Harris Rimmer. "Australians in Guantanamo Bay: A Chronology of the Detention of Mamdouh Habib and David Hicks." *Chronologies Online: Parliamentary Library of Australia.* 2007. http://www.aph.gov.au/library/pubs/online/Australians_GuantanamoBay.htm (accessed December 14, 2008).

Castles, Stephen. *Ethnicity and Globalization: From Migrant Worker to Transitional Citizen.* London: Sage Publications, 2000.

Department of Immigration and Citizenship. *New South Wales: Settlement Trends and Needs of New Arrivals 2007.* Belconnen ACT: DIAC, 2007.

Dowling, Jason. "Howard Move on Muslim Dialogue," *The Age,* September 11, 2005. http://www.theage.com.au/news/war-on-terror/howard-move-on-muslim-dialogue/2005/09/10/1125772732630.html (accessed December 14, 2008).

Dreher, Tanya. "Targeted: Experiences of Racism in NSW after September 11, 2001." *UTS Shopfront Monograph Series,* no. 2 (2006a).

———. "Whose Responsibility? Community Anti-Racism Strategies after September 11, 2001." *UTS Shopfront Monograph Series,* no. 3 (2006b).

Dunn, Kevin, James Forrest, Ian Burnley and Amy McDonald. "Constructing Racism in Australia." *Australian Journal of Social Issues* 39, no. 4 (November 2004): 409-430.

Grewal, Kiran. "The 'Young Muslim Man' in Australian Public Discourse." *Transforming Cultures eJournal* 2, no.1 (November 2007). http://epress.lib.uts.edu. au/ojs/index.php/TfC/article/view/599/546 (accessed December 15, 2008).

Guibernau, Montserrat. *The Identity of Nations.* Cambridge, UK: Polity Press, 2007.

Hage, Ghassan. "Citizenship and honourability: Belonging to Australia Today." Pp. 1-15 in *Arab-Australians: Citizenship and Belonging Today,* edited by Ghassan Hage. Victoria: Melbourne University Press, 2002.

Ho, Christina. "Cronulla, Conflict and Culture." Paper presented at the UTSpeaks Lecture, Sydney, Australia, September 5, 2006. http://www.uts.edu.au/new/speaks/2 006/September/resources/0509-transcript.html (accessed June 1, 2008).

Human Rights and Equal Opportunities Commission. *Racist Violence: Report of the National Inquiry into Racist Violence in Australia.* Canberra: Australian Government Publishing Service, 1991.

———. *Isma-Listen: National Consultations on Eliminating Prejudice against Arab and Muslim Australians.* Sydney: HREOC, 2004.

Humphrey, Michael. "Australian Islam, the New Global Terrorism and the Limits of Citizenship." Pp. 132-148 in *Islam and the West: Rreflections from Australia,* edited by Shahram Akbarzadeh and Samina Yasmeen. Sydney, Australia: UNSW Press, 2005.

———. "Culturalizing the Abject: Islam, Law and Moral Panic in the West." *Australian Journal of Social Issues* 42, no. 1 (Autumn 2007): 9-25.

Jackson, Liz. "Riot and Revenge." *Four Corners*, March 13, 2006. http://www.abc.net.au/4corners/content/2006/s1590953.htm (accessed December 14, 2008).

Kabeer, Naila, ed. *Inclusive Citizenship: Meanings and Expressions*. London: Zed Books, 2005.

Kalantzis, Mary. "Multicultural Citizenship." Pp. 99-110 in *Rethinking Australian Citizenship*, edited by Wayne Hudson and John Kane. Cambridge UK: CUP, 2000.

Lister, Ruth, Noel Smith, Sue Middleton and Lynne Cox. "Young People Talk about Citizenship: Empirical Perspectives on Theoretical and Political Debates." *Citizenship Studies* 7, no. 2 (2003): 235-253.

Marr, David and Marian Wilkinson. *Dark Victory*. Crows Nest NSW: Allen and Unwin, 2004.

Modood, Tariq, Anna Triandafyllidou and Ricard Zapata-Barrero, eds. *Multiculturalism, Muslims and Citizenship: A European Approach*. Oxon: Routledge, 2006.

Noble, Greg. "The Discomfort of Strangers: Racism, Incivility and Ontological Security in a Relaxed and Comfortable Nation." *Journal of Intercultural Studies* 26, no. 1 (February-May 2005): 107-120.

Pell, George. "Islam and Western Democracies." Paper presented at the Legatus Summit, Naples, Florida, February 2006). http://www.sydney.catholic.org.au/Archbishop/Ad dresses/200627_681.shtml (accessed December 14, 2008).

Perrin, Rebecca-Lee and Kevin Dunn. "Tracking the Settlement of North African Immigrants: Speculations on the Social and Cultural Impacts of a Newly Arrived Immigrant Group." *Australian Geographer* 38, no. 2 (July 2007): 253-273.

Poynting, Scott and Greg Noble. "Living with Racism: The Experience and Reporting by Arab and Muslim Australians of Discrimination, Abuse and Violence since 11 September 2001." Report to the Human Rights Equal Opportunity Commission, April 19, 2004.

"Sheik Apologizes for Sexist Comments," *The Age*, October 26, 2006. http://www.theage.com.au/news/national/sheik-sorry-for-sexist-comment/2006/10/2 6/1161749243241.html (accessed December 14, 2008).

Chapter Five
Praying for Food: Class and Indian Overseas Students in Australia
Michiel Baas

This chapter investigates the role of places of worship in the migration experience of Indian overseas students in Melbourne. Indian students do not only come to Australia for higher education, but oftentimes they also have the intention of becoming Australian permanent residents. (Baas 2006, 2007) They are often considered migrants as well as students. This chapter examines how ideas on class and gender intersect with the meaning and function of religious places in the lives of students. I use a personal case where issues such as integration, religion or religious institutions, notions of success and failure, class aspirations, and the role of local migrant communities intersect. My research shows that many Indian students perceive Australia as a stepping-stone to other countries like the United States. Their aim is not so much to integrate in Australian society, but to use their Australian permanent residency (PR) to become transnationally mobile. This desire of transnational mobility appears to be an attempt at global integration that is highly influenced by images, stories and connections with Indians who have already "made it" in that sense. India is increasingly associated with the fast-moving world of information technology (IT) and associated industries and these developments have offered some Indians a lifestyle that consists of constant traveling, working for prestigious global operating companies (e.g., IBM and Microsoft), and earning high salaries. This has added a new dimension to how young recent Indian graduates with bachelor's degrees look at the future. Obtaining an Australian PR is the first step toward fulfilling their dreams.

This chapter focuses on two friends who came to Australia as overseas students. They are both of north Indian middle class backgrounds and have grown up in business families. One (Ajay) is studying textile management; the other (Happy) recently finished his degree in the same field. By following them on their way to a local *gurdwara* (Sikh place of worship)[1] in a suburb of Melbourne, examining what goes on in the prayer hall and after dinner is served, as well as joining them on their way back home, we are in a position to investigate the question of what it means to be a student and migrant at the same time. Talking about other "students," the locally established Indian community, and the implication of obtaining Australian permanent residency, provides a better understanding of how young, well-educated migrants from affluent backgrounds perceive their place in the world. It is important to include gender since majority of Indian students in Australia are not only male, but also have certain ideas on sexuality. The way they talk about their experiences shows something peculiar about their migration trajectory. The gurdwara serves as a nodal point of all aspects of their lives: being students as well as migrants, being highly-educated but often working in lowly-paid jobs, the ambivalent relationship between the locally established Indian community and these newcomers, and issues of migration and "being Australian," come together.

Going to the gurdwara on Wednesday evenings is a popular event among Indian students in Melbourne, especially for its free meals. Other religious institutions, like the Hare Krishna temple in the seaside suburb of St. Kilda, are popular for similar reasons on other days. Interestingly, students with different religious backgrounds are found in all these places. As one Muslim student at Monash University explains, being a Muslim does not stop him from going to the temple. A *Bohri* Muslim himself, and coming from a family that made its money in the paper business, he claims to have many Hindu friends in Mumbai: "Me, being a Muslim has never been a problem till date." He meets most of his friends in Melbourne at the university. "It just matters you are Indian here; that is the community you are from here." He never experiences any particular difficulty in living a religious life: "I sometimes go to the prayer room here at university." In addition, he goes to the Hare Krishna temple on Sunday's around twelve: "They have a free lunch then." Similarly, he goes to the gurdwara on Wednesdays. "We go there for the food most of all. They give *kheer* [rice pudding], we all love that." Other students narrate similar observations.

Religious places of worship sometimes play a marginal role in student's lives. These places are popular for two things: they are seen as meeting places for Indian students and migrants, and to get free food. Arguably, despite the marginal religious role the gurdwara plays, it still performs an important function in the lives of students. The trip to gurdwara with Happy and Ajay is useful in exploring how class and gender operate in a religious setting where religion itself seems to take second place. For this reason, we move away from all too apparent discussions on the way religion itself influences migrants' integration in the host country, the transnational linkages they envision, or how attending religious institutions fosters fanaticism. We now focus instead on how religious institutions sometimes play completely different role in migrants' lives.

Our Way to Gurdwara

In the train from Flinders Street Station (Melbourne's most central train station) to Blackburn, an outer suburb, Happy looks excited. It is a dark, chilly Wednesday evening in June and we are on our way to the gurdwara. Ajay usually goes on Wednesday evenings but Happy's many and frequently changing part-time jobs often prevent him from coming along. Ajay and Happy know each other through loosely connected Punjabi networks, which include overseas students from other parts of India as well. Indian students have a very visible presence in Melbourne particularly on trains, trams and buses. It is not very difficult to meet and make contact with fellow Indian students. In addition, most universities in the Melbourne area have Indian or South Asian themed clubs and societies that are run by students themselves. They regularly organize activities where not only Indian or South Asian students of that particular university come together but students from other universities join in as well. This is also how Ajay and Happy first met and they have been friends since then.

The gurdwara is not only popular on Wednesday evenings among Indian students for the free meals that consequently saves them money but also provides those who travel all the way to Blackburn with a chance to eat "real" Indian food. It is perceived to be an evening when one could be with other Indians, eat real Indian food, and "get a sense of home." Yet, on our way to the gurdwara, this is not the only source of Happy's excitement. "Girls," he smiles happily. He adds: "Many nice girls there, man!" I noticed him looking at his own reflection in the window, rubbing his day old beard, nodding approvingly. He is pleased with the way he looks that evening. Recently, he brags a lot about his latest "conquest": a Chinese girl who kept calling him regularly (or, as he put it: "all the time"), and whom he is more than a little fond of. Yet, he could not help add, it is always good to have some options on the side. The gurdwara is a good place to spot new girls. Nineteen-year-old Ajay listens to it all with a faint smile. He heard Happy's stories more than once before and is not particularly impressed.

Profile of Young Middle Class Indians

By the end of 2006, there were nearly 350,000 overseas students enrolled in Australia, making the country possibly one of the world's biggest sources for education on a commercial basis.[2] The "export education industry"[3] is one of Australia's largest service industries with an annual turnover of around AU$7.5 billion (Morton 2006). There were 38,700 Indian students in Australia in 2006 compared to 27,400 in 2005. This made India the second biggest source country of overseas students after China. Their number continues to grow and was expected to have reached new heights by the end of 2008.

My anthropological fieldwork in Melbourne focuses on Indian students seeking permanent residency in Australia. Based on a year of intensive study in 2005, I interviewed 230 people, of which 130 are Indian overseas students. The other 100 are all connected to their lives one way or another. The group of students in the study is very diverse in terms of place of origin, university and course of choice, but I draw some generalizations about their profile. First, most students are enrolled in so-called masters' programs which means that they are between twenty-one and twenty-five years old, completed a bachelor's program in India, and are often already employed in India before coming to Australia. Second, almost all are of middle class background, with educated parents and grandparents. More than 90 percent have attended "convent" or English medium schools and are conversant in English at home and with their friends. They are multi-lingual, as they speak one or two Indian languages, usually Hindi and another local language. Students are, generally, of a Hindu upper-caste background and only a very small minority comes from Christian or Muslim families.

Generalizations forego internal differences and nuances. Claiming that people are of a middle class background ignores discussions on the meaning of "Indian middle class" (Fernandes 2006; Ranada 2005; Robinson 2001; Säävälä 2003; Shurmer-Smith 2000; Wells 2001; Van Wessel 2004). For some families being middle class is a much more recent phenomenon than for others. During interviews, students sometimes make the distinction between "lower" middle class, "middle" middle class and "upper" middle class. They usually categorize themselves in the latter two yet did, at times, reveal how they perceive themselves, also in relation to their migration status. And as caste and class are inseparable entities in India, this is certainly part of this self-identification as well.

In my study of 130 students, over 10 percent financed their studies in Australia in some other way than a student loan. The rest either financed their studies abroad entirely or in part through a full education loan. Although the Australian government demands that a student proves on paper that he or she can afford to study in Australia, thus, paying for it through private money or a loan, half of the students in my study exaggerate the value of their family's assets (i.e., land, houses, and value of gold owned in terms of jewelry) in order to get a higher loan amount. These students have no intention of actually using the loan in its entirety. They come to Australia with the intention of making most of the money they need locally by working as much as possible. Legally, students are not allowed to work more than twenty hours per week during semesters, but many work much more than that. The only way to do this is by working cash-in-hand so that the hours are not registered anywhere. Regular raids by the immigration authorities not only cause considerable stress among students but also lead to incarceration in migration detention centers, and as a consequence, are forced to leave Australia. Indian students are often in a very complex financial situation. Not only are loans sometimes based on an overvaluation of assets or fictitious amount but, in reality, the bank granted a much lower amount.[4]

Loans taken out from Indian banks come with strict repayment schemes[5] in which students are not only faced with taking care of their living expenses in Melbourne but also of easing the burden off their families back home. Part of this strategy is, very simply put, spending as little money as possible. Going to the gurdwara on Wednesday evening may thus be understood as a way to save money. Yet, regular visits also show that going to the gurdwara has an important function in establishing the status of migrants. This is heavily influenced by the meaning of a successful male Indian student with a plan to become an Australian permanent resident. Class backgrounds impact on the idea of tempering "success" or explaining "failure." Such class backgrounds are constantly performed and reproduced in conversations between them and reflection on the lives of other Indian students. Gender intersects with the performance of a "successful heterosexual Indian man" that is often used as a way to correct a lack in class.

The Manly Indian Student

As the majority of Indian students in Melbourne are male, I will highlight their gendered narratives regarding life in Melbourne and the way they see their future in Australia. Official statistics confirm that 80 percent of Indian students are male,[6] and this is readily visible. At any place where Indian students are found (in classrooms, on campuses, at locally organized "Indian" events, religious institutions, or even simply in the train heading home), it is clear that there are more male than female Indian students in Australia. Such gender gap influences the way the two years that most Indian students stay in Australia is understood. Interaction is mostly with other male students; expectations, impressions, opinions and so on are mostly perceived through a mono-gendered lens. This chapter provides an interesting case in examining the gendered process of migration.

Gender is important in understanding migration (Sharpe 2003; Hartzig 2003; Arya and Roy 2006; Donato et al. 2006; Silvey 2006).[7] As Anna Boucher puts it, "skilled immigration has slipped by as a genderless story in which the androgynous skilled migrant is the central character and economists do most of the storytelling" (2007: 383). Christiane Hartzig calls for the introduction of the *famina migrans* in order to balance with the all familiar and classical *homo migrans* who was also defined in male terms: young, single, independent and unattached, endlessly mobile, in the *prima* of his physical strength (2003: 15, 22). As Pamela Sharpe argues (following Henrietta Moore), "feminist research has shown the ways in which women experience social and economic pressures differently from men" (2003:7- 8). Migration, thus, is a gendered phenomenon (Donato et al. 2006: 4), and understanding migration means that the topic should also be approached with a perspective that takes this into account. Many studies on gender are still about giving women a voice. Although so much has been written on male migrants, they actually do not take into account gender as a factor. In other words, in the world of migration "maleness" is often supposed to speak for itself. I wish to challenge this prevailing situation.

Being part of the migration process as a male Indian very much influences the way this process is experienced. Not only is the world of studying abroad, at least for Indians, male dominated, but the way it is experienced is also a continuation of what it is like in India. Schools and colleges are often all-boy or all-girl, and so are the dormitories and hostels where these students live while completing their undergraduate studies. They have been educated, and one could argue, they have even grown up in an environment often characterized by the lack of the other gender. At the same time, education is still, to a large extent, linked to class in India. Certainly at the higher levels, students of middle class backgrounds dominate the class rooms and lecture halls.

Class, as a variable, is recently introduced in studies of gender and migration. In a study of Indian hotel employees, Adina Keryn Batnitzky and colleagues (2008) demonstrate that class and gender are intricately linked in the way the migration process is experienced. In their study of young middle class men working in a London hotel they demonstrate the process of migration "both challenges and reinforces migrants' gender and class identities in the country of destination by challenging monolithic assumptions about Indian men, as well as Indian notions of class-based masculine identity" (Batnitzky et al. 2008: 52). Indians who find a job in what they apparently consider the "glamorous" hospitality industry of London are, to a certain extent, comparable to the experiences of Indian students I investigated in Melbourne. Like Indian hotel employees, they develop an interest in studying in Australia because of its appealing imagery, which plays both a verbal and physical part in Indian middle class lives at home. Australian universities aggressively market their education services (e.g., campus, location, and amenities) in India, creating the idea of a very attractive destination. In addition, many middle class families have family members abroad (Fernandes 2006), or will at least know of people abroad. Because of such ties and linkages, imagery of an appealing life abroad is often conveyed back to India. It is through an analysis of such imagery that we understand the reason for migrating and studying abroad.

I wish to elaborate on the work of Batnitzky and colleagues on the intricate relations between gender and class, especially in experiencing the migration process. By purposely bringing issues of success and failure both before and after migration into the equation, migration itself is considered both as an ongoing process and one that may have had earlier *avatars* (incarnation) as well. Attempts to migrate are often clouded with an aura of it being the first time that a particular person plans to migrate. Yet, such migration attempt might also be the result of earlier failed effort. This failure affects the experience of class and gender and the way these are performed in both India and abroad. The point is, the way migration-decisions are made is highly dependent on earlier success or failure. Among Indian students in Melbourne this is an important topic of conversation since many had applied for an American study visa before they made the decision to go Australia. Australia often falls in second or third place when it comes to preferred study-abroad decisions. A number of students also attempted to get into one of the top institutes in India itself; something they believe even outranked studying in the United States.

A successful migration path for a male Indian clearly depends on what is perceived to be appropriate for men. This means that to be a middle class Indian with a desire to make it abroad relates to gendered expectations as well as past experiences of success and failure. Class dynamics in India are visible through pressures of "success" in terms of making money, going to the right institute, migrating to the right country and so on. Issues related to success and failure perate at semi-individual levels or what I call "arrival points": imagined moments in the future what one had planned out to achieve will all be achieved. Although gender and class influence such arrival points by themselves, they are also influenced by western and/or global images that further affect what migrants such as these young middle class Indians work for. In that sense, I agree with Batnitzky and colleagues that class-based gender identities change across time and place (2008: 53) but I also argue that we should not understand Indian middle class identities purely as "Indian" but equally also as "global," influenced by the numerous stories of migrant family members, friends and acquaintances bring home, as well as western TV programs, movies and the Internet.

Migrating to Australia

Happy came to Australia because he was not accepted in one of the better universities in India. Although this was also the case of Ajay, he was keener to experience studying abroad. In addition, his parents could easily afford it. For Happy, this is different. True, his family is able to meet the financial criteria demanded by the "immigration people" but once in Australia he has to take care of himself. This means working part-time to make ends meet in terms of groceries, rent and books. Ajay's family, on the other hand, takes care of everything through a generous monthly allowance.

Happy's father is a businessman whom he describes as: "he is into electronics and garments. My father buys electronics from other countries; he imports them." Happy thinks of his family as involved in a typical business. His great grandfather was a laborer but his grandfather had already been in "business." He considers his family upper middle class based on their family income: "Income-wise, we are above average. So that determines it." To that he adds: "We are not rich but we are a good family." Ajay refers to all his extended family as engaged in the same business. His great grandfather, father and his uncles are in the same line of business. Initially, they operated rolling mills and six or seven years ago they diversified into textiles. His grandfather had always been very interested in this line of business and, according to Ajay, his father, the managing director, finally fulfilled the dream of starting it and "the turn-over of the company is now AU$95 million."

Happy and Ajay are both from affluent business families. Yet, the economic prosperity of Happy's family is more recent than Ajay's in terms of fixed assets (i.e., factory buildings, houses, and land). Whenever Happy classifies his family in terms of being "upper middle class," he more regularly brings up his background, upbringing and family's successes than Ajay does. He often claims that he comes from a "good family": they are "good business people" and their business makes "good money." He mentions such things when Ajay is around. It is as if Ajay's position in the class hierarchy is something that both need to challenge and reaffirm at the same time.

Migrants' Schemes

As we stop at each station, more Indians boarded the train, many wearing colorful turbans and sporting traditional Sikh/Punjabi beards. They often greet each other enthusiastically, happily (and loudly) chatting in Punjabi or Hindi,

answering cell phones while looking for more familiar faces in the crowd. I
could not make sense of what they are talking about and asked Ajay about it but
he would tell me once we arrive at Blackburn station. He is clearly intrigued of
the discussion. Happy, on the other hand, seems ill at-ease with the whole
situation. Upon arrival at Blackburn station, Happy insists on taking a slightly
different route than usual to the gurdwara. He explains that he is annoyed with
"all these Indians breathing down his neck." He does not like being among so
many of them. He adds: "They annoy me man, they talk about nothing else . . .
PR, man. Permanent residency. That is all they care about." Ajay agrees with
that assessment: "That is also what I was listening to in the train. They were
talking about some new lawyer; some lawyer who can solve some five-point
problem."

Talk of Migration Issues

To be eligible for a PR, a student needs to score 120 points on a so-called points
test. That is, if one does not have a sponsor in Australia. The issue for most
overseas students is the "final five points." A well-known immigration agent
who often appears in the local Indian media and regularly publishes articles on
changing rules and regulations comments: "Right now you have a lot of students
changing from IT to accountancy because IT is no longer fetching them enough
points." The "five point's issue" is a direct result of increasing the pass mark for
the Skilled Independent Overseas Student visa subclass from 115 to 120 for
those applying after May 2005. This change was announced by the Department
of Immigration and Multiculturalism and Indigenous Affairs (DIMIA) on April
1, 2004 when many students who invested their money on a PR were already in
Australia, or, in the process of coming to Australia, that it no longer made sense
to simply abandon their plans. Obtaining 120 points is a fairly straightforward
and easy process as long as one meets the criteria.[8]

    I met students who based their choice of a particular course of study on the
points they would receive for it. Now that a popular course like IT is no longer
listed on the Migration Occupation in Demand (MODL), many students are
falling behind five points. A popular way to "solve" this problem is to show
proof of work experience in a particular field and claim points for that. The
students on the train were talking about a lawyer who offers "solutions" to the
problem of work experience at a price. Apparently this lawyer is in touch with
some companies, most likely Indian business, Ajay speculates. The thought of it
amuses Ajay because he could not imagine himself making use of such a
scheme. It angers Happy, who claims that such schemes embarrass Indians
overseas.

Who are these Students?

"Do you think that a lot of these guys are also students?" I asked Happy while
walking toward the gurdwara. He replies: "No man, many will have come here a
long time ago." Happy graduated a year ago and, I wonder, to what extent does

he associate himself with them? Ajay interferes by saying: "Some will be students, sure. But not very serious ones. They don't care about their studies much. I am sure most of them are taxi drivers . . . or doing some other lame job." Ajay does not work much. He comes from a large and wealthy industrial family in Amritsar and lives in a nice apartment in the CBD (Central Business District). He studies at RMIT (Royal Melbourne Institute of Technology), a university with a solid reputation.

Happy explains that initially he was not very keen on migrating to Australia but now he is a permanent resident. He always works part-time next to his studies. His first job had been as a waiter with an Indian restaurant. After that he joined a call center. He remembers: "That was for one and a half years. So that was [how I spend] most of the time of my studies." Toward the end of his studies he worked at Safeway, a supermarket chain. He also accepted a job at the computer helpdesk of ANZ Bank while working at Safeway. Happy now works fifty-eight hours a week. He argues that he is saving most of the money for his wedding, but listening to his many stories about girls, he does not seem very eager to marry a girl of his parents' choice in the near future. He drops hints at why he is working so much though. One time, over a beer he talks about Australia as a place to make serious money. He refers to others doing the same and feels it is the most sensible thing to do. Based on observations and interviews with Indian students, many also justify their actions this way. Former students who are young and unmarried work as much and perceive it to be normal and, sometimes, explain this as "taking something back." They refer to the money they paid for their education and discovered that Australian universities depend heavily on such money. Some feel cheated. They argue that Australian universities are only in it for the money, not because they actually like having overseas students. Happy is taking the money back for an education he is not particularly satisfied with. In addition, others are making "serious money" as well, and he feels stupid not to do the same.

The Double Role of Student and Migrant

More than 90 percent of the students I interviewed intend to stay in Australia after graduation. Interestingly, Ajay is a notable exception. From the moment we first met he is quite determined to return home and join his father's company. Happy, after three years in Melbourne, is not keen on returning to India. True, the thought of joining his father's business is in the back of his mind but so is the appeal of living in Australia for at least a couple of years more after graduation. Throughout the years, while studying, he met many students with desires to migrate and their enthusiasm affects him. When his housemate finally decided to apply for PR, Happy paid close attention and did not hesitate when his turn came up. Since then the number of students applying for PR or even coming to Australia for that reason alone increased considerably in his perception. He argues that, at first, when he applied for PR (around the end of 2004) many students did the same. Now colleges seem to cater specifically to those whose primary concern is PR. He listed a number of colleges in the CBD which offer only courses that scored points in the highest category. It seems clear that these colleges are mainly in the business of PR (Birrell 2006; Birrell, Healy and Kinnaird 2007). I met other students of the same opinion and sometimes refer to such places as "PR factories": factories producing permanent residencies (Baas 2006).

Being a student and migrant create awkward conflicts with each other. For an Indian with a middle class background, a good and solid education is seen as very important. PR factories do not only offer that kind of education, their visible presence also forces them to rethink their own attitude toward being both "serious" students as well as migrants. Although Happy did not graduate from a PR factory, he is not very happy with his education in Australia. He opines that the quality of education is much lower than in India. Ajay thinks otherwise. He agrees that an Indian university demands much more from a student, yet the two are difficult to compare since Indian universities expected their students to study from one source, memorize it, and precisely repeat the lectures. Australian universities, however, rely heavily on originality, doing group assignments, using other sources (such as the Internet) aside from required textbooks and so on. An informant once remarked that he feels like he was getting a degree in Google search; a feeling that is shared by many.

The question is not whether Australian education is truly inferior to that offered in India but how such remarks tell us about students' perception of their time as students in Australia. Being unhappy about the quality of education they are receiving coincides with remarks on it as unworthy of their money that is often connected to obtaining permanent residency in Australia. It is through this PR that they are able to pay off their education loans. Yet, as will also become clear from our visit to the gurdwara, the jobs students do or end up in after graduation often do not match their expectations. They imagine their futures to take shape and to be in line with a serious education, yet, the reality of being a migrant and dealing with other migrants interferes with such imaginations and, as a consequence, often results in different expectations. Being a migrant, thus, dampens a student's self-image; being a migrant comes with other priorities that are in conflict with being a serious student. The presence of students enrolled in courses at so-called PR factories further reminds them of the issues they deal with. Having to work next to their studies hinders them from getting the grades they desire. At a PR factory studying is simply about "passing" as grades do not really matter; it is graduating with the least amount of effort and cost to submit the application for PR. Students who are more serious about their education choose a reputable university. Yet, these universities also demand more from them, something that is not always possible considering their financial obligations. Having lowly paid part-time jobs expose them to other migrants with different ideas about a successful future. Keeping a balance between the two, being both migrant and student, comes with a bit of stress, and many find the student role the hardest to maintain in the long run.

Nourishment of the Body and Mind

Entering the gurdwara, we take off our shoes and store them away. Happy and Ajay quickly start shaking hands with several guys they apparently know from earlier visits and we then join them into the main hall. Inside a ceremony is going on and we quietly sit down among the other mostly young Indian men. The occasional girl can be spotted as well, carefully having covered her head and stealing quick glances left and right. Ajay immediately bows down in prayer while Happy remains sitting upright for a while. He then complains a little too loud that he is not able to sit cross-legged like the others. I decided to move over to him for a quick chat. I have been to gurdwaras in India but this place is different. It is basically a huge hall with a large white and gold altar at the end around which a lot of attention is centered. The carpet is soft and clean, but the hall is not particularly well decorated. People continuously walk in and out, getting up, sitting down, and some are even busy with their cell phones.

Meanwhile, a couple of elders picked up the *Guru Granth Sahib* (Sikh sacred scripture) from the altar and carry it into a different room (the bed chamber) next door. Happy asks me to follow him. He suddenly pulls up a very earnest face and is suddenly deeply lost in prayer. The awkwardness he first displayed being among other Indians, sitting upright, somehow not wanting to be associated with them at all, is gone. He now perfectly blends into the praying crowd. Ajay has joined us as well and smiles when he sees Happy. It is, apparently, what he expects. Throughout the train ride to Blackburn Happy is quite outspoken about how little the gurdwara means to him as a religious place. It is a place to get good food and spot nice girls. But now he also seems to make use of the occasion to nourish his mind. This made sense, yet is puzzling. Why the outspokenness first, then the indifference, followed by the act of not knowing what to do as an Indian (sitting cross legged, meditating) and then suddenly the religious devotion?

When the ceremony of putting-God-to-bed[9] is over, we walk toward the direction of the crowd. Slowly we move into a large hall where already hundreds of people are eating, sitting neatly in lines of forty each. In rapid speed volunteers walk by and dump small portions of *dal, gobi, palak* and other Indian food on our plate. The food is kept in large containers and buckets and it clearly seems as if the gurdwara knows how much to prepare. I quickly estimate that there are between six and seven hundred people eating to which Happy adds that they even do a second shift for latecomers. He quickly finishes his plate and asks the volunteer passing by for another scoop. I ask him if he has seen any girls he likes but he shrugs absentmindedly. There are plenty of girls around but inside the gurdwara he does not show any interest. "What about her?" I ask him again pointing to a girl in the crowd. He replies: "I don't know man, I am sure she is some local girl. These are local girls, man; they are not for us students." "Local girls, huh?" I mumble. Happy continues: "Yeah, like these girls who come from local families. They are different." The girl I had pointed at looks like a fairly ordinary Indian girl. She is wearing a pair of tight fitting jeans, white sports socks and a blue sleeveless t-shirt with some colorful print on it.

Draped around her shoulders is a shawl, which does not quite match the ensemble. She must have brought it with her to cover her shoulders upon entering the gurdwara. She looks around in a self-secure manner when she enters the dining hall clearly checking if she knows some people. She then waves at some people. Why Happy categorizes her as from the "local Indian community" and, thus, not being accessible is puzzling.

"Oldcomers" and Newcomers: Issues of Success and Failure

During my fieldwork I noticed that the relationship between the local Indian community and the recently arrived Indian students is less than easy. At best, the relationship is described as ambivalent. The locally established Indian community traces its arrival back to the 1970s through the skilled migration programs after Australia abandoned its White Australia policy. This policy kept Asians out of Australia for the better part of a century. Indian community members and leaders whom I met and interacted with appear to look down on Indian overseas students. They view the students as profiteers, only interested in permanent residency, and not much caring about their studies. While they took pride in having come to Australia as highly skilled professionals and having made a living in a new country where they also thought of themselves as a respected migrant group, Indian students, in their imagination, often simply end up as kitchen hands, petrol station employees and taxi drivers. It is important to understand that the local Indian community appears to look down on Indian students who seem to be aware of this.

In the gurdwara the two groups ("oldcomers" and newcomers) come together and a girl appearing to be from the other group is inaccessible to the other. Happy assumes that the girl we are talking about is a daughter of a local Indian. Using the argument of her "not being an overseas student" is one of which I know was convincing enough.

In my dissertation (Baas 2009) I describe the "Indian community" in different ways. I argue that there is no such thing as *the* Indian community, but that it depends on the view of "others" based on four categories. First, the view of the organizers and members of various Indian associations that the Indian community is composed of successful business owners, highly educated in professions such as doctors, dentists or accountants; they came to Australia under the skilled migration programs whose image is threatened by Indian students. Second, the view, for both Anglo-Aussies and Indian students alike, that the Indian community is based on where Indians are the most visible in day-to-day life—restaurant owners, waiters, petrol pump operators, grocery store managers, and so on—professions not associated with being highly educated. Indian students often look down on this group and consider them "old-migrants," having ended up in professions that they could not imagine themselves settling for. They sometimes even refer to this group as the "Old India," and consider themselves as the "New India." Third, Indian students do not see themselves belonging to either of the two previous categories mentioned. The first category of highly skilled migrants is fairly unknown to them as they often had very weak linkages with people in Australia before they left India. In addition, they are not very interested in participating in so-called community related activities, except for festivals such as *Holi* or *Diwali*.[10] They are, however, very familiar with the second category of whom many have worked for. As stories of abuse of the student labor force abound,[11] they do not share warm feelings toward this category, nor do they see themselves belonging to this category in the future. And fourth, Anglo-Aussies do not make any particular distinction about the Indian community at all. Anybody who looks "Indian" is part of the Indian community. This might also include other South Asians as well. For many Australians, the Indian community refers to those they read about in papers and see in the streets. Indians are usually driving cabs or students crowding trains on their way to work. Yet, the image is not always negative. At times these "same" Indians are their doctors, that man at work (IT department) or that one friendly person who operates the cash register of the Seven-Eleven at the corner.

The separation among these four views about the Indian community is mostly superficial. But it signals the relative place they take up in relation to each other. Indian students remark that they have no real interest in the local Indian community because they are not planning on staying in Australia anyway. They have a more ambitious plan of using Australia as a stepping stone to other places like the United States. The Indian community members also often confirm this idea. Indian students are not only supposed to make use of certain arrangement in the way they did, they are, in some cases, not *supposed* to stay. This hints at the fluidity of integration and how new migrants such as these Indian students form a rather definite break from the intentions of other migrant groups.

Being Indian and Belonging

Washing up our plates after having finished dinner, Ajay runs into some people he has met before. An older gentleman walks up to him and asks him when he will volunteer again. Apparently he has done that before. Ajay shrugs and mumbles something like "sometime soon." He appears unsure. I notice Happy smirking at the thought; definitely not something he ever considers. Just like the girl he saw earlier, the idea of involving himself with a job connected to the local Indian community is something to avoid at all cost. Ajay is not affected by such issues.

When Ajay is finished talking, Happy suggests we leave quickly so that we can take the train back, avoiding the crowds. At the train station, though, it becomes clear that there is no avoiding any crowd this evening. The platform is packed with Indians on their way back to the city. In the train, Happy starts talking about his "girlfriend-worries" again. He is dating a Chinese girl but he is not sure how serious he should take it. He is clearly in love and suddenly starts humming a Bollywood love song. It embarrasses Ajay who begs him to stop. But Happy is in a particular mood and is unable to control himself. Others turn around to stare at him; most of them then smile. They are all Indians, and they all know the lyrics. Ajay shakes his head in disbelief and looks at me with an annoyed smile on his face; singing Bollywood songs in public is, definitely not his thing. The approval of the other Indians in the train seems to strengthen Happy though and he starts singing louder, even having some of the others join in. While Happy is busy performing his "Indianness" in a public place, suddenly clearly at ease with being with and among Indians—creating a sense of *us* instead of *them*—Ajay quietly stares out of the window and pretends not to be there.

Destinations in the World of Indian Student Migration

While inside the gurdwara I observed a difference in attitude between Happy and Ajay. Where Ajay, as a Hindu, is perfectly comfortable with sitting down and praying, seeing it as a form of meditation and coming to peace with himself, the week, his studies, and so forth, Happy (as a "proper" Sikh) seems to have trouble blending in. Ajay is quite comfortable with being seen as an Indian overseas student and thus a temporary resident in Australia. Happy, on the other hand, struggles with the idea that others might look down upon him as a student who has profited from Australia's immigration rules in all the wrong ways. Yet, as a Sikh, the gurdwara was also *his* place and not just in the sense of religion. It is also a place where he is among many who are dealing with similar issues of belonging, becoming, not yet there and so on. Once Happy starts to relax and is lost in prayer, Ajay is hardly surprised. According to Ajay, it has to do with Happy's ideas of the future which do not include staying in Australia. Happy wants to move on to different shores. Ajay is quite sure Happy is thinking of moving to the United States or some country in Europe, possibly the United Kingdom. Many students see Australia as a stepping-stone to even more desirable countries. Many, including Happy, try to enroll in a university in the United States. Australia is not their first choice in that sense. The United States is notoriously difficult to get into. Universities have readily accepted them but the United States immigration authorities turned them down because they are potential immigrants. Students regularly and simply phrase this as: "I got PI (potential immigrant) stamped in my passport." The United Kingdom, another popular destination, is briefly considered but is put aside as an option either because it is too expensive or does not offer the right options to stay-on after graduation. Dreams of ending up in these countries remain very much alive. An Australian PR, so it is argued, makes it much easier to travel to these countries and "go for a job" there.

Ajay plans to return home to Amritsar after he graduates. His father prefers that he pursue a master's degree as well but thinks he had had enough of Australia. He does not like the climate, misses his family and friends, and does not want to settle down in Melbourne. There is no point in staying on. Ajay explains that he comes from a wealthy family and leads a very comfortable life at home. The family company provides plenty of career opportunities and, in terms of traveling, there are many more trips to come. In fact, he was on a holiday to Australia before he migrated as a student. Together with his parents, some uncles and aunts, they traveled around the country for a couple of weeks, getting a feel of the place. His parents and one of his uncles also visited him while studying in Melbourne. Where other students see a PR as a way to explore the world, no longer having to rely on an Indian passport, and being able to make money in currencies worth more than the Indian rupee, Ajay simply wants to go back to his comfortable life in Amritsar and work for his father's company. Whatever traveling comes his way is taken care of by showing the right authorities that his family is more than able to afford going abroad and that there is no risk in them not returning to India. Not becoming an Australian PR holder is almost a symbolic act in this sense.

Gendered Narratives, Class Undertones

Happy listed "to meet new chicks" as one of the "other" reasons for coming to Australia and on the way to the gurdwara, girls are constantly on his mind. "Chicks" are often part of his stories—stories that are mostly meant for making conversation while sitting in the train. Ajay deals with these stories by smiling and frowning, non-verbally communicating that he has heard them all too many times before. While washing our plates, talking to friends Happy barely glances at girls passing by. They belong to the local Indian community. Talking about girls is probably meant more to impress me and Ajay, than his actual lived experiences. His image as a "ladies' man" stands in direct relation to his feelings of insecurity about his background and future plans.

In our discussion regarding both his background and girls, it is clear that the economic windfall of Happy's family is fairly new. They recently started climbing the financial and social ladder and, thus, becoming part of the middle class. India's rapid growth started after the liberalization of the economy in 1992 (Das and Barua 1996; Murty 1996; Bosworth, Collins and Virmani 2007) and this helps the family business grow substantially. They are newcomers to the world of "middle classness," as Ajay sees it. Both Happy's parents are schooled at year ten level. That Happy now completed a university degree is relatively new to the family. Many of his cousins are doing the same, albeit in India, and their parents also never had this opportunity. His making it abroad reflects well on the status of the family in Delhi where they settled, hailing originally from Chandigargh. The family has relatively few members living abroad and Happy is clearly a success story in this regard. Happy's jobs are seen as temporary leading to a much brighter future in business, probably working on his own and creating distribution channels for goods from India to Australia and, hopefully, also to the United States and the United Kingdom.

Hanging Out, Talking About Girls

Ajay knows about young Indian men's fascination with a "western girlfriend" —explained as easy and not too difficult (Mathur 1991; Cullity and Younger 2004). This is hardly important to him. He receives emails from younger cousins in India inquiring if he has "scored" in Australia. This amuses him; it is not his character, rather he is shy and polite. At the same time, he associates this sort of behavior unfitting to his class or his "kind of people" that never fancy "western girls" this way.

Ajay hangs out with Ajith, a student he met at the RMIT library. Ajith is from Hyderabad, Andhra Pradesh, and both are equally serious about their studies. Interestingly, Ajith has little to no interest in staying in Australia after graduation. Ajith's parents are both very scholarly and his father is a well known scientist in India. He describes his family as one that has obtained degrees for generations. The fact that they belong to the upper middle class is uncontested; people also know others in this category. Seeing Ajay and Ajith together made sense. Their families are far from financially compatible (Ajay's being considerably wealthier); yet, where they come from, what they reckon themselves to be part of, is a match.

While having drinks one day, Ajith walks in with a very pretty Indian girl. She is not his girlfriend but somebody he likes to hang out with. Ajith plans to marry a girl arranged by his parents. Like Ajay he regularly receives emails from India about his "latest conquests" of western girls and is expected to "score." He claims he is far too busy with his studies to pay any serious attention to girls. As an Indian middle class man in his early twenties, he is expected to "make some progress in this field."

I interviewed many Indian students who grew up with the idea that western girls are easy, that sex comes without much attachments or consequences. One of the attractions of going to Australia is the idea of sexual adventure that is not possible at home. Western girls, however, are never understood to be much more than that: an opportunity for adventure. In this sense, Happy understands a western girl or the girl at the gurdwara quite differently. Indian girls, having grown up in Australia, are idealized as modest and proper girls that they are supposed to be in their culture. They have families to watch over them that offer less access to flirting with guys like Happy. Interestingly, female Indian overseas students in Australia are not perceived in this manner. They occupy a realm between these two stereotypical female images which create an opportunity to start a relationship. This is how Happy looks at Ajith's Indian "girlfriend": she came to Australia on her own with a liberal upbringing. Ajith is less bothered about this because he imagines his future to be less connected to a life outside India.

Because Ajith plans to marry the girl of his parents' choice he is unsure about having a girlfriend in Australia. It seems this is more for "other" guys like Happy. Happy's "adventures," as well as those of other students, confuses him. He did not want to be seen as a "dork," but, at the same time, amorous adventures with Asian girls are not his type of activity. Happy's behavior is compatible with family values and expectations. On the other hand, a "proper" (i.e., traditional or conservative) Indian girl is unlikely to accept to be a girlfriend either (Krishnaraj and Chanana 1989; Perveez 2002; Ganesamurthy 2008). The pretty girl at Ajith's arm though, watching him with close attention while talking about his week at *uni* (university), is probably considered as such.

She is a safe person to bring along. This is a common practice among students I met in 2005. Many young men, most of whom come from upper-castes and upper middle class families, handle the situation in a similar way. Almost all prefer arranged marriages with girls from their own castes and class backgrounds, but it is acceptable to have a girlfriend in the meantime.

The desire to have a "western" girlfriend is even greater as a way of augmenting one's status. The way this works out depends on class and caste backgrounds. For Happy, a "western" (read white, Anglo-Saxon) girlfriend means that he is a successful male Indian who manages to "get" something others failed to do. This is quite important because his status as new middle class is pushed aside. Yet, this is not all. Since he is so keen on staying in Australia after graduation, it paves the way to increasingly consider himself as an Indian who has permanently left India and its social rules. In more symbolic terms this imaginary girl is also seen as an idealized form of "entering and getting his foot" into the western world. His current Chinese girlfriend is viewed as a stepping-stone on the way to an even more desired girl. It is a complex situation through which Happy navigates his own class-based and gender-infused ideas on life in general, and more specifically on what it means to be a successful migrant in a new world to which he desperately wants to belong— including his dream of making it to the United States.

Becoming and Belonging Transnationally Mobile

"Belonging in and to Australia" is a temporary situation among Indian overseas students in this study. On the one hand, belonging creates a sense of safety, of being where one needs to be. This kind of belonging also relates *to* other Indian migrants in Australia. They are in the same condition as Happy; some of them might offer opportunities leading to a better job. This belonging could never become *too much* since it is temporary.

Happy and Ajay, both from upper middle classes, differ considerably on the meaning of this status. While Ajay's family is considered upper middle class for decades at least, Happy's family is relatively new. Education, social standing (often directly linked to caste), and, for instance, the memory of a "revered" family history, do not play a particularly more important role than money. As a business family, they have been upwardly mobile for a while, and are now getting used to their new position in the Indian class hierarchy.

Yet this new position also creates insecurities. Class and caste hierarchies are rather strict in India and "social climbers" are frowned upon. Interviews with students such as Ajay, Ajith and others who clearly hail from the longer-established upper middle classes often talk about themselves in relation to those whom they consider newcomers to the class. With the extreme growth of the Australian education industry and the rise of smaller colleges that typically cater only to Chinese and Indian students, and seem to offer mostly courses for PR, studying abroad (i.e., Australia) has become available to more Indian students than ever before. The main reason for this is simply money: not only do more

Indians have the money to send their children to study abroad, these new colleges are also typically price fighters, knowing that they cater to a new market unable to afford the traditional and more expensive universities such as Monash and RMIT.

Although students like Happy who completed a degree at RMIT consider working in menial jobs as temporary, many of them are actually hanging on to such jobs, thus creating the image that Indians mostly worked in lowly paid jobs that require less education. This seems to apply to the majority of graduates from less expensive colleges. And it is here that Happy's unease on the way to gurdwara, being among many other Indians, starts to make sense. As a "social climber," a relative newcomer to the world of Indian "middle classness," Happy is clearly aware of other "established" Indians around. At the same time, he recognizes the "newcomers" whom he considers below his class status. He studied at a reputable college and the new generation of Indian students seem to study at much lesser colleges, finally ending up in jobs that Happy considers temporary at best. At the time of our trip to the gurdwara, Happy is still working in one of these jobs. But many of the Indians he heard talking on the train, and later see praying, are also working in similar jobs. They remind him that finding a job that fits more with the way he sees himself as being part of an upcoming business family is a long way to go. These are conflicting issues that affects him. Having a PR partly means being (or having to act) "Australian" now. It also means that one could no longer simply associate with other Indians, or behave in such a way that is not "Australian" at all. Yet India, and its own "Indianness," continues to be part of his narrative as well; proving his personal growth, dating a Chinese girl, and viewing himself differently from newcomers desperately finding ways to obtain permanent residency. These images relate directly to his future as a successful, highly educated middle class Indian having made it abroad.

Happy's case demonstrates similar ambivalence about life among Indian overseas students in Australia. They are in Australia because the country offers a path to permanent residency in a "western" country albeit located in the Southern Hemisphere. One of the goals of getting a PR is to move on to even more desirable countries, most notably the United States. Going to the gurdwara, the Hindu temple in Carrum Downs, or the Hare Krishna in St. Kilda, is, thus, not so much about becoming part of the local Indian community and strengthening a sense of belonging to Australia. These are places where ambivalence about belonging, and at the same time longings to live a transnationally mobile life, resonates. And, these are places where "being Indian" is given its proper place or reconfirmed. Yet, being among other Indians also shows overseas students about avenues inconsistent with their interests and plans: one that is, at least, not bound to either India or Australia and vastly different from the life many Indians regularly attending the gurdwara are living.

Conclusion

The gurdwara is a place where all are welcome and, on the right day, free food is even expected. It is a place where religion and nourishment play a relative role that stands in direct relation to the fact that almost all "worshippers" are still or once were migrants. For Happy, being at the gurdwara means a confrontation of what lies ahead. Conversations about jobs, migration agents, where to get the best spice mixes, the latest Bollywood parties, and so on, start in the train and continue over dinner. This reminds him of how much success and failure work in tandem in the process of migration. The gurdwara does not simply offer free food on Wednesday evenings; it is also a place to pray for success on their migration journeys. Inside the gurdwara one no longer keeps pretense of not being an Indian; they simply indulge in the moment—between success and failure—on one's way to a permanent residency outside India, though not *yet* there.

On the road to and finally inside the gurdwara, Happy and Ajay both cope differently with its "religiousness." It seems that their perception about the place is related to their current status. Being away from home is clearly a temporary matter for Ajay. Yet, taking into account that most Indian students in Australia are also on a migration trajectory, Ajay does not deny that being a migrant is part of his life. As an Indian, he is associated with "others" who are busy planning on permanent migration. On the other hand, Happy is a typical case in this sense. He came to Australia to study and now has obtained a PR, faced with the reality of being in-between; not yet an Australian, no longer "really" an Indian, and so on. Where Ajay could simply let the gurdwara be for what it is— a place of worship and meditation welcoming to Hindus—it is a place for Happy to meet his past and future and where he is one with a group of which he is, at the same time, trying to move away from. His prayer for food is not just for a well-prepared free dish of Indian food but also for success and hope to make it beyond Australia.

Understanding religious places as pathways to integration among Indian overseas students in Australia is complex. Integration is not limited to simply belonging, being comfortable with and fitting in, in Australian society. As a nation of immigrants it is hard to dissociate Australia from the experience of being both a student and a migrant where fellow Indians not only negotiate fitting in with Anglo-Aussies but also with locally-established Indians. This also relates to a much wider framework of imaginations, of becoming transnationally mobile. Indian students do not come to Australia simply to settle as immigrants, something so many of their fellow Indians have done before them. They see themselves integrating in a global world of highly mobile Indians who regularly travel between different countries but never quite commit to any of them. Global integration, thus, seems opposite to local integration, while, at the same time, complying with the prerequisites for accomplishing permanent residency. A visit to the gurdwara symbolizes this contradiction; it gives shape and direction to the mindset that is necessary to accomplish what they had set out to do by coming to Australia.

Notes

1. A *gurdwara* literally means "doorway to the Guru."

2. There are five categories in the Australian education system: higher education, vocational education, school education, ELICOS (English Language Intensive Courses for Overseas Students), and other courses including enabling, foundation and non-award. See Department of Education, Science and Training, http://aei.dest.gov.au/AEI/MIP/Stati stics/StudentEnrolmentAndVisaStatistics/Recent_TableE_pdf.pdf (accessed April 22, 2009).

3. This is typically how Australia describes the industry of selling education to overseas students.

4. There are no earlier studies on fraudulent bank loans among Indian overseas students. For a comparable but slightly different example see Sushi Das, "Our Schools for Scandal," *The Age*, May 22, 2009, http//www.theage.com/national/our-schools-for-scandal-20090522-bic6.html?page=2 (accessed May 25, 2009).

5. On average loans have to be repaid between five to seven years. Repayment starts from the moment a full-time job is found or one year after graduation. Interest rates are often as high as 13 percent to 20 percent.

6. In *Australian Social Trends*, "just 20 percent of all education arrivals from India in 2005 were female, while 66 percent of education arrivals from Japan were female." See "International Students in Australia," *Australian Social Trends 2007*, p. 3, http://www.ausstats.abs.gov.au/ausstats/subscriber.nsf/0/66E07209141CE61FCA25732F 001C9B8D/$File/41020_International%20students%20in%20Australia_2007.pdf (accessed April 5, 2009).

7. For a detailed discussion see, for instance, Kitty Calavita, "Gender, Migration and the Law," *International Migration Review* 40, no. 1 (2006): 104-132; Sara R. Curran et al., "Mapping Gender and Migration in Sociological Scholarship," *International Migration Review* 40, no. 1 (2006): 199-223; Sarah J. Mahler and Patricia R. Pesar, "Gender Matters," *International Migration Review* 40, no. 1 (2006): 27-63; and Nicola Piper, "Gender the Politics of Migration," *International Migration Review* 40, no. 1 (2006): 133-164.

8. Generally, this works as follows: if a student is below thirty years old at the time of application, thirty points is awarded for age. Another twenty points is gained by successfully passing the IELTS (International English Language Testing System) test at level 6. Most Indian students meet both requirements easily. Completing two years of full-time education in Australia can add another five points. The real problem is the issue of particular skills category. The skilled migration program is divided into three different categories, each worth 40, 50 and 60 points. During the period of my research, professions such as IT and engineering are included in the 60 points category. Professions listed in the MODL like accountancy receive an additional 15 points, or a total of 75 points for skills.

9. Temples in Hinduism and Sikhism have specific rituals and timings for putting the deity to bed.

10. *Holi* is called the Festival of Colors. The day is generally celebrated by people throwing colored powder on each other. *Diwali* is known as the Festival of Lights. The festival celebrates the victory of good over evil (light over dark).

11. During academic semesters students are not allowed to work for more than twenty hours per week. However, many work beyond the minimum hours to make ends meet. The competition for the better paying call-center jobs and others is quite tough and,

thus, many end up working as waiters in restaurants, or as petrol pump operators. South Asian business owners allow them to work more hours than is legally allowed by offering "cash-in-hand" wage. They also pay much lower than the prescribed minimum wages. This illustrates that there are often no warm feelings between the two groups.

Bibliography

Arya, Sadhna and Anupama Roy, eds. *Poverty, Gender and Migration*. New Delhi: Sage, 2006.

Australian Bureau of Statistics. "International Students in Australia." *Australian Social Trends* 2007: 1-12. http://www.ausstats.abs.gov.au/ausstats/subscriber.nsf/0/6 6E07209141CE61FCA25732F001C9B8D/$File/41020_International%20students% 20in%20Australia_2007.pdf (accessed April 5, 2009).

Baas, Michiel. "The Language of Migration: The Education versus the Migration Industry." *People and Place* 15, no. 2 (2007): 49-61.

———. "Students of Migration: Indian Overseas Students and the Question of Permanent Residency." *People and Place* 14, no.1 (2006): 8-24.

———. "Imagined Mobilities, Migration and Transnationalism among Indian Students in Australia." Unpublished PhD Dissertation, Amsterdam School for Social Science Research, University of Amsterdam, 2009.

Batnitzky, Adina Keryn, Linda McDowell and Sarah Dyer. "A Middle-Class Global Mobility: The Working Lives of Indian Men in a West London Hotel." *Global Networks* 8, no. 1 (2008): 51-70.

Birrell, Bob. "Implications of Low English Standards among Overseas Students at Australian Universities." *People and Place* 14, no. 4 (2006): 52–64.

Birrell, Bob, Ernest Healy and Bob Kinnaird. "Cooks Galore and Hairdressers Aplenty." *People and Place* 15, no. 1 (2007): 30–44.

Bosworth, Barry, Susan M. Collins and Arvind Virmani. "Sources of Growth in the Indian Economy." NBER Working Paper No. W12901, February 2007. http://papers.ssrn.com/sol3/papers.cfm?abstract_id=966115 (accessed May 25, 2009).

Boucher, Anna. "Skill, Migration and Gender in Australia and Canada: The Case of Gender-based Analysis." *Australian Journal of Political Science* 42, no. 3 (2007): 383-401.

Calavita, Kitty. "Gender, Migration, and Law: Crossing Borders and Bridging Disciplines." *International Migration Review* 40, no. 1 (2006): 104-132.

Cullity, Jocelyn and Prakash Younger. "Sex Appeal and Cultural Liberty: A Feminist Inquiry into MTV India." *Frontiers: A Journal of Women's Studies* 25, no. 2 (2004): 96-122.

Curran, Sara R., Steven Shafer, Katharine M. Donato and Filiz Garip. "Mapping Gender and Migration in Sociological Scholarship: Is It Segregation or Integration." *International Migration Review* 40, no. 1 (2006): 199-223.

Das, Sandwip Kumar and Alokesh Barua. "Regional Inequalities, Economic Growth and Liberalisation: A Study of the Indian Economy." *The Journal of Development Studies* 32, no. 3 (1996): 364-390.

Das, Sushi. "Our Schools for Scandal," *The Age*, May 22, 2009, http://www.theage.com.au/national/our-schools-for-scandal-20090522-bic6.html?pa ge=2 (accessed May 25, 2009).

Department of Education, Science and Training. "Government of Australia Year 2005 Market Indicator Data. Table E: Time Series of Overseas Student Enrolments in Australia by Major Sector, 2002 to 2005." http://aei.dest.gov.au/AEI/MIP/Statistics/ StudentEnrolmentAndVisaStatistics/Recent_TableE_pdf.pdf (accessed April 5, 2009).

Donato, Katharine M., Donna Gabaccia, Jennifer Holdaway, Martin Manalansan and Patricia Pessar. "A Glass Half Full? Gender in Migration Studies." *International Migration Review* 40, no. 1 (2006): 3-26.

Fernandes, Leela. *India's New Middle Class*. Minneapolis and London: University of Minnesota Press, 2006.

Forbes, Geraldine. *Women in Modern India*. Cambridge, UK: Cambridge University Press, 1996.

Ganesamurthy, V. S., ed. *Women in the Indian Economy*. New Delhi: New Century, 2008.

Hartzig, Christiane. "Women Migrants as Global and Local Agents. New Research Strategies on Gender and Migration." Pp. 1-13 in *Women, Gender and Labor Migration. Historical and Global Perspectives*, edited by Pamela Sharpe. New York: Routledge, 2003.

Krishnaraj, Maithreyi and Karuna Chanana, eds. *Gender and the Household Domain: Social and Cultural Dimensions*. New Delhi and California: Sage Publications, 1989.

Mahler, Sarah J. and Patricia R. Pessar. "Gender Matters: Ethnographers Bring Gender from the Periphery toward the Core of Migration Studies." *International Migration Review* 40, no. 1 (2006): 27-63.

Mathur, Anurag. *The Inscrutable Americans*. Delhi: Rupa Publications/New World Library, 1991.

Morton, Adam. "Student Medical Notes Prompt Inquiry," *The Age*, August 18, 2006. http://www.theage.com/au/news/national/student-medical-notes-prompt-inquiry/200 6/07/17/1152988472768.html (accessed April 25, 2009).

Murty, Sudarshan, ed. *Structural Transformation of Indian Economy*. New Delhi: Atlantic Publishers and Distributors, 1996.

Perveez, Mody. "Love and the Law: Love-Marriage in Delhi." *Modern Asian Studies* 36, no. 1 (2002): 223-256.

Piper, Nicola. "Gender the Politics of Migration." *International Migration Review* 40, no.1 (2006): 133-164.

Ranade, Sudhanshu. "The Great Indian Middle Class and its Consumption Level," *The Hindu Business Line,* January 21, 2005. http://www.blonnet.com/2005/01/22/stories /2005012201860700.htm (accessed January 25, 2005).

Robinson, Rowena. "The Great Indian Middle Class," *The Hindu*, January 14, 2001. http://blonnet.com/2005/01/22/stories/2005012201860700.htm (accessed January 22, 2005).

Säävälä, Minna. "Auspicious Hindu Houses: The New Middle Classes in Hyderabad, India." *Social Anthropology* 11, no. 2 (2003): 231-247.

Sadhna, Arya and Anupama Roy, eds. *Poverty, Gender and Migration*. New Delhi: Sage, 2006.

Sharpe, Pamela. "Introduction: Gender and the Experience of Migration." Pp. 1-13 in *Women, Gender and Labour Migration. Historical and Global Perspectives*, edited by Pamela Sharpe. New York, Routledge, 2003.

Shurmer-Smith, Paula. *India: Globalization and Change*. London: Arnold Publishers, 2000.

Silvey, Rachel. "Geographies of Gender and Migration: Spatializing Social Difference." *International Migration Review* 40, no. 1 (2006): 64-81.

Van Wessel, Margit. "Talking about Consumption: How an Indian Middle Class Dissociates from Middle-Class Life." *Cultural Dynamics* 16, no. 1 (2004): 93-116.

Wells, David H. "Milestones: A Road Map to the Indian Middle Class." *APF Reporter* 20, no.1 (2001). http://www.aliciapatterson.org/APF2001/Wells/Wells.html (accessed April 22, 2009).

Chapter Six
Islam as a New Urban Identity? Young Female Muslims Creating a Religious Youth Culture in Berlin
Synnøve Bendixsen

The landscape of European cities has, since the 1960s, been influenced by immigration from former colonies or through working-contracts between European and non-European countries. In the last decade, Islam has become increasingly present in European societies through the global (negative) media focus, increased use of the veil (*hijab*) among young Muslims, and by replacement of the earlier provisory backyard mosques of the 1970s with purpose-built mosques of the late 1990s. Although the urban context is usually associated as a place where people turn away from religion and where religious communities fulfill few social roles,[1] the last decade has seen a return of religion within the urban space. Today, several youths from the second and third generation of migrants[2] in European cities are turning to Islam in a quest for authenticity, an individual identity, and as part of their group orientation. In Germany, the increased visual religious identification of youth with migrant backgrounds has caused surprise, stupefaction and excitement in a society largely believing that being German and Muslim is an oxymoron.

This chapter discusses the "turn to Islam" as a factor of identification among female youths born in Germany and addresses the following questions: How are youths embracing a religious lifestyle in the Western urban spaces compared to their parents? Can a Muslim identity be a way of situating oneself in western modernity, rather than a sign of enclosure or disavowal of the "modern" German?

First, I discuss the kind of identification with Islam among the young generation in Berlin and second, I examine their reasons for turning to Islam as a main reference point of identity. This chapter suggests that there is an increasing individualization of religious belonging at the same time that the German sociopolitical sphere is increasingly shaping the Muslim social field. I propose that a Muslim lifestyle does not necessarily involve segregation from the German society, but can, on the contrary, provide modes of situating oneself in the German social space. The data for this chapter is from an earlier fieldwork that included approximately fifty young female Muslims in Berlin (2004 to 2007).[3] The youths, from thirteen to thirty years old, have parents from Egypt, Turkey, and Palestine and participate in the organization called "Muslim Youth Germany" (*Muslimische Jugend in Deutschland e.V.*, MJD). This religious youth organization arranges weekly meetings in which I participated during my fieldwork.[4]

Muslim Youths in Germany

Islam in Germany is generally represented by the immigrant workers arriving largely from Turkey in the mid 1960s, and their children and grandchildren who were born and educated in Germany. Whereas the German public was less concerned with the religious orientation of their immigrant population up until the 1980s, this situation changed rapidly from the early 1990s onwards (Soysal 2003; Spielhaus 2006).[5] The discursive change in the German media and public discussion in defining its migrant population as *guestarbeiter* (guest worker) to "Turks" and today "Muslims" must be understood as a combination of the end of the "dream of return" both among the migrants and the German population, an increase of visualization of religious markers (i.e., building of mosques and donning the veil), and global events like the terrorist attacks in the United States on September 11, 2001, after which the world turned its focus on "Islam" and "Muslims."

Today, the German Muslim population is around 3.4 million with 213,000 living in Berlin, the capital. These numbers, however, need to be taken with care since statistics on religious belonging is not well designed and do not reflect whether or not the individual actually identifies with Islam (Spielhaus and Färber 2006). When talking about religious belonging among young females in Berlin, the large intra-generational differences must first be noted. While some youths can be called "chic" Muslims as they combine headscarf, strong make-up and sexy clothes; others veil with more modest dress comportment; and again, others are not *visually* practicing Islam, although some might try to lead a religious lifestyle in the sense that they pray and fast. In addition, among the secular youths, some continue to recognize a cultural affinity with Islam. In this paper, I discuss young Sunni Muslims[6] for whom Islam is their main point of identity.

"Identity" is not considered as static or fixed, but continuously (re)created or formed in social interaction—identity is about ascription, both by individuals themselves and of individuals by others (Jenkins 1996). Groups identify themselves and are categorized by others. In modern society, identity is continuously constructed and in flux (Hall 1996). I follow Richard Jenkins (1996) in that others' perception of one's person will affect the perception one has of oneself and one's categorized group. This is particularly true when a person belongs to a minority group which is educationally and socially situated in a position of minor influence in public discourse. Identity formation and influence from peer groups or lifestyle groups are particularly strong among young people, when many seek a "self," and a purpose in life and are dealing with questions on "who to identify with" (Widdicombe and Wooffitt 1995). A *religious identity* tends to be an identity which one was born into and socialized through the family and community. However, one of the characteristics of modern society is the increased leeway to choose and frame political and religious identities (Lipset and Rokkan 1967). A religious identity is not only the adherence to a particular religious or spiritual frame of reference, but also in relation to whether that religious belief becomes a resource which impacts one's daily life, feelings of belonging and representation.

Generational Changes in Religious Practices

Several researchers have pointed out the generational differences in religious identification among Muslim youths in West European societies compared to that of their parents (Nökel 2002; Tietze 2006). Transmission of religion from one generation to the other always implies some change in continuity (Hervieu-Leger 1998). Socialization of youths to religious norms and values takes place as a continuous cultural change, even if a society is tradition oriented (Hervieu-Leger 1998). Movement or migration adds another dimension to religious change as immigration always changes how religion is transmitted. Stephen Warner (1998: 3) asserts that "religious identities, often (but not always) mean more to [individuals] away from home, in their diaspora, than they did before, and those identities undergo more or less modification as the years pass." One main reason for this, is that "[t]he religious institutions they build, adapt, remodel and adopt become worlds unto themselves, "congregations," where new relations among members of the community—among men and women, parents and children, recent arrivals and those settled—are forged" (Warner 1998: 3). Furthermore, social alienation and frustration because of displacement impact ethnic and religious identification, and connected with the very move is the fact that religion and culture no longer are "prearranged identities" (Göle 2003: 813). By changing context, Islam is no longer automatically transmitted from one generation to another or considered as a norm taken for granted. Instead, the former conceptions of social practices are questioned and tested. Migration to societies that are highly modern adds to the escalation of generational change.

The religious identity among the youths in this study is characterized by three partly interrelated aspects which concurrently mark a distinction from their parents' religiosity, namely: an effort to draw a division between "pure" and "traditional" Islam, focus on improving one's knowledge of Islam, and effort to live out Islam in the German language and space. These aspects, as it will be suggested, make it possible for the youths to argue that being a Muslim and a German is not a contradiction.

First, the youth deem their parents as not observing Islam "correctly," but as performing a mixture of religious forms and traditions brought with them from their (Turkish) villages. The youths instead seek a "pure" or "true" Islam (Roy 2004), detached from culture, ethnicity and nation by going back to the sources, particularly the Koran, *Tafsir* (commentary of the Koran), and the *Sunna* (the exemplary practice of the Prophet Mohammed). For example, during one weekly religious youth meeting, Fatwa (twenty-five years old, Egyptian parents) emphasized that some, in particular older women, exaggerate their tears during their prayer in Ramadan or funerals, constituting more of a "performance" or "a competition" of who is feeling the most religiously, or who was the closest to the dead. "This is tradition," she argues, and not "correct religious behavior." Here, the division between "correct" and "wrong" is reflected upon within the framework of distinguishing between "culture" and "religion."[7] Such reflections illustrate that a correct religious performance within this religious group is recognized by certain normative standards, against which flawed performances are distinguished and assessed (Hirschkind 2001). An act "must be described in terms of the conventions which make it meaningful *as a particular kind of activity*, one performs for certain reason and in accord with certain standards of excellence and understood as such by those who perform and respond to it" (Hirschkind 2001: 633).

The emphasis on distinguishing between "pure" and "traditional" Islam is part of religious reform movements as well as among more fundamental religious movements in several European countries (Roy 2004).[8] The youths are part of similar processes taking place in different European societies, and also globally, in what have been called a "revival of Islam." Since the beginning of the 1990s, researchers interviewing young South Asian Muslim women in England find that these females establish a clear division between "religion" and "culture," a distinction which for their parents are largely interchangeable areas (Knott and Khokher 1993).[9] This orientation toward Islam resembles that of the "objectification" processes of the religious imagination in the Muslim Middle East in the 1990s (Eickelman 1992: 643). With the objectification of the religious imagination, Dale Eickelman (1992) points to the consciousness process by which Muslims become aware of their identity as Muslims. In this process the subjects explicitly ask themselves "What is my religion? Why is it important to my life? and, How do my beliefs guide my conduct?" (Eickelman 1992: 643). In the course of this objectification, religion is not becoming uniform or monolithic, even if some religious actors promote this perception. The so-called "objectified consciousness" is realized through *a process of modernization*, where the expansion of literacy, access to education and modern technology, like the internet, contribute to diminish the dependence on more traditional established authorities to make sense of their religion (Ismail 2004: 624-625).

Second, one consequence of seeking a "pure" Islam is an attentiveness to continuously improving ones knowledge of Islam and performing "correct" religious obligations, both internally and externally. The youths consider it insufficient to perform a religious act externally, meaning that one's body movements and comportment of the performance are correct. The internal, one's mind and thoughts, has to be included in the act in order for it to be judged as *a religiously moral act* (cf. Mahmood 2005).[10] I often hear youths point to the idea that if someone performs a good deed "just in order to tell others" and to demonstrate "how good one is," this deed fails to provide "good points" (as a "good deed" for Allah) since such an act must be performed with the "correct" intentions.[11] The following discussion illustrate this further: During one of the weekly religious meetings organized by the Muslim Youths Germany, Fatwa says: "I was thinking that from next Monday on we should fast, but I don't know if people are motivated?"[12] One of the girls exclaims: "If we know that twenty of us are fasting, should that not be motivating enough?" Fatwa agrees, and another young girl enthusiastically suggests that "fasting is also weight reducing" as an incentive to fast. In response, Somaya (eighteen years old, Sudanese parents) wrinkles her nose, stressing that "diet should not be the reason to perform the fast."

Community feelings foster individual incentives to perform a religiously motivated act, like fasting. Moreover, Somaya's comment here reflects the idea that the act of fasting is only religiously "valid" in so far as the person conducts the act with correct motivations and virtues. Cultivating these dispositions, the young participants in the study learn to differentiate between performing practices which are motivated by religious experiences, or coming from religious moods, vis-à-vis those coming from secular, materialistic, traditional or fashion moods. Fasting in itself is not sufficient to count as a compelling religious act. Rather, fasting is only religiously valid in so far as the person conducts the act with truthful motivations.[13] The quest for "correct" bodily and sensory practices is part of what recent Islamist movements are seeking to reinstate or protect (Mahmood 2005; Asad in Mahmood 1996).

Third, in their struggle to live a religiously oriented life, Muslim adolescents emphasize that this religious lifestyle is actually sought *in* German society. Most are particularly preoccupied with how to construct and negotiate a modern life in Germany without compromising what they feel are their religious duties and obligations in their daily life. One of the youth comments: "Living in this society, there are distractions everywhere. It's more difficult to be motivated to keep all the obeisance and religious needs." Consequently, many participate in religious groups and organizations as it aids disciplining themselves, and to be with "similar people." In the religious weekly Muslim Youth Germany meetings, questions concerning how to live as a "good" Muslim in a society that is not only non-Muslim but also largely considered as secular, is a topic of constant concern. For example, during a question round among the youth, some of the females asked, "Is one allowed to show one's hair to a lesbian?" and "How can one avoid being influenced by fashion, or be diverted from their prayers by non-practicing friends or TV shows?"

One consequence of the youths' emphasis on practicing a "pure" Islam is that they seek answers and knowledge in books and through the internet, and are easily rejecting the religious authority of their parents who they believe are following a traditional Islam. This approach to Islam makes it possible for young females to de-legitimize their parents' "religious" positions as based on "culture." To some extent, this situation leads to a "crisis" of their parents' authority (Roy 2004; Khosrokhavar 1997: 144); the youths are not discussing religious issues with their parents and feeling that they know more about Islam than their parents call upon "a higher moral authority and greater Islamic knowledge" (Mahmood 2005: 116; Cesari 2003; Salih 2003; Jacobsen 2006). Sometimes the young women even attempt to influence their own mothers' practices, such as educing them to veil, and assess their parents critically for their lax religious lifestyle. In consequence, the age hierarchy under which textual authority is invoked and, to some extent, the youth can become religious educators of their parents.

However, even if I agree that the youths' individual orientation to Islam leads to some extent to emancipation or more freedom of movement, my fieldwork indicates that this aspect needs to be adjusted or modified. During my fieldwork I realized that the parent's authority is often *re-emphasized* through Islamic discourses. Presentations frequently stress the youths' obligations and duties as daughters (or sons), and the significant role and position of parents within Islam. Breaking with the family is considered as a great sin, and should be avoided as far as possible.

The changed role of religious authority of their parents indicates not only a generational shift, but also an increasing individualization of Muslim identity. How Islam is played out and how the youths are "being Muslims" are negotiated in relation to new religious authorities, including internet blogs, television preachers, books, religious groups and personal judgment. Furthermore, as the youths are not active in ethnic oriented mosques and organizations, they emphasize a universal Islam where the world wide *ummah* (community) is the reference, the youths' religious activities and identification are de-ethnicized. Turning to Islam is not making the youths feel more "Turkish" or "Egyptian." Rather, it detaches their ethnic identity from their religious identity. At the same time, many youths feel that it is difficult to *feel* like a "German" due to continuous framing of Islam as incompatible with German values.

Representing Islam

Typically, the female youths are treated as non-German and/or as "others" by strangers they encounter in daily life and by their school teachers. This representation is related to stereotyping and prefabricated ways of looking at the headscarf by the media (Schiffer 2005). The habits of categorization are often related to second-hand experience, the media. Media is our most important source of information, in particular to themes which we otherwise have little access to, of which consequently media structures our perception (Schiffer 2005). Being German and Muslim is a problematic identification due to the current media framing of "Islamism" (*Islamismus*) and "terror," and the construction of "Islam as strangeness" (*Fremdheit*) (Schiffer 2005) and as representing values incompatible with German values. Islamism and the suppression of Muslim women are symbolized through the continued use of references to or images of the headscarf in the media. A chain of associations, by now unconsciously, has been constructed in that television or newspapers make use of women with headscarves in particular reports. This collective stereotyping or profiling of what "Muslims are" or how they are supposed to behave in which Islam apparently dictates how Muslims behave and think, is not only affecting how the non-Muslim population think about Muslims and Islam, but also how Muslims identify and behave in the European public spheres. This process is gendered in which the image of the veil is constructing an idea of Muslim women as submissive, subverted, traditional and/or passive.

A politician with migrant background is quoted in the tabloid newspaper, *Bild am Sonntag*, as appealing to Muslim women saying, "Arrive today, arrive in Germany. You live here, thus take off the headscarf!"[14] The statement suggests that wearing a headscarf is considered as incompatible with being German, or with having "arrived"—not only physically, but mentally or affectively—in German society. The relation between veiling and being perceived as a non-German becomes particularly clear when talking to German Muslim female converts. Both Muslim and non-Muslim population consider these women as no longer German once they don the veil. Also "born" Muslims feel a difference in the public perception of them after starting to veil. For example, Ines, a seventeen year old of Palestinian background believes that when she started to wear the headscarf, it changed the way her urban surroundings consider her. She narrates:

> Sometimes at the metro, there are like three people sitting across you, and they stare, look at you like this' [she looks at me from head to toe] 'as if they were in the Zoo . . . and I, like, think, come on hey, stop looking at me like that, as if I am a monkey in a cage! And sometimes you are also imagining it, like, that (you think) they are looking, and then there is maybe no one who is really looking at you, it drives you crazy . . . And then they ask why foreigners become criminals? Like, imagine, I feel it like that, and I am not even a foreigner, I am German. And they are still not treating me as a German. Imagine how it must feel for a real foreigner, someone who is not a German! . . . I have been German since I was able to think, and now, since when I started to wear a headscarf, I am not German anymore. They treat you differently, you can just feel it.

Ines feels that there is a clear change in how her immediate surroundings react and behave toward her after she started to veil (Bendixsen 2005). She personally does not see any contradiction in being German and veiled, but experiences that she is treated as a "foreigner" due to this practice. Growing up in a place where she seldom socialized with people of migrant background, Ines had mostly "ethnic" German friends before the age of fourteen. After a turbulent youth, she turned more religious when she moved to Berlin and decided to veil at the age of seventeen. Until then, she says, she had no problems considering herself as a German, a feeling that changed after she visually expressed that she is a Muslim and the subsequent external reactions toward her. In the above conversation, she particularly emphasizes the experiences of being "othered" by gazes from strangers.

"German & Muslim = Good Like That"[15]

Several Muslim youths are trying to combine "being German" with "being Muslim." They employ several tactics[16] in pursuing this endeavor, including learning Islam in the German language, emphasizing certain common values and moralities, and trying to change the negative stereotyping of Islam in Germany. Without the intention of returning to their parents' homeland, many youths of the so-called second generation consciously learn about Islam in the German language in which they are more fluent (Nökel 2002). Consequently, youths can explain Islam to their non-Muslim surroundings in a more straightforward way. Furthermore, the majority focuses on how to best practice Islam, their religious behavior and belief, *in Germany*, which is considered a secular society.

Perhaps paradoxically, the females' religious identification can assist in embracing a German and "modern" identity. The youths encounter daily expectations which they feel are contradictory from those of their parents on the one hand, who fear that their daughters are becoming "too German," and from their teachers and peers, on the other, who they think will consider them as "too Turkish." The clear distinction that the youth make between ethnicity and religion makes it possible for them not to feel "betwixt and between" their parent's home country and Germany. Certain values, such as punctuality, honesty and hard work are appreciated both in Islam and in German culture. By framing these as "Islamic," the youths can negotiate a "third space" (Bhabha 1994).[17] For example, Fatima (thirty years old, Turkish parents) remarks that "religion can be a bridge," because it combines both; "one can say 'I am a Muslim' and it does not matter whether one is German, Turkish or Arabic." When young women look for a marriage partner, it is increasingly important that their future husband is a religiously observant Muslim, without regard for his ethnic background. The majority still marry within their ethnic groups—most likely due to language, social network and expectations from their parents. Nevertheless, a marriage choice is more complex, as Naila (seventeen years old, Egyptian parents) comments: "For sure, I will never marry an Egyptian from Egypt, you know," and explains that it is important that her future husband should not only be a Muslim, but also know the "European lifestyle."

The effort of living out a "correct" Islam by the youths is localized and situated in Germany as a non-Muslim society and as a place where many adolescents feel that "Islam is misunderstood and misrepresented." For example, at one Friday presentation in a German-speaking mosque which the youths often visit, the presenter says "Islam is being criticized because we are doing wrong things. We are mirroring Islam for these people, and when we mirror the wrong things then we are guilty in that they are not coming to Islam because we are mirroring wrong." Such utterance situates the religious practice of youths directly in their physical locality and suggests their larger duty to perform Islam "correctly" in a specific socio-historical context. The representative role the youth's sense as a consequence of "othering" processes cannot be underestimated.[18] Many youths, females in particular, experience being "walking representatives of Islam" in their daily life vis-à-vis both non-Muslims and the Muslim population. With this follows a feeling of obligation to improve the stained (Goffman 1963) image of Islam in the German public where they are depicted as suppressed or victims of patriarchal forces—thus at the same time, portraying "the Muslim man" as a suppressor.

What I call "daily micro-politics" are tactics (de Certeau 1984) the youth make use of in an effort to improve the negative representation of Muslims. Such tactics include a continuous attentiveness to how they behave in the street, such as smiling to strangers, being helpful, or to enhance their Islamic knowledge to improve their answers to questions about Islam. The self-awareness of representing Islam increases social pressure, from themselves, other Muslims and non-Muslims on the young females: as the females try to promote an authentic or ideological image of Islam and Muslims, it involves high demands on their daily behavior in the street. The price for "being in a community" (Bauman 2001: 4) includes self-control and living up to constructed expectations on what it means to be a "good, correct Muslim."

The youths' identification with Islam is not only affected by their status as members of a post-migration religious minority (Cesari 2003), but also by global events, the introduction of technology and opportunities provided in the urban space. The transnational element of the youth's orientation to Islam as a consequence of modern technology cannot be underestimated; figures like Tariq Ramadan,[19] the Egyptian religious scholar al-Qaradawi[20] and the popular Egyptian television preacher Amr Khaled are references and authorities for youths all over the worldwide *ummah* (Mandaville 2005). Through the online discussion groups and cable TV shows, ideas and concepts are spread and discussed between different local spaces. The recent popular Baba Ali figuring in "ummah films" on YouTube is one example of a young, American-Iranian Muslim who creatively contributes to a transnational Muslim youth culture with his funny, satiric clips with titles such as "Culture vs. Islam," "Muslim while Flying," "Looking for a Spouse Online" and "The Parent Negotiations."[21]

Social class and educational level of youths affect how a religious identity is lived out (Ismail 2004; Salih 2003) and where they participate religiously (Bendixsen 2007). Emphasizing knowledge as the only way to live Islam "correctly" seems to attract youths who already are, or in the future will belong to an upward mobile part of the migrant population because of their parents' or own educational success. It can be suggested that educational level has a stronger effect on the youths' relation to Islam (cf. Salih 2003) than merely their economically defined class and migration background.

A Modern Muslim Identity?

The "turn to Islam" is an urban phenomenon in Germany, which can also be found in Cairo (Ismail 2006) and Istanbul (Sanktanber 2002). A city offers a variety of religious spaces representing different religious orientations and congregations providing particular "infrastructures of action" (Ismail 2006: 12). Salwa Ismail suggests that the "turn to Islam" within the urban space is not only a consequence of people moving from rural to urban, thus facing alienation in the urban anonymity and weakening of community structures. More important is mobilizing urban opportunities for a religious organization to situate its message in the social antagonism and positions that have historically always been a part of the urban landscape (Ismail 2006: 112-113). Religion can be practiced alone, by use of the many online groups on the internet, in new religious study groups, or in the more traditional, ethnically oriented mosques. The variety of religious spaces in urban Berlin makes it possible for the youth to pursue a more individual and privatized orientation toward Islam, and consequently, to develop a religious youth culture.

"Turning to Islam" as a focal orientation of identity involves not only a religious moral orientation, but certain aesthetic, search for "pious fun" and religious consumption. Religious businesses or religious consumption are part of the youths' identification with Islam; in "religious shops," particularly in Kreuzberg, Wedding and Neukölln,[22] the youths can purchase CD readings of the Koran, candies without gelatin,[23] Mecca Cola, a counseling book for food purchase for Muslims in Germany, and *hijab*-Barbie (Barbie with a veil) while listening to religious songs by Yusuf Islam or Ammer 114[24] —a German "Islamic" hip-hop artist. Information on which of the "Turkish" or "Arab" *Imbiss* are religiously "correct" is passed via word-of-mouth.[25] Islamic graffiti on the Berliner urban landscape such as "Muslims are the best. Live Allah!" or "Muslims love best" (Kaschuba 2007)[26] both challenge urban spaces and present spaces of belonging (Bendixsen 2007).

Turning to Islam also includes a consciousness on how Muslims dress in public, an effort to behave in a religiously correct manner in terms of gender relation in the public sphere, and refusal to visit places with high alcohol consumption. In this religious identity formation, several seek to improve themselves religiously by increasing their knowledge and enhancing their moral behavior, for example to pray more or to wear the headscarf. There are diverse reasons why young females decide to veil; some of the young women are forced by their parents, for others the headscarf is a fashion or a political statement, and some veil because of religious conviction. In the latter case, veiling is part of a continuous personal effort to improve themselves as "pious subjects" (Mahmood 2005), to please God and to reach Paradise in the afterlife. Seeing other veiled women in the street becomes part of their feeling of belonging in Berlin; "We are always so happy to see someone with a headscarf, particularly here [Reinickendorf] where there are not that many," exclaims one youth during a picnic. It improves their self-consciousness as Muslims and group identification with Islam in Berlin. The veil is not only a religious obligation, but in the sociohistorical climate, it has turned into a symbol of solidarity among female Muslims and by wearing it, creates spaces of belonging in a non-Muslim society.

Salwa Ismail (2006) argues that "[t]he view of Islamism as anti-modern rests on the assumption that modernization is associated with secularization and the retreat of religion from the public sphere. Islamism thus appears as an expression of an anti-modern strand that, for some, is inherent in the religion" (Ismail 2006: 3).[27] Instead of considering Islamism as an anti-modern movement, Ismail refocuses our attention to its rejection of the Western perceived hegemonic ownership or mega-narrative of the modern.

In contrast to this perception, wearing headscarf with jeans and fashionable colors is not about bricolage, but an act through which the youths situate the religious practice in the society in which they live. Further, at a picnic with a group of veiled youths, Rüya says jokingly to her sisters, "We have to be modern, after all we are Muslims!" This narrative of modernity, uttered half playful and half serious, should be understood within a context where Islam and Muslims are considered as "traditional," backward and resisting the modern (secular) society. Even if Rüya recognizes that the non-Muslim German majority consider religious adherence to Islam as traditional, Rüya promotes modernity through her devotion to Islam as a spiritual and social self-fulfillment in Germany.

Living a religious life and seeking modernity is not contradictory for these youths. Scholars point out that even if the traditional systems of believing are rejected by modernity, belief is not abandoned (Casanova 2001; Berger 1999). Individual, self-reflection and search for knowledge are part of the youth's religious identity, an identity which is felt and lived out as a "free" and conscious choice. They continuously distinguish their religious practices from their parents, which they consider traditional. The females, for example, often joke and make fun of their mothers' "unfashionable headscarf," distinguishing their parent's practice from their own. Simultaneously, even if this religious identity is more individualized than their parents, it does not mean the end of orthodoxy or that they are creating a random "pick and choose." The need for legitimacy and validation of the religious practice continues to be largely part of their religiosity. As Danièle Hervieu-Leger stresses "there is no religion without the authority of a tradition being invoked (whether explicitly, half-explicitly or implicitly) in support of the act of believing" (2000: 76).

Push and Pull Factors Illuminating "the Islamic Turn"

The question of why women embrace religious norms and religious communities has been central in studies on Muslim women since the 1990s and has been addressed in different ways. The fact that women embrace Islam and religious organizations regarded as subjecting female bodies to patriarchal gender structures have been considered as a paradox, or representing a "perplexing question" by feminist scholars (Moghadam 1994; Saghal and Yuval-Davis 1992). Some scholars have a tendency to consider women who actively participate in religious organizations as victims of "false consciousness" —disciplined by fundamentalist formations (Grewal and Kaplan 1994).[28] Related to the debate on multiculturalism, Susan Okin (1997), a liberal feminist philosopher, claims that there is an inescapable tension between gender equality ideals and cultural recognition of groups. Continuing in this vein of understanding, other scholars argue in a universalistic feminist matter, that though Muslim girls seem to choose wearing the veil, this does not mean that they are autonomous, as the veil is a (*the*) symbol of subordination (Badinter 1989). In this view, as the content of women's "cultural norms" —such as modesty, self-discipline, and seclusion—is in opposition to personal autonomy, the women risk to be subordinated by adhering to their cultural communities.

Since the 1990s several scholars argue that Muslim youth's "turn to Islam" is part of "identity politics" (Cesari 2003; Khosrokhavar 1997) —a modern phenomenon—with similarities to social movements. Just like other youth subcultures which have developed in the urban spaces throughout the years (Widdicombe and Wooffitt 1995) identification with Islam seems to be a response to socio-economic conditions. It is one possible way to create a space and place within a life-world which does not offer many positive prospects for a socially and economically secure future. As such, "being or becoming a Muslim" is seen as a possible solution toward discrimination (Cesari 2003), and a way out for youths who are more or less excluded or feel rejected from society and search for a purpose in life (Khosrokhavar 1997). Implied in this perception of young Muslims' activities is the idea that Muslims are searching to publicly articulate an "authenticity" (Göle 2003), often through symbols that represent their religious identity as a way to claim *recognition* from the larger society (cf. Fraser 2000).

Identifying with Islam is a way to gain more emancipation from their families. By referring to religious argumentations, youths easily legitimate certain aspirations such as education and working in public. Veiling provides girls more freedom in that their parents will trust their behavior more in public (cf. Jacobsen 2006; Salih 2003; Nökel 2002). Distinguishing Islam from tradition and customs also facilitates their refusal of certain stigmatizing practices, such as forced marriages and "honor killings." By positioning both as the result of tradition and not Islam, the youths argue that "it has nothing to do with me, as it has nothing to do with Islam" both to other Muslims and to non-Muslims.

At the same time, understanding the turn to a religious identification simply as a reaction to external social structures as push factors becomes a too functional analysis and neglects both the specific individual and the global processes of which their religious identification constitutes a part. During my fieldwork with the young females, I realized that one needs to take these youths' religiousness seriously. This includes a stronger focus on the females' religious agency as well as the pull factors from religious organizations. Religious agency, following Laura Leming (2007) is "a personal and collective claiming and enacting of dynamic religious identity. As *religious* identity, it may include, but is not limited to, a received or an acquired identity, whether passed on by family, religious group, or other social entity such as an educational community, or actively sought. To constitute religious *agency*, this identity is claimed and lived as one's own, with an insistence on active ownership" (Leming 2007: 74). This religious agency is, like all agencies, not situated in a vacuum, but is performed within particular socio-historical contexts.

The decision to participate in a Muslim organization or to identify with Islam is shaped by religious and spiritual desires and experiences.[29] Several young women start practicing Islam actively due to a dream related to their—until then—lax religious praxis or because they are feeling confused. "Being a Muslim" and struggling to become a "better" Muslim is also about seeking to identify oneself as a religious person where motivation to becoming a pious or virtuous subject is a vehicle for daily activities, including efforts to perform their five obligatory prayers, struggle to merge internal motivation with external motions, but also forming characteristics which they consider important in Islam, such as modesty and being helpful.

This religious agency is often neglected, perhaps because the "turn to Islam" is considered as an (unfortunate) return to tradition and parental home country's culture. What should be clear by now is that the youths are not (re)turning to a static, unchanging religious tradition. Rather, they are actively pursuing religious morals and values which are situated in their own material and socio-cultural living condition. This does not mean that the youths are creating an individual religion where they pick and choose from Islam as "religion a la carte" or a religious bricolage, which some scholars tend to suggest (cf. Karakasoglu 2003; Khosrokhavar 1997: 128). On the contrary, the youth's quest for a "pure" Islam where validation of the "correct performance" is situated within a search for authenticity makes it necessary to legitimate their practices, for themselves and their peers, by positioning these practices vis-à-vis the religious sources. Most religious actors need a religious community in order to be with "others like them" and to create a universe of meaning where "what makes sense to you also makes sense to me" (Hervieu-Leger 2001: 167). An individual requires confirmation from outsiders for the meanings she/he makes use of in making sense and significance of their daily life (Hervieu-Leger 2001).

One *pull* factor which is often ignored is the effort from religious organizations to attract the youths as these organizations may represent spaces where the youths are not "othered" or considered as abnormal. In continuation, Hans Joas (2004) points to the need for religious people to articulate their faith or their experience of self-transcendence—a practice which is difficult. Religious experiences happen to individuals and are felt or apprehended rather than cognitively recognized. Although these elements contribute to make the experiences real, they make them only real, as the phenomenologist William James ([1902] 1994) suggests, for those who experience them. Consequently, Joas (2004) emphasizes that people need spaces in where they can share these feelings and experiences with others who also experiences them, although in a different way. These *pull* factors from religiousness and religious organization must be included in a deeper understanding of the "turn to Islam."

Conclusion

Is the combination of youth, religion and an urban lifestyle a contradiction? Or, is the urban space opening up for a variety of religious orientation in the twenty-first century, a period depicted as uncertain, ever changing and disintegrating communities? It is my perception that the modern process of individualization takes place (Bauman 2001) at the same time as there is a continued process of ascription, categorization, and "othering" processes. Any individual outwardly resembling a Muslim is expected to represent Islam in any situation. The conditions of community formation are upheld (Baumann 2001), although the form of religious communities has changed. In this process, a new religious lifestyle among the young Muslims is developing in urban spaces.

Without undermining the authentic religious experience of the identification with Islam or Muslim identity, I suggest that this process has similarities to "lifestyle subcultures." The youths' focus on moral values and universality as a reaction both toward the secular, materialistic, and Eurocentric majority in society on the one hand, and a traditional, cultural, local and nostalgic orientation of the "migrant community" on the other. In this space, specialized religious knowledge becomes a kind of "subcultural capital" (cf. Thornton 1995). Noticeably, the youths most attracted to this religious identification are not uneducated youth, but those who in many ways, are the most equipped among the "migrant" youth, in the sense that they master the German language, focus on higher education and have ambitions of a future working career. At the same time as localizing themselves through the urgency of improving the image of Islam in Germany, they also transcend the physically bounded site by drawing on globalized networks and influences, (re)capitalizing on the Islamic notion of community, the *ummah*.

Notes

1. Some sociologists of religion have pointed to the perception that there is a necessary incompatibility between religion and modern, urban life was too quickly taken. Stark argues that in Japan folk religion "flourishes among the young, successful, educated urbanites." It is worth noting that Stark has been critiqued, justifiably so, on his particular selection of statistic and data in order to completely reject the thesis of secularization. See Rodney Stark, "Secularization, R.I.P.," *Sociology of Religion* 60, no. 3 (Fall 1999): 268.

2. The concept of second generation of migrants has been rightly problematized for constructing the idea that people who are born in the country are still "migrant" just because their parents come from a different country. I still use the concept here for lack of a better concept that recognizes the particular socialization in a transnational space, meaning that they, through a *Biografiebildung* (biography formation) in their parent's home country—as well as in the migration "community," are embedded in familial and other relevant social relationships and networks. See Ursula Apitzsch, "Migrationsbiographien als Orte transnationaler Räume," in *Migration, Biographie und Geschlechterverhältnisse*, ed. Ursual Apitzsch and Mechthild (Münster: Verlag, 2003).

3. The participant observation (eighteen months) was conducted as part of my PhD thesis entitled "It's like doing SMS to Allah": Young Female Muslims Crafting a Religious Self in Berlin" in Social Anthropology at the Humboldt University (Berlin) and École des Hautes Études en Sciences Sociales (Paris), 2009.

4. The youth is the main focus of MJD as the stated goal is "to integrate Muslim youths by providing an opportunity to develop their creativity and talents as *young German Muslims* in the German language." See MJD, www.mjd-net.de (accessed February 1, 2008). Similar Muslim youth organisations exist in Austria, Italy, France, Sweden and Norway and MJD is represented at the European level by FEMYSO (Forum European Muslim Youth and Student Organisation) established in Leicester (UK) in 1996.

5. Like most European scholars, German scholars were mostly concerned with how ethnic and national identity and culture continued to have an impact on migrants' life choices up until the late 1980s. Particularly when large parts of the migrant population protested publicly in Britain during the Rushdie affair in 1989 scholars refocused their attention to the (changed) role of religion of migrants and their children born in Europe. See Steven Vertovec, "Religion and Diaspora" (paper presented at the conference on New Landscapes of Religion in the West, University of Oxford, September 27-29, 2000).

6. In Germany, the largest groups are the Sunni (approximately 2.2 million), followed by the Shiite (approximately 400,000), and the Alevite (approximately 340,000). See Susan von Below and Ercan Karakoyun, "Sozialstruktur und Lebeslagen junger Mus-

lime in Deutschland," in *Junge Muslime in Deutschland* (Farmington Hills: Barbara Budrisch, 2007), 33.

7. Hirschkind, performing fieldwork in Egypt, similarly found that many were distressed by people crying during religious sermons for the "wrong" reasons. See Charles Hirsckind, "The Ethics of Listening," *American Ethnologist* 28, no. 3 (2001): 623-631.

8. Hermansen argues that "[i]nternationalist Muslim revivalist movements such as *Jama'at Islami* [Islamic Party] and the Muslim Brotherhood (*Ikhwan al-Muslimin*) have encouraged this concept of a 'cultureless' Islam around the world." They are, she further holds, incorporating the identity element into the organization by insisting on "Muslim and proud of it." See Marcia Hermansen, "How to Put the Genie Back in the Bottle?" in *Progressive Muslims*, ed. Omid Safi (Oxford: Oneworld Publications, 2003), 309.

9. They reject their parents' conformity to ethnic traditions that the parents consider as emblematic of religiosity (e.g., manner of dress), while embracing a Muslim identity in and of itself. Among these young women, Knott and Khokher explain, there is a "self-conscious exploration of the religion which was not relevant to the first generation." See Kim Knot and Sadja Khoker, "Religious and Ethnic Identity among Young Muslim Women in Bradford," *New Community* 19 (1993): 596.

10. Similarities can be found in Christianity.

11. It is the belief that doing "good deeds" (*al-amal al-saliha*) secures God's blessing and aids in the formation of virtuous dispositions. The good deeds must be performed with the right sincerity of intent (*al ikhlas*) in order to perceive "good points" believed to improve a Muslim's chance to enter paradise. See Saba Mahmood, "Women's Piety and Embodied Discipline," (Unpublished PhD dissertation, Department of Anthropology, Stanford University 1998), 102-104.

12. Note that this was not during Ramadan. The youths are sometimes fasting throughout the year as an act that gives "good points," but also in order to complete their past Ramadan as women have to break the fasting month during their period of menstruation.

13. Note here the notion of *niyya* (Arab, "intention"). This notion emphasizes the importance of pronouncing the intention in the heart before performing the outer act in order for it to be a valid religious act in Islam. For example, the prayer, pilgrimage and fast are not valid if the proper intent is absent. One hadith (#1 in *al-Nawawi's* Forty Hadith) states that "actions are according to intent" or "actions are what they are by virtue of intent."

14. Ekin Deligöz, member of the Bundestag of the Green party, is quoted in Spiegel online as saying that prominent German-Turkish have appealed to Muslims in German to take off their headscarf as a sign of their willingness to integrate: "the person who veils is consciously bounding herself off from the German society" (my translation from German). Spiegel, *Deutsch-Türken gegen Kopftuch*, Spiegel, http://www.spiegel.de/politik/d eutschland/0,1518,442656,00.html (accessed October 20, 2006).

15. My translation from the German: "Deutsch & Muslim = Gut so," written in a power point slide presented in the Berlin weekly meeting on the topic "Muslim and German" by one of the national representatives of Muslim Youth Germany (MJD).

16. De Certeau makes a distinction between strategies and tactics: "A strategy assumes a place that can be circumscribed as proper and thus serve as the basis for generating relations with an exterior distinct from it . . . I call a 'tactic,' on the other hand, a calculus which cannot count on a 'proper' (a spatial or institutional location), nor thus on a borderline distinguishing the other as a visible totality. The place of a tactic belongs to the other . . . A tactic insinuates itself to the other's place, fragmentarily, without taking it over in its entirety, without being able to keep it at a distance."

See Michel de Certeau, *The Practice of Everyday Life* (Berkeley: University of California Press, 1984), xix.

17. Third spaces, according to Bhabha, are "discursive sites or conditions that ensure that the meaning and symbols of culture have no primordial unity or fixity; that even the same signs can be appropriated, translated, and rehistoricized anew." See Homi Bhabha, *The Location of Culture* (New York: Routledge, 1994), 37.

18. In postcolonial theory, which is my approach here, the notion of the "Other" refers to "the discursive production of another" —a process typified by the way in which Europe produces an Orient-as-other, also described as "othering." See Gayatri Spivak, "More on Power/Knowledge," in *The Spivak Reader,* ed. Donna Landry and Gerald Maclean (London: Routledge, [1992]1996). There is a general tendency to consider "others" as categorically and essentially different. In this idea of difference, are potentials for hierarchical and stereotypical thinking, which it is why the effect of "othering" bears resemblance to racism. See Slavoj Zizek, "Eastern Europe's Republics of Gilead," *New Left Review* 183 (1990): 50-62.

19. Ramadan in particular encourages young Muslims to regard their position in non-Muslim homelands not as one of weakness, but rather as a source of strength. See Peter Mandaville, "Sufis and Salafis," in *Remaking Muslim Politics,* ed. Robert W. Hefner (Oxford: Princeton University Press, 2005).

20. Al-Qaradawi produces a discourse, which is modern and moderate at the same time. Its more formal dimensions (using more traditional *fatwa* methodology or ruling on a question of Islamic law) preserve the authenticity of Islamic traditionalism. Religious programs on *al-Jazeera* and translations of his books have made him a representative of the most popular contemporary transnational Islamic discourses with devotees from the *banlieus* (suburbs) of Paris to the *pesantren* (Islamic boarding schools) of Southern Asia. See Mandaville, "Sufis and Salafis."

21. See Ummah Films, http://youtube.com/ummahfilms (accessed November 20, 2008).

22. These are neighborhoods in Berlin with a large representation of working class and population with immigrant background.

23. Many groceries contain the additive E441 (used in ice cream, chocolate, candies and different food products) which is produced through swine skin and the E47-E474 contains swine products, considered as *haram* (forbidden) to eat in Islam. There is a difference among Muslims in the degree to how careful one is concerning eating these products.

24. The number 114 refers to the number of *Surahs* (chapters) in the Koran.

25. Mandel has described how shopkeepers in Kreuzberg use the fear of *haram* (forbiden) meat and what is considered obligatory or *halal* (permitted) to their advantage. The result is an increase of shops that cater exclusively to Turks, creating a Muslim space in Germany, subdivided by Sunni or Alevi. She rightly points that this commercial orientation is also creating a place for migrants, on their own terms. See Ruth Mandel, "A Place of their Own," in *Making Muslim Space in North America and Europe,* ed. Barbara Metcalf (Los Angeles and London: University of California Press, 1996), 147-166.

26. My own translation from the German language. Original: "Muslime sind die Besten. Es lebe Allah" and "Muslime lieben am besten." See Wolfgang Kaschuba, "Ethnische Parallelgesellschafen?" *Zeitschrift für Volkskunde* 103 (2007): 83.

27. Islamism is a contested term, and rightly so. Ismail refers to "Islamism" as both Islamist politics and re-Islamisation, the latter of which relates to my usage here. Islamisation is "the process whereby various domains of social life are invested with signs and symbols associated with Islamic cultural traditions, Examples of this process include the

wearing of the *hijab* (veil), the consumption of religious literature and other religious commodities, the publicizing of symbols of religious identity, the reframing of economic activity in Islamic terms." See Salwa Ismail, *Rethinking Islamist Politics* (London: I.B. Tauris, 2006), 2.

28. Bracke suggests how this idea of "false consciousness" is based on a gendered and ethnicized way of thinking. See Sarah Bracke, "Author(iz)ing Agency: Feminist Scholars Making Sense of Women's Involvement in Religious 'Fundamentalist' Movements." *European Journal of Women's Studies* 10, no. 3 (2003): 337.

29. As Rambo correctly intervenes: "[r]eligion and spirituality, like aesthetics, should be considered a domain of life and experience that has its own validity." There are, he continues, "experiences, both cognitive and affective, that are distinctive to religion and spirituality." See Lewis Rambo, "Theories of Conversion," *Social Compass* 46, no. 3 (1999): 264.

Bibliography

Apitzsch, Ursula. "Migrationsbiographien als Orte Transnationaler Räume." Pp. 65-80 in *Migration, Biographie und Geschlechterverhältnisse,* edited by Ursula Apitzsch and Mechthild Jansen. Münster: Verlag Westfälisches Dampfboot, 2003.

Badinter, Elisabeth. "Interview with L. Joffin." *Le Nouvel Observateur,* November 9-15, 1989, 7-11.

Bauman, Zygmunt. *Community: Seeking Safety in an Insecure world.* Malden: Blackwell, 2001.

Bendixsen, Synnøve. "Being Young, Muslim and Female. Creating Space of Belonging in Berlin." Pp. 88-99 in *Hotel Berlin.* Berliner Blätter, Berlin: Gesellschaft für Ethnographie (GfE) und dem Institut für Europäische Ethnologie der Humboldt-Universität zu Berlin, 2005.

———. "Making Sense of the City: Religious Spaces of Young Muslim Females in Berlin." *Informationen zur Modernen Stadtgeschicht* 2 (2007): 51-65.

———."'It's like doing SMS to Allah': Young Female Muslims Crafting a Religious Self in Berlin." Unpublished PhD dissertation, Humboldt University (Berlin) and École des Hautes Études en Sciences Sociales (Paris), 2009.

Berger, Peter. "The Desecularization of the World: A Global Overview." Pp. 1-19 in *The Desecularization of the World: Resurgent Religion and World Politics,* edited by Peter Berger. Cambridge: Wm.B. Eerdmans Publishing Co. 1999.

Bhabha, Homi. *The Location of Culture.* New York: Routledge, 1994.

Bracke, Sarah. "Author(iz)ing Agency: Feminist Scholars Making Sense of Women's Involvement in Religious 'Fundamentalist' Movements." *European Journal of Women's Studies* 10, no. 3 (2003): 335-346.

Casanova, José. "Secularization." Pp. 13789-13791 in *International Encyclopedia of the Social and Behavioral Sciences,* edited by Neil J. Smelse and Paul B. Baltes. Amsterdam: Elsevier, 2001.

Cesari, Joceline. "Muslim Minorities in Europe: The Silent Revolution." Pp. 251-269 in *Modernizing Islam: Religion in the Public Sphere in the Middle East and in Europe,* edited by John Esposito and François Burgat. New Jersey: Rutgers University Press, 2003.

de Certeau, Michel. *The Practice of Everyday Life.* Berkeley: University of California Press, 1984.

Eickelman, Dale F. "Mass Higher Education and the Religious Imagination in Contemporary Arab Society." *American Ethnologist* 19, no. 4 (1992): 643-655.

Fraser, Nancy. "Rethinking Recognition." *New Left Review* 3 (May/June 2000): 107-120.

Goffman, Erwing. *Stigma: Notes on the Management of Spoiled Identity.* New York: Simon Schuster, 1963.

Göle, Nilufer. "The Voluntary Adoption of Islamic Stigma Symbols." *Social Research* 70, no. 3 (Fall 2003): 809-828.

Grewal, Inderpal and Caren Kaplan, eds. *Scattered Hegemonies: Postmodernity and Transnational Feminist Practices.* Minneapolis: University of Minnesota Press, 1994.

Hall, Stuart. "Introduction: Who Needs 'Identity'?" Pp. 1-17 in *Questions of Cultural Identity*, edited by Stuart Hall and Paul du Gay. London: Sage, 1996.

Hermansen, Marcia. "How to Put the Genie Back in the Bottle? 'Identity' Islam and Muslim Youth Cultures in America." Pp. 303-319 in *Progressive Muslims: On Justice, Gender, and Pluralism*, edited by Omid Safi. Oxford: Oneworld Publications, 2003.

Hervieu-Léger, Danièle. "The Transmission and Formation of Socioreligious Identities in Modernity." *International Sociology* 13, no. 2 (1998): 213-228.

———. *Religion as a Chain of Memory.* Malden, MA: Blackwell Publishers, 2000.

———. "Individualism, the Validation of Faith, and the Social Nature of Religion in Modernity." Pp. 303-319 in *The Blackwell Companion to Religion*, edited by Richard K. Fenn. Malden, MA: Blackwell Publishing, 2001

Hirschkind, Charles. "The Ethics of Listening: Cassette-sermon Audition in Contemporary Egypt." *American Ethnologist* 28, no. 3 (2001): 623-649.

Ismail, Salwa. "Being Muslim: Islam, Islamism and Identity Politics." *Government and Opposition* 39, no. 4 (2004): 614-631.

———. *Rethinking Islamist Politics: Culture, the State and Islamism.* London: I.B. Tauris, 2006.

Jacobsen, Christine M. "Staying on the Straight Path: Religious Identities and Practices among Young Muslims in Norway." Unpublished dissertation for the degree of Doctor Rerum Politicarum (dr.polit.), University of Bergen, Norway, 2006.

James, William. *The Varieties of Religious Experience: A Study in Human Nature.* New York: Modern Library, [1902]1994.

Jenkins, Richard. *Social Identity.* London: Routledge, 1996.

Joas, Hans. *Braucht der Mensch Religion? Über Erfahrungen der Selbsttranszendez.* Freiburg: Herder, 2004.

Karakasoglu, Yasemine. "Custom Tailored Islam: Second Generation Female Students of Turko-Muslim Origin in Germany and their Concept of Religiousness in Light of Modernity and Education. " Pp. 107-226 in *Identity and Integration: Migrants in Western Europe*, edited by Rosemarie Sackmann, Thomas Faist and Bernd Peters. London: Ashgate, 2003.

Kaschuba, Wolfgang. "Ethnische Parallelgesellschaften? Zur Kulturellen Konstruktion des Fremden in der Europäischen Migration." *Zeitschrift für Volkskunde* 103, no. 1 (Jahrgang 2007): 65-85.

Khosrokhavar, Farhad. *L'islam des Jeunes.* Paris: Flammarion, 1997.

Knott, Kim and Khokher, Sadja. "Religious and Ethnic Identity among Young Muslim Women in Bradford." *New Community* 19 (1993): 593-610.

Leming, Laura M. "Sociological Explorations: What Is Religious Agency?" *The Sociological Quarterly* 48 (2007): 73–92.

Lipset, Seymour M. and Stein Rokkan, eds. *Party Systems and Voter Alignments: Cross-National Perspectives.* New York and London: Free Press, 1967.

Mahmood, Saba. "Interview with Talal Asad: Modern Power and the Reconfiguration of Religious Traditions." *SEHR* 5, no. 1: Contested Polities, (Updated February 27, 1996). http://www.stanford.edu/group/SHR/5-1/text/asad.html (accessed March 5, 2008).

———. "Women's Piety and Embodied Discipline: The Islamic Resurgence in Contemporary Egypt." Unpublished PhD Dissertation, Department of Anthropology, Stanford University, 1998.

———. *Politics of Piety: The Islamic Revival and the Feminist Subject.* Princeton, Oxford: Princeton University Press, 2005.

Mandaville, Peter. "Sufis and Salafis: The Political Discourse of Transnational Islam." Pp. 302-326 in *Remaking Muslim Politics: Pluralism, Contestation, Democratization,* edited by Robert W. Hefner. Oxford: Princeton University Press, 2005.

Mandel, Ruth. "Turkish Headscarves and the 'Foreigner Problem': Constructing Difference through Emblems of Identity." *New German Critique* 46 (1989): 27-46.

———. "A Place of their Own: Contesting Spaces and Defining Places in Berlin's Migrant Community." Pp.147-166 in *Making Muslim Space in North America and Europe,* edited by Barbara Metcalf. Los Angeles and London: University of California Press, 1996.

Moghadam, Valentine. *Identity, Politics and Women: Cultural Reassertions and Feminisms in an International Perspective.* Boulder, CO: Westview Press, 1994.

Muslimische Jugend Deutschland (MJD). Homepage. www.mjd-net.de (accessed January 2, 2008).

Nökel, Sigrid. *Die Töchter der Gastarbeiter und der Islam. Zur Soziologie alltagsweltlicher Anerkennungspolitiken. Eine Fallstudie.* Bielefeld Transcript Verlag, 2002.

Okin, Susan Moller. "Is Multiculturalism Bad for Women?" *Boston Review,* 1997. http://bostonreview.net/BR22.5/okin.html (accessed October 6, 2008).

Rambo, Lewis R. "Theories of Conversion: Understanding and Interpreting Religious Change." *Social Compass* 46, no. 3 (1999): 259-271.

Roy, Oliver. *Globalized Islam: The Search for a New Umma.* New York: Colombia University Press, 2004.

Saghal, Sita and Nira Yuval-Davis. *Refusing Holy Orders: Women and Fundamentalism in Britain.* London: Virago, 1992.

Salih, Ruba. *Gender in Transnationalism: Home, Longing and Belonging among Moroccan Migrant Women.* London: Routledge, 2003.

Sanktanber, Ayse. "'We Pray like You Have Fun': New Islamic Youth in Turkey between Intellectualism and Popular Culture." Pp. 254-277 in *Fragments of Culture,* edited by Deniz Kandiyoti and Ayse Saktanber. London: I.B, Tauris & Co, 2002.

Schiffer, Sabine."Der Islam in Deutschen Medien." *Muslime in Europa,* Aus Politik und Zeitgeschichte 20 (2005): 23-30.

Soysal, Levent. "Labor to Culture: Writing Turkish Migration to Europe." *The South Atlantic Quarterly* 102, no. 2/3 (Spring/Summer 2003): 491-508.

Spiegel Online. Deutsch-Türken gegen Kopftuch. "Symbol der Unterdrückung." (German-Turks against the headscarf. "Symbol of suppression"). http://www.spiegel.de/politik/deutschland/0,1518,442656,00.html (accessed October 20, 2006).

Spielhaus, Riem. "Religion und Identität: Vom Deutschen Versuch, Ausländer zu Muslimen zu Machen." *Migration und Sicherheit* (März 2006): 28-36.

Spielhaus, Riem and Alex Färber, eds. *Islamisches Gemeindeleben in Berlin*. Berlin: der Beaftragte des Senats für Integration und Migration, 2006.

Spivak, Gayatri Chakravorty. "More on Power/Knowledge." Pp. 141-174 in *The Spivak Reader*, edited by Donna Landry and Gerald Maclean. London: Routledge, [1992] 1996.

Stark, Rodney. "Secularization, R.I.P." *Sociology of Religion* 60, no. 3 (Fall 1999): 249-273.

Tietze, Nikola. "Religiosity among Young Male Muslims in France and German Public Spheres." Pp. 335-369 in *Islam in Public: Turkey, Iran and Europe*, edited by Ludwig Ammann Nilüfer Göle. Istanbul: Bilgi University Press, 2006.

Thornton, Sarah L. *Club Culture: Music, Media and Subcultural Capital*. Cambridge: Polity Press, 1995.

Ummah Films. http://youtube.com/ummahfilms (accessed November 20, 2008).

Vertovec, Steven. "Religion and Diaspora." Paper presented at the conference on New Landscapes of Religion in the West, University of Oxford, September 27-29, 2000. http://www.transcomm.ox.ac.uk/working%20papers/Vertovec01.PDF (accessed May 12, 2004).

von Below, Susanne and Ercan Karakoyun. "Sozialstruktur und Lebenslagen Junger Muslime in Deutschland." Pp. 33-55 in *Junge Muslime in Deutschland. Lebenslagen, Aufwachsprozesse und Jugendkulturen*, edited by Hans-Jürgen von Wensierski and Claudia Lübcke. Farmington Hills: Barbara Budrisch, 2007.

Warner, Stephen R. "Immigration and Religious Communities in the United States." Pp. 3-34 in *Gatherings in Diaspora: Religious Communities and the New Immigration*, edited by Stephen R. Warner and Judith G. Wittner. Philadelphia: Temple University Press, 1998.

Widdicombe, Sue and Robin Wooffitt. *The Language of Youth Subcultures*. Hertfordschire: Harvester Wheatsheaf, 1995.

Zizek, Slavoj. "Eastern Europe's Republics of Gilead." *New Left Review* 183 (1990): 50-62.

Chapter Seven
Female Believers on the Move: Vietnamese Pentecostal Networks in Germany
Gertrud Hüwelmeier

The spread of global Pentecostalism is an intriguing part of contemporary migration and is, thus, part of the "great success stories of the current era of globalization" (Robbins 2004: 117). As many scholars have shown, it is an ever-growing religious movement, not just throughout Africa (Corten and Marshall-Fratani 2001; Meyer 1999; van Dijk 2003), Latin America (Levine and Stoll 1997; Martin 2002; Vasquez and Marquardt 2003) and Asia (Wanner 2004); but also in Europe (Coleman 2000; Adogame 2004; Adogame and Weissköppel 2005; Lauser and Weissköppel 2008). The appealing characteristics of what is commonly understood as gifts of the Holy Spirit, such as speaking in tongues, healing and prophesying, attract millions of people in various countries. Ecstatic experience, a main feature of charismatic Pentecostalism, seems to be one of the reasons why so many people convert to this kind of Christianity.

While Pentecostalism[1] is spreading around the world, regardless of national or cultural borders, the majority of the congregants are women. David Martin reports that about 75 percent of adult evangelicals are women (2002: 8). Considering this fact, it is surprising that to date so little research has been done within this field. In particular, questions of gender have been paid only scant attention.[2] Based on the patriarchal tradition of the Bible, women in charismatic Pentecostal churches are expected to subordinate themselves to God and to male church leaders (Robbins 2004: 132). As most of the leadership positions, including the office of pastor or the roles of evangelists and prophets, are occupied by men, the question arises as to why charismatic Pentecostalism appeals to so many women.

Taking into account the increasing feminist consciousness and women's access to influential positions in various religious groups, such as Catholic sisters in global networks (Hüwelmeier 2008b) or women in the Islamic piety movement (Mahmood 2005), this chapter explores whether or not Pentecostalism enhances women's autonomy. In particular, it investigates the role of charismatic Pentecostal Christianity and its impact on the negotiation of gender conflicts within new migration movements from Asia to Europe.[3]

Pentecostal churches provide a place where women find support for problems in their family and kinship relations. By analyzing shifting gender concepts of Pentecostal Vietnamese migrants in Germany, this chapter argues that the empowerment of women—despite the male dominance in leadership positions —is one of the main factors of the churches' success. Emphasis will be placed on issues of power, in particular on charismatic authority, in relation to changing gender roles. It pursues the question of whether religion is a liberating factor for women within charismatic Pentecostal churches, or whether male authority and power are reproduced.

The first section elaborates on the arrival of Vietnamese migrants[4] in Germany. Due to the division into West and East Germany, there were various waves of Vietnamese migrants with different religious backgrounds. The second part focuses on the emergence of Vietnamese Pentecostalism in Germany and on the split of a Pentecostal church, specifically analyzing the separation of an all-female group. In the last section, the experiences of female believers in their religious journeys as they visit churches in distant areas and their participation in services and prayer camps are investigated. The data was collected through ethnographic fieldwork with Vietnamese migrant women in two Pentecostal networks. Nearly all of them are non-permanent residents. Most of them are single mothers and dependent on the German welfare state. Some have been working as cleaning ladies in public or private offices, others earning a little bit of money in small flower shops. I participated in Sunday services and prayer meetings in house churches as well as traveled to prayer camps with a group of female believers.

Religion and Migration among Vietnamese in Germany

The emergence of Vietnamese Pentecostal networks in Germany is a recent phenomenon and has to be contextualized within different waves of migration. Compared to several African or Latin American countries in which numerous Pentecostal networks have rapidly grown into so-called mega-churches, the situation in Vietnam is very different. Religion in post socialist Vietnam remains a politically controversial topic, despite the fact that a revitalization of religious movements has recently started (Taylor 2007; Endres 2007). The diversity of religious orientations in Vietnam manifests itself in the diaspora. After the end of the Vietnam War in 1975 and the various waves of refugees thereafter, Vietnamese Buddhist, Catholic, and Protestant congregations were founded in many countries, including Europe and the United States. Spirit possession rituals (Fjelstad 2006) and other forms of popular religious culture like fortune-telling or soul-calling (Hüwelmeier 2009a) are both found in Vietnam as well as among the two million Vietnamese who left after the end of the war in 1975.

However, charismatic Pentecostal Christianity in Vietnam and in the diaspora has rarely been the subject of study. One of the main reasons is the fact that this form of Christianity is not allowed in the country of origin. Even though some refugees who left Vietnam after 1975 were already members of Protestant churches, many Vietnamese did not come into contact with charismatic Pentecostalism until after they had migrated. This form of Christianity is spreading with increasing success in Vietnam due to the support of Pentecostal networks based in other countries. A number of Vietnamese refugees who arrived in Germany in the late 1970s as boat people also converted to charismatic Pentecostal Christianity. Nowadays, they evangelize even in Vietnam and in other countries in Asia and Eastern Europe.

During the second half of the 1990s, an estimated number of 2.3 million Vietnamese were living outside of their home country, around 1 million in the United States; 300,000 in France; 200,000 in Australia; 150,000 in Canada; and about 115,000 in Germany (Baumann 2000: 28). Much like in the United States (Gold 1992), there were different waves of Vietnamese migrants entering the Federal Republic of Germany (FRG or West Germany).[5] From 1978 onwards, a number of boat people arrived, due to the political situation in Vietnam. In the late 1970s, the FRG declared it would accept a contingent of 10,000 refugees from Vietnam, Cambodia, and Laos. By 1979 this was expanded up to 20,000; and until 1984 up to 38,000 people from Indochina migrated to the FRG, the majority of the refugees coming from South Vietnam. After 1982 the government of the FRG no longer guaranteed to accept Vietnamese refugees. Within the framework of family reunification policies, by 1990 the number of Vietnamese living in the FRG had increased to 45,779 (Beuchling 2003: 21).

Compared to the situation of the boat people in West Germany, the living and working conditions of the Vietnamese contract workers in former East Germany (GDR) were quite different. Based on contracts between the socialist GDR and Socialist Vietnam,[6] tens of thousands of Vietnamese migrants, most of them from North Vietnam, came to live and work in East Germany since the 1980s. They stayed for five years and eventually went back to their home country because incorporation into the host society was not expected. Aside from a German language course of only two months, the contract workers were not "integrated" at all. Living in specially designated housing, they were ghettoized and watched over by the GDR government and the intelligence service. Contrary to the boat people, for whom family reunion was rather easy according to West German laws, the contract workers, men and women, migrated alone, without their spouses or children. Sexual relations between male and female contract workers were forbidden, and even contacts with local people were not allowed. Despite such contract regulations, these interactions took place in manifold ways. As a consequence, for example, pregnant female contract workers were forced to undergo abortion or to leave for Vietnam (Dennis 2005: 38).

After the reunification of Germany in 1990 the contract workers used their personal and economic networks to build up transnational connections with friends and relatives in Vietnam as well as with former contract workers in East European countries. In the years after the fall of the Berlin Wall, an estimated number of 40,000 contract workers, about two thirds of the Vietnamese population in the GDR, were sent home. Many of them came back in the 1990s, legally or as non-documented migrants, after realizing that living and working in Germany was much easier than in Hanoi or other places in Vietnam (Hillmann 2005). Based on their former networks, they forge transnational relations and maintain political, familial, economic, and religious ties between the home and host country.[7] Today, an estimated number of 120,000 Vietnamese are currently living in reunified Germany.

Vietnamese Pentecostal networks in Germany include former contract workers from former socialist countries such as the German Democratic Republic, Poland, Russia and the Czech Republic, who came as asylum seekers after the reunification of Germany. These networks also include a few German spouses of former contract workers as well as non-documented migrants from Vietnam who only recently arrived. Similar to German Pentecostal believers, Vietnamese Pentecostals gather in so-called "free churches" (*Freikirchen*), who do not pay church taxes to the German government, unlike Catholics and Protestants. While adherents of Vietnamese Pentecostal networks mainly gather with co-ethnics due to preaching and reading the Bible in the Vietnamese language, they also celebrate prayer camps together with people from Latin America, for example. During these gatherings Vietnamese language is translated into German and Spanish. Pastors create transnational ties and personal networks with German preachers and evangelists from various other countries thus establishing trans-border connections and religious networks "beyond the ethnic lens" (Glick Schiller, Caglar and Guldbrandsen 2006).

Women and the Holy Spirit Church

The first Vietnamese Pentecostal network was established in the western part of Germany. Tung, the founder of the Holy Spirit Church and a former soldier in the Vietnam War, was raised as a Protestant, and was not a pastor at the time of his flight from Vietnam. He left his country of origin and arrived in West Germany in 1981.[8] Like many of the refugees, he benefited from special language and social programs offered by FRG and likely incorporated into German society much more easily than the thousands of migrants from Turkey in Germany, for whom such programs did not exist.[9] Soon after his arrival, Tung founded small house cells during the 1980s, and then expanded his church in the 1990s after the fall of the Berlin Wall because he had a vision of evangelizing former socialist countries such as GDR, Russia and Czech Republic, as well as socialist Vietnam.

In Berlin, a branch of the Holy Spirit Church was not founded until 2005. In 2003, a small group of women, former contract workers from the eastern part of Germany, initiated a prayer group not affiliated with the church at that time. The women came to know each other by coincidence while visiting a prayer meeting of about fifteen people in a Vietnamese Baptist church in 2003. Hoa, a woman in her forties, told me about her first contact with the Baptist church: A Vietnamese friend came to visit her at her house, mentioning that she, Hoa, would love music, singing, and playing piano. Her friend invited her to join a meeting in the Baptist church, located in the neighborhood. There she got to know three other women from Vietnam, former contract workers like her, and a strong friendship grew among them. Hoa visited the prayer meeting only twice, but stopped attending because she was dissatisfied with the group. She narrates,

> They were Baptists, you know? Always quiet, always listening. When they were praying, it was monotone, smooth. Not like in the Holy Spirit Church, where praying is much better, much more forceful. Sometimes we pray very loudly.

Hoa missed having positive emotions in her life. She complained that there was no love in her life. Due to certain circumstances, like her marital problems in particular, she felt quite distressed. She had great difficulty with her husband, a Vietnamese who was a gambler and thus had a lot of debts. As she disclosed, there was no more love in the relationship with her husband. Furthermore, she had the feeling of being completely overwhelmed with raising three children in a foreign country, and, as she told me, was very depressed at that time: "I was not a good wife. My life was broken." Only when God came into her life did she feel joy, and she became much happier than before. It was during this time of deep depression that she traveled to a branch of a Vietnamese Pentecostal church and became "born-again."

Along with three other Vietnamese women, Hoa then decided not to visit the Vietnamese Baptist church any more. Finally, the friends met in her home on a regular basis to read the Bible, talk together and discuss it. Within a few months, the group grew to ten women, friends of friends, most of them living as single mothers or divorced women. Others have husbands who live in Vietnam, with little contact between them. In 2004, one of the group members heard about the Holy Spirit Church in the western part of Germany, so they traveled by train from Berlin to a branch of the church in another town (a 300 kilometer ride) once a month to participate in the prayer meetings. Meanwhile, the women continued to meet regularly in the private home of Hoa, studying the Bible, praying, talking about health problems, sharing news, chatting, cooking and having meals together. As mentioned above, in 2005 a branch was founded in Berlin. Pastor Tung appointed one of the women as female leader of the Berlin branch because he lived in a small town in western Germany and was unable to visit Berlin every week, a trip that takes him four to five hours by train. He was very busy organizing all the other branches in various locales in Germany and distant places in Eastern Europe and Southeast Asia.

However, as Hoa explains: In the beginning everything was fine. Her friend, Thuy, the female leader, was a "good woman," she was friendly to everyone, she talked to everybody, and there was a really good atmosphere. The group was growing rapidly so they rented a room and met on Sundays. As time went by, according to Hoa, the female leader changed her attitude and personality. A divorced woman herself, she encouraged other women to leave their husbands if they were not willing to follow Jesus. Hoa was affected by this idea, because she was very unhappy with her spouse and thought about separation. After she realized that a close friend of hers was left by her husband, who fell in love with another woman in the Holy Spirit Church, she thought this could not be what God wants. Hoa then shared her concerns about Thuy with some of the other believers, although Hoa herself was still thinking about separation. During this process, and full of ambivalent feelings, she realized more consciously that the Berlin branch of the Holy Spirit Church, which had grown to forty congregants, was mostly composed of single mothers, divorced women, or those living separate from their spouses. There was only one married couple visiting the church regularly, while other members were married but their spouses never participated in the service.

Many of the women and the few men as well as the female leader visit the church in their everyday clothing. This is not the proper attire for praying, as Hoa explains to me. God would love color and nice hair, but those people in everyday clothing "did not smell good." She complains that they are wearing their working clothes, and sensed the musk of the restaurant or the Vietnamese snack-bar, where some of her co-congregants found jobs. She also dislikes the malodor of the cleaning supplies, which some of the women use while earning their money as cleaning ladies in hospitals. Instead of this they "should have a smile on their faces, they should laugh, they should smell good, they should not look tired and should not wear their everyday clothes," when attending the Sunday services. Contrary to other women in the church, Hoa is always dressed perfectly. She visits the hair salon twice a month, uses make-up, and wears high heels. Her three children, when accompanying their mother to the services, are also dressed trendily. Hoa and her husband, Nguyen, do not have much money because Nguyen, who is working in a restaurant, became seriously ill and could no longer do his job. Therefore, they are dependent on the German welfare state, just like many other members of the congregation. In addition, they have to pay off his gambling debts and are sending remittances to their relatives in Vietnam. Like other migrants, they are expected to support parents as well as brothers and sisters in their country of origin (Levitt 2001). Although Hoa lives very frugally, she invests part of her money in consumer goods. She explains that God always gives her what she needs.

During my participation in the Sunday services, I noticed the female preacher giving instructions to the younger people, some girls between eleven and thirteen years of age, concerning dress codes. She criticized them for wearing their skirts too short, and told them they should cover their naked arms and legs. The girls, second generation Vietnamese, born in Berlin, gossiped about this rebuke after the service. Much of the discourses on the female body and on dress codes in this Pentecostal church are reminiscent of debates about the headscarf in Islam and the proper behavior of Muslim women (Mahmood 2005: 157). However, in the Holy Spirit Church, the girls were quite reluctant to participate further in the religious meetings. All of these conflicts led Hoa and some of the women as well as their children to finally leave the church in early summer 2007. They decided to found a new prayer circle and met on Sundays in Hoa's home. Like two years before, her home became a spiritual place. Again the women started reading the Bible, chatting, cooking, and sharing news: about the church they had left, about problems in their work places, about finances, about health issues, about relatives in Vietnam, and about visas and marriage documents.

After the final separation of Hoas's group from the Berlin branch of the Holy Spirit Church, the women feel free of the paternalism of the male pastor. They are convinced that the church had gone in the wrong direction because of the authoritarian leadership of the pastor and the female leader, and as a result the women did not experience love and understanding. While criticizing the pastor and his style of leadership, they are also bashing the female leader, Thuy, a former close friend of Hoa, in a similar way. She is mainly reproached for encouraging the destruction of marital relations. However, as all fifteen of the women of the splinter group comment during interviews and after prayer meetings, the female leader is only partly responsible because she is instructed by the pastor. Hoa and the group of women, by complaining that they did not feel the presence of the Holy Spirit within the congregation any more, are missing charismatic authority as well as the love and care of its female leader. And where there is no Holy Spirit, they argue, there can be no love. Furthermore, the lack of love and care is one of the reasons why their relationships with husbands, lovers, and children are so unfulfilling. They long for attentive husbands and caring fathers and hope to receive help and assistance from the church in solving family problems.

Despite all of their criticism of the Holy Spirit Church and their relief at deciding to leave the congregation, the women had to deal with great personal conflicts. They suffer from guilt because of the separation from the former church and pray for forgiveness. During the meetings in Hoa's home, where I was invited and participated in services, the women cry loudly while tears ran down their faces. They repent and feel deep sadness in the private prayer circle. Embracing and holding each other, they try to overcome their ambivalent feelings. Reciting passages from the Bible reassure them that they are on the right path. These meetings can be interpreted as the staging of a religious drama as a performance of inner feelings that underlines the separation from the former congregation and simultaneously strengthening the formation of the new group.

In addition to the Sunday gatherings, some of the women also meet during the week to study the Bible in Hoa's place, to read and discuss passages of the "holy book" while reflecting on what had happened in their former congregation. Immediately after the split, some other women from the Holy Spirit Church also join these meetings in Hoa's home. They are attracted to the atmosphere of starting something new, and some of them are close friends with those who have separated. The women want to stay in contact with their previous female co-congregants. Phone calls, in particular exchanges about personal problems, as well as praying and healing via phone, take place and contribute to maintaining contact between the women. Finally, most of the relationships become weaker and break off after some time, due to the fact that after a while, believers have to make a decision about which church they belong to.

For a while about ten women gather to pray on Sundays, enjoying the spirit of solidarity and the sharing of religious sentiments. All of them are quite enthusiastic about the idea that God would help them in establishing a new church. The children, some of them in their teens, also participate in the weekly services. Mai, Hoa's daughter, plays the piano[10] while the adult women sing in loud and enthusiastic voices. Other teenagers take care of small children in the room next door. In the course of several months, up to thirty people gather in the private home of Hoa, a flat of approximately sixty square meters.

Vietnamese women organize the prayer gatherings on their own, including collecting donations from everyone and appointing a treasurer to keep track of the funds. As mentioned earlier, most of the women are single mothers and dependent on the German welfare state, yet at each meeting they contribute a small amount of money. They spend some of this for future investments, like renting a prayer room. In this way, the female believers experiment with quasi-bureaucratic features and, thereby, develop new skills in leadership and organization (Robbins 2004: 134)[11] which are necessary when founding religious and other civil associations in German society.

Moreover, the members of the female prayer group become "religious experts" in various ways.[12] Although they already have some knowledge of the Bible due to their time spent in the Holy Spirit Church, they are autodidacts. None of the women has ever attended a Bible school. For this reason, every Sunday the women select one from their midst who would then choose a Bible passage for the following week, when she would read it aloud and comment on it, giving personal testimonies about what she has read. Within the space of Hoa's home, they develop further skills in literacy and public speaking. In this way, everyone assumes the role of a temporary "female preacher." This role is performed within an egalitarian setting, not assigning responsibility to an appointed pastor. Collectively, the women pray for sick relatives in Vietnam. Included in their prayers are Vietnamese friends, cousins or brothers and sisters who want to migrate to Germany, or are waiting for marriage documents and visas. They also financially support a young woman from the former congregation who needs money to pay a lawyer because her boyfriend is in prison. As a non-documented migrant, the father of her newborn baby is about to be deported to Vietnam.

Members of the female prayer group support each other in various ways. Part of this kind of solidarity is the translation of documents from German agencies, like the applications for welfare or *Kindergeld* (state financial support for children). They enjoy the possibility of daily contact with each other via mobile phone, as well as praying and healing via phone calls. If any of the women suffer from headache, stomach ache, back pain, or any other personal problem, they call each other, praying and reading the Bible together. After this they feel fine.

When Hoa had to go to the hospital for surgery for two weeks, another woman from the prayer group came to stay in her flat and took care of her three children. Some of the co-congregants brought Vietnamese food to the hospital because Hoa did not like and could not eat the meals prepared in that place. Through this the religious group is also a network of social security (Hüwelmeier 2009) or as a network of care (Hochschild 2000). Women provide emotional and material support for each other, supplying the needs that otherwise could not have been met.

The women become experts in organizing their own prayer circle by appropriating religious knowledge, forging new networks, and experimenting with egalitarian ways of conducting religious meetings. In doing so, they practice basic principles of grass-roots democracy that go beyond a solely private religious meeting in a Vietnamese-German living room. Seen from this angle, these gatherings cannot be interpreted as withdrawal from secular society, a view that has sometimes been formulated with regard to Pentecostal churches (Robbins 2004). By establishing a prayer group of their own, independent of male authority, Vietnamese lower-class migrant women, who are non-permanent residents, acquire organizational skills and religious knowledge. Isolated, often without wide-reaching social contacts, overwhelmed with raising children and lacking language skills, disillusioned in regard to male role models of authority, and suffering from various personal problems, the women search for protection and support in a difficult situation. Membership in the prayer group helps them in dealing with their experiences as migrants in German society.

After three months, the small group of female Pentecostal believers felt the need to listen to the preaching of a pastor as well as the need for guidance with their Bible studies. Due to their translocal networks, they decided to contact a Vietnamese pastor in western Germany. This pastor, Lanh, was once a member in the Holy Spirit Church, until he and his relatives as well as a group of about thirty people separated in the late 1990s. They founded their own congregation and officially registered as a religious association with the German state.[13] Shortly after their separation, the newly established congregation led by Lanh purchased a former restaurant in the countryside of north western Germany, and named it the *Lord's Center*. Over the last few years, this group has created several house cells in the region around the Lord's Center, but has also sent its two pastors and male elders to other areas of Germany in order to take over some of the prayer groups that also split off from the Holy Spirit Church.

Traveling Female Believers

Upon the invitation of the new pastor Lanh, some of the women from Hoa's prayer group visit the Lord's Center, which requires a train journey of about 400 kilometers. The preaching of Pastor Lanh differs in substantial ways from the pastor in the Holy Spirit Church. Pastor Lanh preaches love and reconciliation, topics that are quite different from those of the former pastor, who was mainly preaching about sin and repentance. Moreover, the style and personality of the new pastor greatly appeal to the women, especially in their personal conversations with him. They appreciate the warm atmosphere at the Lord's Center and are quite enthusiastic about the place, feeling immediately "at home" not only in the huge house and garden in the lovely landscape, but also among the members of the church, all of them married couples with children. The congregation consists of both former refugees and former contract workers, many of whom have worked in the Czech Republic until 1990 and then applied for asylum in Germany. Interestingly, nearly all of the Vietnamese refugees from the Czech Republic settled in the western part of Germany, unlike the contract workers in East Germany who remained there after the fall of the Berlin Wall.

When Hoa traveled to the Lord's Center for the first time, she took along her husband and her three children, as well as some other members of her prayer circle. While accompanying their group, I realized how relaxed and happy she was in that place. On our way back on the long train journey we talked about her experiences:

> In the Lord's Center everything is different. In the Berlin church you will find only women. Families with women, but without husbands. But in the Lord's Center everything is different. Everything is fine. Everything is okay. Children and so on. Everything is okay. My husband said to me: "Look, everything is okay. A nice congregation. Fine everything. Everything is alright. The children are okay, the kitchen is okay. The Pastor is okay and he has a lovely family." . . . My husband was very happy.

After returning to Berlin, she felt something had happened in herself and in relation to her husband. As she reported during follow up encounters, since the trip they have greatly enjoyed living together. Talking about her experiences with other women of the prayer circle, they became more interested in the Lord's Center and finally decided to take part in the one week "summer conference," a prayer camp organized twice a year. During the prayer camp, many of the women and children chose to join the church and were officially baptized, thereby becoming "born again" Christians.

Compared to about sixty African charismatic Pentecostal migrant churches in Berlin with many pastors and various locations in the city (Hüwelmeier and Krause 2008), the few Vietnamese charismatic Pentecostal churches have only just begun establishing themselves. While migrants from Africa have a number of churches to choose from in Berlin, Vietnamese migrants are dependent on traveling pastors and elders based in other cities and countries and must also travel themselves. The pastors and elders from the Lord's Center usually arrive from the north-western part of Germany by car on Saturday morning, stay overnight in Hoa's home, and teach the Bible in the living room. On Sunday they perform the service, preaching and listening to testimonies as well as practicing healing ceremonies. Nowadays, the Hoa's home is too small for the group of about thirty people. Once, the congregants gathered in a room of a driving school, located on the grounds of a huge Vietnamese wholesale market in a former industrial area in East Berlin.[14] Using their personal networks, the women are able to find a place for worship. For example, the female Vietnamese owner of the driving school is a friend of one of the church members. On another occasion the female congregants rent a room in a Vietnamese restaurant on the grounds of a different Vietnamese warehouse. The pastor only recently decided to visit the women twice a month, namely after they were successful in finding a prayer room in a German Pentecostal church. In order to forge and maintain close contact with the Lord's Center, the Pentecostal Vietnamese women travel to the religious location once a month and spend the weekend there.

Religious experiences are not confined to the sacred place of the Lord's Center; even the train trip is perceived as religious activity by the Vietnamese women. Praying, singing, and talking about personal issues, such as marriage problems, difficulties in raising children, or troubles with "documents," are part of the journey. Each woman tells her story and reflects on how the Holy Spirit helped her in solving one conflict or another. In this way, the train trip could also be considered a pilgrimage where encounter and exchange happen among believers and group solidarity is strengthened on the long journey. Participating in prayer camps twice a year, organized by the Lord's Center, not only introduces believers into "spirit baptism" and deliverance rituals, but simultaneously strengthens their imagination of being part of a global charismatic Pentecostal movement. In the course of the prayer camp, the women encounter Christians from the United States, Latin America, Africa, the Philippines, and various European countries.

Although global outreach is not explicitly on the agenda of the Lord's Center, the members of the church and even the adherents of Hoa's group in Berlin are expected to spread the gospel everywhere, including their relatives in their country of origin. Through phone calls with parents and siblings that take place on a regular basis, the women talk about their new lives, trying to convince the members of their extended kin group to accept Pentecostal Christianity as their faith. They report their religious experiences and how the Holy Spirit helped them to become good Christians. During their visits to Vietnam they bring along the Bible in order to pray with relatives and neighbors. By forging and maintaining translocal and transnational ties (Mahler 2006; Salih 2003), Vietnamese Pentecostal women in Germany are actively involved in coping with the manifold uncertainties both in the home and in the host country.

Conclusion

As migration was, until quite recently, theorized mainly as a male activity (Clifford 1997: 6), I argue that moving, in particular for the purpose of religious journeys, is performed by women as well. Connecting various locales by spreading the gospel, lower class Vietnamese migrant women who are dependent on social welfare, work as cleaning ladies, or run small flower shops, create and maintain religious networks of their own. This chapter highlights the paradox of Pentecostal women being dependant on male church leaders and pastors on the one hand, while simultaneously being quite autonomous with regard to separation from the church and founding an all-female group or joining another congregation.

Confronted with uncertain legal status in the host country, and having material and emotional insecurities, some migrant women join charismatic Pentecostal churches in order to improve their lives. Women perceive themselves to be leading more joyful lives because they believe they are empowered by the Holy Spirit. However, Pentecostal congregations not only function as a substitute for loving and caring familial relationships, but are also places where gender conflicts are negotiated. Pentecostal female believers are actively involved in criticizing religious male authority. As has been analyzed in this chapter, they attentively watch, listen and comment on the preaching, lifestyle and personality of both male and female church leaders. When the women are dissatisfied with their pastors and complain about the lack of charismatic authority, they establish their own prayer circles, thereby obtaining organizational skills and religious knowledge. In Pentecostal churches, women are not simply passive recipients who subordinate themselves to church leaders, but can become powerful agents, able to bring about the split of congregations and found new religious groups under their own control. By doing so, their practices are to be contextualized within the concept of agency, not to be understood as a synonym for resistance to relationships of domination, but as a "capacity for action that historically specific relations of subordination enable and create" (Mahmood 2001: 203).

Compared to many women in Vietnam who live in a patriarchal society characterized by ancestor worship and male authority, Pentecostal Vietnamese women in Germany make a "complete break with the past" (Meyer 1998): abolishing ancestor veneration and removing the altar at home is one of the first duties of the "new born" Christians. In the context of migration, where male dominance is apparently weak and where many Vietnamese men do not take care of their children and families, Vietnamese women in this study find a new home in Pentecostal networks. Moreover, they become experts in religious knowledge and take over various offices within the church. By travelling to remote regions in the host country, viewing video cassettes and DVDs from Pentecostal preachers in Latin America, Africa and Asia, and preaching the Bible on the phone to their relatives in Vietnam, they create and forge translocal and transnational ties, thus generating a sense of belonging to a global Pentecostal movement.

Notes

1. Also known as Charismatic Christianity, Revivalist or the "Born-Again" movement, Pentecostalism is a stream within Christianity that focuses on the gifts of the Holy Spirit, such as speaking in tongues, prophecies, teaching and healing. It emphasizes a personal relationship with Jesus, which is set in contrast to a previous life, declared to be a sinful past. Pentecostalism is assumed to be the fastest growing Christian denomination worldwide. See Philip Jenkins, *The Next Christendom* (Oxford: Oxford University Press, 2002); Allan Anderson, *An Introduction to Pentecostalism* (Cambridge: Cambridge University Press, 2004). Charismatic forms of Christianity appeal to people all over the world due to their capacity to integrate into different local forms. See Birgit Meyer, *Translating the Devil* (Edinburgh: Edinburgh University Press,1999); Joel Robbins, "The Globalization of Pentecostal Charismatic Christianity," *Annual Review of Anthropology* 33, (2004): 121; David Maxwell, *African Gifts of the Spirit* (Oxford, Harare and Athens, OH: James Currey, Weaver Press and Ohio University Press, 2006); Simon Coleman, *The Globalisation of Charismatic Christianity* (Cambridge: Cambridge University Press, 2000); Simon Coleman, "The Charismatic Gift," *The Journal of the Royal Anthropological Institute* 10, (2004): 421-442; André Corten and Ruth Marshall-Fratani, *Between Babel and Pentecost* (Bloomington and Indianapolis: Indiana University Press, 2001); Allan Anderson and Edmond Tang, *Asian and Pentecostal* (Oxford: Regnum, 2005).

2. Elizabeth Brusco is one of the first Marxist and feminist scholars in the field, publishing on machismo and protestant Evangelism in Latin America (Columbia.). She focuses her works on the effects of conversion in the dynamics of family life in the last decade of the twentieth century and how this affects conjugal relationships. Conversion challenges machismo, as expressed by special male behavior such as smoking, drinking, gambling, and having extramarital sexual relations. Converted men are re-integrated into the household and participate in church life, thus adopting a value system that is at odds with those values of the dominant culture. See Elizabeth Brusco, *The Reformation of Machismo* (Austin: University of Texas Press, 1995).

3. This article is a result of my ongoing research project on "Transnational Networks, Religion and New migration," funded by the German Research Foundation. Ethnographic fieldwork was conducted in various congregations of Vietnamese migrants throughout Germany. In order to protect my informants, I have changed all personal and congregational names.

4. Most of the boat people, who came as refugees in the late 1970s, later became German citizens. In this chapter, I mainly refer to contract workers in the former socialist East Germany, who were expected to return to their home country. According to recent debates in anthropology, sociology, and migration studies, a transnational lens departs from differentiating between immigrants and migrants because simultaneous incorporations in more than one local and national context does not contradict integration or the wish to settle permanently. See Nina Glick Schiller, "Transmigrants and Nation-States," in *Handbook of International Migration*, ed. Charles Hirschman, Josh deWind and Philip Kasinitz (New York: Russel Sage, 1999); Nina Glick Schiller and Peggy Levitt, "Transnational Perspectives on Migration," *International Migration Review* 38, no. 3 (2004): 1002-1039.

5. Due to the lack of space I will focus on the boat people and mainly on the contract workers, although a small number of students had already arrived in the late 1960s. See Gertrud Hüwelmeier, "Women's Congregations as Transnational Networks of

Social Security," in *Social Security in Religious Networks*, ed. Carolin Leuthoff-Grandits, Anja Peleikis and Tatjana Thelen (Oxford: Berghan, 2009, forthcoming).

6. In April 1980, the GDR and the Socialist Republic of Vietnam signed a bilateral "Agreement on the Temporary Employment and Qualification of Vietnamese Workers in Companies of the German Democratic Republic." This and other agreements remained valid until May 1990. About 60,000 Vietnamese were present in the GDR in 1989. At the end of 2000, according to the Federal Office of Administration, there were 84,138 Vietnamese living in Germany. It must be noted that neither the large number of naturalizations nor the number of undocumented Vietnamese citizens living in Germany are included in these statistics See Olaf Beuchling, *Vom Bootsflüchtling zum Bundesbürger* (Münster and New York, 2003), 21.

7. Glick Schiller is among the first scholars to theorize transnationalism. See Nina Glick Schiller, Linda Basch and Cristina Blanc-Szanton, eds., *Towards a Transnational Perspective on Migration* (New York: New York Academy of Sciences, 1992); Nina Glick Schiller, Ayse Caglar and Thaddeus C. Guldbransen, "Beyond the Ethnic Lens," *American Ethnologist* 33, no. 4 (2006): 612-633. See also Steven Vertovec and Robin Cohen, *Migration, Diasporas and Transnationalism* (Cheltenham: Elgar, 1999); Ulf Hannerz, *Transnational Connections* (New York: Routledge, 1996); Peggy Levitt, "Between God, Ethnicity and Country," (paper presented at the workshop on Transnational Migration, Princeton University Press, June 30-July 1, 2001); Peggy Levitt, "Redefining the Boundaries of Belonging," in *Everyday Religion*, ed. Nancy T. Ammerman (Oxford: Oxford University Press, 2007b).

8. For a more detailed story of his conversion see Gertrud Hüwelmeier, "Moving East," in *Travelling Spirits*, ed. Gertrud Hüwelmeier and Kristine Krause (New York: Routledge, 2009a, forthcoming).

9. The boat people also benefited from special programs for family reunification. Sometime after their arrival, their spouses and children from Vietnam could join them in Germany. This is quite important compared to the former contract workers, who came alone, without spouses. The separation of the spouses who came as contract workers was a part of government policy of the socialist government in Vietnam to return the workers after the expiration of their contract. In the 1990s, many of these relationships broke off, partly because one of the spouses went back to Vietnam, together with one or two children, partly because either the husband or wife had extramarital sexual relations with other Vietnamese or with Germans.

10. Hoa, a passionate singer, loves the piano and bought this instrument some years ago. Her daughter attends piano lessons once a week.

11. With regard to examples from Latin America, Robbins discusses the role of political culture in Pentecostal charismatic churches. See Joel Robbins, "The Globalization of Pentecostal and Charismatic Christianity," *Annual Review of Anthropology* 33, (2004): 134.

12. On the appropriation of religious knowledge within the women's mosque movement in Egypt, see Saba Mahmood, *Politics of Piety* (Oxford: Princeton University Press, 2005).

13. The process of registering with the German state is necessary in order for associations to undertake various activities, such as the purchase of land and buildings.

14. Finding a place for worship is not at all easy for migrants from Africa and Asia. In London, many migrant churches locate their prayer rooms in industrial areas, miles away from the center of the city. The warehouses of Vietnamese businessmen in Berlin are places of worship not just for charismatic Pentecostals but also for Vietnamese Buddhists, who founded a "warehouse pagoda" in 2006. Many of the shop-owners build

small altars for the "spirits of the territory" to protect their places of business and to guarantee economic success. See Kristine Krause, "Spiritual Spaces in Post-industrial Places," in *Cities, Migrations, and Identities*, ed. Michael Peter Smith and John Eade (New Brunswick, NJ: Transaction Publishers, 2008); Gertrud Hüwelmeier and Kristine Krause, "Götter ohne Pass." Heinrich Böll Foundation, 2008, http://www.migration-boel l.de/web/integration/47_1662.asp (accessed March 30, 2009); Gertrud Hüwelmeier, "Spirits in the Market Place," in *Transnational Ties*, ed. Michael Peter Smith and John Eade (New Jersey: Transaction Publishers, 2008a), 131-144.

Bibliography

Adogame, Afe. "Engaging the Rhetoric of Spiritual Warfare: The Public Face of Aladurain Diaspora." *Journal of Religion in Africa* 34, no. 4 (2004): 493-522.

Adogame, Afe and Cordula Weisskoeppel, eds. *Religion in the Context of African Migration*. Bayreuth: Bayreuth African Studies Series, (BASS), No. 75, 2005.

Anderson, Allan. *An Introduction to Pentecostalism: Global Charismatic Christianity*. Cambridge: Cambridge University Press, 2004.

Anderson, Allan and Edmond Tang, eds. *Asian and Pentecostal: The Charismatic Face of Christianity in Asia*. Oxford: Regnum, 2005.

Baumann, Martin. *Migration, Religion, Integration: Vietnamesische Buddhisten und Tamilische Hindus in Deutschland*. Marburg: Diagonal-Verlag, 2000.

Beuchling, Olaf. *Vom Bootsflüchtling zum Bundesbürger: Migration, Integration und Schulischer Erfolg in einer Vietnamesischen Exilgemeinschaft*. Münster and New York: Waxmann, 2003.

Brusco, Elizabeth E. *The Reformation of Machismo: Evangelical Conversion and Gender in Colombia*. Austin: University of Texas Press, 1995.

Clifford, James. *Routes: Travel and Translation in the Late Twentieth Century*. London, Cambridge: Harvard University Press, 1997.

Coleman, Simon. *The Globalisation of Charismatic Christianity: Spreading the Gospel of Prosperity*. Cambridge: Cambridge University Press, 2000.

———. "The Charismatic Gift." *The Journal of the Royal Anthropological Institute* 10 (2004): 421-442.

Corten, André and Ruth Marshall-Fratani, eds. *Between Babel and Pentecost: Transnational Pentecostalism in Africa and Latin America*. Bloomington and Indianapolis: Indiana University Press, 2001.

Dennis, Mike."Die Vietnamesischen Vertragsarbeiter und Vertragsarbeiterinnen in der DDR, 1980-1989." Pp. 7-49 in *Erfolg in der Nische? Die Vietnamesen in der DDR und in Ostdeutschland*, edited by Karin Weiss and Mike Dennis. Münster: Lit-Verlag, 2005.

Endres, Kirsten. "Spirited Modernities: Mediumship and Ritual Performativity in Late Socialist Vietnam." Pp. 194-220 in *Modernity and Re-enchantment: Religion in Post-revolutionary Vietnam*, edited by Philip Taylor. Maryland, USA: Lexington Books, 2007.

Fjelstad, Karen. "'We have *Len Dong* Too': Transnational Aspects of Spirit Possession." Pp. 95-111 in *Possessed by the Spirits: Mediumship in Contemporary Vietnamese Communities*, edited by Karen Fjelstad and Thi Hien Nguyen. New York: Cornell Southeast Asia Program, Cornell University, 2006.

Glick Schiller, Nina. "Transmigrants and Nation-States: Something Old and Something New in U.S. Immigrant Experience." Pp. 94-119 in *Handbook of International Migration: The American Experience*, edited by Charles Hirschman, Josh DeWind and Philip Kasinitz. New York: Russell Sage, 1999.

Glick Schiller, Nina, Linda Basch and Cristina Blanc-Szanton, eds. *Towards a Transnational Perspective on Migration: Race, Class, Ethnicity, and Nationalism Reconsidered.* New York: New York Academy of Sciences, New York, 1992.

Glick Schiller, Nina, Ayse Caglar, and Thaddeus C. Guldbrandsen. "Beyond the Ethnic Lens: Locality, Globality, and Born-again Incorporation." *American Ethnologist* 33, no. 4 (2006): 612-633.

Glick Schiller, Nina and Peggy Levitt. "Transnational Perspectives on Migration: Conceptualizing Simultaneity." *International Migration Review* 38, no. 3 (2004): 1002-1039.

Gold, Steven J. *Refugee Communities: A Comparative Field Study.* Newbury Park, London, New Delhi: Sage Publications, 1992.

Hannerz, Ulf. *Transnational Connections: Culture, People, Places.* New York: Routledge, 1996.

Hillmann, Felicitas. "Riders on the Storm: Vietnamese in Germany's Two Migration Systems." Pp. 80-100 in *Asian Migrants and European Labour Markets*, edited by Ernst Span and Ton van Naerssen. London: Routledge, 2005.

Hochschild, Arlie Russel. "Global Care Chains and Emotional Surplus Value." Pp. 130-146 in *On the Edge: Living with Global Capitalism*, edited by Will Hutton and Anthony Giddens. London: Vintage, 2000.

Huewelmeier, Gertrud. "Spirits in the Market Place: Transnational Networks of Vietnamese Migrants in Berlin." Pp. 131-144 in *Transnational Ties: Cities, Identities, and Migrations*, edited by Michael Peter Smith and John Eade. New Jersey: Transaction Publishers, 2008a.

———."Formations of the Religious Self-Becoming "Women in Christ" in a Globalizing World." Pp.199-211 in *Religion and its Other: Secular and Sacral Concepts and Practices in Interaction*, edited by Heike Bock, Jörg Feuchter and Michi Knecht. Frankfurt Campus: Verlag, 2008b.

———. "Women's Congregations as Transnational Networks of Social Security." In *Social Security in Religious Networks: Changes in Meanings, Contents and Functions*, edited by Carolin Leuthoff-Grandits, Anja Peleikis and Tatjana Thelen. Oxford: Berghan, 2009 (forthcoming).

———. "Moving East: Transnational Ties of Vietnamese Pentecostals." In *Travelling Spirits: Migrants, Markets, and Mobilities*, edited by Gertrud Hüwelmeier and Kristine Krause. New York: Routledge, 2009a.

———. "Global Sisterhood: Transnational Perspectives on Gender and Religion." In *Untangling Modernities: Gendering Religion and Politics*, edited by Ann Braude and Hanna Herzog. Palgrave Macmillan, 2009b (forthcoming).

Hüwelmeier, Gertrud and Kristine Krause. "Götter ohne Pass. Religiöse Vielfalt und neue Migration in Deutschland." Heinrich Böll Foundation, 2008. http://www.migration-boell.de/web/integration/47_1662.asp (accessed March 30, 2009).

Jenkins, Philip. *The Next Christendom: The Coming of Global Christianity.* Oxford: Oxford University Press, 2002.

Krause, Kristine. "Spiritual Spaces in Post-Industrial Places: Transnational Pentecostal Churches in North-East London." Pp. 109-130 in *Cities, Migrations, and Identities*, edited by Michael Peter Smith and John Eade. New Brunswick, NJ: Transaction Publishers, 2008.

Lauser, Andrea and Cordula Weisköppel, eds. *Migration und Religiöse Dynamik. Ethnologische Religionsforschung im Transnationalen Kontext.* Bielefeld: Transcript Verlag, 2008.

Levine, Daniel H. and David Stoll. "Bridging the Gap Between Empowerment and Power in Latin America." Pp. 63-118 in *Transnational Religion and Fading States,* edited by Susann Hoeber Rudolph and James P. Piscatori. Boulder, CO: Westview Press, 1997.

Levitt, Peggy. "Between God, Ethnicity, and Country: An Approach to the Study of Transnational Religion." Paper presented at the workshop on Transnational Migration: Comparative Perspectives, Princeton University, June 30-July 1, 2001.

———. *God Needs No Passport: Immigrants and the Changing American Religious Landscape.* New York, London: The New Press, 2007a.

———. "Redefining the Boundaries of Belonging: The Transnationalization of Religious Life." Pp. 103-120 in *Everyday Religion,* edited by Nancy T. Ammerman. Oxford: Oxford University Press, 2007b.

Mahler, Sarah J. "Theoretical and Empirical Contributions Toward a Research Agenda for Transnationalism." Pp. 64-100 in *Transnationalism from Below: Comparative Urban and Community Research,* edited by Michael P. Smith and Luis E. Guarnizo. New Brunswick, NJ: Transaction Publishers, 2006.

Mahmood, Saba. "Feminist Theory, Embodiment, and the Docile Agent: Some Reflections on the Egyptian Islamic Revival." *Cultural Anthropology* 16, no. 2 (2001): 202-236.

———. *Politics of Piety: The Islamic Revival and the Feminist Subject.* Princeton and Oxford: Princeton University Press, 2005.

Martin, David. *Pentecostalism: The World their Parish.* Oxford: Blackwell Publishers Ltd, 2002.

Maxwell, David. *African Gifts of the Spirit: Pentecostalism and the Rise of a Zimbabwean Transnational Religious Movement.* Oxford, Harare and Athens, OH: James Currey, Weaver Press and Ohio University Press, 2006.

Meyer, Birgit. "Make a Complete Break with the Past: Memory and Postcolonial Modernity in Ghanaian Pentecostalist Discourse." *Journal of Religion in Africa* 28, no. 3 (1998): 316-349.

———. *Translating the Devil: Religion and Modernity among the Ewe in Ghana.* Edinburgh: Edinburg University Press, 1999.

Robbins, Joel. "The Globalization of Pentecostal and Charismatic Christianity." *Annual Review Anthropology* 33 (2004): 117-43.

Salih, Ruba, ed. *Gender in Transnationalism: Home, Longing and Belonging among Moroccan Migrant Women.* London and New York: Routledge, 2003.

Taylor, Philip, ed. *Modernity and Re-enchantment: Religion in Post-revolutionary Vietnam.* Maryland, USA: Lexington Books, 2007.

Van Dijk, Rijk. "Localisation, Ghanaian Pentecostalism and the Stranger's Beauty in Botswana." *Africa: Journal of the International African Institute* 73, no. 4 (2003): 560-583.

Vásquez, Manuel A. and Marie Friedmann Marquardt. *Globalizing the Sacred: Religion across the Americas.* New Brunswick: Rutgers University Press, 2003.

Vertovec, Steven and Robin Cohen, eds. *Migration, Diasporas, and Transnationalism.* Cheltenham: Elgar, 1999.

Wanner, Catherine. "Missionaries of Faith and Culture: Evangelical Encounters in Ukraine." *Slavic Review* 63, no. 4 (2004): 732-755.

Chapter Eight
Islam: A Dead End for Integration of Female Immigrants in Denmark?*
Helene Pristed Nielsen

This chapter is based on a research project originally entitled "The Mobilization of Muslim Women in Denmark." The project was based on interviews with heads and/or board members of various immigrant women's associations in three different larger municipalities. The women were interviewed primarily about incentives and barriers in forming and participating in immigrant women's associations. The data documents that, while immigrant women are doing everything they can to facilitate integrative ways of belonging, their activities in this regard are *not* based primarily on religious identifications. This finding raises interesting questions on whether faith-based (specifically Muslim) community formations face particular obstacles in Denmark, where church and state are not legally separated, and the current government (in office since 2001 and re-elected in November 2007) finds its support in the right wing Danish People's Party. Many respondents explicitly denounce their Muslim religious heritage, partly because several have fled oppressive Islamic regimes, and express fatigue about continually being queried on their religious practices by members of the ethnic Danish majority. Taking these observations into account, this chapter intends to find out why faith-based Muslim mobilization does not appear to be a preferred strategy for facilitating integrative ways of belonging among immigrant women in Denmark.

The Danish Context

To characterize the Danish setting, this section briefly describes the current Danish integration regime and origin of the immigrant/refugee population, the gender regime, and the state-church arrangement, as these aspects all seem likely to influence questions of faith-based mobilization among female immigrants in Denmark.

Integration regime

Scholarly literature about the Danish integration regime often points to a marked shift in recent years, dating back to the instatement of the present liberal government in 2001. The status and conditions of immigrants in Denmark has been greatly debated within the previous decade, partly because the government bases its majority on the support of the right wing Danish People's Party. However, several authors also point out that the debate emerged in the early-mid 1980s. Flemming Mikkelsen (2003: 98) states that "[f]rom having been preoccupied with regulating *access* to Denmark, the state after 1983 turned its attention towards domestic integration work" (my translation). Mikkelsen calls 1985 a "water shed year in Danish immigration history" (2003: 154), because from this year on, clashes between racists and anti-racists became more frequent and there were a number of demonstrations directed towards the conditions of immigrants *in* Denmark, rather than, as previously, directed towards conditions in their countries of origin. Jørgen Goul Andersen's presentation of statistical material supports the assessment that it is incorrect to talk about a radical turn in the Danes' attitudes to immigrants around the 2001 elections (2002: 8-11).

With the Danish Integration Act of January 1, 1999, regulations regarding housing placement of refugees were introduced, meaning that Danish authorities decide where a refugee who has been granted residence must live. The residence allocation is based on quotas, and the refugee must remain within the assigned municipality for a three year period after obtaining a residence permit (Vikkelsø-Slot 2004: 28-29). As far as more recent changes are concerned, Mikkelsen highlights the role of the present government in tightening the rules and regulations, but he sees this as a trend that already started in the 1990s under the previous social democratic government. Rikke Andreassen and Birte Siim state,

> Immigration became a heavily debated topic from 1997, when the then-Social-Democrat-led government appointed the former mayor of Aarhus . . . as Minister of the Interior. [He] introduced a new [tightened] immigration and integration law . . . In 2001, the Conservative and Liberal [coalition] government, with the support from the Danish People's Party came to power. A central part of their election campaign had been arguing in favour of tightened immigration laws. In 2002, they passed a law stating that family unification was only possible for people over 24 years of age . . . Denmark currently has one of the tightest immigration laws in Europe (2007: 11).

In March 2006 the Danish government once again tightened immigration laws, adding the provision that immigrants applying for citizenship have to sign a declaration obliging them to respect a specified list of "Danish values."[1] Furthermore, non-naturalized immigrants who are found guilty of certain types of crime, risk losing their residence permit after having served their prison sentence.

In so far as the origin of the Danish immigrant population is concerned, Denmark's Statistics provides several figures as of January 1, 2008. The total number of immigrants is 378,665, of which 63 percent originate from non-Western countries. In addition, they cite a total of 199,287 descendants (people whose parents are non-citizens), of which 52 percent are of non-Western origin. The large majority of non-Western immigrants originate from Turkey (31,433 plus 25,696 descendants), followed by Iraq and Lebanon. Although Somali immigrants are highly debated (partly because they are highly visible), they only constitute 10,357 plus 6,193 descendants (www.danmarksstatistik.dk). These figures have to be held up against the total size of the Danish population: 5,447,084 as of January 1, 2008, which means that just fewer than 7 percent of Danish population are immigrants.

Gender Regime

To understand the context of this study on mobilization of Muslim women, it is important to characterize the role of women as it is perceived among the majority of Danish society. Andreassen and Siim note:

> Gender equality has become part of the Danish citizenship model, and the present government defines gender equality as a key aspect of "Danishness" and Danish values. Gender equality and women's rights have become politicised in the struggle for control over migration (2007: 16).[2]

The Danish government speaks about gender equality as something the Danes themselves have already obtained, with efforts now needing direction toward bringing the immigrants on board. This is evident in the following excerpt from Danish Prime Minister Fogh Rasmussen's speech on the re-opening of Parliament after the summer session on October 2, 2007. Speaking on the theme of "the new inequality in Danish society" he stated:

> We want to improve the equality between women and men . . . Not everybody in Denmark enjoys equality. Some immigrant women have no contact with the surrounding society. They are unaware of their rights. They do not decide over their own lives . . . First of all, we want to encourage women of immigrant background to also get a job, get an education, obtain financial independence and participate in associations (www.ft.dk, my translation).

Buffy Lundgren (2007) describes Denmark as a country "in denial" of its ethnic diversity, gender, and ethnic equality issues. She states that gender segregation in the labor market is an issue, and although 27 percent of politicians are women, only 4 percent are leaders in the private sector, education and public administration (Lundgren 2007: 4), while the majority of women are in care giving and social professions. Overall, Lundgren concludes:

> The Danish self-image as a "model society" may actually be an obstacle to Danes' own learning and development. I suspect that its star status as a model welfare state in the 50s and 60s contributes to a pervasive denial . . . Living in the shadow of the past all too often stops countries and organisations from doing the difficult work of building and maintaining internal cohesion (2007: 7).

State-religion Arrangements

State-religion arrangements arguably determine the space for non-majority religions and Denmark's state-religion arrangements are dominated by *Folkekirken* (The People's Church).[3] According to the constitution, Denmark is defined as a Protestant Lutheran country. The People's Church is a state church and has special privileges. For example, the state directly collects church taxes from taxpayers who have not actively requested *not* to pay, and the state also provides additional funding through general taxes. The church is integrated into several institutions; for example, public schools, where Christian studies are taught at the elementary level, and preparation for confirmation is integrated at the junior level. However, students can be excused. Everybody is registered with name, address, and personal number in Denmark, and the church is in charge of this registration, receiving remuneration from the state for this work. This means that all parents, regardless of religious observation or lack thereof, must register their children at the People's Church.

While Denmark is thus the proverbial example of a strong institutionalized connection between state and church, there are also reasons to modify this image of little accommodation of minority religions. First of all, Danes are "passively Christian in large numbers" (Klausen 2005: 138). Secondly, it is possible to become a recognized faith community in Denmark. There are currently more than 100 recognized faith communities (www.familiestyrelsen.dk/11/). Thirdly, the debate about registration of persons has been raging quite heavily since May 1, 2007, resulting in the Minister of the Church giving the option of electronically registering the births of children. This is in response to the previous criticism of the fact that everybody (irrespective of religious convictions or lack thereof) has to register their children with the local Lutheran priest. Considering previous political statements on the issue, this signals a remarkable change.

On the 150th anniversary of the Danish Constitution in 1999, the Danish Council for Ethnic Equality issued a book debating the Constitution and its relation to contemporary Danish society. In it, Jørgen Bæk Simonsen (1999) argues that, although the Constitution does ensure *freedom* of religion in Denmark, people should also debate *equality* of religion—i.e., that no religion ought to be privileged above others. Undoubtedly, the People's Church has a privileged position in Danish society, institutionally, economically, and possibly also in terms of popular support with 85 percent membership (Klausen 2005: 139).

According to the most recent authoritative source on mosques in Denmark, there are currently two purposely built mosques (Kühle 2006: 63), and an additional large one may be under way in Copenhagen. But while local municipal planning authorities have approved the construction of a grand mosque, the project is apparently stalled by lack of funding and disagreements about size among the Muslim population itself. Lene Kühle notes that there are 115 mosques (2006: 65) altogether in Denmark, of which many are so-called "basement mosques."

Another often repeated case of how Denmark has been extremely slow in recognizing the needs of its Muslim population is the issue of a Muslim burial ground (Klausen 2005: 109-113; Zagal-Farias 2002: 95-109). On this front, the first Muslim burial ground in Denmark opened in March 2006. Interestingly, the head of Danish Islamic Burial Fund, Kasem Ahmad, chose, to invite journalists from both abroad and home and reportedly stated that "[t]he burial ground is a sign that Denmark respects Islam" (http:// nyhederne.tv2.dk).

On the whole, it is clear that formally speaking, there is a very strong relationship between state and church in Denmark. On the other hand, Jytte Klausen's point about the Danes being "passively Christian in large numbers" (2005: 138) is rather telling. Although the debate resurfaces from time to time, the issue hardly seems contentious within the Danish setting. Take for example the following reaction by a practicing Muslim woman when I asked about the issue:[4]

> HPN: The fact that the Danish church is paid for by taxes and so on. Is that also a mixing up of politics and . . . [religion]?
> B: I am not agreeing with that. We are equal with the Danes. Because they are not going to take money from ethnic women or ethnic men . . . It has nothing to do with me.

The respondents do not see the Danish state-church arrangement as problematic or in any way interfering in their daily lives. For example, one respondent bases her rejection of Islam on the broad generalization—presumably based on her personal experiences of life in Iraq and Denmark, respectively—that, "If Islam was like Christianity, I would never refuse [the mindset]. Because they [the Christians] do not interfere in your life."

Design and Methodology

During my fieldwork there were no large national associations specifically aimed at ethnic minority women[5] to interview, and those individual women with Muslim background who held the attention of the press were not necessarily reliable sources for the views and experiences of ethnic minority women in Denmark in general. Therefore, the selection of respondents was based on a sample that can be described as "frontrunners" (especially chairwomen in associations), rather than members of association in general, or the presumable majority of immigrant and refugee women, i.e., those not active in associations. In this way, the design excluded interviewing the very politically active immigrant women who were well-known to the media at that time because they often possess an explicit political agenda that would make open-ended interviewing quite difficult. However, it was necessary to find respondents who actually had experience with mobilization and active participation in Danish society, hence the focus on "frontrunners."

Because of the lack of large national immigrant women's associations, I decided to focus on three larger Danish municipalities: Copenhagen, Aarhus and Aalborg (see Table 8.1). These municipalities also enabled local comparisons of whether, for example, municipal practices influence mobilization patterns. The 1999 *Integration Act*, with its quotas for refugee settlement, means that some municipalities tend to have a specific ethnic profile, like for example, Aalborg, where a comparatively large group of Somalis reside. Aalborg has unused quota at the time Somali people were obtaining residence permits. Furthermore, these three cities have a high degree of geographic spread, as far as this is possible within a country as small as Denmark.

Table 8.1 Number of immigrants/refugees and descendants by municipality 2007

Based on data from Denmark's Statistics, final figures for 2007.

	Nationally	Copenhagen	Aarhus	Aalborg
Persons of Danish origin	4,969,384	403,900	258,026	180,804
Immigrants/refugees	360,902	73,289	27,548	10,737
Descendants	116,798	26,510	10,596	2,608
Immigrants/refugees and descendants as total of population	8.8%	19.8%	12.9%	6.9%

Figures for both immigrants/refugees and descendants also cover those of "Western origin."

The associations were selected on the basis of their names, which often included the words "women's association." The search criteria also included the addition of a name of a predominantly Muslim country of origin (e.g., The Afghan Women's Association or Somali Women's Organization Denmark) or a name specifically indicating a cross-ethnic organization (e.g., Multicultural Women's Club or Intercultural Women's Association).

The associations were chosen by searching the internet, looking at city council lists of partners and supported associations, network associations listed by Danish majority women's organizations, plus interviews or telephone calls with integration workers in both public and private contexts. Following these leads and relying partly on a snowball effect among respondents led to twenty-four formal interviews with a total of thirty-four women (some were group interviews) within the primary target group: women of non-Danish origin who were active in ethnic minority associations. In addition, there were nine more or less informal (mostly non-recorded) discussions with other relevant actors. In total, the ethnic minority women within the sample together represent involvement in 26 associations, of which 13 were cross-ethnic, 4 Somali, 3 Kurdish, 2 Palestinian, 2 Iranian, 1 Turkish and 1 Afghan.

The interviews were conducted between August 2007 and January 2008 on locations chosen by the women themselves. They generally lasted about one hour, and most were recorded (with the written consent of the respondents), and all were carried out as relatively open semi-structured interviews with a few recurrent themes. All respondents were given the chance to comment on the transcript of the interview, but only very few took the opportunity to do so.

Based on the selection criteria and the aim of interviewing the "frontrunners," it is clear that their viewpoints and experiences discussed in the next sections do not represent the female immigrant population in Denmark as a whole. It is also important to stress that the respondents do not make up a homogenous group; for example, there are great disparities in the levels of education (ranging from holding a PhD to no formal education), employment within both private and public sectors, as well as being recipients of different types of welfare benefits. In addition, the ages range from sixteen to sixty years, and while the majority either arrived in Denmark as refugees or via family unification laws, fourteen were born and raised in Denmark.

Identifying as Muslim women—or not?

This section presents the perceived relationship between gender, religion, and integration. It discusses two overall themes related to the identity of Muslim women and the meaning of integration. Approximately one third of the respondents identified themselves as Muslims. But rather than focusing on the numbers, the following data relates to *how* this self-identification is expressed. It shows how these women view the relationship between being a woman and being Muslim. Even more interesting is their approach to this issue and how they perceive of the dominant Danish conception of this relationship. Starting with the women who *did* identify themselves as Muslim, the following exchange arguably reveals a prima facie notion that assertive self-identification as a Muslim woman seems self-contradictory to any Dane; even to a Dane who was explicitly contacted to discuss matters of female Muslim mobilization.

> F: Back then in Turkey, we went to Koran school . . . and when I finished the course I was asked by the teacher if I could help him teach some children during the summer.
> HPN: Can I then ask, does that mean that you identify as Muslim?
> F: Yes it does. Although perhaps not everybody would agree with me, but [laughs] . . . You are very welcome to be open and ask about it.

Another woman refers to the Koran to counter some of the prejudices she feels Danes generally harbor about Muslim women. Regarding gender roles, she says, "I am not saying they should have the same roles, because the roles are determined by culture. But the woman has to be treated as a human being of equal worth." She views gender equality as being entirely consistent with the words of the Koran, only adding that more women have to learn to read Arabic to facilitate their own emancipation—a viewpoint consistent with the reasons for her active involvement in the association.

A slightly different take on "Islamic gender roles" is presented by another respondent who says, "if you look at Muslims, you always think that it is the man who decides. He doesn't, the women do too! Of course, the man has the final word in public, but the women decide, too." While this may reveal personal experience, it is all the more interesting in terms of what preconceptions she is *expecting* to find in her various social settings. Another respondent shares that it may be the *expectations* from majority society that are more repressive than any actual *practice* within one's "own" community: "We actually feel repressed when we are always talked about in a negative way." She is the chairperson of one of the very few associations among the sample study group that actively defines itself as religious, finding strength in discussing and expressing their religion together. She refers to the adage, "if you have one branch, it is easy to break, but if you collect a bundle, it becomes much harder."

Other associations have a much more cautious approach to mixing religious discussions with their associational activities. This is shown by one example from this women's group:

> **HPN:** How about religion. Do you discuss it, or?
> **E:** Well, yes. I have great trouble with this, because some of them think a lot about religion, and there are many things that they find wrong for me to do. Otherwise, we are all Muslim, but you know, there are different takes on how much you adhere to religion. So yes, we did discuss, and they did not at all agree with me! . . . Even though I *am* Muslim, and my parents are Muslim . . . But my husband and I do not raise our children in that way. No, we celebrate Christmas with the Danes, and we have other kinds of celebrations. Yes!

Another woman has a much more radical view on the relationship between Islam and womanhood, which she also conveys in her work with the association:[6]

> **I:** I am not Muslim *at all*, and the two others [board members] are not strongly religious. It is more *nationality* than religion . . . We formed this association to take women *away* from slavery, and in my opinion, Islam is pure torture for women. Put on a scarf, and if you say anything along the way, they can kill you. You are on your own they cannot use you as a witness. You need one more—two women for one man; that's what I can't take.

The link between female oppression (even torture) and Islam is also expressed by another respondent. She objects strongly to a formulation in my written letter of consent, which states that "I am at present researching Muslim and other immigrant women's participation in different types of associational and political work." As she rightly points out, one cannot simply find individuals and say "because you come from Iran, you are a Muslim;" which was, of course, never my intention, although I did select her on the basis of the association's name, which includes a reference to Iran.

> G: For example in Iran, when they are whipping somebody, they take the Koran in one hand like this [lifts one arm], and then a whip. The Koran in the left hand, right, and then whiplashes with the other hand. So you whip women . . . what kind of impression can that possibly give other than Koran and whipping, right? I mean, it is very demonstrative, and it makes you experience . . . I believe that more than 90 percent of Iranians are *not* Muslim. They actually feel hurt if you ask them, "are you Muslim?"

She points out, "there are many among my generation, who are not believers . . . For example, my siblings, none of us believe in God or any kind of religion, all are atheists. And all of my acquaintances; I do not know anybody who are believers as such." Most of the other respondents from Iran are approximately twenty to twenty-five years older than this woman, and none of them identify themselves as Muslims either, which very likely had to do with their experiences of the Islamic revolution in Iran in 1979.

In sum, several women do not self-identify as Muslims on the grounds that Islam is repressive to women, whereas those who do self-identity as Muslims are cautious to explain that Islam itself is not oppressive to women— apparently believing that this is a prior assumption of many.[7]

What is "Integration" to these Women?

The alignment between womanhood and Islam is to some extent considered a lost battle in the Danish context. One aspect in which these women generally seem much more ready to struggle relates to the meaning of "integration," and whether or not this is a concept that resonates with being a Muslim living in Denmark. One respondent states: "So we are trying to make Muslim women better integrated into Danish society," repeatedly stressing that being a practicing Muslim and participating in Danish society is not a contradiction in terms. On this note, she also speaks about the concept of *fatwah*— "that which is allowed." She emphasizes that fatwah can be context dependent, hence also dependent on one's need to "integrate"; in the same vein calling for education of Imams in Denmark, so that there would be knowledgeable persons able to present contextually appropriate readings of the Koran. The possibility of aligning Islam and Danish culture is stressed by another respondent:

F: Integration goes both ways. To understand each other's culture and accept who you are and then respect each other. That is integration to me. It has nothing to do with the idea that just because I have moved to Denmark, I have to be a Dane. I accept the culture and religion of the Danes, but I have my own, you see . . . What the media is talking about is *assimilation*; that you have to be a Dane. But even if I am not wearing a scarf, I have some traditions, and I observe Ramadan; but I also work, and I get educated.
HPN: You are saying that the media is talking about assimilation. Is that your general impression?
F: Yes it is. That if you are wearing clothes that look like everybody else's, if you have an education and you speak Danish, then you are integrated.

The idea that appearances matter in terms of whether a person is considered integrated or not is a recurrent theme in women's' responses in the study. Very likely, this is a result of the prolonged and heated debate about the Muslim headscarf in Denmark, which for some time has set the agenda when debating the integration of Muslim women (Siim and Skjeie 2008). But while data above documented rather defensive tactics in terms of the alignment of Islam and womanhood, questions on how "integration" is understood are often met with a much more assertive tactic, as demonstrated by the responses of two women of different ethnic backgrounds, who actively questioned the dominant media and lay depictions[8] of what "well integrated" means:

HPN: What does integration mean to you?
T: I have always been saying that some people think about integration, as if you have to wear trousers and cannot wear a scarf. But that's not it! Integration is that you are able to communicate with people, that you are going out and meet other people . . . I have met many people who said "Oh, you are well integrated." But how can they know if they do not know me? They cannot tell just from how I look. I may not be inside. Maybe I am cross with everybody and xenophobic. But if you can go out and communicate with people . . . it is about being an open person, forming networks. That is what I think integration means to me.
U: If I want to be integrated, it does not mean that I have to drink alcohol or go to a disco or someplace like that. But that I can integrate with Danish language, Danish society, I can learn what things are like within the other culture, the Danish culture. But it is very important that immigrants join each other when having to integrate with the Danes. Because I live here in [neighborhood X] where there are about thirty nationalities, and it is very important that they integrate with each other.

While certainly not all Danish politicians promote the idea that Muslim women have to remove their scarf in order to be "well integrated," one issue on which they generally seem to converge is the idea that the road to integration in Denmark goes through the labor market. This has been a persistent theme for several years[9] that has, of late, been finding expression in the official "Declaration on Integration and Active Citizenship in Danish Society," which, among other points, says that "I understand and accept that the individual citizens and their families are responsible for supporting themselves. I shall therefore endeavor to become self-supporting as soon as possible."

In cases where the Muslim headscarf (not to mention the one actual case of a *burqa*) is seen to stand in the way of labor market participation, suggestions by several politicians have been that labor market interests must override religious preferences (Siim and Skjeie 2008). Interestingly, the following respondent, who here questions the primacy of labor market participation, ran for Parliament elections in 2007 for the Liberal Party, which has taken a key role in promoting labor market participation as a precondition for successful integration.

> H: [T]o me it [labor market participation] does not equal integration, it is a very important *element*, but work in itself is not integrating, because you can be at some factory all by yourself for seven hours a day, not learning anything at all about society. It is an important element in becoming integrated . . . but it cannot stand alone. However, to go out, be part of society, take part in arranging things.

While labor market participation has received great political attention as a means to integration, one debate, which has been notable for its absence from Danish political agenda, is the idea that citizenship could also be considered a *means* for integration. In Lærke Klitgaard Holm's (2006) analysis, this forms a large part of the explanation for Danish politicians' rejection of dual citizenship. Talking about a local ethnic minority community, I received the following rather dejected assessment of citizenship attainment:

> HPN: Did most of them apply for citizenship?
> E: Most of them have it . . . But they are not too pleased with it. Because they say it is only on paper. And that is true. It is *only* on paper that they are Danes.
> HPN: Because they are not being accepted or respected?
> E: Yes, that's how it is. We are Muslims.

This woman does not equate citizenship attainment with integration, and is, in fact, about to use her right as a European Union citizen (*qua* her Danish citizenship) to move to England, where she hopes life is less difficult in terms of impact from the political system.

Conclusion

Faith-based mobilization does not appear to be a preferred strategy for facilitating integrative ways of belonging among immigrant Muslim women in Denmark. The overall reading of the Danish situation is that the dominant discourse on integration in Denmark depicts integration as virtually incompatible with practicing Islam. There are several factors that explain why Islamic-based mobilization among immigrant women in Denmark is so low, among these are the structural and discursive limitations documented above. A third factor could be the fact that Islam, as a religion, is not based on a hierarchical structure, and individual Imams speak only for themselves. This might be one reason for the several failed attempts among the Danish Muslim community as a whole to create a unified group.

Generally, the women downplayed their Muslim cultural and religious heritage, but had strong views on what integration is, and wanted to challenge the dominant conceptions or discourse about their Muslim identity. In this way, they indirectly (and sometimes also directly) challenged the perceived incompatibility between integration and being a practicing Muslim. Using a metaphoric description of this state of affairs, the conclusion is that seeing faith-based Muslim mobilization as a first step toward integration is a road that is cut off by Danish political and media discourse. Rather than choosing this (dis)connection as their battlefield—partly because some of the respondents did not personally identify as Muslim—the respondents rather chose to focus on attempting to challenge the dominant conception of the end goal, namely what "integration" supposedly entails.

Notes

* I would like to thank Professor Hege Skjeie of Oslo University, Norway and Martin Bak Jørgensen of Aalborg University, Denmark for their critical commentaries and suggestions for this article.

1. See "Declaration on Integration and Active Citizenship in Danish Society," Danish Ministry for Refugees, Immigrants and Integration, http://www.nyidanmark.dk/ NR/rdonlyres/7A32FAD0-E279-467C-91E3-3074249ED586/0/integrationserklaering_e ngelsk.pdf (accessed May 26, 2008).

2. This assessment of the Danish situation is supported by Langvasbråten (2008), while Roggeband and Verloo (2007) suggest that this is probably a general European phenomenon, which certainly applies to the Netherlands. See Trude Langvasbråten, "A Scandinavian Model? Gender Equality Discourses on Multiculturalism," *Social Politics* (Spring 2008): 32-52; Conny Roggeband and Mieke Verloo, "Dutch Women are Liberated, Migrant Women are a Problem," *Social Policy and Administration* 41, no. 3 (June 2007): 271-288.

3. This is the popular name for The Danish National Evangelical Lutheran Church.

4. "HPN" marks my own questions in interview quotes, whereas respondents have been assigned a random letter.

5. There are some large national associations for people with a Muslim background. These tend to be divided into either religious ones (e.g., The Islamic Faith Community, from 2004 and Danish Muslim Union, from 2008) or non-religious ones (e.g., Forum for Critical Muslims, from 2001 and Democratic Muslims, from 2006).

6. This statement came following a question about whether the association was for Iraqi women in general, to which she responded that it was only intended for Kurdish Iraqi women, as she saw Iraqi women in general as more religiously observant.

7. This observation opens up a number of issues about interviewer/interviewee relations, which I unfortunately do not have the opportunity to explore further here.

8. According to World Economic Forum, out of twenty surveyed countries, Denmark is the country in which most people (79 percent) see greater interaction between the Muslim and the Western world as a threat. Furthermore, Denmark is the only country in the report in which there are no recorded findings of a positive tone in the media toward "the other." Concerning a negative tone toward "the other," Denmark is only surpassed by Lebanon, Namibia, Palestine and Iran. See World Economic Forum, "Islam and the West: Annual Report on the State of Dialogue." January 2008. www.weforum.org/pdf/C100/Islam_West.pdf (accessed May 26, 2008).

9. This convergence on labor market participation as the road to social integration goes also for ethnic Danes, a logic whereby youth below the age of twenty-five since 1993 have restricted access to some welfare benefits to encourage their full labor market participation.

Bibliography

Andreassen, Rikke and Birte Siim. "Country Report Denmark." Unpublished report for the VEIL Project: "Values, Equality and Differences in Liberal Democracies. Debates about Female Muslim Headscarves in Europe." 2007.

Bæk Simonsen, Jørgen. "Fra homogenitet til Pluralisme. Religionsfrihed og Islam i Danmark." Pp. 11-27 in *Visioner for Religionsfrihed, Demokrati og Etnisk Ligestilling*, edited by Lisbeth Christoffersen and Jørgen Bæk Simonsen. Copenhagen: Nævnet for Etnisk Ligestilling, 1999.

Danish Ministry for Refugees, Immigrants and Integration. "Declaration on Integration and Active Citizenship in Danish Society." http://www.nyidanmark.dk/NR/rdonlyre s/7A32FAD0-E279-467C-91E3-3074249ED586/0/integrationserklaering_engelsk.p df (accessed May 26, 2008).

Danish Parliament "Folketinget." http://www.ft.dk/doc.aspx?/Samling/20071/salen/R1_B EH1_1_1_1.htm (accessed October 4, 2007).

Denmark's Statistics. www.danmarksstatistik.dk (accessed April 16, 2008).

"Familiestyrelsen" [Family Affairs]. www.familiestyrelsen.dk/11/ (accessed June 24, 2008).

Goul Andersen, Jørgen. "Danes' Attitudes towards Immigrants: An Overview." AMID Working Paper Series No. 17, 2002. http://www.amid.dk/pub/papers/AMID_17-200 2_Goul_Andersen.pdf (accessed June 24, 2008).

Klausen, Jytte. *The Islamic Challenge: Politics and Religion in Western Europe*. Oxford: Oxford University Press, 2005.

Klitgaard Holm, Lærke. "Migration, National Tilhørsforhold og Statsborgerskab." Pp. 299-327 in *Bortom Stereotyperna? Indvandrere och Integration I Danmark och Sverige*, edited by Ulf Hedetoft, Bo Peterson and Lina Sturfelt. Gothenburg: Makadam Förlag, 2006.

Kühle, Lene. *Moskeer i Danmark – Islam og Muslimske Bedesteder*. Højbjerg: Forlaget Univers, 2006.

Langvasbråten, Trude. "A Scandinavian Model? Gender Equality Discourses on Multiculturalism." *Social Politics* (Spring 2008): 32-52.

Lundgren, Buffy. "Diversity in Denmark: An American Diversity Practitioner and Colleagues Share Their Observations." *The Diversity Factor* 15, no. 2 (Spring 2007): 1-8.

Mikkelsen, Flemming, ed. *Indvandrerorganisationer i Norden*. Aarhus: Phønix Trykkeriet a/s, 2003.

Roggeband, Conny and Mieke Verloo. "Dutch Women are Liberated, Migrant Women are a Problem: The Evolution of Policy Frames on Gender and Migration in the Netherlands, 1995-2005." *Social Policy and Administration* 41, no. 3 (June 2007): 271-288.

Siim, Birte and Hege Skjeie. "Tracks, Intersections and Dead Ends: Multicultural Challenges to State Feminism in Denmark and Norway." *Ethnicities* 8, no. 3 (September 2008): 322-344.

TV2 Nyhederne. "Muslimsk gravplads Snart Færdig." http://nyhederne.tv2.dk/article.php /id-3591076.htm (accessed May 29, 2007).

Vikkelsø-Slot, Line. *Migrants, Minorities, Belonging and Citizenship: Glocalisation and Participation Dilemmas in EU and Small States. The Case of Denmark*. Bergen: BRIC, University of Bergen, 2004.

World Economic Forum. "Islam and the West: Annual Report on the State of Dialogue." January 2008. www.weforum.org/pdf/C100/Islam_West.pdf (accessed May 26, 2008).

Zagal-Farias, Pedro. "At Sige Ordentligt Farvel—På Muslimsk Vis." Pp. 95-109 in *Medborgerskabets Mange Stemmer*, edited by Jonathan Schwartz. Aarhus: AKA-PRINT A/S, 2002.

Chapter Nine

Muslim Immigrants in France: Religious Markets and New Mechanisms of Integration

Jamel Stambouli and Sonia Ben Soltane

In this chapter we explore the role of religion as a pathway to integration by examining the entrepreneurial strategies of immigrants in developing ethnic and religious markets in France. In the last few years, a public debate concerning the incompatibility of republican values, mainly secularism, with some expressions of sectarian or communitarian behaviors, has been revived in France. The universalist values of the French nation set up by *les idées des lumières* (the philosophical ideas emanating from the Age of Enlightenment) during the revolution of 1789[1] appear to be in conflict with the requirements of certain individual liberties like religious freedom. This debate concerns the cultural and religious practices adopted by Muslim immigrants in France, specifically those of African and North African origins. The third generations of immigrants who are French citizens, still face an acute confrontation between a culture transmitted by their parents through memories of their homeland, where culture is widely shaped within an Islamic register,[2] and the values of their native society.[3]

At the end of the 1960s, Europe, particularly France, witnessed a massive migratory wave from their former North African colonies. This migration consisted of an exclusively male population in response to the labor shortage in some French industries. These men were not recruited to engage the French public space, or to hold a place within it as social actors. Rather, they were only supposed to be workers in French industries.[4] Few social interactions existed among French, employers, neighbors, or workplace colleagues, and the "Arabs." The presence of foreigners became the focus of studies in the social sciences during that time.[5] However, some activities related to wars of independence in the former French colonies, especially those related to *la guerre d'Algérie*,[6] generated suspicion and mistrust toward immigrant workers coming from the other shore of the Mediterranean. They were often suspected of complicity with the independence movements of their countries.[7]

The issue of colonial memory[8] has provoked a major controversial debate in the last few years. The debate not only heightens individual memory for those who lived this epoch and have lost a parent, an entire family, or their fortunes, with the public debate bringing forth issues loaded with memories. These debates accompany the process of "inflaming" particularities linked to some communities and minorities within the republican public space by putting forward the injuries, the memories, and competing historical claims.

French authorities envision the relationship of North African male immigrants to the French territory[9] in terms of a provisional status justified by the immediate need for labor force. In the last two decades, most of the French migration studies focusing on male migrations from 1950s to 1970s,[10] describe an essentially working-class male population, whose everyday life was shaped by promiscuity, poverty, and solitude. Pierre Bourdieu and Abdelmalek Sayad (1964),[11] forerunners of French studies on North African migrations, adopt a subjective position that highlights the central role of immigrants in understanding migration paradigms. The notion of exile explored by French migration scholars [12] is widely reflected in North African literature[13] that uses this theme. The concept of "double absence" developed by Sayad (1999: 438)[14] is, to this day, a constant element in the analysis and comprehension of North African migration discourse. Immigration results in the feeling of loss or uprooting (*déracinement*) in men's lives both in native and host societies. Sayad's contribution lies in the novelty of his idea toward immigrants as central to the analysis of migration processes and allows him to detach the figure of the immigrant linked to work, and represented as "work force," to establish it, as "social fact," as social agent.

More recent studies raise newer forms of North African migrations revealing new dynamics and complex immigrants' profiles that include women. The influx of women, spouses, and daughters of the first wave of male immigrants after the promulgation of French family reunification law in 1974, modified North African migration movements. It has a more lasting impact on French society and has coincided with the emergence of issues linked to ways of life, values, and to religious practices from the private to the public sphere. The settlement of North African families[15] with their social, moral and religious values that compete and sometimes contradict French values produced, over time, frictions that crystallized around social objects that, in turn, became emblematic of these debates: the veil or *hijab*, prayer spaces, and certain forms of violence linked to suburbs populated by Muslim[16] immigrants who were referred to as *les banlieues* (French popular suburbs). In this situation, the immigrants' practices are viewed as threatening to the republican order and its founding ideas. Paradoxically, other aspects in the lives of North African immigrants merely pass unnoticed. This is the case of economic and entrepreneurial strategies that define trajectories of social ascension and the emergence in the French society of a *beurgeoisie*[17] constituted by successful immigrants.

Since the second half of the 1980s, French social scientists have been exploring the connections between immigration and the economy. The economic crisis that began at the end of the 1970s contributed to growing visibility of immigrants whose presence was no longer required as workers, and was increasingly considered as persona non-grata. French migration authorities then decided to close the frontiers to North African labor migrations and even promoted legislative measures to encourage the repatriation of these workers.[18]

The first studies on migration and economy relates to remittances and its reinvestment in the immigrant's country of origin. The immigrants are viewed as a link to their native countries who engage in return projects. For example, a range of practices and strategies are developed by North African immigrants for economic advancement. At present, the economic sectors where immigrants have invested and demonstrated particular entrepreneurship in the French territory remains underexplored. Studies by Alejandro Portes (1999: 15-25), Emmanuel Ma Mung (1990: 138) and Alain Tarrius (2002: 220) examine the rise of ethnic economic enclaves. They construct the profile of immigrant' entrepreneurs, trace economic routes, and feature the economic strategies developed within globalized networks following heightened human mobility.

In this chapter we explore the policies through which French society tried to integrate North African Muslim immigrants during the last two decades. We pay attention to the political discourses and positions taken by both the French left and right political parties on their perception of religion, particularly Islam, as in conflict with republican values, and as incompatible with the requirements of citizenship. The practices required by religions, especially Islam, are considered threatening to individual liberties. The French position is not exclusively reserved to Islam and Muslims, but is addressed to all religions. This is the result of a long ideological and political process of secularization of the state's actions and structures, and of the policies and political discourses initiated during the French revolution of 1789 that culminated in the Cultural Revolution of May 1968. These historical and ideological processes definitively eliminated social conservatism and the interference of religious morality and dogmas in political and social life.

Muslims are perceived to be out of touch with modernity and their adherence to Islam in relation to certain issues is considered backward. Some French, especially the individual civil rights militants, feel that they are obliged to endure specific social behaviors of immigrants. Democratic values and republican laws at times usher negative effects when sectarian and sometimes freedom-alienating behaviors such as forced marriages and virginity imposed on women[19] paradoxically, and in some extreme cases, are tolerated. The tension between the two is evolving in a strange way. We argue that, somehow, North African Muslims do not need to be integrated; they develop a sort of autarchic way of living in accordance with their faith. French public opinion accepts this situation as long as the tolerance zone instituted between discrete faith practice and secular French public space is not violated.

We want to note here the specific definition of integration adopted in France.[20] It is observed in other societies that individuals are free to behave in accordance to their own cultures and religions; it is so in France. However, the individual's freedom to practice one's own culture and religion in everyday life is limited by some specific boundaries. For example, religion and culture are not transferable into the public and political sphere. Universalism is a founding ideal of the French nation and of French republican values. Implementing universal-

ism benefits individuals regardless of their race, beliefs, or cultures. People have
the same rights and the same obligations, and, under specific conditions, can be
considered as citizens granted with supplementary political competences. However, universalism is also a frontier; particularistic practices, faith or beliefs
could not prevail one on the other, neither can Islam.

We are particularly concerned with the everyday life of female immigrants,
and the ethnic and religious markets developed by the immigrants' entrepreneurial strategies in France. The existence of such markets proves that both communities could coexist with Islam without conflict. The economy could be a
pathway for integrating Islam and Muslims in French society. We start our discussion by deciphering the processes that allow North African Muslim immigrants' integration into French society, and their creation of ethnic enclaves for
special markets centered on Islam and Islamic consumerism. These processes
are linked to the introduction of new categories of migrants. This type of successful integration is also, and paradoxically, linked to the failure of the French
conceptions and politics of integration intended for this group of people.

Migration is not mobility per se, but it has its own logic and paradigms. A
look at actual North African migration data reveals the introduction of new lo-
gics and new goals; the studies of Pierre Robert Baduel (1983) on the earlier
periods show that some populations were "put on the road" by the deconstruc-
tion of traditional social structures. Such was the case of the first labor migrants
that shared the profile of single, unqualified poor men recruited as workers for
the French industry in the 1970s. The newcomers, however, have different profiles. The new migration trajectories and strategies, the increase in the number of
departures, are proofs of how the sending societies are changing, and of how
social factors contribute to the migration of certain individuals. On the other
hand, immigration experiences, the paths taken, the support given by networks,
and the way each immigrant is received by the host society are all relevant in
understanding how the host society positions itself toward immigration.

In this chapter, we present two major sections. The first section explores the
new directions chosen by immigrants, establish the new immigrants' profiles,
and examine the way these profiles or characteristics interact with French society through the creation of milieus with proper rules and ethics. The second
section examines religion as vector of entrance into the economy and the case of
the *hajj* (pilgrimage) market, and the way it is accommodated in French economic life. The existence of the hajj market is the result of acute social negotiations and challenges some social a priori always evoked concerning Islam such
as women's rights and positions in Muslim society. The *hajj* market and its links
to specific social structures is not a linear manifestation of multiculturalism in
French society. The way immigrant communities inscribe their economic and
social practices in French society points to two main observations. First, immigrants negotiate the social and moral (religious) values from their native cultures
and societies which include gendered identities and competences. Second, the
values and practices of immigrants have an impact on the host society.

New Roads and New Migrants

The emplacement of the North African immigrants in French society is confirmed by their numbers, the growth of the second generation, marriages, and alliances. The arrival of new categories of immigrants for studies or for business from North Africa as well as their religious and cultural practices widely marked by Islam is fixed definitively in the French public space. Muslims are no longer perceived as a minority, and the presence of Islam provokes incidents and confrontations in a recurring way.

Although people with less skills and qualifications made up the first waves of migration from North Africa to France, the migratory roads diversified considerably during the last three decades. The political and "social facts"[21] that have dominated the Maghreb during this period, particularly the violence that has risen in Algeria, coupled with an advantageous legal frame,[22] gave the immigrants reasons to leave their countries of origin in North Africa. These streams of people include intellectuals, academics, persons with liberal convictions, businessmen, students, unemployed persons, farmers escaping poverty, and women coming alone. The North African countries[23] are generally peaceful, but oftentimes regional politics, sartorial crisis situations, and the repercussions of international economic crises or pressures on the local markets drive people to seek better living conditions elsewhere. They may not be poor, desperate and indigent immigrant, but "free navigators"[24] seeking better life opportunities. The biggest catalyst for the departure of new immigrants is, in our view, a relational factor, family and/or emotional factor. The dreams of success and the desire to liberate oneself from the severely alienating traditions and social norms are at the heart of new immigration movements.

The above mentioned reasons, juxtaposed with an ensemble of other elements,[25] contribute to the creation of new categories of qualified immigrants for whom the migratory project is justified outside of economic motivations. Among these new migrant groups are qualified or non-qualified female immigrants.[26] In this situation, the departure is not conditioned by a constraint, but by an obligation, in the sense that the potential immigrant preserves certain autonomy of decision and action. It is basically a question of investigating the influence of, as Constance de Gourcy notes, the "family and relational configurations in which, female migrants are, more particularly, engaged" (2004: 514).

While academic as well as political discourses on immigration tend to standardize the profile of the North African immigrants, this profile has changed considerably in the last thirty years: immigration is hereafter gendered. We now see a very diverse group of immigrants who have taken a variety of previously unforeseen migratory routes. Many of the immigrants are Muslims, but their Islam is not a uniform faith with a unique expression. Rather, in a way, it is a reinvented faith, negotiated and mixed with cultural variations brought by im migrants. This faith is often mobilized for constructing and supporting identities, for challenging emigrational experiences and difficulties. This last function is made necessary by the fragility of identity construction induced by experiences of migration.

Integration of Muslims in French Society: "the noise and the smell"

In reaction to the intensification of migration, the French politics of integration is not really a resounding success (Noiriel 2006) as long as it requires immigrants to assimilate and to abandon their communitarian particularities. For some immigrants, especially the second generation North African immigrants, the challenges they face is likened to apartheid. For some French, with right or extreme right political convictions, immigrants are still perceived through the schema of the emblematic Jacques Chirac phrase "the noise and the smell."[27] Certainly, some children of immigrants experience relative success and demonstrate an ideal integration into French society but social facts such as urban revolts in certain suburbs, high unemployment rate, and spatial segregations[28] concerning North African (and African) immigrants in France, moderate the results of these policies and point to the rarity of success stories. Success— presumably to have a job, a house, and social status—does not benefit a greater number of immigrants. The relative failure of diverse policies of integration pushes the immigrants, especially the newcomers, to rely on their own community to be able "to make it"—to live, have a job, rent a house, and so forth.

In France, debates on integration raise issues of definition and interpretation. Amin Maalouf (2001: 189) and Michel Wieviorka (1995) advance the hypotheses of return to religion or of religious revival. Some scholars show that the consumption of *halal* (lawful/permissible) goods is conditioned by the desire to be a better Muslim and to be closer to Islamic precepts. The Islamic references demonstrated by second generation immigrants derogate the parents' Islamic practices. The emphatic behavior displayed by the second generation, in their clothing and religious practice, in the public sphere is perceived by some other Muslims[29] as foreign to the Islam they learned in their respective cultures.

In a sense, the stigma derived from a set of a priori clothing modes, attitudes, and practices rightly or abusively associated with Muslims· and Islam conveyed worldwide[30] become an element of self-definition for Muslims. These stereotypes associated with Islam are not only evoked by occidental societies which are supposed to ignore what the "real Islam" presumably known and understood exclusively by Muslims, is also evoked by some Muslim factions themselves. The first generation of immigrants who are separated from their native societies are no longer able to transmit valid religious practices, having a social sense or utility[31] to their children. Furthermore, globalization contributes to the spread of dominant interpretations of Islam that respond to the quest for identity of the second generation immigrants who feel uprooted and are convinced that Islam is a fundamental element of their identity. The fervor is so strong that this image of an Islam fighting for recognition in the West is opposed to the reality of some Muslim countries where people are no longer concerned with religion.[32] The religious factor then becomes, in a sense, a new mechanism of "integration" used as a resource by Muslim immigrants for identity construction. This conversion is, paradoxically, made possible by the republican principles. Alain Tarrius describes clearly this process:

> The integrationist constitutional generosities of our national states, built during two or three centuries of relationships with strangers and addressed to the newcomer to whom we offer the choice of "being one of us" or to leave, carry more and more a synergy: many current social trajectories of integration are not in accordance with the historic models we defined anymore (2000: 265).

The diverse forms of social and urban segregations shape the everyday lives of immigrants and reinforce feelings of isolation. Several scholars explore this feeling of strangeness, difference and exclusion, indeed of double exclusion (Sayad 1999: 438). Islam is the major recourse for this seemingly hopeless community as they construct their new identity that is "neither from here, nor from there." This identity centered on Islam is reinforced by religious practices as well as by certain imams who assert that being Muslim is being better, in contrast to the "nonbelievers." Islam is represented to the young, disadvantaged generation as a manner to emphasize their identity and their personality, in order to get a better position in society.

Muslim immigrants demonstrate a sort of "social intelligence" which allows them to define themselves, to build an otherness, and to propose it to their host society. It is certain that such an "assembly" edified on a controversial base—because it has a religious basis cannot be enthusiastically greeted by the political and intellectual circles as well as French public opinion. However, it challenges our understanding of the situation and points to a process of renewing social life and diversification, which is inevitable in French society. Alain Tarrius notes:

> Naturally, this "third status," this knowledge of being from here and from there at the same time, produces original territorial constructions, on the mode of social networks convenient to circulations, where the criteria of recognition of the others are in break with quiet and "evident" drawn borders, ethnic in particular, produced by the local societies (2000: 7).

Some authors reveal the existence of political and ideological processes that are at the heart of the construction of Muslim identity and its underlying significations. They denounce beyond this "Muslim otherness" in gestation, the historic and ideological evolution which produced it. Sophie Bessis (2007) notes the culturalist and differentialist[33] literature produced in Europe and in the West, about the Muslim world and Islamic ideology. Islam has been contained on the borders of Europe for a long time. Now, Islam is a European concern because of the large number of Muslim immigrants and converts. The author decodes the postures surrounding the question of the interference of Islam in the public sphere and in the formulation of European and French laws and policies on subjects such as wearing the veil, prayer time, food prohibitions, or other sorts of religious constraints. Bessis (2007) refutes the thesis of clash of civilizations and cultures, but she deciphers the way in which globalization has produced perverse and paradoxical effects and has contributed to strengthening conflicting social processes which reflect definitively the same phenomenon:

> Without being afraid of the paradox, we are attending to an acceler-
> ated globalization of specific ideologies. Everything happens as if the
> essentialization of societies operated by the western postmodern theo-
> ries had for oriental mirror the construction of "the Muslim identity,"
> presented as unbendable to the other identities by the new Islamic
> mouvance (2007: 168).

This position enlightens the way French policies on Islam could accelerate the phenomenon of withdrawal into "Muslim identity" taken by certain immigrants.

Regulation of Religious Practice in the French Public Space

Notwithstanding the fact that Islam and Muslims are not new in French public space and that North African former colonies are spaces of encounter between the two cultures, France is one of the few European countries that tries to frame Islam as a "new" religion. In 1926, the French government founded a focal insti-tution, the Paris Mosque that played a major role in the supervision of Islam in France. The French government which is very interventionist in religious prac-tices did not have a coherent plan for supervision of Muslim populations. The government engaged in instantaneous reactions to certain behaviors that were more "disturbing" than illegal such as the opening of prayer rooms or mosques in small transformed sheds arranged for such use, or sheep sacrifice for the *aïd al idhà* feast (Vieillard-Baron 2004).[34] Later on, it became necessary to create guidelines and principles of this supervision, and the French state looked for allies and partners for its policy. Bilateral Algerian-French conventions allowed a fruitful partnership in some domains where French authorities were unable to act. This was the case of the regulation of the mission of the spiritual guides: imams. Imams were formed and their mission was organized in France, with the collaboration of Algerian experts and officials authorities.

The French government, with Algerian "technical and ideological" assis-tance and help from other North African countries, created the Islamic supervi-sion coalition, and developed policies geared toward regulation and control of Islamic practice by immigrants on French soil. In our view, the major effect of these policies was to make visible and apparent in the public space a faith and its practice that was done in the private space. Islam then penetrated French public space and, at the same time, gained legitimate visibility as the object and subject of interest for republican discourse. The issue became important since the con cerned immigrant populations were no longer foreigners but French citizens of immigrant descent.

In this section, we want to emphasize a special issue where immigration, religion, and identity relate to each other. In fact, French immigration policies, especially concerning North African immigrants, induce certain "perverse effects." These policies reinforced within the second generation immigrants in France a feeling of uprooting and of difference that they compensate for by rebuilding their identity around Islam, which is the only common and binding element of identity among communities having cultural, linguistic and ethnic disparities. A single major event has, in our opinion, released an identity and religious revival among Muslim or Arab immigrants in France. This event is the Gulf War, the first and the second. It may not seem to be mentally or morally close to populations living in Europe, but it has a moral implication on Muslims all over the world. The Gulf Wars awakened a sense of membership in the Arab nation through Islam.[35] This process of identity construction is, of course, justified by a return to religion, but our observations allow us to suggest that it is rather a strategy of identity and social ascension. Second generation immigrants, as well as new immigrants, have feelings of self-esteem and superiority. Islam is for them a means to surpass the negative image of inferiority and poverty linked to the first wave of immigrants. In this way, they promote in the French republican discourse a new and positive image drawn by the family and communitarian memory and history widely nourished by Islam.

One of the most important sectors where Muslim immigrants operate their positive social status is the economy. Because French market and economic operators were not aware of the possibilities of ethnic demands, a new group took advantage of the situation. This new category of immigrants has strong social capital and determination to succeed. They rely on their personal culture, their knowledge of Islam, Arabic language and their specific cultures[36] to develop a range of goods and services for the ethnic demands of Muslims. After witnessing the success of these new businesses, French institutions are now trying to capture this new market. The French Central Bank is even trying to introduce Islamic banking rules in the range of knowledge and skills of local banking operators.

Religion as Vector of Entrance into the Economy: The Religious Market v. the Market of Religion

The new ethnic markets reveal the economic dynamism of immigrants, and demonstrate the way they transform their culture and often their differences in commodities, in capital to be invested, and in productive resources. Thus, ethnic entrepreneurship seems to be one of the most important factors of integration. Florence Bergeaud-Blackler (2005), a French sociologist working on *halal* markets and products in France, points to the cultural and economic processes which result in ethnic demand for certified *halal* products and describes the way some immigrant entrepreneurs shape this market in what she calls, "*halal* business." In these new markets and new models of Islamic consumption investigated by

Bergeaud-Blackler, religion intervenes as an argument of marketing and qualification of an ethnic demand. We want to assert here that religion does not intervene only as a factual element in this type of markets, but that it is often, a product itself. Religion intervenes in the modulation of these new ethnic markets as a constant element in the definition of some market standards, consumer methods, and as marketing argument.[37] It also intervenes as a moral rule organizing the economic relationship inside the market. Gradually, and as Bergeaud-Blackler notes concerning the evolution of the halal label, the status of religion evolved. It is no longer evoked only as marketing argument but as a good to sell in itself. Religion in itself (i.e., faith, practices, and objects used in religious practices) is sold just like any other commodity. The pilgrimage to Mecca is a perfect illustration of the transformation of a religious practice into a business. The mechanisms of this new business reflect the complex negotiation involving economic rules, social relations, and gendered roles.

Economic Market and Religion

The study of ethnic enterprises based on religion demonstrates the progressive construction of an Islamic market in France offering Islamic goods and religious services. The economic operators of this market are recruited among the new category of immigrants discussed in the first part of this chapter. These entrepreneurs are young and skilled immigrants who invested their academic, social, and cultural capital to satisfy an ethnic demand untapped by traditional French businesses.

The hajj market operators in France portray certain characteristics. These entrepreneurs are self-made men and women who started the operations of the business after their pilgrimage. Historically, the hajj was organized by non-profit associations. But the organizers we meet, in most cases, are young, immigrant students presumably without any competence in business administration. They venture into the business not only to fulfill a religious obligation but also to help others in the community prepare for the pilgrimage. Young entrepreneurs follow a successful marketing strategy: mobilize family, neighbors, and friends to advertise their services. Funds are collected inside the community and, because they monopolize the market, they are able to increase their assets rapidly.

Because of historical conditions, the operators of hajj market continue to exist outside the mainstream French market. The operators adopt and implement economic rules, strategies, and finance practices from their native cultures. They rely on new partners, particularly Middle Eastern entrepreneurs, who are familiar with this type of business. The opportunities in the French market enable the integration of new economic routes, establish associations with operators to Mecca, such as Syrian and Saudi airline companies, contribute to the financial success of these enterprises and growth outside of France. Hajj operators are now able to sell religious and pilgrimage services anywhere in Europe and even in countries of origin. It is obvious for us that we are confronted with non-conformist entrepreneurial trajectories.

The Pilgrimage Market, Entrepreneurship and Commercial Places

In this section, we present the immigrant entrepreneurs that transform Islam into a business. They appear to have succeeded in integrating themselves in the receiving countries, in this case, France. They follow multiple paths to success. They often pass through unskilled work experiences as laborers in French factories (as first waves of immigrants from which some of them came from). Some of them moved to France to study and, over time, become businessmen, depending on the opportunities they encounter. The last category, which is a most recent addition to these two "classical" trajectories, are successful businessmen in their native countries looking to enhance their social status and economic success by settling in France. These three categories have in common the fact that they join together persons who developed business opportunities and constituted a new market having its own operators, and its own norms and values; a market that French investors had not envisioned. Immigrant entrepreneurs encounter extraordinary social and economic improvement by exploiting the resurgence of a religious identity, and a religious practice among Muslims in France. An example of this is the pilgrimage ritual to Mecca and faith practices linked to it. This pilgrimage market led to a spectacular and unexpected boom, hitherto an unexplored market based on religious products designed for Muslims, within which they created their favorite niches. Pilgrimage, however, is not an isolated example. These entrepreneurs set up a real Islamic consumerism model, based on religious food prohibitions. The religious norm becomes a consumer norm, production norm, and manufacturing label: halal is a commercial institution.

A pilgrimage to Mecca is compulsory for every Muslim man or woman who is physically fit and who has sufficient financial resources to undertake the trip. In France, many immigrants in the mid-1970s felt the need to fulfill what is expected of every "good Muslim." On the one hand, these immigrants have achieved economic success in their countries of origin; they have secured social standing as part of the upper class. However, this goal was insufficient. It was deemed necessary for them to constitute for themselves a new nobility, to have a reputation in a country where they had been absent for a long time. Thus, and on the other hand, a *hàjj*[38] is a person one can confide in, and is also considered to occupy a very prestigious position in the community.

Gendered Images in the Pilgrimage Market

The group of businessmen in this study is exclusively male. The pilgrimage to Mecca as a product offered to Muslims in Europe, and strongly impregnated by a new Muslim identity, raises several problematic friction points about gender. In the pilgrimage market, women are also present as consumers of this service just as men are. Gender differences arise at the level of reinvestment of this moral capital in social mobility. If, for women, making the pilgrimage is a matter of moral prestige and personal satisfaction, or even of travels abroad, for men, the issue is more important: the issue is to construct for oneself a privileged place in one's community.

In certain traditional societies, like Egyptian or Mauritanian society, it is common for women to be engaged in business, and pilgrimage then could be a guaranteed activity. In Muslim societies, contracts are often concluded orally, and economic transactions rely on honor and morality of the contracting partners. Women's inability to contract and to be in business can be imputed to religious and legislative factors, as the theory of proof in Islamic laws grants the man's testimony the doubled value of that of a woman's. This is aside from the fact that in the majority of legal subsystems in Muslim societies women are legally considered as minors unable to contract. However, we believe that the real reason is situated elsewhere.

French sociologist Anaïk Pian (2007) explores the entrepreneurial activities of Senegalese women in Morocco through the figure of the adventurer. Her work demonstrates clearly that Senegalese society, as well as other African Muslim societies, allows women to contribute to economic life and in some ways, business is more accessible to them than in some other societies in North Africa. The figure of the adventurer crossing the desert and countries for business is supported by women entrepreneurs. We opine that Pian (2007) demonstrates clearly that religion is not the real basis of women's exclusion from the economy. We argue that the reason for exclusion is more linked to social traditional structures. In Mauritania, for example, the matriarchal social structures benefit the women who possess and transmit all the familial wealth. This is why they are over represented in economy.

Germaine Tillion (1966: 10), French anthropologist, examines traditional Mediterranean societies (North Africa) and concludes that women as well as lands form part of the familial patrimony. The patriarchal structures and management of wealth in North African societies explain the exclusion of women from economic domains. Islam was then interpreted and used to justify misogyny (Tillion 1966).

A nonfocused observation of the pilgrimage market and its operators reveals the absence of women as active operators, but, in reality, they are as active as the *rabatteurs* (prospectors).[39] The hajj organizers often have recourse to rabatteurs to constitute small groups that function as mini communities united to help pilgrims hurdle the administrative, financial, and physical[40] difficulties of undertaking the pilgrimage. These rabatteurs are exclusively men. Nevertheless, in the study group, we note that females comprise the majority of pilgrims. The principal reason for this is because the laws in Saudi Arabia deny a single woman the right to trample the holy grounds. All women must be accompanied by a *mohram*, a sort of guardian whose proximity is guaranteed by a family relationship or marriage. The right to perform the pilgrimage without a mohram is reserved to women of more than forty-five years of age, who are supposed to be beyond temptation. Elderly women, mothers, grandmothers who are often widows, or women whose husbands are not able to accompany them, find refuge in these groups to make their departure to Mecca easier.

Most female pilgrims are discretely organized and closely supervised by rabatteurs' spouses. If women are absent in the supervision level they are over-represented as candidates for the pilgrimage. Our study reveals complex religious and economic motivations for women to embark on a pilgrimage. This finding parallels Pian's work, as she demonstrates that Morocco is only a step in the trajectory to Europe and to Saudi Arabia, Kuwait, and several other Arab places of business. Their motivations reflect the status of commerce and money in Islam. In particular, the prophet Muhammad was a businessman and so was his first wife Khadija, who is referred to as the "Muslims' mother." Commerce is considered as a noble profession that does not contradict with the responsibilities of motherhood.

Often, the women present in the hajj market are more experts than their husbands—we encounter single women in these milieus—in the art of negotiation and finance. They subtly lead negotiations and arrangements with the hajj organizers. This is often the case of many African women who have mastered the art of trading. We attended some negotiations with prospectors who were discretely advised by their wives present during the negotiation, sometimes using signs. Women attend silently and intervene when necessary. They also often possess the money necessary to conclude transactions.

In our study, women create ingenuous ways to bypass the legal restrictions that prevent single women from this international (religious) sojourn, for example, by providing the Saudi Arabian embassy in France with false documents proving marriages or fictitious links with men (*mohrams*) to undertake the pilgrimage. The hidden goal is commerce. Women finance their travels with *tantines*[41] and reimburse the cost by sales. The presence of a large proportion of women among the candidates for the pilgrimage is justified by the dynamic prospectors among females in the family, neighborhood, and friends.

Women as regular consumers and discreet operators having an influence on the pilgrimage market, profiting from their activities, and taking advantage of the market opportunities, are surprising realities. If any woman is publicly invested by a responsibility, it is not (only) because of masculine domination, but explicitly because they are taking advantage of the discretion of their status. Scholars like Véronique Nahoum Grappe (1996: 137) views discretion as consubstantial with femininity, a sort of female way of doing things. We do not really agree with this point of view, but it is certain that discretion enable these women a sense of liberty and power of action within a masculine market.

The primacy of male-led international mobility is at the base of gender relations which reproduces the social structure of their communities. The marriage alliances, economic strategies, and constitution of patrimonies reflect the continuity of male domination in the processes of social and spatial mobility. This gender dissymmetry gives advantage to men. However, we affirm that women are negotiating a new role and position toward Islam and in diasporic Muslim communities. Precisely, in this case study, women are developing at the very core of this market a sort of feminine praxis that allows them to take advantage of their status as invisible economic operators. Are we confronted with what seems to be a bastion of sexism with the rise of a new feminine Muslim identity? Does it mean that the traditional gender differences as they are perceived in North African Muslim societies are moving under the influence of spatial mobility? We cannot really provide the answers. But, it is obvious for us that the economic enclaves constituted by ethnic and religious markets in France succeed in some ways in integrating Muslim immigrants.

Conclusion

The economic strategies and the dynamism of economic relations in facilitating the integration of immigrants show more than economic integration. It points to the way immigrants reconstruct their communities by negotiating at the same time the values of their native society and those of their host society, and, in the process, attain the enrichment of both communities. Somehow, this process demonstrates a sort of "immigrant social intelligence."

Religion, and more precisely Islam, is investing in the public space in France. Based on our study, we are convinced that French politics and laws target only migration managements and regulation. French authorities then did not formulate any pertinent political or collective project that envisages the issue of coexistence with immigrants having different cultural and religious background in concrete ways. Grassroots activities and spontaneous social acts grow because of the lack of political projects on integration in France. Grassroots activities succeed in transforming the stigma of North African immigrants in the community with valuable ethics. Exploring the hajj market, among a range of other examples like Islamic banking and financing, suggests the social capacities of individuals and in the dynamism of the new category of immigrants, that Alain Tarrius (2000: 254) calls the strangers' abilities and skills (*les competences de l'étranger*).

Religion appears to be an important pathway for integration. The rise of hajj market and the development of its structure and operators demonstrate the immigrant's capacity to challenge at the same time the rules imposed in their original societies and in their host societies. The emergence of Muslim women as entrepreneurs in such a market is proof of negotiating social gendered relations within a community where women are supposed to be deprived of their elementary liberties.

Notes

1. The universalist values are *liberté, égalité, fraternité*: "freedom, equality and brotherhood." These are fundamental in the French conception of citizenship.

2. We intentionally use this formulation instead of saying that the culture in question is shaped simply within Islam. We assert in this chapter that contemporary Muslim societies are interrogating what Islam could be in a modern context. The appearance of Mus-

lim youth movements, of Islamic feminisms, or of the European or French suburban Islam (*l'Islam des banlieues*) is a recurrence of this phenomenon. Hence, Islam, in itself, has nothing to do with the cited situation. We consider it as a simple Islamic register because it consists of elements drawn from Islamic history, culture, historical figures, and liturgy.

3. We want to specify here that not all black immigrants, often considered as Africans, (although not necessarily from Africa) are Muslims. But majority of North Africans are Muslims, and therefore, Islam is more often associated with North African immigrants, than with black immigrants.

4. North African workers were imposed a sort of "social and spatial apartheid." They used to live in places where they work and many French enterprises like Renault, provided housing to their employees. The lodging provided consisted of rooms shared by several men. Public offices called SONACOTRA even specialized in providing rooms to immigrant male workers. When the first immigrant families arrived in France a program called "transit housing" (*cites de transit*) was provided for their use. Azouz Begag, a former state secretary, novelist and social scientist, used to live in such *cité*. He wrote an autobiography inspired by his childhood in the *banlieues* (suburbs) of Lyons. See Azouz Begag, *Le Gone du Chaâba* (Novel, Paris: Le Seuil, Coll. 2001).

5. The major reference here is devoted to Bourdieu and Sayad who introduced the exploration of North African migration as a matter of sociological investigation. Other authors like Pierre Robert Baduel explored migration routes inside the colonial Maghreb and on the road to France. More recent authors like Gildas Simon looked at the quantitative aspects of this migration. Since the beginning of the 1990s some authors largely inspired by critical assessments of the Chicago school, started to study the interactions (economic, cultural, and political) between North African migrants and French society. At Aix-Marseille University, Alain Tarrius conducted empirical research on that subject for a long time and was succeeded by other scholars like Michel Peraldi, Lamia Moussaoui, and others.

6. This refers to the Algerian war of independence. The terminology of *guerre d'Algérie* is linked to a historical fact, but the way it is evoked in French literature conceptualizes the reference to the war, so we prefer to cite it in French.

7. We refer to the doctrinal positions of the French historian Benjamin Stora, on the topic of memory of the Algerian war of independence, and on what he calls memory wars that are marking French politics, as well as laws. The author describes the manner in which memory discourses are introduced by the minorities in the public space, and are erected as integral part of a national memory, a memory of repentance toward the injustices committed in the past (memory of slavery, the memory of the French Jewish community handed over to the holocaust, and colonialism). See Benjamin Stora, *La Gangrène de l'oubli, Mémoire de la Guerre d'Algérie* (Paris: La Découverte, 1991), 369; and *Entretiens avec Thierry Leclere* (Paris: Editions de l'aube 2007), 107.

8. This colonial memory concern North African French colonies as well as other African and overseas colonies (French Guyana, Guadeloupe, Reunion, Martinique, St Pierre and Miquelon, Mayotte, New Caledonia, Wallis and Futuna, French Polynesia, which are still under French authority). Algerian war of independence is a much discussed issue but it is not exhaustive of the debate.

9. There were public French offices organizing the recruitment and repatriation of the North African workers.

10. This luxurious period is called in French academic theories, *les trente glorieuses*, which means the thirty years of glorious and prosperous economy and good living.

11. See also Abdelmayek Sayad, *L'immigration ou les Paradoxes de l'altérité* (Bruxelles De Boeck Université, Paris : Éditions Universitaires, 1991), 331.

12. The theme of exile is omnipresent in French migration studies because these studies were dealing with single men, living in solitude and feeling uprooted.

13. This refers to North African literature in both French expression and Arabic languages. We note the novels of North African authors as Mohamed Dib, Mouloud Feraoun, Tahar Ben Jelloun, Assia Djebar, Kateb Yacine, Taos Amrouche, and other authors.

14. The concept of double absence is extracted from the eponymous work of Sayad. See Abdelmalek Sayad, *La Double Absence: Des Illusions de l'émigré aux Souffrances de l'immigré* (Paris: Seuil, 1999), 438.

15. Noria Boukhobza, asserts that a North African family structure is a subject matter that is underexplored in French social sciences. In substance, women, mothers, wives or immigrants' daughters are indeed forgotten and invisible. The comprehension of certain phenomena related to immigration management in the French suburbs is closely centered on the exploration of male behaviors and attitudes, while an exploration of female practices would lead to the enrichment of the knowledge on that issue. See Noria Boukhobza, "Les Filles Naissent Après les Garçons: Représentations Sociales des Populations d'origine Maghrébine en France," *Revue Européenne des Migrations Internationales* 21, no 1 (2005): 227-242.

16. It is a specific violence exerted over women. A number of autobiographies revealed during the last few years the existence of symbolic and physical violence of which women were the prime victims. This image of the North African boy as rapist and violent is relayed by the French media, despite its disputable probity. This violence was denounced and analyzed by several scholars, notably Nacira Guénif-Souilamas. See Nacira Guenif-Souilamas and Eric Mace, *Les Féministes et le Garçon Arabe* (Paris: Editions L'aube, 2004), 107.

17. This term means Arab bourgeoisie. A vernacular language adopted by young North African immigrants often designated as Arabs, is here pronounced in the reverse side. This language is called *le verlan*, which means reverse side: *envers*, pronounced in the reversed way.

18. We want to specify that the first waves of North African immigrants scarcely acquired French nationality. The second generation born in France, in accordance to French laws, acquires French citizenship on demand, and only at the age of majority.

19. We refer here to some *faits divers* (news brief) that crystallized the conflicting positions between Muslim immigrants and French public opinion. We want to give particular attention to a recent affair concerning a civil trial presented to a French civil court concerning marriage annulments. The conditions of this requirement were possible under French laws, but public opinion put a great pressure on the justice minister Rachida Dati (who is of Moroccan descent) to deny the husband his right to ask for wedding annulments, because of the reason evocated by him: the spouse was not a virgin.

20. Each time we refer to the notion of public space, we point to the intersubjective public space developed by Jürgen Habermas, as a space for public and political debate, and as a space for construction and diffusion of political opinions. See Jürgen Habermas, *L'espace Public: Archéologie de la Publicité Comme Dimension Constitutive de la Société Bourgeoise* (Paris: Payot, 1988), 324.

21. By "social fact" we introduce a personal translation of the French notion of "fait social."

22. This refers to bilateral conventions signed during the sixties between France and certain countries of the Maghreb, especially with Algeria. These conventions planned advantageous conditions of entrance and of settlement to Algerian citizens, who are often exempted from the obligation to obtain an entrance visa or a working authorization. However, it is necessary for us to admit that the evolution of diplomatic relations between the two countries, as well as, the evolution of European legislation on extra-European migrations, has strikingly shrunk all these advantages. We evoke here the bilateral convention concerning circulation employment, and the settlement in France of Algerian nationals and their families, dated December 27, 1968. We also cite the Franco-Tunisian convention on manpower on August 9, 1963.

23. North Africa or what is generically known as "Maghreb" is a geographic area representing a relative social, cultural and geographical homogeneity. It includes Tunisia, Algeria, and Morocco.

24. The metaphor is from Manuel Castells. See Manuel Castells, *The City and the Grassroots* (London: Hodder Arnold, 1983), 480.

25. It is about situations of mourning, losses, or family conflicts, or even about symbolic violence. Constance de Gourcy investigates female migrations and tried to enlighten female immigration as an active process in which women formulate a migratory project and are not content with conforming to a family will. The author does not work particularly on North African migrants. See Constance De Gourcy, "D'un Lieu á l'autre: les Femmes dans le Processus Migratoire," in *Femmes et Villes, DENÈFLES. (dir).* (Tours: Presses Universitaires Francois-Rabelais, MSH, 2004), 513-527.

26. These figures are rather recent, and they are still not studied enough. We shall refer essentially to the work of Nassima Moujoud concerning Moroccan women immigrating alone. Nassima Moujoud, "Partir Seules...Heurs Et Malheurs De Marocaines En France," *Gradhiva* no. 33 (2003).

27. On June 19, 1991, during the speech of Orléans and on the occasion of a debate dinner of the *Rassemblement pour la République* or RPR (political party, main representative of the French right) in Orléans city, and with the presence of 1,300 activists and sympathizers, Jacques Chirac, then president of the RPR and mayor of Paris, delivered his speech concerning a possible revision of the French immigration policies. In this speech Jacques Chirac claimed he had given up political doublespeak by "expressing any height of what many people think quite low" with regard to the Muslim immigrants in France. In the same occasion, he pronounced his famous phrase, "the noise and the smell" which marked people's minds to the point that the interethnic rap group Zebda took it as a title for a popular song. See Guyotat Regis, "Le Débat sur l'immigration le Maire de Paris: Il ya Overdose," *Le Monde*, June 21, 1999, 40; Zebda, http://www.zebda.fr (accessed June 25, 2009).

28. On the question of urban segregations see Jacques Danzelot, Catherine Melvel and Anne Wyvekens, *Faire Société: La Politique de la ville aux états unis et en France* (Paris: Editions du Seuil, 2003), 264. On the question of revolts of the suburbs we give the following reference, but it is not exhaustive of the subject, which has spilt a lot of ink, but it is because of the brief and hard-hitting character of the article. See Béatrice Giblin, "Fracture Sociale ou Fracture Nationale? De la Gravité des Violences Urbaines de l'automne 2005, " *Revue Hérodote* 120, (2003): 77-95. The article of Noria Boukhobza is

very revealing of the gendered structure of these riots in the region of Toulouse which the author describes. See Boukhobza, "Les filles naissent après les garcons," 227-242.

29. Recent immigrant Muslims may have experienced prejudices to their personal liberties because of some orthodox Islamic beliefs in their countries. We point here to the divergence of interpretative traditions that arise between Muslims from different countries and/or persuasion. The devout and strict practice of religion is for some Muslims obsolete and reactionary and, for others, the essential message of Islam.

30. The most notable event is September 11, 2001 among other events where violence is associated with demands with strong religious content. In this respect the notion of *jihad*, which is much evoked in this debate, is not systematically associated by Muslims with war or armed struggle or any form of violence. According to a *hadith*, the supreme jihad is undertaken against oneself, against one's own instincts.

31. Social norms and what is called in Islamic tradition *mouàmalàt* (social interactions) are strictly codified in order to maintain a social order in harmony with Islamic ethics. It is obvious that these social ethics are inoperative in migration context and in a French society having its own norms and ethics.

32. The French weekly, *Le Courrier International*, cites an article from the newspaper Al-Watan that says: "Too much religion kills the religion." Its author, Hamza Al-Mizaini, expresses himself in the following terms: "In France and in the other western countries, as well as in the other laic Muslim countries as Turkey, there are Muslims who fight to have a place of prayer or to wear the veil." See Hamza Al-Mizaini, "Trop de Religion tue la Religion," *Le Courrier International*, July 2008, 26.

33. Differentialist positions define Muslims and Islam as different and opposed to the liberal societies. Sophie Bessis considers Samuel Huntington's theory of "the clash of civilizations," for example, as differentialist. These positions are essentialist in the sense that they define Islam and Muslims by some of their particularities and differences without interrogating the essence of these categories.

34. Literally *aïd* means feast in Arabic. *Aïd al idhà* is the feast of sacrifice to remember Abraham's sacrifice by scarifying a sheep. In the Islamic calendar this feast intervenes to mark the end of hajj's pilgrimage to Mecca.

35. The religious argument had taken a preponderant place in the event, while the conflict focused around the violation of Kuwait's territorial sovereignty as well as on the control of the oil wells in the region.

36. We refer to specific culinary, clothing, and festive habits and uses. Muslims in France have different origins, cultures and cultural practices. Middle Eastern Muslims, Turkish Muslims, and North African Muslim immigrants have different habits, social practices, consumption models, and so forth, from each other.

37. The use of Qur'an verses on shop windows of ethnic businesses like restaurants, works as messages of appeal for a targeted category of consumers.

38. A *hàjj* is here the person who did the pilgrimage. The difference with *hajj* lies in a stress put on the first syllable. We prefer here to adopt the Arabic appropriate pronunciation instead of some other close formulations like *hajji*.

39. Literally, the term means prospectors.

40. In Saudi Arabia the climatic conditions are extreme. They are also worsened by the strong concentration of the pilgrims and by pollution.

41. It consists in jackpot system of common capital, which profits randomly to each one of them.

Bibliography

Al-Mizaini, Hamza. "Trop de Religion tue la Religion," *Le Courrier International*, July 2008, 26.

Baduel, Pierre Robert. "Migrations Internes et Émigration: Le cas Tunisien." *Annuaire de l'Afrique du Nord* (1983): 169-186.

Bastian, Jean-Pierre. "La Nouvelle Économie Religieuse de l'amérique Latine." *Social Compas* 53, no. 1 (2006): 65-80.

Begag, Azouz. *Le Gone du Chaâba*. Novel, Paris: Le Seuil, Coll. "Point-Virgule," 2001.

Bergeaud-Blackler, Florence. "De la Viande Halal au Halal Food: Comment le Halal S'est Développé en France." *Revue Européenne des Migrations Internationales* 21, no. 3 (2005): 125-47.

Bessis, Sophie. *Les Arabes, les Femmes, la Liberté*. Paris: Albin Michel, 2007.

Boukhobza, Noria. "Les Filles Naissent Après les Garçons: Représentations Sociales des Populations d'origine Maghrébine en France." *Revue Européenne des Migrations Internationales* 21, no. 1 (2005): 227-42.

Bourdieu, Pierre and Abdelmalek Sayad. *Le Déracinement: La Crise de l'agriculture Traditionelle en Algerie*. Paris: Édition de Minuit, 1964.

Castells, Manuel. *The City and the Grassroots: Cross-cultural Theory of Urban Social Movements*. London: Hodder Arnold, 1983.

Chiffoleau, Stephane. "Un Champ á Explorer: Le Rôle des Pèlerinages dans les Mobilités Nationales, Régionales et Internationales du Moyen-Orient." *Revue Européenne des Migrations Internationales* 19, no. 3 (2003): 285-289.

Danzelot, Jacques, Catherine Melvel and Anne Wyvekens. *Faire Société. La Politique de la Ville aux États Unis et en France, la Couleur des Idées*. Paris: Editions du seuil, 2003.

de Gourcy, Constance. "D'un Lieu á l'autre: Les Femmes dans le Processus Migratoire." Pp. 513-527 in *Femmes et Villes, DENÈFLES. (dir)*. Tours: Presses Universitaires Francois-Rabelais, MSH, 2004.

Giblin, Béatrice. "Fracture Sociale ou Fracture Nationale? De la Gravité des Violences Urbaines de l'automne 2005." *Revue Hérodote* 120 (2006): 77-95.

Grappe, Vèronique Nahoum. *Le Féminin*. Paris: Hachette, 1996.

Guenif-Souilamas, Nacira and Eric Mace. *Les Féministes et le Garçon Arabe*. Paris: Editions de l'Aube, 2004.

Habermas, Jürgen. *L'espace Public: Archéologie de la Publicité Comme Dimension Constitutive de la Société Bourgeoise*. Paris: Payot, 1988.

Maalouf, Amin. *Les Identités Meurtrières*. Paris: Éditions de Poche, 2001.

Ma Mung, Emmanuel and Gildas Simon. *Commerçants Maghrébins et Asiatiques en France*. Paris: Masson, 1990.

Missaoui, Lamia. "Petit ici, Notables là-bas." *Revue Européenne des Migrations Internationales* 11, no.1 (1995): 53-75.

Moujoud, Nassima. "Partir Seules... Heurs et Malheurs de Marocaines en France." *Gradhiva* no. 33 (2003): 93-101.

Nahoum Grappe. *Véronique. Le Féminin*. Paris: Hachette, 1996.

Noiriel, Gérard. *Le Creuset Français Histoire de l'immigration Xixe—Xxe Siècle, Collection Points*. Paris: Éditions du Seuil, 2006.

Peraldi, Michel. *Cabas et Container: Activités Marchandes Informelles et Réseaux Migrants Transfrontaliers*. Paris: Maisonneuve et Larose, 2001.

Pian, Anaïk. "Les Sénégalais en Transit au Maroc. La Formation d'un Espace-temps de l'entre-deux aux Marges de l'Europe." Unpublished PhD dissertation, Université Paris 7 Denis Diderot, 2007.

Portes, Alejandro. "La Mondialisation par le Bas. L'émergence des Communautés Transnationales." *Actes de la Recherche en Sciences Sociales*, no. 129 (1999): 15-25.

Regis, Guyotat. "Le Débat sur l'immigration le Maire de Paris: Il ya Overdose," *Le Monde*, June 21, 1999.

Sayad, Abdelmalek. *L'immigration ou les Paradoxes de l'altérité*. Bruxelles: Bruxelles De Boeck Université, 1991.

———. *La Double Absence: Des Illusions de l'émigré aux Souffrances de l'immigré*. Paris: Seuil, 1999.

———. *L'immigration ou les Paradoxes de l'altérité*. Paris: Raisons D'agir Éditions, 2006.

Simon, Gildas. *Géodynamiques des Migrations Internationales dans le Monde*. Paris: PUF, 1995.

Stora, Benjamin. *Entretiens Avec Thierry Leclère, La Guerre Des Mémoires. La France Face á Son Passé Colonial*. Paris: Editions de l'Aube, 2007.

———. *La Gangrène de l'oubli: La Mémoire de la Guerre d'algérie*. Paris: La Découverte, 1991.

Tarrius, Alain. *La Mondialisation par le Bas: Les Nouveaux Nomades de l'économie Souterraine*. Paris: Balland, 2002.

———. *Les Nouveaux Cosmopolitismes: Mobilités, Identités, Territoires*. La Tour-d'Aigues, Vaucluse: Éditions de l'Aube, 2000.

Tillion, Germaine. *Le Harem et les Cousins*. Paris : SEUIL, Collection ESSAIS, 1966.

Vieillard-Baron, Hervé. "De la Difficulté á Cerner les Territoires du Religieux: le cas de l'islam en France." *Annales de Géographie* 640 (2004): 563-87.

Weber, Max. *L'éthique Protestante et l'esprit du Capitalisme*. Paris: Flammarion, 2000.

Wieviorka, Michel. "Plaidoyer Pour un Concept." Pp. 209-220 in *Penser le Sujet: Autour d'Alain Touraine*, collectif, Francois Dubet et Michel Wieviorka. Paris: Librairie Arthéme Fayard, 1995.

Zebda. http://www.zebda.fr (accessed June 25, 2009).

Zingales, Luigi. "In God We Trust? Comment les Attitudes Religieuses Influencent l'économie." *Dieu et les Sciences* no. 14 (2004): 56-60.

Chapter Ten
Muslim Women in Brazil: Notes on Religion and Integration
Cristina Maria de Castro

This chapter focuses on the role of Islam in the integration of immigrant Muslim women in Brazil. Being a Muslim in this context has both positive and negative impacts on the process of immigrant integration. Brazil hosts the largest Muslim community of Latin America, a religious minority originating mainly from Lebanon, which has achieved truly successful economic survival strategies (Castro 2007a). Through a shared Islamic identity, former immigrants have been induced to help newcomers overcome linguistic, cultural and social obstacles. However, the minority status of Muslims imposes the need for negotiation with the Brazilian host society, which is characterized by the strong presence of Catholicism, the growth of Protestantism, a secular state, a basically Western culture, dependence on the United States, and the Brazilian tradition of absorbing immigrants in a very strong process of assimilation (Castro 2007b).

Men and women have different experiences and reactions in the migration process. Muslim women in Brazil face a broader range of consequences from the Orientalist view spread by the media than do men, since their religiousness is more visible when they wear the *hijab*. Brazilians consider them "victims of gender oppression" or even "gender traitors," in the case of converted women who have *chosen* to adopt a religion "that preaches the submission of women." Exposure to the values of Western host societies, such as gender equality and individual freedom, also influences the treatment received by Muslim women from the immigrant community itself. On the one hand, gender-oppression may increase, but on the other, a progressive view may develop in an attempt to bring Islamic and Western ideas closer together (Roald 2001).

The interpretation of social issues like gender relations in Islamic sources is clearly affected by its interaction with social structures around it. Factors such as the time of residence in the host country, level of contact with society as a whole, social class, educational models, and lastly, personal disposition should be taken into account (Roald 2001). The central argument here is that the development of a successful ethnic economy helps preserve cultural aspects in a migration context (Light 2005), including those involving a more traditional religious view of women. An ethnic economy can weld together an immigrant

167

group, reducing the opportunities for deeper contact with the host society. Hypothetically, the outcome of this is the preservation of a less flexible religiosity. To test this hypothesis, two Muslim communities in the state of São Paulo are analyzed: one that frequents the Islamic Center in the city of Campinas and the other involving the Islamic Youth League in the Brás neighborhood of the city of São Paulo. The latter is deeply affected by the ethnic economy, while members of the former act independently[1] in the economic sphere. The main research technique used in the study was participant observation from 2004 and 2006. I attended Friday sermons, Arabic and religion classes on Saturdays, lectures, religious celebrations, marches and events organized by leaders and members of both mosques to gain a deeper insight into Muslim life in São Paulo.

This chapter is divided into three sections and followed by a conclusion. The first section includes a brief overview of the Islamic presence in Brazil. The second section provides details about the ethnic, occupational and spatial distribution profiles of the two aforementioned communities, and their relationships with the local religious fields. And, the third section compares the prescribed and experienced social roles of gender in the Muslim communities of Brás and Campinas.

Muslim Presence in Brazil

Several local Muslim religious leaders claim that the Islamic presence in Brazil dates back to the Age of Discovery (Jerrahi n.d.). This may be a strategy to create a place in the "founding" history of this country and to legitimate the claim that Muslim presence is as old as Christianity in Brazil. However, it was only with the beginning of slave traffic to Brazil that a substantial number of Muslims arrived in the country. *Malês*, Africans of Yoruban[2] descent, are the most well known of Muslims in that period. In 1835, they organized an uprising, based on the Islamic right of self-defense, which they took to the streets of a very important northeastern city (Salvador) for many hours, leading to repercussions that were felt as far away as Europe. Some of the participants of this uprising were deported, while others were arrested, beaten or even condemned to death (Reis 2003).

As a consequence of the uprising, Islam was seen as something to be feared and controlled, and it all but disappeared from Brazil's religious scene, returning only with the arrival of new Syrian and Lebanese immigrants, especially after the 1940s. These immigrants represent the majority of Muslims in Brazil today. However, it should be noted that there were several phases in the Syrian-Lebanese immigration to Brazil, the first of which was marked by the almost exclusive arrival of Christians (Truzzi 1993). This migratory movement began in 1880, when the "Great Syria"[3] was dominated by the Ottoman Empire. At the root of the emigrational movement were demographic, political, economic and cultural factors. The successful experiences in "America," described in letters sent to relatives and friends in Lebanon (along with substantial sums of money), encouraged many people to come to the New World, even if they did not know exactly where that was. Many believed that the United States, Argentina, and Brazil were the same country. Others came to Argentina or Brazil because somebody had told them that those lands were America, too. Finally, some went to the United States but were refused entry due to poor health or because of stricter immigration laws. To avoid a complete waste of time and money spent on traveling, they were persuaded to settle in South America. The decadence of the Ottoman Empire and the subsequent French dominion prompted the emigration of increasing numbers of Muslims who felt belittled by the preferential treatment of Christians in Lebanon (Gattaz 2001).

Unlike Italian, Portuguese, Spanish and other European groups, Syrians and Lebanese did not receive financial support to immigrate to Brazil. An immigration system was set up by the Brazilian government to recruit workers for rural labor and, starting in the early twentieth century, for the industrial sector. However, Syrians and Lebanese were excluded because they did not satisfy the criteria of Brazil's immigration policies, aimed primarily at "whitening" the country's population. Although they did not pose a threat to the ideal of "whitening," as did Africans and Asians, they were not the ideal immigrants the government was looking for. Therefore, they did not receive support from the Brazilian government, but neither did they encounter obstacles to entering the country.

Since the Lebanese immigrants arrived without contracts to work either on farms or in industry, they became merchants. Most of them had no capital to invest, but street peddling presented a possible path to rapid riches (Osman 1998). This soon became their main activity in the host country. After saving a little money, they started opening small shops and inviting friends and relatives to work for them, selling their goods through consignment. Successful shopkeepers invested their savings in wholesale businesses and later in industry. The process came full circle as older immigrants who had become wholesale merchants or manufacturers then supplied goods to the more recent immigrants working as street peddlers or shopkeepers.

Lebanese immigration to Brazil was, on the whole, a male worker phenomenon. When temporary immigration became permanent, wives, brides, sisters and daughters were brought over to join their men. Lebanese women were given incentives to immigrate to Brazil to help men with "female tasks" (Osman 2006). However, their contribution transcended house and child care. Reports collected by Osman (2006) reveal their active and direct participation in their husband's business, even though the man was considered the primary family provider. Citing one response from Osman's study, "while my husband peddled, I took care of our store," said Sara Toufic Abou Jokh, a first generation Muslim immigrant (Osman 2006: 6). Her support made the expansion of the family business possible. Other female Lebanese immigrants from Christian and Muslim backgrounds were also responsible for this kind of contribution to their own families. Despite the apparently strict definition of the social roles of gender, i.e., women caring for the home and men being the providers, some women subtly crossed these roles.

The arrival of Lebanese immigrants in Brazil coincided with the beginning of the country's urbanization process. This contributed to the immigrants' commercial success, which was much greater here than it was, for example, in the United States (Truzzi 1993). Lebanese immigrants attempted to do the same thing in the United States, but the context was different since the urbanization process was already well advanced and other immigrant groups already occupied those commercial activities. According to Muslim leaders like Mohamed Habib from the Islamic Center of Campinas, the majority, or 90 percent, of Muslims in Brazil are of Lebanese descent. Syrians make up the second largest group, followed by Palestinians. The latter came to Brazil mostly after the creation of the state of Israel. Egyptians, Moroccans, Sudanese, Nigerians, South Africans, and Mozambicans represent other nationalities of Muslim immigrants who settled in Brazil, albeit in fewer numbers.

There are no reliable statistics about the number of Muslims in Brazil for they are classified under a generic category called "others" in censuses. Islamic organizations claim they are almost a million; however, according to geographers Philippe Waniez and Violette Brustlein (2001), the real number may be as few as 200,000 individuals, including the category "others." Muslims in Brazil are concentrated mainly in the states of São Paulo, Paraná, and Rio Grande do Sul. São Paulo is Brazil's wealthiest and most industrialized state and its capital is home to the country's largest Muslim community. On the other hand, most of the Muslim immigrants in Paraná and Rio Grande do Sul live in cities other than the capitals of those states. Their main host cities are Foz do Iguaçú in Paraná and Uruguaiana in Rio Grande do Sul because these locations are geographically favorable for commerce. Both cities lie on the border with Argentina, and Foz do Iguaçú also borders on Paraguay. Almost 60 percent of the Muslims in Brazil engage in commercial activities. Wealthier and better educated than the average population, many own their business, and about 40 percent are employers in Brazil (Waniez and Brustlein 2001).

The next sections describe in greater detail the ethnic and occupational profiles of the two communities of this study. The first, the Islamic Youth League, has a more typical profile considering the majority of Muslims in Brazil, i.e., a Lebanese background and dedication to commerce. The Islamic Center of Campinas, on the other hand, is a very interesting case for comparison, since it comprises heterogeneous ethnic backgrounds and members concentrated on educational activities. This comparative analysis is important because it brings to light the diversity of roles Islam can play in the same host context, from the standpoint of Muslim women's integration.

The Islamic Youth League

The Islamic Youth League Mosque is located on the border between the neighborhoods of Brás and Pari[4] in São Paulo, the main host city for Muslims in Brazil. This mosque was built in 1995 to provide a place of prayer for recently settled immigrant businessmen. Arab countries such as Egypt, Saudi Arabia, the United Arab Emirates, and Kuwait contributed to institutionalize Islam in that community, not only financially but also by offering its leaders religious training and education. The main source of funding, however, was provided by the community's own successful members residing in Brazil. The community consists of about 200 families, most of them from Tripoli, Lebanon. These Muslim families followed the example of the first Lebanese immigrants in Brazil: the entry in commercial activities, based on a system of mutual cooperation, whereby the earlier immigrants help recent ones to learn the language, obtain goods to sell through consignment, or get a job. Their region of origin has directed Muslims to specific neighborhoods and cities in Brazil and the socialization offered to newcomers has led them to concentrate their activities in the same type of business. Muslim immigrants who settled in the city of São Bernado do Campo, for example, sell furniture. Recent immigrants who are members of the Islamic Youth League specialize in blue jeans business in a region currently dominated by the clothing industry and commerce.

Mohammed Chedid, one of the League's founders, states in an interview that the support successful Muslim immigrants offer to newcomers is a religious duty (Castro 2007b). The region of origin played an important role in directing immigrants to certain cities and neighborhoods and Islam has completed the link, encouraging solidarity and mutual cooperation. However, it should be noted that the immigrants' network of solidarity has expanded to help individuals with no ethnic or national connection to that group apart from the same religious affiliation. During my fieldwork, I saw a considerable number of converted women, migrants from Brazil's northeastern states, being absorbed into the immigrants' network of solidarity. After facing disadvantages in the labor market due to their lack of social capital in São Paulo, and religious discrimination because of their use of the veil, these girls are usually hired by immigrant Muslim businessmen. Brazil's northeast is the poorest region of the country and a typical region of emigration. The Brás and Pari neighborhoods, on the other hand, are traditional hosts of migrants from Brazil and abroad and are commonly marked by interethnic and religious frictions.

Pentecostalism[5] represents the second-largest segment in Brazil's religious groups, with its followers representing 13.59 percent of the population. The last two national demographic censuses, in 1991 and 2000, indicated that Pentecostalism is the fastest growing religion in the country. In metropolitan São Paulo, 30 percent of the population are Pentecostals, and, most of them are concentrated in the eastern part of the city where Brás and Pari are located (Almeida 2004). This region is marked by the presence of northeastern migrants, who are strong devotees of Pentecostalism.

There is a strong presence of Pentecostals (especially from God's Assembly) at the League in Saturday classes for converts and the curious. Although the original religious background of several women converts was Pentecostal before they embraced Islam, it is a well known fact that many visitors, particularly men, have no intention of changing their religion. Introducing themselves as Christians interested in a dialogue between religions and the opportunity to attend free Arabic classes, they invariably polemicize religious classes, asking controversial questions that coincide with the media's view of Islam and Muslims. For instance: "Is it true that if a bomber kills himself he goes to heaven and is rewarded with seventy-two virgins? What about women? What do they receive for that?"

Arabs seem unaware of the real intentions of visitors on Saturdays, but recent converts know, probably because of their earlier experiences with Pentecostal religions. Some evangelicals may attend Islamic classes in the mosque in order to prevent new conversions to Islam or even as a form of training for proselytizing missions to Africa and/or Asia. Discrimination and verbal attacks from evangelical members against Muslim women in São Paulo were observed during my fieldwork, as well. Muslims are criticized for not believing that Jesus is the son of God, and are sometimes seen as being "anti-Jesus." The "devil nun" is an example of the verbal aggressions Muslim women are subjected to by Pentecostals in Brazil.

The youthful dynamism of the League, run by twenty- to thirty-year-old leaders, allied to its high economic capital, is used for disseminating God's word in the host country. In another work, I observe that:

> Arabs have been successful in getting fatayers to be sold in every snack bar on every corner, but what about God's word? It has not even reached the first corner. We have failed in this, and it must be our contribution to Brazilians, to take God's word to them (Castro 2007b).

Pentecostals are aware of the Muslim proselytizing attitude in Brás and try to fight against it. Pentecostalism is followed predominantly by women and formerly presented the most combative profile among all religious groups in Brazil. Generally, more women profess a religion than men, but this difference is even more marked among Pentecostals. About 63 percent of Pentecostals are women, and some denominations show an even higher number. For example, almost 80 percent of the members of the Universal Church of the Kingdom of God (IURD) are women (Almeida and Montero 2001). Many women converts to Islam have had previous experience in evangelical institutions such as the IURD and God's Assembly (Castro 2007b). Labeling Islam as gender-oppressive is one of the main Pentecostal strategies against Muslim conversion, not only due to the influence of an Orientalist view spread by the Brazilian media—which is strongly influenced by the American media—but also because the Islamic Youth League is attracting the main clients of Pentecostalism, mainly women.

A male member of God's Assembly who used to attend religious and Arabic classes at the League confides that Muslim women are "slaves": "They are not allowed to drive cars or even to go outside their homes alone, without the presence of a man of the family" (Castro 2007b: 77). His perception is based on a folder distributed by a local church of God's Assembly about how Muslims treat their women. It is interesting to note that the young man's ideas about Muslim women are based solely on information disseminated by his church rather than on his personal experience with the Islamic League. He is unaffected by the ideology of the Muslim group, according to which Islam is the most respectful and protective of religions when it comes to women. Neither does he acknowledge the daily examples displayed by the community, like the female Arabic teacher—a married second-generation Lebanese—who habitually drives her own car to the mosque, as well as that of several converts, single or married to Arab immigrants, who do the same.

The better economic conditions of Brazil's Muslim community do not protect it from the stereotypes disseminated by the Brazilian media and which rival groups manipulate to their own advantage. However, the strong ethnic economy developed by Muslim immigrants in Brás and extended to Brazilian converts has, to some extent, helped women overcome discrimination, albeit in differing degrees according to their national and social backgrounds. Immigrant Muslim women in Brás are more protected from prejudice than are converted Brazilian women. The Arab women can count on the financial support of fathers or husbands, since most of them engage primarily in the roles of housewife and mother. Using private cars, they are better protected from verbal aggressions and disapproving looks or sneering. Brazilians consider Arab women "victims of gender oppression" and converts are seen as "gender traitors" because they have *chosen* to adopt a religion that "preaches female submission." Non-Arab women converts can count on the help of Muslim businessmen to get a job, but they nevertheless occupy a lower position on the economic scale and are obliged to use public transportation. Some of them marry Muslim immigrants and ascend socially, but face discrimination by Arab women, who see them as competitors in the matrimonial market of Brás' Muslim community.

The Islamic Center of Campinas

The Islamic Center of Campinas was founded in 1977 on the initiative of its current president, Ismail Hatia, a South African immigrant of Indian descent. In the 1970s, Hatia decided to travel to South Africa to raise funds to institutionalize Islam in Campinas. A donation of twenty-five thousand dollars from the Indian Muslim community was used to buy land and start the construction of a mosque. Subsequently, continuing support of the project was provided by Muslims residing in Campinas and the surrounding region, comprising immigrants of Lebanese, South African, Palestinian and Egyptian descent.

The Muslim community of Campinas is exceptional for various reasons, one of which is the greater ethnic and national heterogeneity of its members compared to other Islamic centers in the state of São Paulo. According to Mohamed Habib, the leader of this community, this heterogeneity is explained by the presence of the State University of Campinas (Unicamp).[6]   Many Egyptians fled their country due to the political persecution of Nasser's regime and some of them became professors at Unicamp. One of these professors is the community leader and current pro-rector for extension and community affairs, Prof. Mohamed Habib. Libyans moved to Campinas to join graduate programs as research fellows or members of the teaching staff in the same university. Other groups, like the South Africans of Indian Gujarati background, make up the community. They fled apartheid and settled in Campinas, many as English teachers. Some of them have set up their own English language schools. Immigrants from Malaysia and the Guyanas also settled in Campinas and the surrounding region, albeit in fewer numbers.

At one point, Mozambicans of Indian Gujarati background were the majority Muslim group in Campinas. However, according to informants from the Islamic Center of Campinas, most of the Mozambican immigrants became disenchanted with Brazil's economic crises, so they gave up their "American dream" and left the country between 1985 and 1990, during the administration of President José Sarney. This abandonment may be explained by the lack of a supportive ethnic economy and the fact that their cultural capital[7] fell short of that of other Muslims associated with Unicamp, thus preventing them from being assimilated into the university as members of the teaching and graduate research staff. Unlike the Gujarati Indians from South Africa, they did not speak fluent English, which largely explains why they were unable to follow the example of their fellow South African Muslims. In addition, the economic recession of the times was unfavorable for the development of a new ethnic economy.

The poor mobilization of internal social capital for developing an ethnic economy in the aforementioned Muslim immigrant community was not the result of ethnic heterogeneity, but was in fact due to its members' particular cultural capital. Even more so than in other Islamic centers of the country, the common religious identity in Campinas' Muslim community suffices to justify marriage between immigrants of different ethnic backgrounds. Since their religious identity is enough to encourage this type of connection, there is no reason to believe it would not also suffice to articulate those individuals around the same economic activity. The main reason for the poor use of internal social capital for economic purposes by that group is the differentiated cultural capital of its members, which enabled them to become part of the teaching and graduate research staff of Unicamp and to embark in the English language teaching business.

The ethnic heterogeneity in Campinas emphasizes the ideal of *ummah*[8] since it appears to be practically the sole reason for the construction of a collective identity for the members of that group. As for the presence of Brazilian converts, this is quite rare in Campinas, where there are only about six converts according to one informant of the Islamic Center, and eighteen according to another one, in a group of three hundred people. The Islamic Center of Campinas does not offer religious classes or any other event to attract new followers from outside the borders of the immigrant community. Its members are scattered around the city of Campinas and in smaller towns nearby. Moreover, they work independently, mainly in educational and research activities. There is no ethnic economy based on interdependent commerce, nor is there a concentration of immigrants in any particular neighborhood. The use of the veil is exceptional in Campinas, and only four women wore it in during the time of this research. The *hijab* has become the "prayer clothes" in Campinas. Taken together, these factors render Muslims in Campinas almost invisible. Hence, no verbal attacks from Pentecostals were reported in that city during my fieldwork. Between January 2004 and January 2005 only one group of six evangelical women visited the Islamic Center once. Islam in Campinas remains an immigrant religion and this situation is not expected to change, at least in the foreseeable future.

Social Roles: Mother, Wife, Student and Professional

This section discusses social roles of gender in Campinas and Brás, pointing out the impact of a successful ethnic economy vis-à-vis the preservation of a traditional religious view of women within the context of migration. Among several social roles available to Muslim women in Brazil, two are privileged in the discourse among religious leaderships, namely, the roles of mother and wife. The leaders of the Islamic Youth League are extremely concerned about stressing biological reasons to justify the differences between male and female social roles, which are recommended by Islamic teaching.

Women are considered naturally suited to some kinds of activities, such as housework and childcare, while men, out of respect for "women's delicate and fragile nature," are responsible for being the family provider. The discourse of the League's leaders, presented in sermons and websites, recognizes women's right to work outside the home, but "only if their obligations towards their family are fulfilled." Women's right to an education is also mentioned in the official leadership discourse, published in the Islamic Youth League's website, in answer to Western critics, who claim that Muslim women live confined in their homes until they are released by death.

In Campinas, the roles of wife and mother are also highly valued. However, the leaders' discourse does not make such an explicit division of male and female roles, possibly because this group consists almost entirely of Muslim immigrants, so everyone is already completely familiar with traditional Islamic family roles. Be that as it may, children are described as the responsibility of both parents. The leaders in Campinas also recommend the participation of sons and daughters in family decisions. The acceptance and recommendation of Western values such as individual freedom is probably the result of greater contact between the immigrants and Brazilian host society. Finally, the Campinas leaders do not talk about women's right to an education in sermons or informal conversations. They refer, instead, to women's *duty* to study: "The quest for knowledge is an obligation of every man and woman in Islam."

The discourse among the leaders of the two Muslim communities, in Campinas and Brás, reveals significant differences in terms of social roles of gender, as does the daily religiousness practiced by ordinary people. The educational level of the Muslim community in Campinas is higher than in Brás, even considering the types of occupations of its members. The same applies to women's education. Based on my fieldwork, it is observable that considerable investments are normally made in the education of Muslim girls in Campinas, where a university education seems to be a shared goal and destiny among those young women. Engineering, Biology and Law are some of the courses they attend at outstanding institutions like Unicamp and the Pontifical Catholic University of Campinas.

In the community of the Islamic Youth League, however, attending university is not so common, particularly in the case of women because marriage usually comes earlier. It seems that some twenty-one year-old girls are deeply concerned about getting married as soon as possible, fearing that, at that age, they would already be considered too old. Samira Osman (1998) and Oswaldo Mário Serra Truzzi (2006) point out the differences in the attitude of Lebanese immigrants in São Paulo regarding the education of their sons and daughters. In her masteral thesis, Osman goes even further, declaring that the daughters of Muslim Lebanese immigrants who decide to continue their studies face resistance from their own fathers.

In terms of work, there are also differences in the experiences of women in Campinas and Brás. In Brás, it is common to see girl converts working for Arab shopkeepers. Some of them marry immigrants and may continue to help their husbands, as some immigrants do. Working in the family business and as a volunteer Arabic teacher in the mosque is more acceptable than working outside the confines of the immigrant ethnic economy. Thus, the role of male as provider in the family continues unchallenged. According to fieldwork informants, the majority of the female immigrants in Brás are fulltime housewives and mothers.

It is interesting to note that, in Campinas, even when Muslim women have jobs, men remain the family providers in the social imaginary of that community. In an interview with a thirty-eight-year-old second-generation housewife, she declares that, "women have the right to be supported by men." A twenty-two-year-old female university student also states that, "Muslim men do not abandon their women (financially)." Her mother, a South African immigrant of Indian descent and a teacher of English for high-school students, proudly backed up her daughter's statement. When describing potential husbands, they both repeatedly emphasize the men's ability to earn a living and support a family, notwithstanding the fact that they themselves are perfectly qualified to do so as educated and employed women. The roles of mother and wife are highly valued in both communities, but women are sought at a younger age in Brás. This makes it even more difficult for Muslim women in Brás to pursue higher education and possible financial independence.

However, a few Brazilian converts object to the male provider role like a thirty-five-year-old woman employee of a Lebanese shopkeeper: "Almost nobody knows I'm married because my husband cannot support our family and Islam does not allow a man in such circumstances to marry. But I love him so I married him. I am not an Arab, I'm Brazilian! I can work and support myself!" This case is an example of the individualization of Muslim religiosity in a Western context of migration. It shows the Muslim convert's independence in face of the leaders' discourse about one of the key aspects of gender relationship, locally defined. The finding of an individualized Islam is similar in most studies in Europe, particularly in France (Frégosi 2004; Khosrokhavar 1997) and in Spain (Martin Muñoz 2003; Peter 2005). Nevertheless, this does not mean that the religious leadership discourses have lost their validity (Amir-Moazami and Salvatore 2003). Individualization of Islam must be examined together with institutionalized Islam, since "theology changes in interactions with the spread of eclectic beliefs in order to restore its cultural credibility in a secular environment," (Hervieu-Léger cited in Peter 2005: 9). The analysis of social roles of gender in the state of São Paulo, highlights not only the discourse of leaders but also practices and statements of ordinary members of these communities, for their religiosity is also forged in their daily lives.

Conclusion

Muslims in Brazil are richer and better educated than the average population. The "Muslim immigrant economic threat" is not perceived as an issue here, as has been the case in Europe, for example. On the contrary, Muslims are often employers in Brazil. Unlike some European countries that still seem to find it difficult to consider themselves as permanent immigrant host societies, Brazil sees immigrants as people who bring progress, not deterioration (Oliveira 2000). The idea that Brazil is willing to receive every immigrant without distinction and with open arms is even part of the myth of Brazilian national identity.

There is quite a strong trend in Brazil to limit the affirmation of identities and to dilute diversity. In Europe, as in Brazil, Islam is seen as a "foreign religion," an element that belongs to neither "the Brazilian identity" nor "the European identity." According to José Casanova (2005), more than a foreign religion, Islam is the "other," not exactly of a Christian Europe but of an increasingly secularized Europe. Secularization is understood in terms of privatization of religion and not so much as the absence of faith. In Brazilian society, in turn, professing belief in Catholicism, and even more so, in Christianity, is almost tantamount to recognizing oneself as a human being

(Carneiro and Soares 1992). Therefore, there is not much space for other religions according to the criterion of "normality" held by Brazilian society. In the imaginary of most of the country's population, being Brazilian means being a Christian as much as being Muslim means being an Arab.

Muslim women, converts or not, face strong pressures of assimilation from Brazilian society when using the *hijab* in public. They do not face prohibitive laws like those imposed in France, but are subjected to verbal harassment or mockery. Muslim religiosity displayed in public, as in the case of the hijab, is also not accepted in Brazil. This aversion stems not so much from religious privatization pressures but from the fact that Islam is not seen as part of "Brazil's national identity myth" and because it is associated with terrorist and gender-oppressor stereotypes spread by the Brazilian and American media (Castro 2007b).

Even so, the empirical data from this study indicates that the presence of a successful ethnic economy helps preserve cultural and religious aspects in a minority context. This can be explained, among other things, by the fact that such an economy fosters more intense contact within the immigrant community and only superficial contact with the host society. Anne Sofie Roald (2001) notes that the intensity of contact with social structures around immigrants influences the Islamic interpretation of social issues, like gender relations. Several responses of immigrants are highly revealing, and range from progressive to coercive views of women. In Campinas, for example, women receive a bigger investment in their education and child care is seen as a responsibility of both parents. In Brás, on the other hand, girls are encouraged to get married sooner and constitute a traditional Islamic family, marked by well defined gendered social roles.

According to theorists in the area of ethnic economy, like Roberto Grün (1992), it is more advantageous to remain within the borders of the immigrant community and its values when a successful ethnic economy is in place than to become assimilated into the host society. Therefore, it is especially important to follow certain signs of differentiation that are symbolically meaningful for the minority group in order to be considered a trustworthy member of the group. The more traditional religious treatment dispensed to women is part of this strategy of differentiation from the Brazilian host society.

Obviously, it is not only economic interests that affect religiosity. A personal inclination to follow a more disciplined religious life must also be taken into account. However, one should not ignore the fact that the spatial distribution of a group professing a minority religion as stigmatized as Islam can truly influence its members' disposition to face assimilation pressures from segments of the host society. Pious Muslim women wishing to wear the hijab in Brazil may feel much more comfortable doing so in a neighborhood frequented by Muslims, as in the case of Brás. This neighborhood has its own ethnic economy, an advantage for Muslims in Brás who are recent immigrants and who can also count on an Islamic school for their children. The time of residence and educational models also affect the Islamic interpretation of social issues (Roald

2001). The high economic capital of Arab immigrants has even been used to persuade a Catholic school in the neighborhood to offer, by means of additional payment, extra Arabic and Islamic religion classes for Muslim descendants.

In Campinas, Muslim immigrants work relatively independently of each other, and there is no ethnic economy that might otherwise unite them. Their situation as immigrants in Brazil is much more long-standing than that of the Muslims in Brás. Furthermore, they are scattered around Campinas and in small nearby towns. Islamic schools are not an alternative for their children. In short, all these factors make this community more susceptible to influences from the Brazilian host society. The Muslim community of Campinas is an example of flexibility achieved through intensive contact with Western values founded in Brazil. A progressive Muslim view concerning women has developed there, while Brás represents fertile ground for conservative and traditional religious interpretations about women and gender relations.

To conclude, the presence of a solid ethnic economy can weld together an immigrant group, helping immigrants not only to defend themselves from cultural and economic disadvantages, but also, to preserve cultural aspects in the context of migration, including those concerning traditional religious views of women.

Notes

1. In other words, Muslims in Campinas do not use their ethnic social capital to get a job.

2. An ethnic group from West Africa.

3. "Great Syria" corresponds to the current territories of Syria, Lebanon, Jordan and part of Iraq.

4. Like other blue-collar neighborhoods in São Paulo, Brás and Pari display a strong ethnic and cultural diversity. Italians, Portuguese, Spanish and Lebanese were already numerous there in the early 1930s. Starting in the mid-1940s, large numbers of migrants from northeastern Brazil started arriving in São Paulo's Brás neighborhood, fleeing a water crisis of major proportions in their native states. The 1970s saw the arrival of Korean immigrants, followed soon thereafter by Bolivian, Paraguayan and Peruvian immigrants to work in the Korean immigrants' garment factories. See Sidney Silva, "A Praça é Nossa!' Faces do Preconceito num Bairro Paulistano," *Travessia Revista do Migrante* 18, no. 51 (Janeiro-Abril 2005): 32-37; Paulo Cursino de Moura, *São Paulo de Outrora: Evocações da Metrópole* (São Paulo: Editora da Universidade de São Paulo, 1980).

5. The main religion in Brazil is still Catholicism, professed by 73.9 percent of the population. This is followed by Pentecostalism and traditional Evangelicalism representing a total of 15.6 percent. Other religions such as Kardecism, Esotericism and Afro-Brazilian, represent less than 3 percent of the population. See Instituto Brasileiro de Geografia e Estatistica, *IBGE Demographic Census 2000*, www.ibge.gov.br/censo (accessed July 20, 2008).

6. In 2007, Unicamp joined the ranks of the world's top 200 universities, according to The Times' Higher Education Supplement. Unicamp ranks in the 177th place, while the University of São Paulo (USP) ranks as the 175th best university. Unicamp was founded in 1967 and is considered new compared to USP, the alma mater of the Brazilian State

University, and therefore more open, while USP was established in 1934. European universities are centuries old, while the oldest universities in Brazil were established in the 1920s. Before that, the country had only a few independent institutions of superior education founded after 1808, upon the arrival of the Portuguese Court. See José Tadeu Jorge, "USP, Unicamp e o Ranking Universidades," http://www.unicamp.br/unicamp/div ulgacao/2007/11/25/reitor-comenta-inclusao-de-unicamp-e-usp-entre-as-melhores-do-mundo (accessed July 20, 2008).

7. Cultural capital corresponds to the set of intellectual qualifications produced by the educational system or transmitted by the family. See Pierre Bourdieu, *A Reprodução: Elementos para uma Teoria do Sistema de Ensino* (Rio de Janeiro: Francisco Alves, 1975).

8. A native concept that means "the world Muslim community."

Bibliography

Almeida, Ronaldo. "Religião na Metrópole Paulista." *Revista Brasileira de Ciências Sociais* 19, no. 56 (October 2004):15-27.

Almeida, Ronaldo and Paula Montero. "Trânsito Religioso no Brasil." *São Paulo em Perspectiva* 15, no. 3 (July/September 2001): 17-35.

Amir-Moazami, Schrin and Armando Salvatore. "Gender, Generation and the Reform of Tradition: From Muslim Majority Societies to Western Europe." Pp. 52-77 in *Muslim Networks and Transnational Communities in and across Europe*, edited by Stefano Allievi and Jorgen Nielsen. Leiden: Brill, 2003.

Bourdieu, Pierre. *A Reprodução: Elementos para uma Teoria do Sistema de Ensino.* Rio de Janeiro: Francisco Alves, 1975.

Carneiro, Leandro Piquet and Luiz Eduardo Soares. "Religiosidade, Estrutura Social e Comportamento Político." Pp. 9-58 in *O Impacto da Modernidade Sobre a Religião*, edited by Maria Clara Lucchetti Bingemer. São Paulo: Edições Loyola, 1992.

Casanova, José. "Immigration and the New Religious Pluralism: A EU/US Comparison." Paper presented at The New Religious Pluralism and Democracy Conference, Georgetown University, April 21-22, 2005.

Castro, Cristina Maria de. "Anotações Sobre Economia Étnica e Resistência à Assimilação entre Muçulmanos em São Paulo." Paper presented at the First Thematic Seminar Centrality and Frontiers of Enterprises in the 21st Century, UFSCar, 2007a.

———. "A Construção de Identidades Muçulmanas no Brasil: Um Estudo das Comunidades Sunitas da Cidade de Campinas e do Bairro Paulistano do Brás." Unpublished PhD dissertation, Post-Graduate Programme of Social Sciences, Federal University of São Carlos, 2007b.

Frégosi, Franck. "L'imam, le Conférencier et le Jurisconsulte: Retour sur Trios Figures Contemporaines du Champ Religieux en France." *Archives de Sciences Sociales de Religions* 125 (2004): 131-146.

Gattaz, André Castanheira. *História Oral da Imigração Libanesa para o Brasil – 1880 a 2000.* Unpublished PhD dissertation, Social History Department, USP, 2001.

Grün, Roberto. *Negócios e Famílias: Armênios em São Paulo.* São Paulo: Editora Sumaré, 1992.

Hervieu-Léger, Danièle. *Le Pelerin et le Converti. La Religion en Mouement.* Paris: Flammarion, 1999.

Instituto Brasileiro de Geografia e Estatistica. *IBGE Demographic Census 2000.* Brazil: Ministry of Planning, Budget and Management.www.ibge.gov.br/censo (accessed July 20, 2008).

Jerrahi, Muhammad Ragip al. "História da Presença Islâmica." http://www.mubar.org/jerrahi/Artigos___Palestras/Historia_da_presenca_Islamica_/historia_da_presenca_Islamica_.html (accessed April 20, 2006).

Jorge, José Tadeu. "USP, Unicamp e o Ranking das Universidades." http://www.unicamp.br/unicamp/divulgacao/2007/11/25/reitor-comenta-inclusao-de-unicamp-e-usp-entre-as-melhores-do-mundo (accessed July 20, 2008).

Khosrokhavar, Farhad. *L'islam des Jeunes.* Paris: Flammarion, 1997.

Liga da Juventude Islâmica. "Quem Somos." http://www.ligaIslamica.org.br/quem_somo s_.htm (accessed April 20, 2006).

Light, Ivan. "The Ethnic Economy." Pp. 647-671 in *The Handbook of Economic Sociology,* 2nd ed., edited by Neil Smelser and Richard Swedberg. New Jersey: Princeton University Press, 2005.

Martin Muñoz, Gema, F. Javier Garcia Castaño, Ana López Sala and Rafael Crespo. *Marroquíes en España: Estudio Sobre su Integración.* Madrid: Fundación Repsol YPF, 2003.

Moura, Paulo Cursino de. *São Paulo de Outrora: Evocações da Metrópole.* São Paulo: Editora da Universidade de São Paulo, 1980.

Oliveira, Lúcia Lippi. *Americanos: Representações da Identidade Nacional no Brasil e nos EUA.* Belo Horizonte: Editora UFMG, 2000.

Osman, Samira. "Caminhos da Imigração Árabe em São Paulo: História Oral da Vida Familiar." Unpublished Master's thesis, History Department, USP, São Paulo, 1998.

_____. "O Papel da Mulher Árabe no Processo Imigratório entre o Brasil e o Líbano." Paper presented at the VII Seminário Fazendo Gênero, Florianópolis, August 28-30, 2006.

Peter, Frank. "Individualization and Religious Authority in Western European Islam—A Review Essay." Paper presented at the workshop on Muslim Religious Authorities in Western Europe, ISIM, Leiden, September 30- October 1, 2005.

Reis, João José. *Rebelião Escrava no Brasil: A História do Levante dos Malês (1835).* São Paulo: Companhia das Letras, 2003.

Roald, Anne Sofie. *Women in Islam: The Western Experience.* London and New York: Routledge, 2001.

Silva, Sidney. "A Praça é Nossa!' Faces do Preconceito num Bairro Paulistano." *Travessia Revista do Migrante* 18, no. 51 (Janeiro-Abril 2005): 32-37.

Truzzi, Oswaldo Mário Serra. "Patrícios – Sírios e Libaneses em São Paulo." Unpublished PhD dissertation, Unicamp, Campinas, 1993.

———. "Configurações e Valores Familiares entre Muçulmanos em São Paulo." Paper presented at the 30th Annual Encounter of ANPOCS, Caxambu, October 24-28, 2006.

Waniez, Philippe and Violette Brustlein. "Os Muçulmanos no Brasil: Elementos para uma Geografia Social." *Revista Alceu* 1, no. 2 (January-July 2001): 155-180.

Chapter Eleven
Polish-Catholic Religiosity in California
Krystyna Błeszyńska and Marek Szopski

Polonia (Polish diaspora) is one of the largest in the world comprising twenty-one million in 2008. Most Polish immigrants are found in the United States and are identified by their Catholic faith. In this chapter, we examine Polish Catholic religiosity, gender and migration in relation to the parish and parochial communities in California. We use published surveys to analyze Polish religiosity and our research conducted among Polish immigrants in central California from 1994 to 2008 in cooperation with Stanford University and San Francisco State University with a grant from the Kosciuzko Foundation. Our discussion is divided into two parts: Polish religiosity and Polish religious life in the United States.

Polish Religiosity

Polish religiosity has undergone very significant changes in the course of the country's history. Initially, until the loss of independence and partitions by the neighboring empires at the end of the eighteenth century, the notion of Polish identity was much closer to the idea of today's citizen or a subject in monarchies, where it described membership in a political entity rather than national or ethnic identity (Davies 1981). However, after the partition, the notion of ethnic identity was coupled with membership in the Catholic Church and, thus, the cluster of the "Pole-Catholic" was born.

The conception of Pole-Catholic was strengthened in the second World War and its aftermath, under the Communist rule, which, associated with Soviet domination and an atheist state, gave the Catholic Church in Poland the vestige of the shelter of "Polishnesness." The shift from a multi-religious pre-partition society to post-war made Poland one of those rare states that are practically homogenous ethnically and religiously, i.e., about 95 percent of population is identified as ethnically Polish and Polish speaking, and Roman Catholic at the same time. It seems that we are dealing with a sort of national Catholic cluster as far as the Polish contemporary identity is concerned.

According to Norman Davis, "Poles . . . belong to a community which has acquired its modern sense of nationality in active opposition to the policies of the states in which they lived" (1981: 11). Viewed from this perspective, the Roman Catholic Church functioned for the last 200 hundred years not as *Ecclesia* but rather as a sect, according to Benton Johnson's classification (1963: 542; cf. 1957, 1971), in which the religious community is in opposition to the socio-political environment in which it exists. This paradoxical condition of the Roman Catholic Church in Poland has very few parallels, with Ireland, possibly, being one of them.

Another aspect of Pole-Catholic identity is a certain non-reflexive attitude toward religion. Most Poles seem to take for granted their adherence to the Catholic faith and do not try to investigate its deeper meanings or question the possible contradictions between belief and everyday practice. A religious commitment that is concentrated on belief and ritual practice dimensions (Stark and Glock 1968) and associated with the agrarian way of life is often referred to as "folk religion," which typifies Polish religiosity. It is being criticized for the relative weakness or even absence of such dimensions as knowledge of the dogmas or consequences of the faith in everyday life. Hence, in spite of religious education, formerly in Sunday schools and, since 1991 as a part of public schools' curriculum, the actual knowledge of the Church's doctrine and teachings and the Bible are quite superficial. Also, displays of faith beyond the church setting such as "saying grace" or public prayer tend to be rare.

Recent surveys conducted by the Public Opinion Research Center or CBOS (Boguszewski 2008) show that in spite of transformations in socio-economic life the image of the "Polish-Catholic" has not become a relic of the past. The Roman-Catholic faith is still an important element of Polish self-image and constitutes a part of Polish identity. Immutably, about 95 percent of the inhabitants of Poland declare their adherence to the Catholic Church, while belonging to other denominations. Religious indifference or atheism is quite seldom declared.

Declaration of faith is not the only constitutive aspect of Polish identity but also religious commitment. Based on the above cited survey report about 89 percent consider this a typical characteristic of Poles, while 25 percent believe that it also forms part of European identity. The belief that religiosity is a permanent feature of Polish identity has not changed since 1992. Interestingly enough, over 74 percent hold the opinion that the accession to the European Union (EU) has no influence on Polish religiosity.

Belief and Religious Practices

High level religious commitment finds its proof in the general declaration of faith and participation in religious practices. The last twenty years did not see a significant change in the general declaration of belief in God among Poles. In the CBOS (Boguszewski 2008) survey, almost all respondents declare their religiosity and about 10 percent consider their faith to be deep. However, the percentage of non-believers remains the same, rather insignificant range, at about 5 percent.

A characteristic feature of Polish religiosity is adherence to religious practices. Again, the level of commitment has not changed significantly in the last twenty years and still remains high. A majority of the respondents declare regular weekly church attendance; while one in five declare such participation once or twice a month. Only about 8 percent declare permanent absence from religious practices. Some fluctuations in those attendances are related to special events, such as papal pilgrimages, for instance. Nevertheless, the level of commitment seems to be steady over time. There is no indication of any tendency of decline even among young people, between eighteen and twenty-four years old, and the urban population.

CBOS confirms the high attachment of Polish population to religious ceremonies related to the rites of passage—birth, marriage, and death. Almost nine in ten Poles believe that funerals, baptisms, and weddings are of great importance. The participation in those rites of passage has declined in the last twenty years only by a small margin. Another dimension of religious fervor is found in devotional practices, such as private prayer and Bible reading. In the CBOS survey very few respondents do not pray at all, while every second person declares some form of prayer practice.

A factor indicating strong ties of Poles with the institutional Catholic Church is the strong attachment to the parish, the intensity of which does not change over time. Over 80 percent of those polled by CBOS consider themselves members of the parish in which they live. About 45 percent show very strong attachment to it. Of the 18 percent who do not declare such ties over one fourth identify with a parish away from their home. Moreover, every fourth person not participating in religious practices declares attachment to their parish.

In the same vein, the Church as a social institution enjoyed high levels of social confidence during the Communist rule with over 80 percent. The Church was the paramount authority compared to other state or public institutions at that time. After 1989, as a result of the change in its official position within the country, the Church's popularity declined. The lowest level was recorded in 1993 when only 38 percent of the respondents found it trustworthy. However, positive opinion of the Church has steadily been going up since then and, according to some recent studies, it might be as high as 74 percent today.

As far as subjective assessment of religiosity is concerned, 69 percent of Poles surveyed in 2006 responded that they are religious, while one in six declared high levels of religiosity. Only 17 percent viewed themselves as religiously indifferent and 4 percent declared a total lack of religiosity. The shift here is into the more decisive self-evaluation with the decline in the group of religiously indifferent (from 25 to 17 percent). Although in this survey it was clearly stated that participation in religious practices was not a decisive measure, most clearly considered this factor as the most significant. Thus, religiosity for the Poles is most strongly correlated with the participation in religious rituals and practices.[1]

The Role of Religion in Life

The secularization hypothesis or the notion that religion tends to be less important as societies become modernized is apparently not confirmed in contemporary Poland. In spite of dramatic changes in the socio-economic and political spheres, levels of religiosity remain high. Using the same CBOS survey, about a third of the respondents believe that religion in the world is growing while another third believe that it is declining.[2] Therefore, it can be surmised that religion in personal and family life among the Poles is seen as stable or on the rise. Over 77 percent of the respondents view religion as an "important" value in their lives, and 44 percent consider it as "very important." Only 12 percent seem to be rather indifferent to its role while 4 percent has a negative opinion of religion. However, and this seems to be characteristic of Polish religiosity, when compared with other values religion loses precedence to peace and quiet, respect of other people, work and sincerity in that order.[3] In this ranking, religion is considered important by slightly over one fourth of the respondents (28 percent) Traditionally in Poland, the highest value is attached to two aspects of life: health (80 percent) and family happiness (79 percent).[4]

In everyday language people declare their adherence to the Catholic religion but they do not seem to practice what the Church preaches. It is particularly evident in the case of the attitude toward Pope John Paul II. Poles almost unanimously declare their love for the Pope but do not follow his admonitions and teachings. That opinion is universally shared by the Poles. Only one in ten respondents objects to such a statement. There is a basic inconsistency between declarations of faith and actual behavior in life as well as acceptance of Catholic teachings. Thus, although 90 percent of Poles declare faith in God, only 74 percent believe in heaven and only 70 percent believe in life after death. About half of the Poles believe in the existence of hell or of Satan. There is also high level of belief in astrology and soothsayers, i.e., the influence of Zodiac signs on human fate.

In the area of norms and values the discrepancy between declaration of faith and actual beliefs and attitudes is even more dramatic. Only slightly more than one third of the respondents declare that there is a clear distinction between good and evil. Over half of those polled are of the opinion that there are no objective dimensions of good and evil (Boguszewski 2008). In general, it can be stated that only about one third of the population believe that there are fixed and clear moral principles and values, and the majority find them contingent and relative. As a result, there is widespread acceptance of such behavior that is obviously considered faulty or sinful in the Catholic morality. The examples do not only include premarital sex, contraception, but also divorce, cohabitation, euthanasia, or even cheating at exams or buying counterfeit goods (Boguszewski 2008).

Religion, Social and Civic Attitudes

Research shows that there is a positive correlation between religious participation and civic activity. Respondents declaring regular participation in religious practices more often vote in elections than those who are less active in their practices. Also, the commitment to religious practices correlates positively with the belief that people, acting collectively, can help solve problems of the community. There is also evidence that the civic commitment of citizens increases with their participation in religious practices to the ratio of two to one (Wciorka 2008).

Strong attachment of Poles to the ritual aspects of religious life is a proof that religiosity thus understood will remain a permanent feature of social life. On the other hand, in the doctrinal and pragmatic sense, Polish religiosity presents a different picture. The declarative and factual aspects of religious life differ significantly and it can be safely argued that the Catholic ideal of morality operates at the level of declaration and not application in life. Thus, the thesis that Poland is religiously homogenous should be modified by the perspective one adopts. Viewed from the outside and in ritual dimension it appears to be uniform and homogenous—the "Pole-Catholic" stereotype. However, viewed from inside, this religiosity becomes more differentiated. In the final analysis, religiosity in Poland, associated with high levels of church practices, is an autotelic value unrelated to the interiorization of Catholic dogmas and moral norms. Paradoxically, this declarative and performative attachment to religion seems to support the involvement of Poles in their civic and social life.

Polish Religious Life in United States

Migration is perceived as the psychological process of uprooting, acculturation, and adaptation that is developed in a dialogue between the individual, community and society (Ward 1996). The phenomenon of religion and spiritual life has been analyzed in categories of an organized institution, a faith-based community as well as an individual spiritual experience (Johnstone 2006).

Our research aims to identify strategies of acculturation and social inclusion of immigrants in a multicultural society as well as to identify the crossroads of gender and religion as factors of social integration. The study is interdisciplinary and applies both psychological and sociological approaches. We used qualitative and quantitative methods to collect data: case study and survey. The case study focusing on the processes of social inclusion employed longitudinal observation, interview and document analysis of thirty-one cases (18 males and 13 females). The survey, conducted in the states of New York and California, was concerned with problems of acculturation and included the research sample of 137 Polish immigrants (59 males and 78 females). All respondents migrated to the United States during the period of the Solidarity movement (1980-1990). They were between the ages of thirty-five and fifty, with educational backgrounds ranging from high school to university levels. Information used in this chapter was obtained from the case studies.

Parochial Community and Polish Immigrants

Polish immigrants show both high adaptability and high resistance to assimilation processes (Polzin 1973; Sandberg 1974). Their integration capacity has depended on their education and expectations toward the host country. William Thomas and Florian Znaniecki (1996) describe uneducated peasants as less able to integrate fairly well compared to the educated political refugees. Immigrants who perceive the host country as a final objective of their plight integrated better than those who saw immigration as temporary. All groups, however, displayed the same need to maintain their cultural identity.

Since the occupying powers in Poland at the end of the Second World War, after its partition, had different state religions, Roman Catholicism was an essential element of the Polish identity (Poser-Zielinski 2003). Alongside with secularization and socio-political changes in Poland the role of religion as a national identity marker began but seems to fade as it underwent privatization and began to acquire the nature of political orientation (Błeszyńska 2002). The arrival of new, mostly young, immigrants in the 1990s to the United States has brought these tendencies to the *Polonia* communities.

The weakening of religion's position as the Polish identity marker did not influence the position of the Catholic Church in the Polish diaspora. Historic conditions, specific situation of the immigrant (e.g., social isolation, the necessity to reconstruct one's life, acculturation stress) and needs of affiliation associated with the immigrant experience make parish communities the reference groups, which replace the ones that remained in the home country. Following Steven Vertovec (2001), integration in the faith-based communities stimulates religious revitalization even with those who showed low interest in religion at the home country.

Religiosity and Choices

Reconstruction of life in a new country requires immigrants to make numerous choices. One of them is their religious affiliation. Polish society is ethnically and religiously diverse. These differences, perceived as negligible in the home country, become significant after the immigrants' arrival in the United States, thus, dividing Poles according to their ethnic and religious identities. Our study shows that religious non-Catholic Poles join their own religious communities, loosening ties with Polonia while Catholics participate in the religious, cultural and social life of the Catholic parish. Most of the Catholics continue their ties to the homeland by choosing Polish Roman Catholic parishes. Much less frequently, the choices are Polish-Catholic, Mariavit or other Catholic parishes.

Changes in parish affiliation are more often initiated by women than men. Many Polish women usually emphasize the convenient location of the new parish or the objections toward the functioning of the Roman Catholic parishes (e.g., politicization or conservative approach toward women) in their decision to change parishes. Two women in our study consider their religious fundamentalism unacceptable within the Polish community. Most of the respondents have satisfied their spiritual needs within their parish or other Christian churches. In few cases, the respondents went beyond in their spiritual search to explore other religions like Buddhism. Their attempts did not result, however, in religious conversion.

A frequent phenomenon we observed was the loosening of ties with the religious community and privatization of religiosity by immigrants staying in the United States for longer than two years. It seems that this change results from individualization of spiritual experience, and suspends selective participation in religious practices of the parish. This phenomenon pertains to both men and women alike and is intensified with mobility as well as the length of stay in the United States. On the other hand, numerous non-practicing believers, as well as some atheists and agnostics, mostly women, revive their religiosity by returning to the fold of the Polish parish community. However, some respondents, mostly men, maintain a distance to matters of religion.

Choices that Polish immigrants face in America also relate to the religious doctrine they have internalized in the home country. Confrontations of individualism and human rights with the Catholic vision of the family and society, challenges of a liberal and consumer society, pluralism of ideas, diversity of spiritual life as well as weakening mechanisms of social control stimulate many Pole-Catholics to review and transform their attitudes and choices under the pressure of American values. The most questioned topics are "the right of individuals to the pursuit of happiness" and the social role of women. The specific Marian character of Roman Catholicism in Poland, stressing motherhood as a woman's task and emphasizing piety in women often could not stand the test of American ways. Many Pole-Catholic women reject the Marian model of self-sacrifice and adopt a pragmatic approach, distancing themselves from the unaccepted standards while maintaining membership in the parochial community. In some cases, however, these contradictions result in departure from the community.

The frequency and forms of religious practices present another area of choice. Transformation of religiosity among contemporary Poles combined with the dispersal of Polish settlements in California tend to develop alternative patterns of religious behaviors. One of these is the selective commitment in religious practices such as weddings, funerals, Easter and Christmas Masses. It appears that the basis for the development of an alternative pattern is the privatization of religious experience adopting the shape of personal and dialogical relation with God enhanced by reflexive thought and cherishing of religiosity in the non-ritualized forms of prayer. Male respondents expressed these attitudes with such statements as: "in order to pray I do not have to go to Church" or "I am closer to God in the mountains or on the seashore." These statements were accompanied by the decline or disappearance of participation in religious practices and life in the parochial community.

Internalization of spiritual life as a matter of individual concern also results in the dislike of majority Polish immigrants to demonstrate religiosity in an ostentatious way. Polish religious ceremonies rarely go beyond the boundaries of the parish. The respondents in our study rarely display religious symbols outside of their homes, contrary to the Polish rural practice of little shrines and crosses placed in the courtyard. Also, domestic religious practices are private and usually do not involve visitors. There is little difference in these attitudes when gender comes into consideration. The exception is in the religious holidays celebrated in the household. Preparation and organization of the activity are mostly in the hands of females continuing the traditional role of women as the spiritual, cultural, and social leader of the family while men perform auxiliary functions at best.

Identifying the choices in the lives of Pole-Catholic immigrants in the United States is a continuing discourse. Spiritual searches beyond the Polish diaspora usually open access to resources of non-Polish origin. They support the development of English language communication and intercultural competences facilitating interactions with the American community. In the case of communities with members of high social status they also contribute to immigrants' successes in the American society. They deprive, however, some immigrants from the support of their compatriots thus intensifying their feeling of disintegration and uprooting. On the other hand, associating with small, separatist or fundamentalist faith-based communities also pose a threat of social marginalization or potential manipulation.

Rejection or complete privatization of religiosity pushes respondents beyond the faith-based communities. Among people living alone, it increases the risk of isolation and emotional stress. This situation is very rare in our study though, and concern mainly males, while women choosing that strategy rely on social networks which compensate for the lack of support from faith-based communities.

The optimal strategy from the point of view of integration is inclusion and moderate participation of immigrants in the life of the Polish parochial community while keeping open and developing contacts with other groups. General preferences concerning that strategy are not gender-related. However, men more often establish friendships within their ethnic group, while women more often show tendencies to establish intergroup relationships.

Religion, Experience and Migration

Migration as a social phenomenon generates long-term physical, psychological and social stresses. Isolation and social marginalization, change of living conditions and the necessity of adaptation to a new environment as well as continuing stress and deprivation of needs result in psychological crises threatening the physical and mental health of the immigrant (Haavio-Mannila 1973). All these factors seem to hinder the process of integration of immigrants into the host society.

The basic conditions of coping with the challenges of migration are the development of competences facilitating the survival, acquisition of a desired form of life, socio-economic status as well as establishing satisfying relations with other people. Existential concerns play a more significant role in the lives of immigrants contributing to the specificity of the migration experience. Our study affirms many challenges in the lives of Polish immigrants in the United States. Their reflections on their migration and life in a new country are one of the most important dimensions in reconstructing their lives and careers. These include questions related to the meaning of migration, choices made, fear and hope, uprooting, and the ability to cope with difficulties. The confrontation of the Polish *habitus* with the American way of life possibly results in the collapse of the immigrant internal normative order that might lead to the development of anomie (Błeszyńska 2008).

Collected data show that regardless of gender, almost all respondents have experienced a normative crisis. Due to their belief system the respondents who declared to be religious could cope with problems more easily than non-believers or agnostics. The changes in lifestyle that Pole-Catholics adopt are more superficial and do not affect the core values of their worldview.

The level of immigrant's integration is determined by their ability to cope with psychological problems. These problems include acculturation difficulties, anxiety and uncertainty, pressure of the pursuit of success, and related frustration as well as the sense of disorientation, non-competence and loss of control of one's life (Berry 2006). There are also problems related to the reconstruction of identity and the erosion of self-esteem due to the loss of social status upon migration, perceived stigma and marginalization, and experience of cultural incompetence in dealing with the host society. Another set of problems relates to the difficulties in relations with other people. These include the sense of guilt toward relatives left in Poland, responsibility for the accompanying persons, loneliness and social isolation, as well as problems with integrating in the multiethnic local communities. Some negative experiences of these relationships result in ethnic prejudices. It is possible that certain prejudices result from the affirmative action policies of the United States causing among immigrants from post-communist Europe, especially among men, the sense of discrimination and social injustice compared to other groups.

The problems associated with migration are often reflected in the tendency of many Polish immigrants to withdraw from social activities in various ways: social withdrawal, psychological breakdown, psycho-somatic diseases and, sometimes, addictions. Significantly, four out of five males even declare experiencing suicidal thoughts. Efficient handling of such conditions depends, amongst many others, on the personal religiosity of the immigrant and his/her attachment to the faith-based community. Based on our study, immigrants who maintain their Catholic religiosity made reference to their belief system as a framework for reorganizing the immigration experience and providing emotional support. A female Polish immigrant describes the function of religion as: "faith protected me from despair . . . in the most difficult moment, when all things seemed to be going against me, when I was all exhausted, I felt that God was with me and helped me carry that burden . . . and that let me survive." The sense of divine proximity seems to give comfort and internal peace. Many identify belief in God as important, seen as next to relation with parents and/or mentor. It brings hope and a sense of security, develops a distance from one's experience and places this experience within the framework offered by the religious doctrine. Challenges of immigration are perceived as tasks set by God. The sense of guilt and self-accusation seems to be alleviated by pangs of conscience, repentance, and belief in forgiveness. The norm of forgiveness, coupled with the Christian imperative of love, helps to neutralize negative feelings toward oneself and others.

As declared, faith protects Polish immigrants from the collapse of their Catholic worldview upon migration, stabilizes the system of moral values, and prevents a sense of alienation. Internalized moral norms serve as the bases from which one becomes oriented and directs one's behavior in a multicultural society like America. However, Polish immigrants with no declared religion experience more problems of alienation. The sense of moral confusion, relativism or rift between the values imposed by the new society and action objectives that are accepted in society and accessible to the actor are some issues they have to deal with.

Religious norms shape the immigrants' social attitudes. The norms of human equality and positive attitudes toward others as well as Christian personalist openness to others, even promoted by John Paul II, provide a sense of protection among many respondents from racism, ethnic prejudice, and discriminatory practices. In many cases, religious views contribute to the ways in which non-Catholics are treated by Pole-Catholic immigrants. For example, a female respondent in our study states that "I could not host a person not being a Catholic." The supportive role of religion in the integration of immigrants also includes the issue of group image and status. The historically low position of Polish immigrants in the United States and the individual sense of social degradation and humiliation (e.g., Polish jokes) make it difficult for many immigrants to reconstruct a positive image of oneself and one's group (Olzak 1994). However, this positioning seems countered by their improved social status or economic success. A change in the construction of Polish identity took place after the election of a Catholic Polish pope in 1979 and the collapse of the communist system ten years later. The popularity of John Paul II as well as the recognition of the role played by Poles and the Polish Church in the fall of communism contributed to the perceived boost in self-esteem among Polish immigrants in United States. Moreover, the development of interests in Poland and Polish affairs in American society apparently limit the sense of marginalization among Polish immigrants.

Integration and the Parish Community

The parish community is one of the most important reference groups of Polish immigrants in the United States. Inclusion in parish community life is usually the first step toward integration in American society. It also meets many needs of the immigrants, providing them with a sense of belonging and security as well as social and emotional support. Its supportive role has been greatly expressed by a female respondent: "Each of us, leaving Poland, got the same advice: if you need help in America, look for a Polish church."

Ties with members of the faith-based community initiate reconstruction of immigrant's social capital, provide access to resources and means, and facilitate the immigrant's adaptation. Parochial community members provide new arrivals with assistance in the search for housing and employment and offer advice for problems appearing in the life of each immigrant. Those who are in dire conditions could obtain legal, medical and material help. The above mentioned support absorbed the shocks of the early stages of immigration. If the religious community is ethnic, it also helps to maintain the immigrants' cultural identity.

Participation in parochial community life facilitates the acquisition of social rules and the civic commitment of immigrants in American society. The specificity of the functioning of the parochial communities, such as personal commitment of members, participation in the decision making process and varied forms of activity, taking responsibility for problems in the parish, stimulates both social and political interests of Polish immigrants. It also enriches their social networks, sparks interest in volunteering and sense of common responsibility for the parish and its members. The necessity of getting involved beyond the parish and maintaining contact with other religious institutions, organizations, or American administrative institutions help Polish immigrants acquire knowledge of the ways the state and society function, thus, shaping their ability to operate in new conditions, and contribute to the social inclusion of others.

Civic attitudes are demonstrated by involvement in activities geared toward benefiting the home country. During the period of this research, there were reported activities that motivate immigrants of Polish citizenship to participate in Polish presidential and parliamentary elections, collective actions supporting Poland's accession to North Atlantic Treaty Organization, as well as legal actions aimed at correcting misinformation of Nazi concentration camps in Polish territory. These engagements introduced Poles into the American political space and developed in them the skills to use the mechanisms of civil society. Extensive commitment to the Polish parochial communities, however, did not always favor social integration among immigrants in our study. The focus on political issues affecting Poland or concentration of activities, including the professional and social limited to the Polish diaspora, usually marginalized immigrants reporting this kind of involvement (Błeszyńska 2008).

In terms of gender, the behaviors of men and women suggest a traditional differentiation of their participation in the life of parochial communities. Men tend to be more actively committed to the legal and political actions going beyond the boundaries of the parish. The social ties men create are rather weak and rarely involve interethnic relations. Women's participation, on the other hand, involve intra-group and interethnic activities concerning mostly the areas of culture, education, and preparations for festivities. There is no gender difference, however, in the tendency to limit oneself to the boundaries of the parochial community.

Catholic Church, Integration and Polish Migration

The attempts to define the role of the Catholic Church in the process of social inclusion of Polish immigrants suggest that there is a nationality-related gap between the actions undertaken at the level of the Polish parishes and the activities of the American ecclesiastical authorities. The priests and the nuns operating at the parish level have Polish origins and represent the missionary orders preparing them to work with immigrants. Their services include ministry, social work and counseling. As community members, they participate in its life and activities as well as provide support and help to members of the parochial community. Authorities of the Roman Catholic Church in the United States seem less involved in the integration of Polish immigrants. Many Polish immigrants in our study view these churches as lacking in interest in the social inclusion of immigrants. It appears that these institutions act indifferently or are even considered hostile to immigrants in their own communities. Representatives of Roman Catholic churches are, in their opinion, mainly concerned with conflicts and religious celebrations and not with the lives of immigrants.

In the course of our research two serious conflicts took place concerning property rights. These conflicts, which were eventually adjudicated in favor of Poles, unified the members of the Polish community and made them familiar with legal procedures in the United States. For the immigrants raised in Communist Poland, these were lessons in civic education that enabled them to acquire principles of law as well as establish emotional ties and trust toward the state.

Paradoxically, conflicts with the American Catholic Church authorities seem to contribute to the development of civic attitudes and participation of Polish immigrants. The duality of the church's nature as being both the hierarchical institution of the *Gesselschaft* type as well as a community, that is *Gemeinschaft*, has forced Poles to choose between obedience to the church hierarchy and the sense of subjectivity and American civic engagement. These conflicts have appeared since the early stages of the establishment of Polish ethnic enclaves in the United States (Posern-Zieliński 1982). It produced a systematic growth in the bonds, subjectivity and autonomy of community members, gradually limiting the interference of church authorities and stimulating the development of secularized institutions within the Polish diaspora. In terms of conflict with value systems, demands or mutual resistance also resulted in the defection of the individual or occasionally of the whole parish communities.

Both men and women equally participated in resolving conflicts with the Catholic Church, although there were cases of local concern. Comparison of their behavior indicated, however, some gender-related differences. Men showed a greater commitment to the formal action taking place at the public forum. Women, on the other hand, were more willing to join the preparatory work and support activities conducted behind the scenes such as mobilizing, canvassing and running errands.

Conclusion

Religion and its corresponding belief system and rituals among faith-based communities facilitate the social inclusion of Polish immigrants in the United States. While the path toward integration seems to be under the control of the immigrant, our study demonstrates these basic patterns of integration: the Polish parochial community-mediated integration, the integration through transfer to another faith-based community and, the individual integration beyond any religious communities such as privatized religiosity or rejection of religion. The support of the faith-based communities tends to be more effective and productive than the attempts at neglecting mediations of any of the three groups. Avoidance of the group mediation, particularly in cases of people with limited social competences, carries with it a threat of isolation and social exclusion.

Religion, religiosity and religious communities support the integration of immigrants in the following dimension: existential, functional, psychological, social and political. Existential dimension refers to providing meaning to the immigrant experience and normative stabilization of the worldview. Functional dimension addresses counseling, assistance in adaptation processes and organization of life in the new country. Psychological dimension includes emotional support, facilitation of the acculturation and identity transformation processes. Social dimension is instrumental in shaping positive attitudes toward other ethnic groups, social support, reconstruction of the immigrant's social capital, mediation in the relations with other groups and local social environment. Political dimension is responsible for the development of civic attitudes and engagement. Limiting one's activities to the ethnic parochial community creates a barrier in the social integration process. Our study shows that participation in church activities leading to social integration of immigrants was rather limited. Nevertheless, the priests and nuns operating within the parochial community displayed significant commitment and competences in these activities. On the other hand, institutions with hierarchical structures show a relative lack of such commitment.

Gender seems very significant in diversification of religious behavior and the forms of participation in faith-based communities. Women are often likely to engage in religious rituals or participate in social, educational or cultural activities within the community. They are more willing to build ties with representatives of other faith-based communities. Women tend to be autonomous in their decisions regarding changes in their attitudes toward religious affiliations. Men show more restraint in their religious activities. They are largely engaged in the political programs of the community or in collective action in the public arena, seldom leave the parochial community for good, and are less prone to build ties with other ethnic groups on the basis of religious beliefs.

Women are more flexible and show greater tendency to deal with problems related to acculturation than men. The gender difference may be attributed to women's greater mobility, their ability to display expressive behavior, and create social networks. Women tend to attribute protective, cathartic, and consolatory functions to religious experiences. It seems that this attribute stabilizes any disruption in women's lives more than men.

Religiosity is one of the essential factors shaping the psychological and social situation of immigrants. It is instrumental in supporting immigrants to cope with the challenges of their migration experience. Religion establishes a framework which shapes the overall meaning of their migration to another country. Commitment to religious life compensates for the alienating experience and threat to one's positive self-valuation; protects the normative structures and value systems; directs moral choices; and facilitates the integration to the new environment. Furthermore, it reduces the sense of anxiety and apprehension, making possible the immigrant's coping of adversity. The religious experience and ties with religious communities are significant in alleviating the culture shock upon migration and in facilitating social inclusion as shown by Pole-Catholics in diaspora.

Notes

1. Like other countries, levels of religiosity differ from region to region. If the frequency of participation in practices is the measure of religiosity, then it is quite differentiated territorially. Thus, the most religious are the inhabitants of the Carpathian Piedmont (84.4 percent) and Little Poland (76.5 percent). If we move from the most religious south-east westward, the least religious region is Western Pomerania with 38.6 percent, or about half of the participation level compared to Piedmont. Another factor differentiating the levels of religiosity is the size of the settlement. Highly urbanized areas show much lower levels of religiosity. In terms of gender, there is greater religiosity in women, with elderly people showing higher commitment to religion, as well as among poor people with lower levels of education. Men who reside in cities, the youth, and those with higher education and income status tend to be less religious.

2. About 40 percent of the respondents view the present status of religion as higher than it used to be, while 23 percent believe it has declined somewhat.

3. Religion in Poland ranks fifth after such values as peace and quiet (42 percent), respect of other people (42 percent), work (45 percent) or sincerity (53 percent). See Rafal Boguszewski, "Polak – na Zawsze Katolik? Polska Religijnosc w Latach 1989-2008 na Podstawie Badan, CBOS," *Wiez* 9, no. 599 (September 2008): 5-26.

4. Education (23 percent), patriotism (21 percent), friendship (17 percent), freedom of speech (17 percent) and wealth (12 percent) are valued less than religion. Other values of less significance include participation in cultural life (6 percent), adventures and experiences (6 percent), participation in socio-political life (5 percent) or success and fame (3 percent). See Boguszzewski, "Polak."

Bibliography

Berry, John W. "Stress Perspective on Acculturation." Pp. 43-58 in *The Cambridge Handbook of Acculturation Psychology*, edited by David L. Sam and John W. Berry. New York: Cambridge University Press, 2006.

Błeszyńska, Krystyna. "Nationalism and Criteria of Establishing National Identity." Pp. 211-234 in *New Directions in Cross-Cultural Psychology*, edited by Pawel Boski, Fons J. R. van de Vijer and Anna M. Chodynicka. Warsaw, PL: IP PAN, 2002.

———. "Polscy Amerykanie." In *Wspólnoty a* Migracje, edited by Jerzy Nikitorowicz. Bialystok: Trans Humana, 2008, forthcoming.

Boguszewski, Rafal. "Polak – na Zawsze Katolik? Polska Religijnosc w Latach 1989-2008 na Podstawie Badan. CBOS. " *Wiez* 9, no. 599 (September 2008): 5-26.

Davies, Norman. *God's Playground: A History of Poland.* Oxford: Clarendon Press, 1981.

Foley, Michael and Dean Hoge. *Religion and the New Immigrants: How Faith Communities Form Our Newest Citizens.* New York: Oxford University Press, 2007.

Haavio-Mannila, Elina. *Immigration and Mental Health.* Helsinki, SU: University of Helsinki, 1973.

Johnson, Benton. "A Critical Appraisal of the Church-Sect Typology." *American Sociological Review* 22, no. 22 (1957): 88-92.

———. "On Church and Sect." *American Sociological Review* 28, no. 28 (1963): 539-549.

———. "Church and Sect Revisited." *Journal for the Scientific Study of Religion* 10, no. 10 (1971): 124-137.

Johnstone, Ronald L. *Religion in Society: A Sociology of Religion.* New Jersey: Prentice Hall, 2006.

Olzak, Susan. *The Dynamics of Ethnic Competition and Conflict.* Stanford, CA: Stanford University Press, 1994.

Polzin, Teresa. *The Polish Americans: Whence and Whiter.* Pulaski, WS: Fransiscan Publishers, 1973.

Posern-Zieliński, Aleksander. *Etnicznosc a Religia.* Poznan, PL: Wydawnictwo Poznanskie, 2003.

———. *Tradycja a Etnicznosc: Przemiany Kultury Polonii Amerykanskiej.* Wroclaw, PL: Zaklad narodowy im. Ossolinskich, 1982.

Roguska, Beata. *Zmiany w Wizerunku Polaka i Europejczyka po Trzech Latach Czlonkostwa Polski w UE,* komunikat z badan CBOS. Warsaw, PL: CBOS, 2007.

Sandberg, Norman C. *Ethnic Identity and Assimilation: The Polish-American Community. Case of Metropolitan Los Angeles.* New York: Praeger, 1974.

Stark, Rodney and William Sims Bainbridge. *The Future of Religion.* Berkeley: University of California Press, 1985.

Stark, Rodney and Charles Y. Glock. *American Piety.* Berkeley: University of California Press, 1968.

Thomas, William and Florian Znaniecki. *The Polish Peasant in Europe and America.* Chicago, IL: University of Illinois Press, 1996.

Vertovec, Steven. *The Hindu Diaspora: Comparative Patterns.* New York: Routledge, 2001.

Ward, Colleen. "Acculturation." Pp. 124-147 in *Handbook of Intercultural Training*, edited by Dan Landis and Rabi Bhagat. Thousand Oaks, California: Sage, 1996.

Wciorka, Bogna. *Spoleczenstwo Obywatelskie 1998-2008*. Warsaw: CBOS, 2008.

Chapter Twelve
Acculturation of Kenyan Immigrants in the United States: Religious Service Attendance and Transnational Ties
Lilian Odera

The United States continues to be a favored destination of many foreign nationals entering as temporary workers, refugees, students and permanent residents. Nationally, the number rose from 11.1 percent of the United States population in 2000 to 12.4 percent in 2005 (United States Census Bureau 2005). These rising numbers demonstrate a continuing trend toward diversity in immigrant populations in the United States with immigration patterns challenging the definition and categorization of minority groups.

The last three decades of the twentieth century witnessed significant immigration of Africans to North America (United States Census Bureau, 2004, 2005), a trend that has often been due to political crises, civil wars, ethnic conflict, and economic deterioration (Arthur 2000). By the year 2000 Africans comprised more than 5 percent of the documented immigrants in the United States, up from less than 2 percent in 1991 (Arthur 2000). Hugo Kamya (1997) contends that limited attention has been given to the study of immigrants of African descent, such as continental Africans and Caribbean-born Blacks in the United States. Perhaps this dearth of a research focus on this population has been due to a lack of understanding of the diversity that exists among foreign-born Black immigrants. Immigrants of African descent do not form a homogeneous group. On the contrary, they have great cultural, historical, religious, and linguistic diversity. Kenya is a multilingual and multiethnic nation consisting of forty-two ethnic groups stratified in society (Ogot 1979).

The culture-specific orientation of immigrants of African descent needs to be addressed with respect to their specific country of origin (Dyal and Dyal 1981). Studies in this area have focused mainly on the cultural adjustment of South Africans (Segel 1996), Ethiopians (Kibour 2001), and Moroccans (Ourasse and Vijver 2004). However, none has so far focused on immigrants from East African nations like Kenya. This study seeks to expand existing research on cultural adjustment by investigating the effects of various demographic factors, religious service attendance, and transnationalism on the cultural adjustment of Kenyan immigrants.

Many Kenyans migrate to the United States as students, workers, visitors, and permanent residents. Their migration is very selective, and a significant number of these immigrants are highly educated. For example, Frederic Docquier and Abdeslam Marfouk (2006) note that in 2000, about 82 percent of Kenyan immigrants in the United States had post-secondary education compared to only 38 percent of Kenyan immigrants in fifteen countries of the European Union. The 1990 *Immigration Act* and the 1998 *American Competitiveness and Work Force Improvement Act* emphasize the selection of highly skilled workers (Docquier and Marfouk 2006). Consequently, in 2004, Kenyans accounted for 704 out of the total 1,541 temporary workers granted with H1-B visas (United States Office of Immigration Statistics, USOIS 2006). Kenyans also enter the United States on visitors' visas which allow multiple entries for limited periods (USOIS 2004). Other Kenyans arrive in the United States as legal permanent residents (LPR) or "green card" recipients. In 2007, a total of 7,030 Kenyans were granted legal permanent residence in the United States which comprised 3,429 males and 3,601 females. In the same year 1,396 Kenyans consisting of 679 males and 717 females were granted United States citizenship (USOIS 2007).

Acculturation Model

Acculturation is the process of psychological and behavioral change that individuals and groups undergo as a consequence of long-term contact with another culture (Berry 1997; Berry and Sam 1997). John Berry (1997) developed a model that explains this process of living within two different cultures. This model consists of four types of acculturation orientations: assimilation, separation, integration and marginalization. *Assimilation* is the orientation in which the dominant/host culture is favored while the traditional culture diminishes. In *separation* the individual favors, and maintains the traditional culture and the dominant/host culture is diminished. *Integration* is characterized by maintenance of the host and traditional cultures. Finally, *marginalization* involves diminishing both cultures, that is, the loss of the original culture without establishing ties with the new culture.

Studies focusing on immigrants show that integration is the most preferred orientation of acculturation among adults and adolescents (Berry and Sam 1997; Phinney et al. 2001). The strategies of separation and marginalization produce poor cultural and psychological adjustment in most circumstances. In a study that examines acculturation among first generation South Africans in the United States, Martin Segel (1996) reveals that participants are well integrated to American culture, as most respondents endorsed items indicating integration, with a few endorsing assimilation. None of the respondents endorsed items that placed them in marginalization or separation categories of acculturation.

Similar to Berry's model of acculturation (1997), the framework for this study posits that demographic factors and transnationalism influence the acculturation process. However, rather than focusing on the four distinct types of acculturation proposed by Berry (1997), this study examines the adaptation of American cultural values, retention of Kenyan values, and an adaptation that involves the choice of both cultures. Additionally, gender difference in religious service attendance is examined.

A total of 209 self-identified first generation Kenyan immigrants in the United States participated in this study. They included 94 males and 114 females ranging in ages between eighteen and fifty-five. Other demographics are detailed in Table 12.1. *The Abbreviated Multidimensional Acculturation Scale* (Zea et al. 2003) is a measure of acculturation that was modified to measure cultural identity, language competence, and cultural competence among Kenyans in the United States. This measure consists of forty-two items rated on a four-point Likert-type scale. Composite American, Kenyan, and bicultural acculturation scores were obtained from the measure. *The Transnationalism Scale* (adapted from Murphy and Mahalingham 2004), which was originally created for Caribbean immigrants, was modified to assess Kenyan immigrants' transnational activities. The twenty-one items in the scale includes activities grouped into four different domains: family, cultural, economic, and political ties. Religious service attendance was assessed using a single item with the response ranging from one (*never attend*) to four (*attend very often*). Data analyses included regressions, which were conducted to examine impact of predictor variables on acculturation, and independent sample t-tests, which were conducted to assess gender differences in acculturation, religious service attendance, and other variables.

Demographics and Acculturation

Acculturation is impacted by demographic factors such as age, gender, immigration status, and length of stay in the host country. Among first generation immigrants, older individuals are less likely to adapt to new cultural values while younger immigrants are more culturally flexible and easily adaptable to the culture of the host country. The choice to adapt new or retain old cultural values is also determined by gender. Women tend to acculturate slower than men because of greater conservatism within traditional roles (Ghuman 2000). However, this may only be true for immigrants originating from cultures where women have conservative traditional roles. That is, women in cultures where there is a strict adherence to traditional female roles such as child-rearing responsibilities and household maintenance may not readily acculturate.

With the increase of exposure to Western cultures through media and technology, fewer Kenyan women who migrate to Western nations such as the United States adhere to traditional gender roles. For example, as they join the workforce and seek employment outside the home, Kenyan women may be less likely to adhere to traditional gender roles. It is important to note that, although

Table 12.1 Study Sample Characteristics

Variable	Frequency (n)	Percentage (%)
Age		
18-25	41	19.7
26-35	122	58.6
36-45	30	14.4
46-55	15	7.3
Age of Migration to the USA		
11-15	10	4.8
16-20	63	30.2
21-25	76	36.5
26-30	43	20.6
31-35	10	4.8
Above 35	6	2.9
Length of Stay in the USA		
Less than 1 year	6	2.9
1-5 years	60	28.8
6-10 years	89	42.8
More than 10 years	53	25.5
Socioeconomic Status		
Do not have income	16	7.7
Less than $15,000	16	7.7
$15,001 - $25,000	36	17.2
$25,001 - $50,000	70	33.5
$50,001 - $75,000	43	20.6
$75,001 - $100,000	8	3.8
$100,001 and above	9	4.3
Missing data	11	5.2
Education Level		
High school/GED	15	7.2
Associates degree/trade school	40	19.1
Bachelor's degree	68	32.5
Master's degree	70	33.5
Doctoral/Professional degree	14	6.7
Missing data	2	1.0

Continued on next page

Table 12.1 — Continued

Immigration Status

Green Card/Legal Permanent Resident (LPR)	71	34.0
Student visa	63	30.1
Work visa	30	14.4
Naturalized USA citizen	25	12.0
Other visas (diplomatic, dependent, visitors)	13	6.2
Missing data	7	3.3

Kenyan women culturally ascribe to the role of primary caregivers, traditionally there is a higher expectation on men to initiate an adherence to such roles and maintenance of cultural values. The basis for this difference in cultural expectation is the idea that women are expected to adopt and adhere to the culture of their spouses while the women that Kenyan men marry are expected to adopt Kenyan cultural values. Therefore, it is often expected that despite acculturating to American culture, Kenyan men will be more likely to retain Kenyan cultural values compared to women.

Religious Service Attendance

Religion is an important factor that many immigrants employ while adjusting to a new society. Religious service attendance, for instance, may enhance expansion and maintenance of social support networks (Pargament 1997). Based on national survey data, frequent Christian churchgoers report larger social networks, more frequent social interactions outside the church, and more positive perceptions of their social network members than persons who attend religious services less often (Bradley 1995).

The role of religious service attendance during the acculturation process has particular relevance for Kenyan immigrant research given the emphasis on religiosity in African societies (Mbiti 1991). National surveys have shown that 66 percent of Kenyans embrace Christianity, 26 percent embrace indigenous beliefs, 7 percent embrace Islam, and 1 percent embraces other types of faith (Republic of Kenya 2002). The two main religions practiced in Kenya are Christianity and Islam, but apart from the traditional Christian dichotomy of Catholic and Protestant, there are many sects emerging (Kiima et al. 2004). Involvement in religious activities is a salient strategy for adjustment among Kenyans as evidenced by utilization of religiosity to cope following the 1998 United States embassy bombing in Nairobi (Njenga et al. 2004). Religiosity is also related to the overall cultural adjustment of African students in the United States (Pruitt 1978).

The consistency of religious service attendance provides an anchor to other aspects of lives of many immigrants. Charles Hirschman (2004) posits that religious values provide support for traditional beliefs and patterns such as intergenerational obligations, gender hierarchy, and customary familial practices. The combination of culturally attuned spiritual comfort and material assistance heightens the attraction of membership and participation in churches (Hirschman 2004). Churches and religious organizations often play an important role in the creation of community as a source of social and economic assistance. There is an increasing number of ethnic churches and Kenyan congregations across the United States. Peggy Levitt (2003) argues that immigrants, such as those from Kenyan, may be drawn to the fellowship of ethnic churches where primary relationships among congregants are reinforced with traditional values such as cultural dialects, ethnic foods, and customs.

Transnationalism

Transnationalism is defined as the maintenance of occupations or activities that require social contacts over time, across national borders and/or across cultures (Portes, Guarnizo and Landolt 1999). This is important following migration, especially since, upon arrival and eventual adjustment to a new country, familiar social ties are lost (Vega et al. 1991). Transnationalism provides an avenue for immigrants to maintain familiar connections to their home countries such as religious practices and ties to religious organizations that could be important agents in their adjustment. Prior to migration, Kenyans normally turn to their extended family and the larger community for social interaction and spiritual nurturance. However, following migration involvement in churches and religious organizations may be essential in creating a community that would serve as a major source of social interaction and spiritual growth.

Transnational religious ties among immigrants include retention of customary religious practices as they migrate to the United States. But these activities take on new meanings after migration. Familiar religious rituals, such as hearing prayers in one's native tongue, provide an emotional connection for Kenyan immigrants living away from their home country, especially when shared with others. The feelings of loss associated with being away from home are accentuated from time to time when individuals are faced with adversity, such as the death of a family member or some other tragedy (Hirschman 2004). During such difficult times traditional religious practices are performed. Examples of religious practices that are still upheld among Kenyan immigrants in the United States are the daily community gatherings called *maombolezis* following the death of a family member, and overnight prayer gatherings called *keshas*.

Familial ties are one of the most salient aspects of transnationalism among Kenyan immigrants because of their Afrocentric roots and communal worldview that is characterized by maintenance of social networks. Transnational ties relate to serial migration, as in the case of Caribbean immigrants (Foner 1998). This often occurs when family members leave the family to obtain employment and "pave the way" for those left behind (Crawford-Brown and Rattray 2001).

Monica Nyamwange (2005), in her study on students and workers, shows the strong ties that remain between Kenyan immigrants in the United States and their families in Kenya through informal networks. These networks include women's groups, village associations, and extended family networks that engage in activities such as building orphanages, churches, and health centers, among other projects. Kenyans foster transnational ties through personal communication and regular remittances. Remittances not only include sending money to family but also to support religious organizations, missionary work, or other causes that Kenyans abroad adopt.

Transnationalism also affects the level and type of acculturation among Kenyan immigrants by enabling them to maintain cultural values and knowledge of the country of origin. Because of participation in both the host and traditional cultures, Kenyan immigrants develop a bicultural style of acculturation where they live and function daily within the host culture and maintain transnational activities in the country of origin. Traditional religious practices are fostered by continual contact with religious organizations that may involve exchanges such as invitation of religious leaders from Kenya to speak to those abroad or missionary trips by Kenyans in the United States to their home country.

Results and Discussion

Independent sample t-tests were conducted to assess gender differences in study variables. Results showed that male participants reported significantly higher levels of American (t [194] = 2.78, $p < .01$), Kenyan (t [194] = 2.34, $p < .05$), and bicultural acculturation (t [194] = 3.67, $p < .001$). Results also revealed that Kenyan male immigrants in the United States tend to be older (t [206] = 2.57, $p < .01$), migrate at an older age (t [206] = 2.22, $p < .05$), and have higher socioeconomic status (t [196] = 2.83, $p < .01$), compared to females. On the contrary, females reported frequent attendance in religious services (t [160] = 2.06, $p < .01$), compared to males. A summary of statistics on gender differences are presented in Table 12.2.

A three-step hierarchical multiple regression analysis was utilized to assess the effects of demographic factors and transnationalism on types of acculturation. Demographic factors, length of stay, and transnationalism were entered in the first, second, and third step of the regression model respectively. Regressions for the three types of acculturation were conducted separately.

The results from the final step of the regression examining effects of various factors on American acculturation revealed that this model was significant, F (10,168) = 4.88, $p < .001$. Although transnationalism did not have a significant effect on American acculturation, length of stay in the United States ($\beta = .39$, $p < .001$) and age ($\beta = -.37$, $p < .001$) emerged as factors with significant effects. The independent variables together accounted for 19 percent of the variance in American acculturation. A summary of these regression results are presented in Table 12.3.

Table 12.2 Descriptive Statistics for Variables by Gender

Variables	Males M (SD)	Females M (SD)
Age	33.13 (8.23)**	30.42 (6.24)**
Age at Migration	24.15 (6.72)*	22.39 (4.65)*
Socioeconomic Status	3.98 (1.08)**	3.51 (1.27)**
Length of Stay in the United States	8.87 (5.71)	8.02 (4.54)
Transnationalism	2.84 (.81)	2.78 (.79)
American Acculturation	2.95 (.42)**	2.79 (.38)**
Kenyan Acculturation	3.40 (.44)*	3.24 (.44)*
Bicultural Acculturation	3.17 (.29)***	3.02 (.28)***
Religious Service Attendance	3.26 (.99)*	3.56 (.80)*

*p < .05, **p < .01, ***p < .001

Results from the final regression step examining effects of various factors on Kenyan acculturation revealed that the model was significant, $F(10, 168) = 6.23$, $p < .001$. Transnationalism ($\beta = .33$, $p < .001$), gender ($\beta = -.23$, $p < .01$), length of stay in the United States ($\beta = -.39$, $p < .001$), and all immigration statuses emerged as significant correlates of Kenyan acculturation in this final step of the regression model. The independent variables together accounted for 24 percent of the variance in Kenyan acculturation in this sample. Table 12.4 presents a summary of these regression results.

Results from the final regression step examining effects of various factors on bicultural acculturation revealed that the model was significant, $F(10, 168) = 3.57$, $p < .001$. Transnationalism ($\beta = .29$, $p < .001$), gender ($\beta = -.25$, $p < .01$) and all immigration categories emerged as significant correlates of bicultural acculturation. The independent variables together accounted for 14 percent of the variance in bicultural acculturation in this sample. A summary of regression results are presented in Table 12.5.

This study aims to expand existing research on acculturation by investigating the effects of various demographic factors, religious service attendance, and transnationalism on acculturation among Kenyan immigrants. Overall findings reveal that all three types of acculturation are impacted by transnationalism and demographic variables while attendance in religious services differ by gender.

Gender and Religious Service Attendance

Kenyan women in this study frequently attend religious services compared to their male counterparts. Evidences for gender differences in religiosity are found in other studies that have shown religiosity and religious activities tend to be more prominent among women than men (Jagers, Boykin and Smith 1994;

Table 12.3 Hierarchical Regression Model Examining the Effects of Independent Variables on American Acculturation

Variables	Demographic Factors Step 1 β	Length of Stay in the USA Step 2 β	Transnationalism Step 3 β
Age	-.15[+]	-.35***	-.37***
Socioeconomic Status	.15[+]	.08	.07
Gender (female vs. male)	-.08	-.12	-.12
INS Status (LPR vs. other)	.64*	.56[+]	.54[+]
INS Status (student vs. other)	.44	.42	.39
INS Status (work vs. other)	.24	.25	.23
INS Status (visitor vs. other)	.21	.20	.19
INS Status (citizen vs. other)	.57*	.44*	.42[+]
Length of Stay in the USA		.39***	.39***
Transnationalism			.05
R^2	.16***	.22***	.23***
Adjusted R^2	.12***	.18***	.19***
F-Statistic	4.04***	5.34***	4.88***
ΔR^2		.07***	.00
ΔF-Statistic		13.23***	.85

[+]$p < .10$, *$p < .05$, **$p < .01$, ***$p < .001$

Table 12.4 Hierarchical Regression Model Examining the Effects of Independent Variables on Kenyan Acculturation

Variables	Demographic Factors Step 1 β	Length of Stay in the USA Step 2 β	Transnationalism Step 3 β
Age	.08	.27**	.17[+]
Socioeconomic Status	-.14	-.07	-.13
Gender (female vs. male)	-.24**	-.21**	-.23**
INS Status (LPR vs. other)	.76*	.83**	.70*
INS Status (student vs. other)	.86**	.88**	.72*
INS Status (work vs. other)	.75***	.74***	.66**
INS Status (visitor vs. other)	.38*	.38*	.31*
INS Status (citizen vs. other)	.45*	.57*	.49*
Length of Stay in the USA		-.37**	-.39***
Transnationalism			.33***
R^2	.13**	.19***	.28***
Adjusted R^2	.08**	.13***	.23***
F-Statistic	3.08**	4.19***	6.23***
ΔR^2		.06**	.09***
ΔF-Statistic		11.94**	21.21***

[+]p < .10, *p < .05, **p < .01, ***p < .001

Table 12.5 Hierarchical Regression Model Examining the Effects of Independent Variables on Bicultural Acculturation

Variables	Demographic Factors Step 1 β	Length of Stay in the USA Step 2 β	Transnationalism Step 3 β
Age	-.07	-.04	-.12
Socioeconomic Status	-.01	.00	-.05
Gender (female vs. male)	-.24**	-.24**	-.25**
INS Status (LPR vs. other)	.99***	1.00***	.89***
INS Status (student vs. other)	.94***	.94***	.81*
INS Status (work vs. other)	.72**	.72**	.65**
INS Status (visitor vs. other)	.42**	.42*	.36*
INS Status (citizen vs. other)	.71**	.72*	.65**
Length of Stay in the USA		-.02	-.04
Transnationalism			.29***
R^2	.11*	.11*	.18***
Adjusted R^2	.07*	.06*	.14***
F-Statistic	2.62*	2.31*	3.57***
ΔR^2		.00	.07***
ΔF-Statistic		.03	13.27***

*p < .05, **p < .01, ***p < .001

Taylor, Mattis and Chatters 1999). Previous studies of African Americans demonstrate that women attend church more frequently, and participate in church-related activities more than men (Chatters, Levin and Taylor 1992; Jagers, Boykin and Smith 1994). It has been suggested that women often have less access to secular resources and power in American culture. For this reason religious practices such as service attendance represent an alternative resource that is easily accessible (Pargament 1997). Perhaps as Kenyan women continue to live in the United States, the awareness of their limited access to secular power leads to frequent attendance in religious services.

The sample group of Kenyan immigrants maintains transnational ties with their home country. Contact with cultural aspects of the home country provides access to familiar religious practices such as prayer in native languages. Additionally, transnational ties involve connections to religious organizations in the country of origin that may encourage involvement in religious services. Levitt (2003) argues that religiosity is universal and, therefore, transnational. This characteristic of religious service attendance may, therefore, not necessarily require immigrants to develop new religious faith and allegiance upon migrating to a new country, but maintain native languages and styles of practicing their faith.

Transnationalism and Acculturation

A positive association emerges between transnationalism and both Kenyan and bicultural acculturation styles. This implies that as Kenyan immigrants engage in transnational activities such as sending remittance and maintaining social networks in Kenya, they continue to be in contact with and retain Kenyan cultural values and norms.

Transnational immigrants often live aspects of their social, economic and political lives in at least two settings. Silvia Pedraza (2005) posits that transnational immigrants establish themselves in the host country while they continue to vote, operate businesses, and earn and send money to their countries of origin. In this regard, they develop bicultural identities and live their lives by being involved in more than one culture. Dual contact and activities in two different countries and cultures foster a bicultural style of acculturation.

Kenyan immigrants engaging in transnational activities are able to maintain competence in both Kenyan and American cultures. For example, immigrants develop competence in American culture and engage in American churches in order to receive social and economic assistance. American churches have a long tradition of community service, particularly directed at those in need such as new immigrants (Hirschman 2004). These charitable works are often directed to fellow congregants and, as such, immigrants are potential recipients if they attend religious services. Immigrants may engage in American religious church services and religious organizations but maintain competence in their own culture by packaging their involvement in a familiar linguistic and cultural context. They could also be drawn to fellowships of ethnic churches where primary relationships among congregants are reinforced with traditional foods, music, language, and customs (Hirschman 2004).

Gender and Acculturation

Gender comparisons reveal that Kenyan men have higher levels of American acculturation compared to their female counterparts. Perhaps Kenyan men are obligated to adopt American cultural values and attain competence in navigating networks in the host country because of the economic expectation placed on them. Previous research has associated socioeconomic success with structural assimilation to mainstream society and has been documented among Cuban exiles in Miami. Alejandro Portes and Alex Stepick (1993) report that Cuban immigrants only assimilate structurally but not culturally, such that they have access to socioeconomic benefits in American society but preserve their cultural values by living in ethnic enclaves. Kenyan men are similarly positioned to structurally assimilate to American society and gain access to socioeconomic benefits.

Kenyan men in this study also have higher levels of Kenyan acculturation compared to women. Cultural and familial expectations placed on men in Kenyan society behoove them to maintain Kenyan cultural values. Culturally, Kenyan men are expected to pass cultural values to subsequent generations. Notably, even when length of stay is accounted for, gender still emerges as a strong positive correlate of Kenyan acculturation. This implies that, regardless of how long Kenyan men live in the United States, many still maintain strong cultural values of their home country, while women may be less likely to do so. According to Kenyan traditional cultural practices, women adopt the culture of their spouses regardless of the spouse's culture, whereas men are expected to pass on Kenyan cultural values to their spouses and children regardless of whether the spouse is from a different culture.

Gender comparisons show that Kenyan men have higher levels of bicultural acculturation compared to their female counterparts. As previously discussed, Kenyan men strive to negotiate the host culture for economic success as well as maintain a Kenyan cultural identity despite living abroad. Because of these dual responsibilities, Kenyan men are obligated to maintain Kenyan cultural values, learn and adopt American cultural values, and be competent in both cultures. On the other hand, Kenyan women do not have cultural expectations to adopt and maintain either culture.

Demographic Correlates of Acculturation

A positive association emerges between age and both American and Kenyan acculturation. In Erik Erikson's developmental theory (1980), older individuals have a fully developed cultural identity, while younger individuals have a malleable identity and may choose to adopt cultural identities other than that of their country of origin. Consequently, younger immigrants are more likely to explore American cultural styles compared to older immigrants. Often young professionals and younger immigrants seek to navigate mainstream lifestyles and seek competence in American cultural ways. Younger immigrants are often likely to be students and, as such, exposed to American college settings and, therefore, learn aspects of mainstream society that are useful in their academic interactions and eventual success (Constantine et al. 2005).

Age also contributes to the maintenance of traditional cultural values. Older Kenyan immigrants migrated as adults and therefore developed stable Kenyan cultural identities prior to migration. Notably, the average length of stay in the United States for the sample study group was eight years and the average migration age was thirty-one years, implying that most study participants migrated as adults. However, age is only a salient correlate of Kenyan acculturation when length of stay in the United States is accounted for. This implies that Kenyan cultural values become more important and valuable when Kenyan immigrants have been away from their home country for a prolonged period of time. Although over time immigrants settle in the new society and create new social ties and networks, these networks and culture may still differ from the culture of origin. For this reason, they may hold on to cultural values and practices, particularly those which are unique to their home country. This includes religious service attendance and practices that Kenyan immigrants observe prior to migrating.

In this study, length of stay in the United States is positively associated with American acculturation. This is consistent with previous studies which maintain that length of residence in the host country increases social contacts and interactions, which, in turn, lead to improved communication skills and ability to negotiate the new society (Dawson, Crano and Burgdoon 1996; Tran 1990). As Kenyan immigrants continue to live in the United States they are exposed to and acquire knowledge of American culture. There is a negative association between length of stay and Kenyan acculturation as a result of less interaction with Kenyan culture.

Kenyan immigrants retain the culture and values of their country such as competence in the Swahili language as well as knowledge and practice of cultural roles. Findings from this study show that, despite length of stay, or magnitude of transnational ties, Kenyan immigrants' cultural knowledge, identity and competence do not fluctuate. This means that Kenyans have a strong cultural identity and competence, such that changes in their environment and aspects of their lives do not affect their cultural preferences. They also demonstrate competence in American cultural values and practices. This solid bicultural acculturation may be a result of Kenyans' historical experience with European colonization. During this period Kenyans were able to simultaneously function both within their indigenous culture by engaging in traditional and religious practices while also adhering to colonial British cultural expectations. Consistent bicultural acculturation style has been found among Caribbean immigrants as well (Henke 2001).

Conclusion

This chapter presents research findings that provide important insight into the experience of Kenyan immigrants living in the United States. It demonstrates that demographic factors influence acculturation and religious service attendance in various ways. Religious service attendance is a gendered experience among Kenyan immigrants. Age and length of stay are also important factors that impact acculturation in complex ways. Immigration status appears to be a significant determinant of acculturation, implying that immigration regulations/restrictions play a role in how Kenyan immigrants interact with the American system. Transnationalism and religious service attendance—factors not frequently studied among African immigrants—emerged as important elements in the acculturation process. The effects of these variables on acculturation may be useful in broadening the scope of immigration research and underscore the need for continued research on determinants of acculturation in this population.

Bibliography

Arthur, John A. *Invisible Sojourners: African Immigrant Diaspora in the United States.* Westport, CT: Praeger, 2000.

Berry, John W. "Immigration, Acculturation and Adaptation." *Applied Psychology: An International Review* 46, no. 1 (January 1997): 5-68.

Berry, John W. and David L. Sam. "Acculturation and Adaptation." Pp. 291-326 in *Handbook of Cross-cultural Psychology 3. Social Behavior and Applications*, 2nd ed., edited by John W. Berry, Marshall S. Segall and Cigdem Kagitcibasi. Needham Heights, MA: Allyn and Bacon, 1997.

Bradley, Don E. "Religious Involvement and Social Resources: Evidence from the Americans' Changing Lives Data." *Journal for the Scientific Study of Religion* 34, no. 2 (June 1995): 259-267.

Chatters, Linda M., Jeffrey S. Levin and Robert J. Taylor. "Antecedents and Dimensions of Religious Involvement among Older Black Adults." *Journal of Gerontology: Social Sciences* 47, no. 6 (November 1992): 269-278.

Constantine, Madonna G., Gregory M. Anderson, LaVerne A. Berkel, Leon D. Caldwell and Shawn O. Utsey. "Examining the Cultural Adjustment Experiences of African International College Students: A Qualitative Analysis." *Journal of Counseling Psychology* 52, no. 1 (January 2005): 57-66.

Crawford-Brown, Claudette and Melrose J. Rattray. *Parent-child Relationships in Caribbean Families. Culturally Diverse Parent-Child and Family Relationships: A Guide for Social Workers and Other Practitioners.* New York, NY: Columbia University Press, 2001.

Dawson, Edwin J., William D. Crano and Michael Burgdoon. "Refining the Meaning and Measurement of Acculturation: Revisiting a Novel Methodology Approach." *International Journal of Intercultural Relations* 20, no.1 (1996): 97-114.

Docquier Frederic and Abdeslam Marfouk. "International Migration by Education Attainment in 1990–2000." Pp. 151-200 in *International Migration, Remittances, and the Brain Drain,* edited by Caglar Ozden and Maurice Schiff. Washington, D. C.: The World Bank, 2005.

Dyal, James A. and Ruth Y. Dyal. "Acculturation, Stress and Coping." *International Journal of Intercultural Relations* 5, no. 4 (1981): 301-328.

Erikson, Erik. *Identity and the Life Cycle.* New York: Norton and Company, 1980.

Foner, Nancy. "Immigrant Women and Work in New York City, Then and Now." Pp. 231-252 in *Mass Migration to the United States: Classical and Contemporary Periods,* edited by Pyong Gap Min. Lanham, MD: AltaMira Press, 1998.

Ghuman, Singh P.A. "Acculturation of South Asian Adolescents in Australia." *British Journal of Educational Psychology* 70, no. 3 (September 2000): 305-316.

Henke, Holger. *Patterns of Migration to the United States in the Twentieth Century: The West Indian Americans.* Westport, Connecticut, London: Greenwood Press, 2001.

Hirschman, Charles. "The Role of Religion in the Origins and Adaptations of Immigrant Groups in the United States." *The International Migration Review* 3, no. 3 (2004): 1206-1233.

Jagers, Robert J., Wade A. Boykin and Paula Smith. "A Measure of Spirituality from an Afro-Cultural Perspective." Unpublished manuscript, 1994.

Kamya, Hugo A. "African Immigrants in the United States: The Challenge for Research and Practice." *Social Work* 42, no. 2 (March 1997): 154-165.

Kibour, Yeshashwork. "Ethiopian Immigrants' Racial Identity Attitudes and Depression Symptomatology: An Exploratory Study." *Cultural Diversity and Ethnic Minority Psychology* 7, no. 1 (February 2001): 47-58.

Kiima, David M., Frank G. Njenga, Max O. Okonji and Pius A. Kigamwa. "Kenya Mental Health Country Profile." *International Review of Psychiatry* 16, no. 1-2 (February-May 2004): 48-53.

Levitt, Peggy. "You Know Abraham was Really the First Immigrant: Religion and Transnational Migration." *The International Migration Review* 37, no. 4 (2003): 847-873

Mbiti, John S. *Introduction to African Religion.* Oxford: UK. Heinemann, 1991.

Murphy, Eleanor J. and Ramaswami Mahalingham. "Transnational Ties and Mental Health of Caribbean Immigrants." *Journal of Immigrant Health* 6, no. 4 (October 2004): 167-178.

Njenga, Frank G., P. J. Nicholls, Caroline Nyamai, Pius Kigamwa and Jonathan R. T. Davidson. "Post-traumatic Stress after Terrorist Attack: Psychological Reaction Following the US Embassy Bombing in Nairobi." *Journal of Psychiatry* 185, no. 4 (October 2004): 328-333.

Nyamwange, Monica. "International Migration and the Brain Drain of Students and Workers." *National Social Science Journal* 24, no. 1 (January 2005): 97-103.

Ogot, Bethwel A. "Review: Pre-colonial Kenya." *Journal of African History* 20, no. 4 (1979): 580-588.

Ouarasse, Otmane A. and Fon J. R. van de Vijver. "Structure and Function of the Perceived Acculturation Context of Young Moroccans in the Netherlands." *International Journal of Psychology* 39, no. 3 (June 2004): 190-204.

Pargament, Kenneth I. *The Psychology of Religion and Coping: Theory, Research and Practice.* New York: Gilford Press, 1997.

Pedraza, Silvia. "Assimilation or Transnationalism? Conceptual Models of the Immigrant Experience in America." Pp. 419-429 in *Cultural Psychology of Immigrants,* edited by Ramaswami Mahalingam. Mahwah, NJ: Lawrence, Erlbaum, 2005.

Phinney, Jean S., Gabriel Horenczy, Karmela Liebkind and Paul Vedder. "Ethnic Identity, Immigration, and Well-being: An Interactional Approach." *Journal of Social Issues* 57, no. 3 (2001): 493-510.

Portes, Alejandro, Luis E. Guarnizo and Patricia Landolt. "Introduction: Pitfalls and Promise of an Emergent Research Field." *Ethnic and Racial Studies* 22, no. 2 (1999): 463-478.

Portes, Alejandro and Alex Stepick. *City on the Edge: The Transformation of Miami.* Berkeley: University of California Press, 1993.

Pruitt, John. F. "The Adaptation of African Students to American Society." *International Journal of Intercultural Relations* 2, no. 1 (1978): 90-118.

Republic of Kenya. *Economic Survey.* Nairobi: Ministry of Commerce, 2002.

Segel, Martin D. "Acculturative Stress and Depression among First Generation South African Immigrants in the United States." *Dissertation Abstracts International* 56, no. 10-B (1996): 5817.

Taylor, Robert J., Jacqueline Mattis and Linda M. Chatters. "Subjective Religiosity among African Americans: A Synthesis of Findings from Five National Samples." *Journal of Black Psychology* 25, no. 4 (November 1999): 524-543.

Tran, Thahn V. "Language Acculturation among Older Vietnamese Refugee Adults." *Gerontologist* 30, no. 1 (February 1990): 94-99.

United States Census Bureau. U.S. Department of Commerce, 2004. http://www.dhs.gov /ximgtn/statistics/publications/YrBk04TA.shtm (accessed February 8, 2007).

———. U.S. Department of Commerce, 2005. http://www.census.gov/population/www/ socdemo/foreign/index.html (accessed February 8, 2007).

United States Office of Immigration Statistics (USOIS). *Annual Flow Report* .U.S. Department of Homeland Security, 2004. http://www.dhs.gov/xlibrary/assets/statist ics/publications/IS-4496_LPRFlowReport_04vaccessible.pdf (accessed February 8, 2007).

———. *Annual Flow Report.* U.S. Department of Homeland Security, 2006. http://www .dhs.gov/xlibrary/assets/statistics/NatzProfiles/2006/COBBook109.xls (accessed February 8, 2007).

———. *Annual Flow Report.* U.S. Department of Homeland Security, 2007. http://www. dhs.gov/xlibrary/assets/statistics/publications/lpr_pe_2007 (accessed February 8, 2007).

Vega, William A., Bohdan Kolody, Ramon Valle and Judy Wei. "Social Networks, Social Support, and their Relationship to Depression among Immigrant Mexican Women." *Human Organization* 50, no. 2 (1991): 154-162.

Zea, Maria C., Kimberly Asner-Self, Dina Birman and Lydia P. Buki. "The Abbreviated Multidimensional Acculturation Scale." *Cultural Diversity and Ethnic Minority Psychology* 9, no. 2 (May 2003): 107-126.

Chapter Thirteen
Ethno-Religious Power: Yoruba Immigrant Women in the United States
Abolade Ezekiel Olagoke

The Yoruba people of southwestern Nigeria live with a highly religious worldview. Their traditional religious beliefs have five basic components: belief in God, belief in deities or divinities, belief in the reality of the spirit world, the ever-present nature of the ancestors, and practice of magical incantations and medicinal herbs. These elements did not die with the advent of Christianity or any of the universal religions. These belief systems have provided the fulcrum to a better understanding of theological, spiritual, ethical, and social dimensions of the Christian faith among the Yoruba people of Nigeria, and those who have migrated to countries of the West.

The 1965 *Immigration Act* made it much easier for non-Europeans to immigrate to the United States. For the most part, more men than women have emigrated from African countries to the West in pursuit of education and greener pastures. As more men leave their countries of origin, their wives, children or fiancées eventually join them. The "push and pull factors" of emigrating to the United States have also impacted women as they desire to further their education, seek the American dream, and professional development abroad. Some who came as wives desire to maintain family continuity and community even in a foreign land.

Older women usually come to help in taking care of their grandchildren whose parents maintain the rigorous schedules of combining education with jobs and professional development. Some came to the West as students, and eventually settled after completing their education. Others are part of the new immigrants who moved to the West as nurses, engineers, doctors, and professionals. While some might have decided on very limited years of sojourn in a foreign land, political or economic conditions in their home countries have often discouraged them from making the final decision to go back "home." In this regard, it is not unusual for women of faith, especially among the Yoruba women, to invoke traditional as well as Judeo-Christian parallels to the Jewish people when they were in exile during the time of the prophets of Israel.[1] These Yoruba women are usually divided into two opposing camps regarding their viewpoints on immigration: advocates of permanent residency, and those who maintain that "home is home" no matter how long any sojourn in a foreign land may last.

Theoretical Overview

The natural, cultural, and nurturing roles that women perform in Africa such as socio-cultural constructions of realities, religious education, identity formation, and intercultural dynamics have been examined by globalization theorists, theories of modernization, Marxists, feminists, and even the newly emerging scholars on immigrant religious communities (Ebaugh and Chafetz 2000; Olupona and Gemignani 2007; Yanagisako and Delaney 1995). This study provides both emic and etic[2] perspectives on gender and power among Yoruba immigrant women in the United States.

The resurgence of religion, especially the Christian faith in the South, that is, Asia, Latin America, and Africa, has also been explored in recent years, with most of the works dealing with the cultural, theological, or missionizing effects of migration from non-Western countries. Of particular importance is the explosion of Christian religion in Africa with mission outreaches in Western countries (Sanneh 2003). In a personal interview with Lamin Sanneh (July 21, 2008) at Calvin College, Grand Rapids, he emphasized the relevance of his earlier works (Sanneh 1996, 2003), and the importance of the mother tongue in missionary projects. Another prolific author on the changing face of Christianity, Philip Jenkins (2006, 2007), examines the role of stories and parables of Jesus in the New Testament in providing liberating effects from cultural and structural patterns of "evil" especially affecting African women. Jenkins' poignant examples are particularly drawn from experiences of women from Zimbabwe and Kenya.[3]

While aiming to understand the complex nature of gender, sex, identity, and religious relationships, considerably lacking in the above studies is the role of immigrant women in shaping and forming gender relationships in their newly adopted homes in the United States. The paucity of work on women under this category is underscored by a statement from a Yoruba woman during one of my interviews, *Kikere labere kere, ki se mimi fun adie* (a needle may be small, but that does not make it something a chicken can swallow with impunity). The import of this proverb is that one should not underestimate people, especially women, simply because they have been culturally conditioned to inferior status; they have their worth and their talents remain untapped. This chapter examines aspects of ethno-religious power and attributes of Yoruba immigrant women in the United States.

Methodology

Data for this chapter is based not only on graduate work (Olagoke 2002) among African immigrant communities in the United States and England, but also on the results of a two-year participant observation, ethno-cultural experience (I am

Yoruba myself), and intercultural dialogue among various members and groups in the African diaspora. This is spurred by a class in Sociology of Feminine Theory and Dynamics which I taught at Arapahoe Community College in the fall of 2007. The class enabled me to look more closely into gender and sexual stratification as I knew it in Nigeria, and as it plays out among the African immigrant churches, students, groups and organizations that I have been associated with over the last twenty years. This chapter, thus, envisions a cross-cultural comparative perspective in the intersection of ethnicity, religion, and power among the Yoruba immigrant women in the United States.

I have visited over a dozen churches and mosques, including ethnic organizations, homes, and groups in Denver, Dallas, Chicago, and London between 2006 and 2008. These visits have enriched my theoretical and practical perspectives on the powerful and manifold roles of immigrant women in this age of globalization. Periodic visits (the latest being in March through April 2006) to some of the core cities like Ibadan, Lagos, Oyo, Abeokuta, and Ijebu Ode in Nigeria where most of these Yoruba women emigrated from have also been undertaken. I interviewed six women pastors in Denver and Dallas, including six deaconesses, two of which have a Muslim background, from December 2007 to June 2008. I also interviewed Yoruba women who are housewives, church members, and recent arrivals from Nigeria from June 2007 to August 2008. Altogether, sixty Yoruba women in the United States took part in this project. I correlated some of their responses with thirty interviews conducted in Lagos and Ibadan, Nigeria during my visits in 2006 and 2007. The project was not simply an academic exercise but one of listening to stories of a new mosaic of cultures, adaptive mechanism, and dynamic of religious exchanges in the United States that have often been understudied, under-theorized, and perhaps little understood.

Yoruba Women of Southwestern Nigeria

The Yoruba population of over thirty-five million occupies the southwestern part of Nigeria. Some of them are also scattered in many countries of West Africa. Their history is one of migration from one place to another prior to their final settlement in southwestern Nigeria. Traditions had it that the Yoruba migrated from north-east Egypt and Saudi Arabia to their present place between the seventh and tenth centuries (Lloyd 1974). In *The History of the Yoruba*, Samuel Johnson and Obadia Johnson (1969) argue that one popular myth indicates Yoruba sprung from Lamurudu, one of the kings of Mecca. One of his offsprings was Oduduwa, the father and the founder of Yoruba people (Johnson and Johnson 1969: 3). They opine that cultural, religious and economic rivalries prodded descendants of the Yoruba to emigrate to the western part of Africa.

Whether in pre-colonial, colonial or post-colonial times, the important roles of Yoruba women cannot be overstated. Traditionally, they have occupied powerful and profound religious leadership roles in their communities. Their predecessors have been prophets, mediums, diviners, seers, medicine persons, and priestesses who also fulfilled traditional roles of motherhood, educating children, training younger women, and being the spiritual and communal bond for future generations. However, their roles in the communities are not restricted to the religious milieu alone. Simi Afonja observes that Yoruba society in general, and Yoruba women in particular, have consistently grappled with, "how and through what mechanisms women exercised control over their own lives, over issues which affected their lives, and over the lives of others" (1986: 136). In essence, Yoruba women fulfilled various roles as rulers, traditional chiefs, palace officials, leaders in women's associations, and were presumably endowed with supernatural powers that oversaw the affairs of the state and society. In dealing with traditional Yoruba political system, Bolanle Awe underscores the patrilineal aspect of Yoruba society, arguing that women's participation in the affairs of state have been marginal at best. He asserts:

> The ubiquity and energy of the Yoruba market woman, like her sisters in many parts of West Africa, have caused scholars to focus primarily on her economic role in society to the neglect of her contribution in other spheres. Thus her political participation has often been regarded as indirect and incidental to her economic interest (1977: 145).

At the crux of the debate is how a society stratifies its citizens either through ascription, class, caste, or achievement. Social stratification, in essence, implies the existence of a system of classification, and of structuring people into layers in a given society. The Yoruba is not an exception. According to Arthur Tuden and Leonard Plotnicov, "stratification is essentially a structural phenomenon, only secondarily is it cultural, and then in terms of ideological supports or ways of rationalizing and comprehending the structure" (1970: 4).

In a society where there is no separation between religion and the state, the powerful and profound roles of Yoruba women imbued with such supernatural powers remained and still remains the engine that drives the stability of society. These roles may have been blurred, or effaced after conversion to Christianity or Islam, but they have not been completely erased despite androcentric or patriarchal interpretations of these universal religions and some aspects of sexual or gender stratification in the Yoruba society.

Approaches to Roles of Yoruba Women

In the current debates on globalization, theories of development, and the expanding impact of women in development locally and globally, the religious milieu in which women now find themselves is giving a new face to theoretical and policy scholars in many areas of academic discipline (Summerfield 2006). The historical context of recent immigration of Yoruba women demands a reworking of the changing gender roles and relationships of African immigrant women in general and the Yoruba women in particular. For example, despite the commendable efforts of scholars like Helen Rose Ebaugh and Janet Chafetz (2000), the analysis conveys static conception of immigrant religious communities. The work of Jacob Olupona and Regina Gemignani (2007) are rather instructive, but limited to Pentecostal churches. The Yoruba women in this study belong to other denominations, religions and traditional milieu.

Though dealing with women in diverse societies, Irene Tinker's work (1990), like other researches, has its limitations. It follows the Enlightenment paradigm that as societies become secularized, the influence of religion will fade or wane. Tinker echoes the secularization thesis that pushes aside the importance of religion as societies become more enlightened—a thesis that has faced serious obstacles in recent years (Berger 2003; Haar 1999). In fact, the resurgence and renewal of religion in many non-Western societies, delimits the scope of Tinker's work, notwithstanding the erudite nature of this scholarship from various theoretical perspectives. Looking at the dynamics of social change in many parts of the world, I argued elsewhere (Olagoke 2002) that religion matters considerably, and essentially underscores the limitations of Tinker's thesis and the enlightenment prejudice against religion.

The earlier conception of the "autonomy thesis" highlights the important roles of African women in their societies. This theory sees the positive roles of African women, not as "hewers of wood and drawers of water" but as co-equal, if not more than that in some settings in Africa. Under this paradigm, key women groups in Nigeria, especially the Yoruba and the Igbo were known to have exercised considerable amount of power especially during pre-colonial times. For example, Yoruba women like Funmilayo Ransome Kuti and Tinubu wielded considerable powers in challenging the subjection and subjugation of women in southwestern parts of Nigeria. In Nigeria today streets, squares and public parks have been named to honor these women (Johnson and Johnson 1969). I noticed the acknowledgement of the roles of these women during my travels in Ibadan and Lagos in March through April in 2006 as public squares and streets in these cities were named after them. These key studies emphasize the important roles of women in socio-religio-public realm; yet, sexual stratification in the domestic spheres is still notable in these societies. Simi Afonja points the weakness and inadequacy of the autonomy thesis and states:

> Yet the persistent low status of women in the domestic domain and the disadvantaged position of all categories of women in spite of development pointed to weakness of the autonomy thesis. Literature about African women's autonomy emphasized their role in the public domain only. It overlooked the division of labor in biological and social reproduction, and the resulting sexual stratification (1990: 199).

Religious Milieu of Yoruba Women

The religious underpinning of Yoruba women in this study do not exist in a vacuum. While most of them professed to be Christians, one cannot dissociate the effect of their traditional Yoruba religious upbringing and subsequent conversion to Christianity or Islam before coming to the United States. Three areas of their traditional belief systems that are carried over in the United States and which are germane to this project are: first, the belief in existence of the supernatural; second, the place of pithy sayings, or proverbs in the lives of these women, and third, how this background contributes to their adaptive mechanism in the many facets of life in the United States. It is safe to say that atheism or agnosticism is very foreign to the African religious landscape. It is not that agnosticism or atheism is completely lacking, as there are Africans in diaspora as well as in the continent who by choice, critique, or intellectual honesty, have seen universal religions as more of an incubus than a blessing especially in their practice.[4]

None of the women express any doubt about the existence of God or the supernatural world in shaping and intervening in human affairs. In response to a question on why one should even believe in God in the face of all the adversity in a foreign land, a woman quoted a Yoruba proverb: *A ki ba Olorun sowo ka padanu* (one does not trade with God and come up a loser). This proverb underscores the fact that any venture or anything done where God is taken into account and put first, will surely prosper. Another elderly woman stated that, *Bi alagba ba juba f'Oluwa, ona a la* (whenever an elder pays homage or obeisance to God, the path will be open and be straight). This saying emphasizes the place of the deity in human affairs, as with God nothing shall be impossible—a saying which is invariably not far-fetched from the New Testament admonition by Jesus, that with God all things are possible. The woman was quick to point to the chapter and verses in the Bible where there are parallels to this saying such as Luke 1:37, Jeremiah 9:23-24 and Jeremiah 32:37.

Conversely, another woman who had gone through very difficult times of not finding a job in United States, losing a loved one in Nigeria and not being able to attend the funeral service was so distressed with her plight, that she invoked the traditional Yoruba saying, *Orisa bi o o le gbe mi, se mi bi o ti se ba mi* (if the gods or deities will not save me or deliver me from my predicament, please leave me as you found me). The statement means that if help does not come in time, at least one should not be left worse off than the previous condition. The state of unbelief or the predicament of the woman was also given a different perspective by another woman present at the interview, when she responded, again with Yoruba proverbial saying, *Malu ti ko niru, Oluwa ni nba l'esin* (a cow that has no tail can count on God to help it drive away menacing flies). This is to encourage the distressed person to still believe in the goodness of God and to have faith that there is always some help even for those whose backs have been driven against the wall, especially the aliens, the orphans, the disinherited, and the poor. This is the kind of traditional background that reinforces their life in the United States.

While it is true that these women are nurtured by such traditional proverbs from their countries of origin, certain aspects of the place of gender and proverbs in Yoruba culture can be disturbing. According to Oyekan Owomoyela, "[t]he presence in the Yoruba proverbial corpus of derogatory (at least on the surface) statements about women deserves some comment (2005: 14).[5] This is because such sayings, like: "I have paid dowry on that woman, and she completely belongs to me" (*mo ti san owo ori obirin na, temi ni patapata*) and, human beings have not had a place to sleep, and the dog is seen snoring (*enia ko ti ri ibi sun, aja nhanrun*), denote the disadvantage in investing in women's education as they will eventually leave the home and get married. Such traditionally androcentric thinking is seriously challenged by women because these are viewed as demeaning to women, womanhood, and the accompanying maternal and cultural power that have supposedly accompanied the roles of Yoruba women before migration. It is these latent and overt powers that I will explore in relation to their experiences of migration and adaptation in a new society.

Yoruba Women and Household Economy

More than half of the women interviewed for this study are professionals (i.e., teachers and nurses) and owners of salons. In some of these families, women's incomes seem to be much higher than that of their husbands. This situation has created a deeply disturbing stress on the families. It is not unusual for professional women to make more money than their husbands in Nigeria. However, the fact that these men have been marginalized because of the impact of racism in their inability to get decent jobs in the professions, or other cultural factors preventing upward mobility, made some of them settle down for driving cabs, working in janitorial services, or at airports as baggage handlers or security personnel. The newly discovered economic power and advantage on the part of the women can be hard on the family. One husband whose wife is now a nurse, making more than thrice what he is making, emphasized the impact of his wife's income on their household when he states,

> Our women have become too Americanized now. As soon as my wife started making more money than I am, the tension began: she now shops like Americans; she commands me around like American women; she is now driving a BMW; she is now so high minded, that I do not even know the woman I married in the church in Nigeria any more. That is what America has done to our women. I am even regretting bringing her to the United States; even my father will turn on his grave if he sees what is going on. I am completely emasculated.

The above scenario illustrates how transition to a new environment has positive or negative impact on the family. Even though the couple in this interview are members of the Foursquare Gospel Church in Nigeria before coming to the United States, yet the husband cannot reconcile the newly found freedom of his wife to what was culturally or even biblically expected by traditional patriarchal interpretations now undergoing a new hermeneutic in the United States. When I decided to speak to the wife, who had moved out of their house, the husband stated, "maybe you can speak some sense into her head, but she is gone too far now."

The struggle to maintain balance of expectations between what the culture requires in Nigeria, and the demands of life in the United States is filled with tensions and conflicts that sometimes lead to breakdown of relationships such as separation and divorce. From the cultural standpoint, this husband's request for me to speak to his wife was another effort to intervene in a bad relationship before it gets worse. As a researcher, I had to maintain this balance of coming from an emic or outsider perspective for the sake of my project. About a week later, I had the opportunity to speak to the wife, and obviously she had a different take on the situation as she made her point clear and succinct:

> My husband still behaves as if nothing has happened since we came
> to America. I come home and he is expecting me to be in the kitchen
> and prepare pounded yam with the usual *egusi* soup; he has no clue
> that after working over sixty hours a week, I need to be pampered
> too; I need for him once in a while to take care of the children, bathe
> them, put them in bed, prepare food once in a while, and also not
> expect too much sex from me.

The case of the estranged wife is not necessarily the plot of every Yoruba woman in United States. In the face of adversities and transition in a new environment, these women have found ways to adapt, nurture, educate, and leave a legacy for the coming generations. Their communal involvement is not limited to their church settings, but also beyond the walls of the church to other Africans irrespective of their religious background. In most of these cities, there are also other African immigrant organizations that cater to other needs that are not necessarily spiritual.

Ethno-Religious Power

It is necessary at this juncture to examine how these women exercise power, control, or influence not only in their own lives, but also in the lives of others in the communities in the United States and Nigeria, where most of them originally came from. According to Robert Dahl (1970), the concept of power or influence is defined as the relation in which actors influence or induce other actors to act, behave or do something in a way they would not have otherwise acted. Afonja delineates between the concept of power and authority when he asserts that, "influence derived from authority differs from that based on power in that it requires cultural legitimation" (1990: 199). He further argues that,

> Power is conceptualized as the ability to act effectively on persons or
> things, to make sure favorable decisions which are not formally
> recognized as part of an individual's role (1990: 199-200).

The concepts of Yoruba ethnicity, religion, power, and how they intertwine and interrelate in the complex roles played by Yoruba women are examined further in the following areas: traditional versus modern Yoruba households, power from cell groups, food preparation and cultural continuity, reproduction/formation of identity, and politics.

Traditional Versus Modern Yoruba Households

The relationships between husbands and wives among the Yoruba are ideally of reciprocal respect. While the basic structure of society does not claim to be egalitarian, there is, however, the tension between submission expected from the woman, and her autonomy as well. As a result of migration, the tensions in these relationships are further exacerbated when the husband is unable to perform expected cultural roles, and when the positive influence of extended family is lacking. Among the women in this study, it is not unusual for both parties to refer to the aphorism common in most African countries, like "for every successful man, there is a woman, and vice versa." The delicate role of the women as the "sheep rather than the goat" is usually underscored. But the situation depends on individual households: whether the husband is flexible and not too culturally demanding on the wife; whether he does not place too much cultural expectations on the wife; whether he is able to adjust to a new role that may be vastly different from what he is used to in Nigeria. Whatever the situation, it is noted that women have had to exercise wisdom to ensure the smooth running of the homes in terms of domestic duties as well as stability of familial relationships. Oftentimes, it is not unusual for them to exercise such wisdom to other extended family members.

A woman from Denver refers to the powerful role played by Oya, the wife of Sango, the Yoruba god of thunder, in ensuring that when Sango was in his fiery temper or mood, Oya's coolness, wisdom, and ability to defuse tension ensured order and stability in the home. Women, whose husbands' mood swings rather occasionally, also appeal not only to cultural norms and nuances, but also scriptures. One woman states that, "I have to just ignore my husband when he is in the 'I am the head mindset' because I convinced myself that if he maintains that he is the head, I am the neck, and the head has to pay homage to the neck as the neck is responsible for the movement of the head." For this woman, she has always accomplished something or has her way when she recognizes this role expectation and how it operates under such motto. While to some, this may appear as "giving in," traditionally, it is seen and praised as wise and worthwhile. Power in essence, is not just about conquering in the physical sense of the word, but building up, planting lives, and maintaining them through empathetic ability that is common among women and often unrecognized.

Power from Cell Groups

Cell groups among Yoruba women are comprised of small, house fellowship groups where members in a particular geographic location meet regularly to discuss issues that may not be appropriate for discussion in their respective congregations. Cell groups usually meet during the week in the evenings. Since they meet in homes, women's roles here comprise of extending hospitality, welcoming new members of the church or newcomers into the area, and providing spiritual guidance during the one or two hour meeting. I attended about eight different cell groups, and one commonality among them is the spirituality of the group and the way this is usually related to church issues, functions, and the congregation at large. Most of these churches are so-called spiritual churches. Not a few of the members belong to Foursquare Gospel Churches (Dallas and Los Angeles), Mountain of Fire Churches (Aurora, Colorado, Philadelphia and London), and the Redeemed Christian Churches (Denver, Colorado, Dallas and Texas), and others who belong to other non-denominational churches.

The concept of power reverberates throughout the cell group meeting. It is noteworthy that the Yoruba translation of power, *agbara*, not only deals with issues of physical coercion, but also transcendental powers. The power of God, power of the gospel, power of the word, power of the blood of Jesus Christ, power in the name of Jesus Christ are usually referred to as they pray for humanly impossible situations. A woman once prayed to this effect:

> The issue of our sister's visa is not something that any human power can do. It has to be done by the power of God. He alone can instruct the clerks at the Immigration and Naturalization Service to pick up our sister's file and deal with that file favorably. We can have faith that it will be done because this is the same God that raised Lazarus from the grave, the same power that set the captive free, the same power that was with Joseph in the land of Egypt. The earth is the Lord and the fullness thereof.[6]

Pervasive in this concept of power is also the belief that there is a spirit assigned not just to every human being but also to nations to determine their destiny. It is, therefore, not unusual for them to incorporate this in their prayers as they request specific favors for each member and each nation during the prayer session in the cell groups.[7] Most of these cell groups comprise of women, and it is not unusual for references to be made as well that since God is impartial, power is given not just to men, or pastors, or people of a particular ascribed status. The priesthood of all believers is underscored rather profoundly irrespective of class, race, sex, or ethnicity. Relevant scriptural verses that are appealed to in this regard are Galatians 3:28 and Acts of the Apostles 1:8. The Galatians verse is in reference to the Pauline epistle in the New Testament where Paul asserted that there is no difference between male and female, Jews and Gentiles, that all stand before God as free individuals wonderfully and uniquely created. The Lukan verse in Acts 1:8 confirms the power promised by the risen Christ to those who waited upon him in prayers and supplication for future services in different parts of the world.

Power of Yoruba Women in Food Preparation and Cultural Continuity

Whether it is a birthday celebration, wedding anniversary, cell group meeting, cultural visit and home visit, food is central to the culture of the Yoruba and hosts serve food liberally during these occasions. Ancient biblical and traditional African practices are often invoked to underline the significance of food in human interaction. While encouraging members to visit one another and be open to others from a different cultural tradition the pastors in these congregations often allude to places where Jesus met people as usually saturated with food. Biblical examples include the wedding at Cana, the visit to Peter's house, the visit to Mary and Martha, the last supper and, when Jesus resurrected, his gathering with the disciples was around a breakfast meal.

In the African tradition, especially among the Yoruba, food also takes on a very important role in gatherings—from the womb to the tomb. During birthday celebrations, marriage, business success, house warming, purchase of a new car, invitations to share in one's promotion, and even in death, parties and food consumption can last for days. In some African cultures, like the Yoruba, it would be offensive to visit somebody's house and refuse to eat what is hospitably offered. Tedros Kiros (1992) examines the traditional African approach to food in the community as an inalienable right as opposed to the modern view, which treats food as a commodity. Kiros' description below also suggests that certain aspects of traditional worldviews also have Christian underpinnings:

> There was a period in the history of Africa prior to its penetration by colonialism and by the global world economy during which African food producers circulated and consumed food among themselves. The tendency to look at food as a commodity, accessible only to those who have the means to buy food, thereby securing an everyday existence, and to look at those who fail to have the means as predestined victims of poverty famines, starvation, and malnutrition has become almost second nature in the modern age (1992: 175).

Two points need to be made here about the nature and the context of food production and cultural underpinnings behind it in the traditional African milieu. First, during the interviews, most Yoruba women expressed amazement at the abundant food supply in the United States where less than two percent of the population farm and yet there is enough food for a population of over 300 million. Respondents also recognized that, despite this country's material prosperity, food, shelter and the pursuit of happiness are hard to come by for those who are hard-pressed.

The commodification of food in the modern economies often makes these immigrants long for the "good old days" in African villages where oranges, mangoes, bananas and apples are never placed in the market for purchase. It is in this light that food becomes an essential part of fellowship for Yoruba women and other immigrants. They reminisce about the traditional landscape. I remember a gathering of the Abeokuta Grammar School Alumni in Dallas, Texas where a significant amount of African food was provided. Quite a number of Yoruba men and women who were alumni of this school in Nigeria now live in the Dallas Metro Area. I asked the host if his wife had spent an entire week preparing the food for the fifty church members and their children who came to visit in the house. He responded that women of the church join together at such times to prepare food and make sure that more than enough is provided.

When members contrast the abundance of food in the United States to famines in Ethiopia and Somalia, they often invoke moral lessons of the traditional African worldview through stories, which often look at the current political climate in many parts of the continent. For example, the collapse of the agricultural sector in Zimbabwe under President Mugabe as well as the pillage and plundering of the treasury by the elites in some of these countries are deeply regretted and critiqued. At the same time, they also do not fail to address the paradox of material poverty on one hand and spiritual poverty on the other. Most members express the view that even underdeveloped Africa can contribute to Western values, especially in areas that are not measured in terms of economic or material quantification. Kiros' statement in this regard is particularly germane and instructive:

> In the traditional African life-world technocratic backwardness and the resistance to modernization is balanced by moral richness and charity. Modernity needs to revitalize the moral richness of the pre-reflective stages of the life-world. Whereas the African peasant's resistance to science as a whole may be criticized, his moral sentiments are admirable, so admirable that they can serve as the foundation of African philosophy (1992: 175).

During gatherings when food is prepared and served, prayers are made for those who cannot afford to eat. In addition, concrete measures are undertaken to insure that jobless members are provided for, measures that are reminiscent of the traditional African milieu, especially in the villages where a significant number of poor people still live in Nigeria.

Gatherings around food create fun and fellowship and it also engenders other forms of con-associational life-world. For example, it is during these gatherings that the names of volunteers for the next meeting are announced. Secondly, it is also a time when the African concept of collective *Harambe* (traditional collective economics) is implemented. The Swahili word *Harambe* has a Yoruba equivalent *Ajo. Harambe* encourages six or eight persons in a group to contribute equally so that every month, one person in the group is given the money to start a business venture or to send home to start building a house or fulfill other family responsibilities. Each participant takes a turn in contributing and collecting at the end of the month until all participants have collected a sum of money. Members who have participated in *Harambe* say that this form of enterprise has enabled them to do concrete things that would have been impossible otherwise. This is a typical traditional African economics. Traditional African economics also encourages thrift and savings for the new immigrants in their transition process to a new society. Yoruba women take active part in this form of economics, and most of them have been able to use the proceeds as down payment on houses, sending children to colleges, and other family endeavors. Women's empowerment is demonstrated in how norms and beliefs shaped and formed in Nigeria are inculcated into the new generation of Africans born in the United States. Ebaugh and Chafetz sums up their role:

When meals are prepared communally, women often use the opportunity to relate information, discuss problems, and provide mutual support, turning meal preparation into a broader experience of shared sisterhood. To the extent that women virtually monopolize this role, they constitute a critical lynch-pin in the reproduction of ethnicity within immigrant congregations (2000: 399).

Role in the Reproduction/Formation of Identity

The respect accorded to age among Yoruba women cannot be overstated. First, older women play a critical role in inculcating Yoruba tradition and culture to the new generation: they are the repository of knowledge and wisdom. It is often believed and expressed by the current generation of educated Africans that when an old person dies in Africa, a virtual library is lost. Such is the extent of the sagacity often accorded or associated with age in traditional Yoruba culture. Not only is it traditionally unacceptable to call them by their first name, one also has to use a specific form of salutation and address while talking to them. Second, even among married women who are younger, it is considered disrespectful to call them by their first name. Addressing married women with children is often prefaced with "Mama James" —meaning the mother of James.

In further elucidation of the powerful role women play in the Yoruba diaspora community, a woman states: "women are the pillars of the home, men are just like caterpillars." The context here is that women are like pillars of the house in the manifold ways they keep the family together, whereas men through their aggressive, violent, and often disruptive behaviors are compared with the destructive machine, "caterpillars" which are used to demolish buildings and old structures. Another woman concurred with her stating, "women are gold, men are only reflections like a mirror" (*Iya ni wura, baba ni digi*). This saying basically refers to the enduring image of womanhood just as gold is an enduring metal compared with mirror, which is breakable and comparatively of diminishing value. Therefore, it places a high premium on women's role in Yoruba society. Ebaugh and Chafetz stress the role of reproduction of ethnicity and identity germane in the Yoruba context:

> Along with participating in the ethno-religious education of children, women's most ubiquitous role within their congregations is that of ethnic food provider. Whether for formal, congregation-wide social events, less formal religious meetings, or family centered but religiously oriented practices, ethnic food consumption marks the most gatherings of fellow ethnic congregational members. Along with the use of native tongue, the collective consumption of traditional foods constitute what are undoubtedly the most significant ways by which members of ethnic groups define cultural boundaries and reproduce ethnic identities (2000: 399).

Politics of Yoruba Women

Yoruba women interviewed in this study are involved in intercultural dialogue between Yoruba culture and American culture. This is more so among women whose first major of study before going into nursing or other profession were in the areas of humanities or the social sciences in colleges and universities. Some of them obtained degrees in sociology, political science, or economics back in Nigeria and are aware of women's struggles against oppression or are familiar with women's movement in other parts of the world. As one woman from Denver states:

> Oppression is oppression, whether it is on the basis of race, gender, sex, color, or national origin. In Africa, we are socialized not to question aspects of our oppression as women to some extent, but we live in a culture here where even children have the right to question their parents. It is part of learning, to be able to question any form of oppression.

The above attitude and worldview, while not expressly shared by the large majority of Yoruba women, is common among younger generations of women especially those in their early twenties and thirties. In this age bracket, it is not unusual for them to be vociferous in critiquing typical Yoruba sayings, like "my husband is my head, no matter what; the one who paid my dowry is the owner of my life; the wife who respects her husband will be respected by the community." For such women, personal fulfillment, and earning respect usually take precedence over ascribed attributes of age, traditional social class, sex, or the fact of just being a husband. They will even go further to critique the concept of wife's submission to husbands preached in some churches, and argue that respect and submission should not be a one way process but rather reciprocal.

While in Denver during the 2008 Presidential Campaign, I had a few discussions on the current political landscape, especially in regards to Hillary Clinton and Barrack Obama. While a good number identified with Obama because of his mixed heritage, and the fact that the father was from Kenya, East Africa, not a few wondered why it took the United States over 200 years for a woman to even aspire to the highest office in the land (at the level of Clinton), when a country in Africa like Liberia had their own woman President. Some of them drew copious examples from traditional milieu where women were not just home leaders but also community leaders especially before the colonial times. Despite having a woman President in Liberia other African nations still have a long way to go. Women holding important and powerful positions, however, seem to be the wave of the future. This means then that Africa in general and Yoruba people in particular should not lag behind in the education and progressive attitude toward uplifting the status of women. One of the women suggests:

> Maybe this is the time for women to lead, afterward men have been leading the world for thousands of years, and they have given us

nothing but wars, poverty, oppression, racism, sexism, and inhumanity to each other. I am sure when a woman leads, there should be a difference as women are seldom prone to shoot first and ask questions later. Women bring good attributes that if utilized will be good for the world.

Concluding Postscript—The Future

The obstacles that women have to surmount are seemingly prodigious, and this is ably stated in the women's conference of the Migration Policy Institute and the Woodrow Wilson International Center for Scholars in 2002:

> Many immigrant women find themselves caught up in conflicting obligations as they struggle to function simultaneously as wage workers, wives, and daughters while negotiating patriarchy and gendered hierarchy in their new homeland . . . Lack of connections to social support networks and institutions in the mainstream society (Zhou 2002: 32).[8]

To illustrate, just three days before the conclusion of this chapter, a Yoruba family whose house I had visited over half a dozen times called to update me on the progress of their daughter who is twenty years old and was recently admitted into the school of pharmacy. Like in many other instances of celebrations where there is an important occasion, this was important enough for the family to invite neighbors, other Africans and Yoruba people to rejoice with the family. On arrival at the house, what I discovered was almost tragi-comic. The woman of the house, an elderly Yoruba woman in her mid-fifties, indicated that if I had visited them a week ago, she would have been dead. Her story was profoundly touching:

> My brother, it is only the grace of God that I am not yet six feet under. On Monday night, the pain on my side was so intense I had to wake up my husband, and then the pain went from the side to the back. It was like a flaming fire. My husband prayed, everybody in the family prayed and nothing happened. Around four in the morning, when the pain did not subside, my husband had to rush me to the nearest hospital. They gave me some medication and I came home yet, the pain got worse. I called my place of work and let them know that I could not make it for work that day. Later in the day, my husband had to rush me to the hospital again, in fact to the emergency room. It was another time for more prescriptions. Finally when we got home, I told my husband, this is beyond Western medical care, so we called Nigeria, and the brethren there started intensive intercession. Still nothing happened. That was when I decided to call all my three children to let them know that the time had come for me to go home, to the place of the ancestors, and also to meet with Jesus. My husband dissuaded me, and said all will be well. He had to rush me to the hospital the third time where finally they had to conduct an

X-ray to determine what was the problem. To God be the glory that I
am alive today and I am telling you this ordeal. It was terrible, but we
serve a living God and I am a living witness to the power of prayer. I
will live to see the goodness of the Lord in the land of the living.
Amen.

The woman's story is representative of the plight of most Yoruba immigrant
women, especially those without professional jobs that would enable them to
enroll in their employers' health insurance: no adequate health insurance for the
family; having to play the role of nurturer, provider, and essential contributor to
the welfare of the family, remitting money home on regular basis, and even
becoming future sponsors for members migrating from Nigeria to the United
States, thus maintaining substantial link between the family here and those
across the Atlantic. Current political debates on the issue of health insurance,
outsourcing, women's plight, immigration policies, sexism, and racism, all strike
at the core of how the government can ease some of the problems associated
with health and physical well being of not just foreigners but U.S. citizens as
well.

The above quotation also reflects the holistic roles of women in a foreign
land. Their roles are not just spiritual catering for the souls of others, but also
catering to the body and emotions. I observed in my interaction and discussions
with them during the meetings in their churches and homes, that when any of
these immigrants are sick, much emphasis is placed on the spiritual dimension
of sickness, therefore, prayers are offered for the sick members. Even in cases
where a couple of students in Denver were afflicted with serious depression and
stress, these women were quick to go beyond psychological diagnosis to a larger
Yoruba worldview of addressing the issue from not just one perspective, but
from a rather holistic perspective. This grid on life is integral to most African
worldviews where there is no dichotomy between the secular and the sacred in
daily activities. The woman was quick to enjoin me to underscore the fact that
"Our Christianity here is not a cerebral Christianity that tends to separate the
spheres of life, but one that includes and incorporates the whole person." I could
not but affirm that what she said was reminiscent of the roles and communal
responsibilities of Yoruba women diviners in Nigeria, not just in pre-colonial
times but even today. It is just in a new garb, with a new twist, and religious
language in a new world.

Notes

1. Two major prophets who were also exilic prophets of Israel (Ezekiel and
Jeremiah), enjoined the scattered Jewish community not to think of going back to their
land as a matter of urgency; the prophet encouraged those in exile to plant crops, build
houses, and multiply as their sojourn in Babylon and other cultures was not going to be a
temporary one. The Yoruba women parallel was first illustrated by a Yoruba proverb:
Oni Mo nlo, ola Mo nlo, ti ko je ki alejo gbin awusa. This is transliterated as: "Today, I
am leaving; tomorrow I am leaving, which keeps the sojourner from planting

awusa."*Awusa* is usually translated in English as "walnut" which takes years to mature and to bear fruit. A counterpoint to the permanent settlement paradigm is usually given by older women who would constantly reiterate using the analogy of the Yoruba proverb, *ajo ko le dun ki odidere ma rele, ile ni eiye agbe nke* (trip should not be so palatable that we should not aspire to return to our native land, just as return to the source is the constant desire of the bird named *odidere*). See Oyekan Owomoyela, *Yoruba Proverbs* (Lincoln: University of Nebraska Press, 2005).

2. Emic and etic perspectives stem from cultural anthropological understanding of culture from both insider's or native's point of view (emic) as well as the external factors (etic) such as economic or ecological aspects including those that the researcher may also interrogate, if s/he is an outsider.

3. There are significant parallels between women from Kenya and Zimbabwe and the Yoruba women addressed in this paper. It is interesting to note that some of the stories and examples given by Jenkins are also reminiscent of the those expressed by Yoruba women in this paper, i.e., the story of the raising of Lazarus in John 11; the woman with the issue of blood, and the story of Deborah, and the loosening of the donkey tied to a pole on the instruction of Jesus. Furthermore, there are also significant parallels with the biblical understanding and interpretation between women from Eastern/Southern Africa and Yoruba women. See Philip Jenkins, *The New Faces of Christianity* (Oxford: Oxford University Press, 2006).

4. Two prominent Africans, V.Y. Mudimbe of Congo, and Wole Soyinka of Nigeria have expressed their agnostic stances on issues of religion. Their criticism of Christianity, colonialism, and commerce (the three Cs), have had a profound effect on African scholars in the continent and in the diaspora. See the works of V. Y. Mudimbe, *The Invention of Africa* (Bloomington: Indiana University Press, 1988) and *Tales of Faith* (London: Athlone Press, 1997).

5. See Owomoyela, *Yoruba Proverbs*, 14. Certain aspects of cultural respect for women seem to be contradicted by some of the celebrations in Yorubaland (especially Oke 'Badan festival) that tend to be irreverent or disrespectful in their disdainful references to women or the female genitalia. The context of these celebrations, which is usually once a year, however, should not negate other expressive and respectful proverbs that literally venerate women or womanhood among the Yoruba. Examples include: *Iya ni wura baba ni digi* (Motherhood is golden; the father is just like a mirror, a mere reflection). Owomoyela underscores this importance and reverence accorded to womanhood when he further states that "she is the only pathway through which people come into existence, and whatever a man's contribution to the process, it cannot compare in importance or in the awesome psychic implications to the truth that every human being begins incarnation as an anatomical part of the woman."

6. "The earth is the Lord and the fullness thereof" is a scriptural reference to Psalm 24:1, echoing the fact that since God is the Lord of creation, He is not limited in what He can do in any part of the world.

7. See a detailed discussion of cell groups in African churches in Abolade Ezekiel Olagoke, "Pan Africanism and the New Diaspora: African Christians in the United States." Unpublished PhD dissertation, Iliff School of Theology, University of Denver, 2002.

8. This is part of the conference proceedings. See Philippa Strum and Danielle Tarantolo, eds., "Women Immigrants in the United States," Woodrow Wilson International Center for Scholars and the Migration Policy Institute, September 9, 2002.

234   *Olagoke*

Bibliography

Afonja, Simi. "Women, Power and Authority in Pre-Colonial Yoruba Society." Pp. 136-
    157 in *Visibility and Power: Essays on Women in Society and Development*, edited
    by Leela Dube, Eleanor Leacock and Shirley Ardener. New York: Oxford
    University Press,1986.
———. "Changing Patterns of Gender Stratification in West Africa." Pp. 198-209 in
    Persistent Inequalities: Women and World Development, edited by Irene Tinker.
    New York: Oxford University Press, 1990.
Awe, Bolanle. "The Iyolabe in the Traditional Yoruba System." Pp. 145-148 in *Sexual
    Stratification: A Cross-Cultural View*, edited by Alice Schlegel. New York:
    Columbia University Press, 1977.
Berger, Peter. *Questions of Faith: A Skeptical Affirmation of Christianity*. Oxford:
    Blackwell Publishing Company, 2003.
———. *The Desecularization of the World: Resurgent Religion and World Politics*.
    Grand Rapids, MI: W.B. Eerdmans Publishing Company, 1999.
Dahl, Robert. *Modern Political Analysis*. New Jersey: Prentice-Hall, 1970.
Ebaugh, Helen Rose F. and Janet S. Chafetz. *Religion and the New Immigrants:
    Continuities and Adaptations in Immigrant Congregations*. Walnut Creek, CA:
    AltaMira Press, 2000.
Haar, Gerrie ter. *Halfway to Paradise: African Christians in Europe*. Cardiff: Academic
    Press, 1998.
Jenkins, Philip. *The New Faces of Christianity: Believing the Bible in the Global South*.
    New York: Oxford University Press, 2006.
———. *The Next Christendom: The Coming of Global Christianity*. New York: Oxford
    University Press, 2007.
Johnson, Samuel and Obadia Johnson. *The History of the Yorubas: From the Earliest
    Times to the Beginning of the British Protectorate, 1st ed.* London: Routledge & K.
    Paul, 1969.
Kiros, Tedros. *Moral Philosophy and Development: The Human Condition in Africa*.
    Athens, Ohio: Center for International Studies, Ohio University, 1992.
Lloyd, Peter Cutt. *Power and Independence, Urban African's Perception of Social
    Inequality*. London: Routledge and Kegan Paul, 1974.
Mudimbe, V. Y. *The Invention of Africa: Gnosis, Philosophy, and the Order of
    Knowledge*. Bloomington, IN: Indiana University Press, 1988.
———. *Tales of Faith: Religion as Political Performance in Central Africa*. London:
    Athlone Press, 1997.
Olagoke, Abolade. "Pan Africanism and the New Diaspora: African Christians in the
    United States." Unpublished PhD dissertation, Iliff School of Theology, University
    of Denver, 2002.
Olupona, Jacob O. and Regina Gemignani. *African Immigrant Religions in America*. New
    York: New York University Press, 2007.
Owomoyela, Oyekan. *Yoruba Proverbs*. Lincoln: University of Nebraska Press, 2005.
Sanneh, Lamin O. *Piety and Power: Muslims and Christians in West Africa*. New York:
    Orbis Books, 1996.
———. *Whose Religion is Christianity? The Gospel Beyond the West*. Grand Rapids,
    MI: W.B. Eerdmans Publishers, 2003.

————. *Disciples of All Nations: Pillars of World Christianity.* New York: Oxford University Press, 2008.

Schlegel, Alice. *Sexual Stratification: A Cross-cultural View.* New York: Columbia University Press, 1977.

Strum, Philippa and Danielle Tarantolo, eds. *Women Immigrants in the United States.* Washington, DC: Woodrow Wilson International Center for Scholars, 2002.

Summerfield, Gale, Pyle Jean and Desai Manisha. "Preface to the Symposium: Globalizations, Transnational Migration, and Gendered Care Work." Pp. 281-295 in *Globalizations*, edited by Barry Gills. Milton Park, UK: Routledge Taylor & Francis Group, 2006.

Tinker, Irene, ed. *Persistent Inequalities: Women and World Development.* New York: Oxford University Press, 1990.

Tuden, Arthur and Leonard Plotnicov. *Social Stratification in Africa.* New York: The Free Press, 1970.

Yanagisako, Sylvia J. and Carol L. Delaney. *Naturalizing Power: Essays in Feminist Cultural Analysis.* New York: Routledge, 1995.

Zhou, Min. "Contemporary Female Immigration to the United States: A Demographic Profile." Pp. 23-34 in *Women Immigrants in the United States*, edited by Philippa Strum and Danielle Tarantolo. Washington, DC: Woodrow Wilson International Center for Scholars, 2002.

Chapter Fourteen

New Guadalupanos: Mexican Immigrants, a Grassroots Organization and a Pilgrimage to New York

Patricia Ruiz-Navarro

"Virgin of Guadalupe, grant us legalization" reads a sign held by a Mexican immigrant outside St. Patrick's Cathedral in New York City during the celebration of Mexican Catholics' main patron saint (field notes December 12, 2002).

Wade Clark Roof, in his presidential address to the Society for the Scientific Study of Religion in 1997, posed the following question: "Who defines the meaning of a symbol?" In his response, Roof spoke of the significance of religious borderlands and the reshaping of American Catholicism, which included a discussion on what it means to be living in a pluralistic religious world with porous borders. He declared that: "from the perspective of the borderlands, symbols have emergent qualities [whereas] meaning . . . rises out of the re-creations and reinterpretation of symbols" (Roof 1998: 4). Rather than taking place as isolated processes, new religious symbols, and meanings provided by immigrants are keys to how religious congregations become reconfigured. At the same time, these congregations, as in the case of American Catholicism, are reshaped to serve the new immigrants. In this context, there is growing interest in the study of immigrants' faiths, religious practices, and their interpretation of objects, symbols and religious dogma. In a sense, Roof's question on the meaning of symbols continues to be relevant today.

While religious practices and identities have been the subject of study of scholars of religion for quite some time, interests have expanded to the study of unfolding present events, such as immigration and religion. In the case of the latter, interests include the study of religious practices, religious affiliation, and religious identities. In this chapter, I examine how Mexican Catholic immigrants' religious practices, identities, and affiliation to a grass-roots organization exemplify the reshaping of the American Catholic Church. I use ethnographic data and interviews conducted with Mexican immigrants who are participants in a pilgrimage celebration across the Mexico-U.S. border.

New Immigrants, New Practices

Scholars trying to define the meaning of symbols and identities among immigrants are looking more closely at religious congregations as they influence the construction of immigrants' religious beliefs and identities (Ammerman 2001; Bacon 1996; Badr 2000; Carnes and Karpathakis 2001). For nineteenth century immigrants from predominantly Catholic countries (e.g., Irish, Polish and Italians), a strategy for survival was centered, not so much on a collective class action, but on a common religious identity as "religious labels were the quickest ways to summarize and to contest cultural differences" (Moore 1991: 239). That is to say, Irish and Polish immigrants were generally Catholics and religious in their home countries, yet, in response to American Protestantism, these early European immigrants became more committed Catholics than they were in their homeland.

While immigration to the United States consisted almost entirely of Europeans a century ago, Asian and Latin Americans represent the largest wave of immigrants in recent times (Foner 1997; Foner, Rumbaut and Gold 2000; Massey 1995; Miller, Miller and Dyrness 2001). At the same time, the fluid exchange of ideas and goods in a global context has made it easier for immigrants to remain in contact with their places of origin. Immigrants find it easier to remain close to people, ideas, culture, the political climate, and even religious celebrations back home. Individually and collectively, immigrants impact both the economy and the ideological prospect of the home and host countries. In sum, waves of recent immigrants to the United States are changing the way scholars and people in general interpret immigrant assimilation (Alba and Nee 1997; Gans 1997; Suarez-Orozco 2000).

David Rieff, in an article entitled *Nuevo Catholics*, notes that Hispanics in the United States account for 39 percent of the total Catholic population. A considerable majority are foreign-born immigrants from Latin America, mostly from Mexico who arrived in the United States in the past three decades legally and illegally (Rieff 2006). The American Catholic Church not only accepted, but began to promote a new model of assimilation among Latino Catholics. The inclusive attitude toward immigrants' native language, patron saints, ways of worship and the existing mix of folk religiosity with Catholic symbolism fitted the description of a "gentler, kinder notion of Americanization" (Diaz-Stevens and Stevens-Arroyo 1998: 167). At the same time, for Mexican Catholics, the suffering nature of folk religiosity mirrors the life of Mexican immigrants, and is often manifested in religious festivities. Such suffering nature is almost exalted in rituals like the Stations of the Cross in which Jesus is beaten, mocked, and denied by his friends on his way to the cross; or, the self-inflicted pain of pilgrims who arrive at the Shrine of Guadalupe in Mexico City on their knees during the feast of the Virgin of Guadalupe. Anthropologist Janet Abu-Lughod (1991) speaks of the way unifying symbols help define cultural groups. In this regard, the Virgin of Guadalupe has brought together people from different ethnic, cultural, socio-economic and geographical backgrounds within Mexico, and conveys a resourceful, empowering, transnational identity for Mexicans abroad.

Transnational Perspectives

Nowadays communication and transportation give way to fluid borders and shortened distances, all of which allow immigrants to remain connected to the home country in emotional, social, economic, and even political ways. Such home ties exemplify challenges to an assimilation model which, in principle, states that immigrants assimilate as they come to understand and adopt the mainstream social and cultural dynamics of the host country (Alba and Nee 1997; Guarnizo, Portes and Haller 2003). The opposite occurs, as some scholars would argue, when immigrants reproduce ethnic enclaves in the host country and if they engage in transnational practices (Abusharaf 1998; Ebaugh and Chafetz 2000; Guest 2003). Transnational migrants are those for whom social, economic, political, and even religious life is lived between two places. In the case of religious transnationalism, Peggy Levitt (2001) asserts that communication and transportation technologies heighten the immediacy of contact between transnational migrants and their communities. Elsewhere, Levitt adds that transnational migrants "establish themselves in their host countries while they continue to earn money, vote and pray in their countries of origin" (2003: 850). This bidirectional exchange of practices and relationships accounts for processes scholars have labeled as "transnational social networks" (Guarnizo, Portes and Haller 2003; Portes 1996), and "transnational life" (Levitt 2001; Smith 1998). Crucial to the understanding of immigrants' life dynamics is the need to deepen the knowledge of how practices (e.g., religious and social) and relationships (e.g., cultural, political and gendered) unfold. At another level, individual and collective identities shape the transnational life of immigrants and their families in a way that "practices and relationships [link] immigrants and their descendants abroad with the home country" (Smith 2001: 1). Just as a transnational perspective has changed the study of immigration (Itzigsohn 2001), transnational interaction have changed the everyday life of immigrants.

Mexican migration has grown into a bidirectional process and its geographic proximity to the United States has allowed for a more dynamic physical mobility. However, for those unable to travel back and forth, and this is particularly true for undocumented immigrants, migration from rural Mexico to the United States is more than a movement between places with distinct ways of life and different sets of social relations (Rouse 1991). In such cases, migration reveals nuances of life processes and redefinition of identities. This is how anthropologist Roger Rouse 1991) shows, from interviews with Mexican immigrants, that national and ethnic identities shift in multiple contextualized directions. As one of his interviewees declared: "My identity now possesses multiple repertoires: I am Mexican but I am also Chicano and Latin American" (Rouse 1991: 8). Thus, the "multidimensionality" and "interdependency" of Mexico-U.S. relations (Smith 2003) relies on similar interdependent relations of those who emigrated and those who stayed behind. These relations do not exist in a vacuum. Oftentimes, religious congregations also work as transnational bridges for immigrants living between their home and host countries.

Communities, Practices and Identities

Many immigrant groups join religious congregations to cultivate social networks with a community which preserves their ethic and cultural identity (Min 2003). Likewise, grass-roots organizations provide immigrants with social and economic support, as well as opportunities to enhance their network system. Many immigrant groups in the United States find that religious communities and organizations provide more social and economic networking than other agencies. [1] Perhaps immigrants see in religion that "kinder and gentler Americanization," especially when assimilation is no longer seen as a prerequisite for immigrants to become part of American society.

On the contrary, Catholic immigrants do not favor assimilation when, in fact, their culture, language, practices, and patron saints are all welcome in their American Catholic parishes (Diaz-Stevens 2003). Scholars studying other religious immigrant groups, such as Korean Protestants (Min 1992; Chai 1998), Chinese Christians (Yang 1998), Cuban Catholics (Tweed 1997), Sudanese Muslims (Abusharaf 1998), and Dominican Catholics (Levitt 2001) explore the role that religious congregations play in immigrants' lives. In such case, the social and political aspects concerning members of the community are incorporated into the congregation's agenda. Oftentimes, religious organizations provide spaces and opportunities for its members to celebrate religious festivities as well as national holidays. *Asociación Tepeyac* of New York (hereafter also referred to as *Tepeyac*) is a community-based organization that pays close attention to safeguarding Mexican traditions and culture, offers legal and human rights advice to undocumented immigrants, as well spaces for Mexican immigrants to celebrate religious and cultural events. Tepeyac has used the image of Virgin of Guadalupe as its insignia. Its efforts, and those of its executive director, a Jesuit priest, are directed toward creating an atmosphere where Mexicans can become socially, culturally and politically active (Solis 2004).

For Mexicans, the Virgin of Guadalupe exemplifies a connection between "the Aztecs and Spanish Catholicism" (Benavides 1989). According to popular belief and church documents, the apparitions of the Virgin of Guadalupe to Juan Diego date to 1531. Virgin Mary (in her *persona* of Guadalupe) appeared before Juan Diego, an indigenous young man, and commissioned him to communicate to the Spanish bishop her intent to have a place of worship built for her. Eventually, a sanctuary was consecrated in 1621 in the hill of Tepeyac in what was then the outskirts of Mexico City (Brading 2001). The bond between the indigenous Mexican people and the Virgin of Guadalupe was subtly established first by her appearance, her brown skin, the subtle, loving way she addressed Juan Diego in his native Nahuatl language, and how she presented herself as a mother and protector of the helpless (Brading 2001; Rieff 2006). Octavio Paz, the Mexican poet and Nobel Prize awardee who wrote extensively on Mexican identity, expressed in 1977: "the Virgin of Guadalupe had succeeded in capturing the minds and hearts of all Mexicans . . . her cult is intimate and public, regional and national. The feast of Guadalupe, 12 December, is still the central date in the emotional calendar of the Mexican people" (Brading 2001: 330). In the United States, as in Mexico, many Mexicans remain faithful to the Virgin of Guadalupe, although not always faithful to the official teachings of the Catholic Church. An example is the confluence of a religious celebration that mobilizes millions of Guadalupanos (faithful followers of the Virgin of Guadalupe) with a socio-political march intended to promote social justice for immigrants.

Members of Tepeyac affirm that the protection of the Virgin of Guadalupe[2] helps them deal with the dreadful and dangerous experiences of crossing the border and daily life struggles. On both sides of the Mexico-U.S. border, being Guadalupano, as some have claimed, conveys a message of unity and hope under the protection of the Virgin of Guadalupe. Religious beliefs and practices are not always interpreted as leaders of the hierarchical Catholic Church envision (Wolf and Hansen 1978). Religion permeates the lives of people at many levels, and since it is public and private, individual, and social (Casanova 1994), it has also been a cultural ingredient as well as an element of faith.[3]

This brings us back to the critical question of who defines the meaning of a symbol. In this chapter, I explore the following questions: 1) to what extent do religious communities and/or organizations play a role in framing immigrants' identities? 2) why and how do religious practices acquire new meanings? and, 3) to what extent does the study of religious celebrations unveil immigrants' religious, ethnic and national identities?

Data and Method

This study consists of ethnographic field notes and semi-structured interviews with participants of a pilgrimage called *Antorcha Guadalupana* (Guadalupano torch-run) that traveled from the Shrine of Guadalupe in Mexico City to St. Patrick's Cathedral in New York City. In researching the religious life of Mexican immigrants, first, it is important to understand the role of Tepeyac, a grass-roots organization, in the religious life of Mexican immigrants. Second, I explore individual motivations to participate in the pilgrimage of Antorcha Guadalupana. Finally, I examine how Mexican immigrants' speak of their national and religious identities as well as how they understand the relationship and shared meanings between these two identities. Through this data I examine the role of Tepeyac in the life of Mexican immigrants to show how religious practices are recreated and religious identities constructed and understood by these immigrants.

Ever since Asociación Tepeyac of New York organized its first Antorcha Guadalupana, a local torch relay-run in 1997, young runners began carrying torches from St. Patrick's Cathedral in the borough of Manhattan to parishioners' churches across the five boroughs of New York City. The torch is a symbol of light and protection brought by the Virgin of Guadalupe into the community. Accordingly, the Virgin of Guadalupe is, among members of this community, the "patron saint of the oppressed and exploited." In 2001, during the December 12th Mass in celebration of Virgin of Guadalupe, Cardinal Edward Egan of New York invited participants of the torch-run to expand this local celebration into a transnational event. He encouraged runners to initiate the torch-run at the Shrine of Guadalupe in Mexico and bring it across the Mexico-U.S. border to the people of New York. Thrilled by the challenge, a year later in 2002, Asociación Tepeyac of New York coordinated the first *Carrera Internacional Antorcha Guadalupana* (International Guadalupano Torch Relay-Run) in 2002. This pilgrimage, which brings together Mexican Guadalupanos from both sides of the border, has grown to become a unique religious/political celebration that spans the Mexico-U.S. border. It embodies multiple levels of a social, religious, and political transnational liaisons, celebrates Virgin of Guadalupe as the patron saint of the oppressed and exploited, and is a symbol that conveys the identity and history of Mexicans' struggle then and now.

In 2003, during its second year as a transnational event, over two thousand runners traveled across cities and towns in eight states of Mexico and fourteen states in the United States as part of the torch relay-run pilgrimage Antorcha Guadalupana. As part of an exploratory study I followed and interviewed eight *corredores de la Antorcha Guadalupana* (runners of Guadalupe's torch relay-run). Four men and four women, all undocumented immigrants from Mexico between the ages of sixteen and thirty-six[4] and currently living in the New York metropolitan area, agreed to participate in this study.

Mexican immigrants were contacted at weekly meetings at local churches in the four boroughs of New York (Manhattan, Brooklyn, Queens and The Bronx) and in Union City, New Jersey in September 2003. First, I distributed flyers seeking volunteers who might want to share their intentions and experiences as runners of Antorcha Guadalupana. Each participant was interviewed twice between October and December of that year, once before and once after their assigned segment of the torch relay-run. Participants ran in one of the following states covering the route of the torch-run, including Texas, Louisiana, North Carolina, Washington, Pennsylvania and New York.

Mexican Catholics have used Carrera Internacional Antorcha Guadalupana to cross not only the geographical Mexico-U.S. border, but the boundaries of a traditional pilgrimage that moved beyond a religious celebration and became a platform in which popular religiosity and socio-political concerns have been equally voiced. Although religious and political agendas are expressed simultaneously via this religious event, it is not a homogeneous religious-political participation. Mexican immigrants who join the torch relay-run organized by Tepeyac may or may not share an interpretation of the event and the meaning of being Guadalupano. The feast day of the Virgin of Guadalupe is the most important and well attended Catholic festivity in Mexico. The Shrine of the

Virgin of Guadalupe (Basilica de Guadalupe) receives more visitors and pilgrims in the world than any other Catholic sanctuary, even more than Saint Peter's Cathedral in Rome (Notimex 2008). In 2006, the 475th anniversary of the apparition of the Virgin of Guadalupe before the indigenous man, Juan Diego, nearly twenty million people visited the Shrine of Guadalupe. On December 12th alone, six million people as part of more than 600 pilgrim groups arrived at the Shrine of Guadalupe (Noticias Eclesiales 2006).

In 2004, I followed the Antorcha Guadalupana transnational pilgrimage. On the U.S. end of this pilgrimage, participants ran a leg of the torch-run somewhere between Texas and New York. Mexicans living in Mexico brought the torch from Mexico City in central Mexico to the state at the Texas border. The torch that was lighted at the Shrine of Guadalupe in Mexico City and two big paintings with the image of the Virgin of Guadalupe and Juan Diego were handed over to Mexican immigrants in the U.S. who continued the pilgrimage to the northeast of the United States. The pilgrimage covered over 3813 miles from the Shrine of Guadalupe in Mexico City to St. Patrick's Cathedral in New York City.

Analysis

From the data collected through ethnography of Asociación Tepeyac of New York and interviews with participants of Antorcha Guadalupana, I identified emergent topics that deal with how Mexican immigrants recreate religious and national identities and reshape American Catholicism. I discuss them in three sections. In Discourses on Crossing Borders, I present an analysis of Asociación Tepeyac in its role as a grass-roots organization and as intermediary for immigrants with public and private institutions (e.g., government, schools, and unions) and individuals (e.g., school teachers and employers). The following section, Discourses on Crossing Boundaries, emerges as a parallel to the physical crossing of national borders through the Antorcha Guadalupana. Here I examine how members of Tepeyac crossed societal boundaries and understand their participation in this torch-run pilgrimage. Lastly, in Discourses about Life beyond Borders and Boundaries, I explore how participants in this study speak of negotiating and reshaping religious and national identities. These three sections are an exploration of the emergent qualities of symbols, reinterpreted meanings, and a renegotiation of national and religious identities by Mexican immigrants.

Discourses of Crossing Borders

Members of Asociación Tepeyac note that this grass-roots organization has opened its doors to immigrants, and is instrumental in mediating relations between immigrants and public and private institutions. Since its foundation in September 1997, Brother Joel Magallán has been the Executive Director of

Asociación Tepeyac of New York. Magallán is a Jesuit priest who seems more interested in promoting social justice than complying with Catholic Church doctrine. He is a strong advocate and supporter of the Mexican community in New York. The name Tepeyac is the name of the hill in Mexico City where the Virgin of Guadalupe appeared to Juan Diego and where the Shrine of Guadalupe was built. It is not a coincidence that Asociación Tepeyac has used the Virgin of Guadalupe as its banner, in the same way that Father Miguel Hidalgo, a Catholic priest and hero of Mexico's independence, employed it against the Spaniards in 1810.

Tepeyac is dedicated to empowering the Mexican community in New York, to preserving Mexicans' cultural identity, promoting and supporting Mexican entrepreneurs, and teaching about legal and human rights of immigrants, particularly undocumented immigrants. Tepeyac also encourages the Mexican community to preserve its identity by organizing cultural events and celebrating religious festivities. Educational programs that Tepeyac offers include English as a Second Language (ESL) courses for adults, leadership training classes, labor advocacy programs, computer training, after-school programs and psychological counseling. In all, Asociación Tepeyac of New York, educates, empowers, and supports its members who are often seen outside the community as simply low skilled, poorly educated and undocumented immigrants.

As far as advocacy for undocumented immigrants is concerned, Tepeyac advises them to know what their labor and human rights are, and how to put those into effect. Maria is a woman in her forties who migrated from Mexico more than ten years ago and has been a member of Tepeyac since its foundation in 1997. She explains the role of the organization in negotiating issues with political and religious institutions on behalf of Mexican people. For example, Maria observes how Tepeyac empowers men and women, young and old, when they join political rallies in Washington, or participate in religious celebrations in St. Patrick's Cathedral in New York City. She states:

> [i]n former times, here at the [St. Patrick's] Cathedral, Mexicans were not allowed inside . . . now thanks to Tepeyac we are welcomed and act as lay ministers and conduct the readings. It has all been little by little. Before . . . it was not allowed for those without experience and preparation to participate as ministers. But then, Tepeyac started to open doors for us, we were able to [become active participants] join and do the readings, distribute communion and ushering. I got to read the psalms the first year the mass [of Virgin of Guadalupe] was celebrated there. I felt shivers down my spine.

Mario, another member elucidates on how Tepeyac has also contributed to immigrants' self-worth and self-confidence. He believes that Tepeyac helps its members feel enlightened. He notes:

> When someone is in one of these groups, you do not hide who you are. I do, I am in this group, and in this group [Tepeyac] they've

taught me to value my worthiness as a human being, the value of my work, [and] to love thy neighbor.

Tepeyac has opened its doors and embraced immigrants who find themselves in vulnerable conditions and feel isolated in the host country. Members of Tepeyac speak of ways in which they feel empowered since joining the organization, from learning about their labor and human rights to using and appropriating public spaces. However, not all participants in the study share the same views about the opportunities provided by Tepeyac. For Daniel, the day to day conflict of undocumented immigrants could be easily resolved with a little bit of help from organizations like Tepeyac. Daniel comments:

> For example, if we had stronger support from Tepeyac or the [Mexican] Consulate, beyond being issued an official ID, if they could sponsor us, if they could say "alright he does not have documents but he pays his rent on time." [That they could] offer a recommendation. If they [Tepeyac and the Mexican Consulate] could at least help us in this way. Do you know what I mean? If you do not have a Social Security Number but you are an honest, hard-working person who pays his bills. See, that we could count on them, the Consulate or Tepeyac.

Daniel discussed further how undocumented immigrants who are in a vulnerable situation might not be in a position to change their circumstances, but when a community organization or an institution is willing to represent and stand on their behalf, this representation allows its member to have a voice, and offers them an opportunity to transform things for the better. Daniel argues that Tepeyac and the Mexican consulate could, for example, collaborate and issue official IDs for undocumented immigrants but do more than that. In fact, Asociación Tepeyac and state-represented organization such as *Casa Puebla* and *Casa Mexico* are already seen as intermediaries willing to help immigrants (Galvez 2007).

Discourses of Crossing Boundaries

Participants of Antorcha Guadalupana express different intentions—social, religious and political—in participating in this event. This activity serves as a metaphor for a space of flexible borders. In a public space, the massive celebration of Antorcha Guadalupana unveils the multiple layers of a transnational religious event.

Laura, a sixteen-year-old girl, relates her experience on crossing the border and how people put their trust in the Virgin of Guadalupe during this dangerous journey. Unlike the threatening and difficult experience of other undocumented migrants, Laura considers herself fortunate and blessed for having had a safe crossing with her mother and her older sister. She remembers vividly her experience of crossing the Mexico-U.S. border illegally when she was only six years old, and credits their successful journey to being under the protection of the Virgin of Guadalupe.

Stories of feeling safe under the protection of the Virgin of Guadalupe are common among Mexican Catholics. Diana, a thirty-six year old immigrant and runner of Antorcha Guadalupana, asserts that her participation in this event fulfills a promise she made to the Virgin of Guadalupe after she was miraculously healed from a kidney tumor. She explains:

> I am very determined to give my all at these events; not only when it comes to the torch relay-run but all church events and everything that is connected to the Virgin of Guadalupe. I feel that she has performed a huge miracle for me . . . I was going in and out of hospitals during four months . . . Doctors found a tumor . . . in the beginning they told me it was cancer.

Diana further explains how her illness progressed. Since the tumor was found near the time of the celebration of the feast day of the Virgin of Guadalupe, she felt that she might not be well and able to run in the torch relay-run. She was disappointed, but ultimately decided she was not going to miss the celebration and ignored a doctor's recommendation to have surgery in early December. After the celebration of the Virgin of Guadalupe, on December 12th, Diana checked into the hospital. She was taken into the operating room and was shortly released. Diana recalls what the doctor told her:

> Well, I don't know what happened, I don't know what you did, but there is no sign of any tumor. [Diana continued] at the hospital they made more tests and scans and there was nothing, nothing, nothing. I cried, I laughed. From then on I have surrender to her. I told her; I will always be with you, in all your celebrations, all your events I will always be there with you.

By participating in Antorcha Guadalupana, Mexicans on both sides of the border claim to be the "new messengers of a people divided by a border." As Juan Diego, an outcast indigenous man was chosen by the Virgin of Guadalupe to deliver a message to the Spaniard bishop, Asociación Tepeyac has also called on Mexicans to be the new Juan Diegos and become the new "messengers for the dignity of a people divided by borders." Therefore, the appeal by Mexicans to the Virgin of Guadalupe to grant them legalization leads us to better understand how politicized interpretations of religious practices become socially constructed. Participants in this pilgrimage who view themselves as the messengers of good news offer a promising future for undocumented immigrants. They embody a multi-vocal, multipurpose celebration across the Mexico-U.S. border as they claim dignity, human and labor rights, and condemn violence, injustice and discrimination against undocumented immigrants. While there are those for whom this is solely a religious celebration, for others, it is an opportunity to voice their claims of labor and human rights for undocumented immigrants. Juan explains the reasons that lead him to participate in this celebration:

> I want the lives and rights of all of us to be respected in this country [the United States]. I want people to come together and fight for the rights of all immigrants that live in New York and elsewhere in the United States, you know? Eventually, laws that support and protect immigrants' rights might come into place.

In Daniel's account, the support of a community like Asociación Tepeyac of New York, assists immigrants in coping with everyday conflicts and provides tools to help immigrants cope with psychological distress and provides social well-being. At the same time, Tepeyac, as do other religious communities, provides a platform in which immigrants can reenact cultural and religious festivities. The torch relay-run, as mentioned by a participant, helps immigrants connect with their traditions. For Daniel, this event reminds runners of the importance "of remembering one's roots and Mexican customs." He further states, "I feel good about participating in the torch run and express through these means who I am as Mexican."

Discourses about Life beyond Borders and Boundaries

Mexican immigrants and members of Tepeyac share the highs and lows of their experiences as immigrants, and the conflicting positions of negotiating multiple identities. Based on the responses of participants in the pilgrimage run, Mexican immigrants seem to be living transnational lives beyond the borders of nation-states, a position from which they contest the boundaries of religious and political institutions as well. Mario frames his experience in the United States as follows:

> I am never going to forget this country. I will never forget it, because it has given me good things, all the good things, and all the bad things. The bad experiences refer to not having a family [because he is the only one who migrated], of getting involved with gangs, with alcohol and drugs . . . of getting involved with women or going places where you can offend them . . . On the other hand, the good side of being [here] in the United States is that I met people I never thought I would meet. Also, I haven't done so bad, not so bad. As I was telling you, I have been very brave.

The way immigrants interpret new meanings as to who they could be or have become has ultimately shaped their experiences in the host country and vice versa. Likewise, experiences and identities are not solely based on first hand experiences, but have been shaped by learning about attributions given to their group, from stereotypes and in negotiating with people's positive or negative perceptions. For example, Juan observes how Mexican immigrants we have met, have changed, and have adopted American values. He suggests that these people have embraced "this country's currents" (*las corrientes de este*

país). In Juan's view, it is important for immigrants to remain strong and not
feel hurt even if acquaintances, friends or even family turned their backs on
them because they have changed and become individualistic. Juan narrates:

> Life is not better, it is not better because here [in the U.S] if you don't
> work, you don't eat. And it is hard because sometimes your own
> people would not give anything to you. Sometimes not even your
> own family. Your people [Mexicans] will not only not help you; they
> will even ignore you . . . here human beings allow themselves to be
> changed by the currents of this nation. [In the United States] if you
> don't have money you are worth nothing.

Worthiness and people's value are consistent themes raised during my
interviews. These are elements people identify with, and analyzing people's
perceptions of them have shaped what immigrants might come to identify or
have come to struggle with. Such is the case of Juan who spoke of immigrants
who have dealt with relatives not willing to help them. The same is true with
immigrants as their views of the host country, its people and its values, become
critically assessed. Mexican immigrants who participate in Antorcha
Guadalupana, and carry signs to St Patrick's Cathedral that read "No Human
Being is Illegal," are at one level eager to communicate their struggle and to find
a place in society that judges others not only by their legal status as
undocumented.

Psychologist Jocelyn Solis (2002) explores the concept of illegality as an
identity among children and youth living in New York City. In her study,
conducted at Asociación Tepeyac with children and youth of undocumented
migrants, Solis avers that being illegal is something her participants have come
to understand as a political tool with individual and societal implications. Solis
argues that illegality "comes to function as an identity when it is adopted by
individual people for a purpose, such as to understand the organization of U.S.
society and their own place of silence and invisibility in it" (Solis 2002: 3). That
sense of invisibility is interpreted as being outcasts, although for some it is also
an opportunity to feel safe as they would not draw much attention that might
translate to them being deported.

As participants of Antorcha Guadalupana, runners intentionally come
forward and make themselves visible. Here they do not disregard their
vulnerability or their outcast position in society. On the contrary, Guadalupanos
who participate in Antorcha Guadalupana consider themselves as the new Juan
Diegos entrusted by the Virgin of Guadalupe to be "the new messenger for the
unity of a people divided by a border" (*mensajeros por la unidad de un pueblo
dividido por la frontera)*. Maria, one of the interviewees, mentioned that
undocumented Mexican people, who are at the bottom of the socio-economic
ladder, are like the "Juan Diegos" of today. Like Maria, other Mexican
immigrants feel that they are being excluded from reaching high positions in
society whether it is within the hierarchical Catholic Church or the job market.
For example, Diego states:

> Juan Diego was not welcomed because of his language and the same
> is true for us here. If we don't speak English, they won't let us in [the
> church]. We need to find a translator so he/she could guide us with
> regards to what we are going to say.

Many of the participants also expressed their concern about abuses and
neglectful treatment of Mexican workers, especially for those who have no
proper documents to work in the United States. Again Mario, a thirty-year-old
man who migrated from Mexico four years ago, condemns the attacks and
misconstrued views of Mexican immigrants:

> Because many people here in the United States, especially the
> authorities, look at us as if we were terrorists, they see us as invaders
> of this country; that we have come to take their jobs, to take things
> away from Americans, when in reality that is not true.

Oftentimes, devotees of the Virgin of Guadalupe offer prayers in requests
and responses to miracles (e.g., people ask for the Virgin's help, offer prayers,
ask favors, and give thanks for having healed or for feeling protected).
Immigrants pray and make promises to the Virgin of Guadalupe as they ask for
her protection of family members in their journey across the border, or as they
ask for her help in getting family reunification granted to themselves or
relatives. The Virgin of Guadalupe is seen as the intermediary to get amnesty
which might guarantee better jobs and fair salaries. I listened to stories of
immigrants who worked for weeks without pay and were later threatened by
employers to have them deported when they insisted on getting paid. Others
concerned with the political implications of being "illegal" in the United States,
seek the intercession of the Virgin of Guadalupe on behalf of all undocumented
peoples so that one day they might be granted amnesty. Participants in this study
seem to agree that if granted the opportunity to work legally, without fears of
harassment, deportation or exploitation, work opportunities and living
conditions will also improve. As a result, the immigrant's initial expectations of
coming to the United States to work and earn enough money to live, remit and
save, would perhaps enable them to go back home in a shorter period of time, as
initially planned. In informal conversations, undocumented immigrants disclose
that coming illegally is not their first choice; they would have preferred to come
legally, with work permits. In the end, as one person affirms, there are jobs to
fill and work to do, why would not the government want to issue work visas?
Another participant contends that it is much easier if would-be immigrants
"could just do what they came to do, and then go back to their country."
Unfortunately, as Daniel has experienced, there are many barriers that delay
their plans to return:

> Well, for me, the downside, personally, is that as a Hispanic and as
> an illegal, as a person who does not speak English, well it is very
> hard to make it . . . it is here that one is born again. You have to

> teach yourself to speak, you teach yourself to ask for food and you
> teach yourself how to walk. Those are the three steps that a child
> learns when he starts to grow, [eat, talk and walk].

Using the label "Hispanic" and "illegal" as shared identities is, for Daniel, as it is for other undocumented Latin American immigrants, a strategy that enables them to consider the shared nature of struggles in their community. Meanwhile, there are those who see considerable differences in substance and interpretation of identities. Not all Mexican Catholic immigrants in the United States view being Guadalupano and being Mexican in a uniform way. Overall, there is a shared sentiment among participants in my study that Mexicans are a chosen people for the Virgin of Guadalupe. Laura who considers all Mexicans privileged for having the Virgin of Guadalupe as the nation's patron saint, said that not all Mexicans are true to the Virgin. In terms of their level of commitment and devotion, one can distinguish between "true Guadalupanos" and others. Laura states:

> The only thing is that many Guadalupanos, the true Guadalupanos are
> there twelve months of the year. There are many others who are there
> only on the twelfth [of December]. Those might be Guadalupanos,
> but not 100 percent. Maybe because [they have] work obligations, but,
> they don't get together as often as we do—all twelve months of the
> year as a community, every weekend we gather to pray the rosary to
> the Virgin of Guadalupe.

While Laura made a distinction between who among Mexicans is a true Guadalupano, for others, national and religious identities merge into one. For Maria, being Mexican and Guadalupano "is pretty much the same thing." Likewise, for Daniel, these are "sort of the same flag, the same sentiment . . . that is how I feel. I feel the same by being Guadalupano and being Mexican."

In a globalized era in which immigrants have adopted a wider, translocal view of where they live, hybrid identities are also more common references to heterogeneous interpretations of the self (Arnett 2002). For the American Catholic Church at the crossroad of rapid changes brought about by the increasing number of a Catholic Latino population, particularly Mexican immigrants, new references, identities and interpretations have come into place.

Conclusion

The new Catholic immigrants transcend the boundaries of mainstream religious practices; the parishes serving Polish, Italian and Irish now welcome the ethnic, language and cultural differences of Latin American Catholics. This exploratory study unveils a new dimension as to why immigrants join religious communities and how meaning, practices and identities are constructed in a multi-dialogical conversation. It presents how immigrant's experiences and religious identities are not individually constructed, but are shaped by interactions and conversations with other individuals and larger institutions. A qualitative approach to the study of immigration offers an opportunity to learn about the experiences of individuals that complement quantitative data on Mexican immigrants.

As immigrants cross physical borders, their interpretations of religious and national identities are called into question. Within the universality of the Roman Catholic Church, there are nuances that make religious beliefs and practices very distinct depending on where and how they are performed. In addition, with immigration, religious beliefs and practices have also changed "from below," from the experience at the micro level (Smith and Guarnizo 1998). Likewise, the American Catholic Church has shifted to a micro level approach in that, instead of promoting a hierarchical model of assimilation (from above) as was done with Catholic immigrants in the early twentieth century; the Church has accommodated the religious and social needs (from below) of its multicultural, multilingual immigrant congregations. Among early ninetieth century European Catholic immigrants, religious cultural symbols were used to maintain "ethnic personalities" (Min 1992). Nowadays, Mexican immigrants, along with other Latino immigrants, have invigorated American Catholicism with their own language, devotions and religious practices (Diaz-Stevens and Stevens-Arroyo 1998).

The American Catholic Church, instead of promoting assimilation to an exciting community, has welcomed newcomers, their distinct practices of worshiping and has even found ways to better serve immigrants. Stories I collected from members of Tepeyac suggest that a multilevel convergence of a national and religious celebration, of what it means to be Mexican and Guadalupano, takes place during the celebration of Antorcha Guadalupana. In this space, physically and symbolically, Mexican immigrants pray and claim, religiously and politically, for inclusion and for opportunities that might crystallize their dreams for a better life.

Notes

1. Beyond the scope of this paper is the role that religious Muslim communities have played for Muslim groups after the attacks of 9/11, and the polarizing experiences and discriminating views associated with them (from its role as a support network in strengthening religious identities to accusations of financing terrorist activities).

2. The term Guadalupano refers to a devotee of Virgin of Guadalupe. Among Mexican Catholics, being a devotee of Virgin of Guadalupe means that she is seen as the preferred intermediary with God. The Brown Virgin embodies Virgin Mary with Mexican characteristics.

3. Two good examples of ways the church in Latin America plays cultural and political roles are Napolitano's accounts of the girls' fifteenth birthday celebrations in Mexico and Levitt's descriptions of Dominican Republic (DR) churches as sites of local-level political activity. In the former, Napolitano explains how the fifteen birthday

celebration is charged with symbolisms of an "illusory time" and which gender roles are socially expected. In the latter, Levitt explains Miraflореños from DR praising the bishop's intervention with the government getting roads paved and prostitute-bars closed. See Peggy Levitt, *The Transnational Villagers* (Berkeley: University of California Press, 2001); Valentina Napolitano, "Becoming a *Mujercita*: Rituals, Fiestas and Religious Discourses," *The Journal of the Royal Anthropological Institute* 3, no. 2 (June 1997): 279-296.

4. I acknowledge the limitations inherent in the small sample size; however the stories shared by participants provide a valuable insight into the reality of Mexican Catholics and undocumented immigrants in the United States.

Bibliography

Abu-Lughod, Janet L. *Changing Cities: Urban Sociology.* Harper Collins, 1991.

Abusharaf, Rogalia, M. "Structural Adaptations in an Immigrant Muslim Congregation in New York." Pp. 235-264 in *Gatherings in Diaspora: Religious Communities and the New Immigration,* edited by Stephen Warner and Judith Wittner. Philadelphia: Temple University Press, 1998.

Alba, Richard, and Victor Nee. "Rethinking Assimilation Theory for a New Era of Immigration." *International Migration Review* 31, no. 4 (1997): 826-874.

Ammerman, Nancy T. *Congregation and Community.* New Brunswick, NJ: Rutgers University Press, 2001.

Arnett, Jeffry J. "The Psychology of Globalization."*American Psychologist* 57, no. 10 (2002): 774–783.

Bacon, Jean. *Lifelines: Community, Family and Assimilation among Asian Indian Immigrants.* New York: Oxford University Press. 1996.

Badr, Hoda. "Al-Noor Mosque: Strength through Unity." Pp.193-229 in *Religion and New Immigrants: Continuities and Adaptations in Immigrant Congregations,* edited by Helen Rose Ebaugh and Janet Saltzman Chafetz. Walnut Creek, CA: Altamira Press, 2000.

Benavides, Gustavo. "Religious Articulations of Power." Pp. 1-13 in *Religion and Political Power,* edited by Gustavo Benavides and M. W. Daly. New York: State University of New York Press, 1989.

Brading, David A. *Mexican Phoenix. Our Lady of Guadalupe: Image and Tradition across Five Centuries.* Cambridge: University Press, 2001.

Cano, Gustavo. "The Virgin, the Priest, and the Flag: Political Mobilization of Mexican Immigrants in Chicago, Houston and New York." Paper presented at the 62nd Annual Conference of the Midwest Political Science Association, San Diego, April 15-18, 2004.

Carnes, Tony and Anna Karpathakis, eds. *New York Glory: Religions in the City.* New York: New York University Press, 2001.

Casanova, José. *Public Religions in the Modern World.* Chicago: University of Chicago Press, 1994.

Chai, Karen. "Competing for the Second Generation: English-Language Ministry at a Korean Protestant Church." Pp. 295-332 in *Gatherings in Diaspora: Religious Communities and the New Immigration,* edited by Stephen Warner and Judith Wittner. Philadelphia: Temple University Press, 1998.

Diaz-Stevens, Ana Maria. "Colonization versus Immigration in the Integration and Identification of Hispanics in the United States." Pp. 61-84 in *Religion and Immigration*, edited by Yvonne Yazbeck Haddad, Jane I. Smith and John L. Esposito. Walnut Creek, CA: Altamira Press, 2003.

Diaz-Stevens, Ana Maria and Anthony Stevens-Arroyo. *Recognizing the Latino Resurgence in U.S. Religion*. Colorado: Westview Press, 1998.

Ebaugh, Helen Rose and Janet S. Chafetz, eds. *Religion and the New Immigrants Continuities and Adaptations in Immigrant Congregations*. Walnut Creek, CA: Altamira Press, 2000.

Foner, Nancy. "The Immigrant Family: Cultural Legacies and Cultural Changes." *International Migration Review* 31, no. 4 (1997): 961-974.

Foner, Nancy, Ruben G. Rumbaut and Steven J. Gold, eds. *Immigration Research for a New Century: Multidisciplinary Perspectives*. New York: Russell Sage Foundation, 2000.

Galvez, Alyshia. "'I too was an Immigrant': An Analysis of Differing Modes of Mobilization in Two Bronx Mexican Migrant Organizations." *International Migration* 45, no. 1 (2007): 87-121.

Gans, Herbert. "Toward a Reconciliation of 'Assimilation' and 'Pluralism': The Interplay of Acculturation and Ethnic Retention." *International Migration Review* 31, no. 4 (Winter 1997): 875-892.

Guarnizo, Luis Eduardo, Alejandro Portes and William Haller. "Assimilation and Transnationalism: Determinants of Transnational Political Action among Contemporary Immigrants." *American Journal of Sociology* 108 (2003): 1211–1248.

Guest, Kenneth J. *God in Chinatown: Religion and Survival in New York's Evolving Immigrant Community*. New York: New York University Press, 2003.

Itzigsohn, Jose. "Living Transnational Lives." *Diaspora* 10, no. 2 (2001): 281-285.

Levitt, Peggy. "You Know, Abraham was really the First Immigrant: Religions and Transnational Migration." *International Migration Review* 37, no. 3 (2003): 847-873.

———. *The Transnational Villagers*. Berkeley: University of California Press, 2001.

———. *God Needs No Passport: Immigrants and the Changing American Religious Landscape*. New York: The New York Press, 2007

Massey, Douglas. S. "The New Immigration and Ethnicity in the United States." *Population and Development Review* 21, no. 3 (Sep. 1995): 631-652.

Miller, Donald, Jon Miller and Grace Dyrness. *Immigrant Religion in the City of the Angels*. The Center for Religion and Public Culture, 2001. http://www.usc.edu/schools/college/crcc/private/docs/publications/immigrantreligion.pdf (accessed March 12, 2004).

Min, Pyong Gap "The Structure and Social Functions of Korean Immigrant Churches in the United States." *International Migration Review* 26, no. 4 (1992): 1370-94.

———. "Immigrants' Religion and Ethnicity: A Comparison of Indian Hindus and Korean Protestants." Paper presented at the annual meeting of the American Sociological Association, Atlanta, August 16, 2003. http://www.allacademic.com/meta/p106478_index.html (accessed March 19, 2008).

Moore, Robert L. "The End of Religious Establishment and the Beginning of Religious Politics: Church and State in the United States." Pp. 237-264 in *Belief in History Innovative Approaches to European and American Religion*, edited by Thomas Kselman. Notre Dame: University of Notre Dame Press, 1991.

Napolitano, Valentina. "Becoming a *Mujercita*: Rituals, Fiestas and Religious Discourses." *The Journal of the Royal Anthropological Institute* 3, no. 2 (June 1997): 279-296.

Noticias Eclesiales. "Seis Millones de Peregrinos Visitaron Basílica de Guadalupe." 2006. http://www.eclesiales.org/noticia.php?id=000644 (accessed April 20, 2009).

Notimex. "Basílica de Guadalupe, Santuario Mariano más Visitado del Mundo." *El Excelsior*, September 10, 2008. http://www.exonline.com.mx/diario/noticia/primera/pulsonacional/basilica_de_guadalupe,_santuario_mariano_mas_visitado_del_mundo/347714 (accessed September 10, 2008).

Portes, Alejandro. "Global Villagers: The Rise of Transnational Communities." *The American Prospect* 25 (March- April 1996): 74-77.

Rieff, David. "Nuevo Catholics," *New York Times,* December 24, 2006. http://www.nytimes.com/2006/12/24/magazine/24catholics.t.html?_r=1&sq=nuevo%20catholic&st=cse&oref=slogin&scp=2&pagewanted=all (accessed February 12, 2007).

Roof, Wade C. "Religious Borderlands: Challenges for Future Study." *Journal for the Scientific Study of Religion* 37, no. 1 (1998): 1-14.

Rouse, Roger. "Mexican Migration and the Social Space of Postmodernism." *Diaspora* 1, no. 1 (1991): 8-23.

Smith, Michael P. and Luis Eduardo Guarnizo, eds. *Transnationalism from Below*. New Brunswick, NJ: Transaction Publishers, 1998.

Smith, Robert. "Diasporic Membership in Historical Perspective: Comparative Perspectives from Mexican, Italian and Polish Cases." *International Migration Review* 37, no. 3 (2003): 724-759.

———. "Local Level Trasnational Life in Rattvik, Sweden and Ticuani, Mexico: An Essay in Historical Retrieval." Pp. 37-59 in *New Transnational Social Spaces*, edited by Ludger Pries. New York: Routledge, 2001.

———. "Transnational Localities: Community, Technology and the Politics of Membership within the Context of Mexico and US Migration." *Comparative Urban and Community Research* 6 (1998): 196-238.

Solis, Jocelyn. "No Human Being is Illegal: Counter-identities in a Community of Undocumented Mexican Immigrants and Children." Paper presented at the Fifth Conference of The International Society for Cultural Research and Activity Theory, Amsterdam, Holland, June 18-22, 2002. http://www.psy.vu.nl/iscrat2002/solis.pdf (accessed June 7, 2008).

———. "Narrating and Counternarrating Illegality as an Identity." Pp. 181-199 in Narrative Analysis: Studying the Development of Individuals in Society, edited by Colette Dauite and Cynthia Lightfoot. Thousand Oaks, CA: Sage, 2004.

Suarez-Orozco, Marcelo. "Everything You Wanted to Know about Assimilation but were Afraid to Ask." *Daedalus* 129, no. 4 (Fall 2000): 1-30.

Thomas, William I. and Florian Znaniecki. *The Polish Peasant in Europe and America: A Classic Work in Immigration History*, edited by Eli Zaratsky. Urbana: University of Illinois Press, 1996.

Tweed, Thomas. *Our Lady of the Exile: Diasporic Religion at a Cuban Catholic Shrine in Miami*. New York: Oxford University Press, 1997.

Warner, R. Stephen and Judith G. Wittner. *Gatherings in Diaspora: Religious Communities and the New Immigration*. Philadelphia: Temple University Press, 1998.

Wolf, Eric R. and Edward Hansen. *The Human Condition in Latin America*. New York: Oxford University Press, 1978.

Yang, Fenggang. "Tenacious Unity in a Contentious Community: Cultural and Religious Dynamics in a Chinese Christian Church." Pp. 333-363 in *Gatherings in Diaspora: Religious Communities and the New Immigration*, edited by Stephen Warner and Judith Wittner. Philadelphia: Temple University Press, 1998.

Chapter Fifteen

Building Communities through Faith: Filipino Catholics in Philadelphia and Alberta

Glenda Tibe Bonifacio and Vivienne SM. Angeles

More than eight million Filipinos reside outside of the Philippines with over three million in Canada and the United States as of December 2007 (Commission on Filipinos Overseas, CFO). The "culture of migration" (Asis 2006) in the Philippines or the "migration of a mentality" (Lott 1976) also reflects the "feminization of migration" (UN Instraw 2007) because more than half of Filipinos in the global labor diaspora are women who paved the way for the eventual reunification of their families as nurses, teachers, or caregivers. Aside from contributing to the labor pool in host societies, Filipinos enable the building of communities in distant shores; one of which is through religion or shared faith beliefs.

Religion has always been very much a part of Philippine life long before the advent of Spanish colonization. Indigenous religions, as well as Islam was already practiced in some parts of the country when the Spaniards came in 1521. Spain's colonization coupled with Christianization that included forced conversions dramatically altered the Philippine religious landscape and, with the colonial conflicts against Muslims particularly in southern Philippines, religion became a salient feature of Filipino identity (Steinberg 2000; Constantino 1976). Filipino indigenous beliefs in the power of a great god *Batala,* in spirits and other gods or goddesses that could be provoked or pacified through elaborate rituals therefore merged with Spanish Christian ideas of God and salvation. The result is a Christianity that is highly ritualistic where devotions to images of saints figure prominently. Catholicism also became an important component of the identity of most Filipinos. By the time the Americans occupied the Philippines in 1898, these religious beliefs and practices had become very much part of Philippine life. Today, the Philippines is the only Christian country in Asia with 81 percent of the population professing Catholicism (BBC News 2005). Filipinos, however, are said to be very religious and spiritual people regardless of their attachment to any religious institution (Root 1997).

When Filipino Catholics travel or migrate to other countries, this religious orientation is expressed in some ways in their new environment. They find places of worship, form prayer groups, and hold novenas in their homes as a way of perpetuating traditions and rituals learned as children. More importantly, religion and this sense of community fulfill important functions in the life of migrants. As Filipinos try to adjust to life in the United States (U.S.), for example, they also cope with the issue of creating and transforming their identities as Filipinos and Filipino-Americans (Almirol 1985; Strobel 1996). In so doing, they find themselves negotiating their cultural orientations, revising inherited traditions and practices in order to fit the new environment and lifestyles and, at the same time, to establish themselves in the host society.

We argue that gender and religion intersects in the integration of Filipinos in host societies like the United States and Canada. Because Filipino migration is highly gendered, this follows that the pathway of integration into host societies is likely gendered. This means that there are different ways in which religion impacts the subjective lives of Filipino men and women in migration. In the Philippines, women comprise the largest group of churchgoers and volunteers although the priestly Catholic hierarchy is reserved for men. Social codes prescribed by Catholic dogma permeate into the roles of men and women in the private and public spheres (Mananzan 1987; Rodriguez 1990). In particular, the ideology of female domesticity and male superiority have been ingrained in education and politics (Sobritchea 1996; Aguilar 1992). However, these roles are changing in more recent times with increasing democratization and economic globalization.[1]

Upon migration, religion becomes a refuge during the adjustment process and, at the same time, an agency through which Filipinos negotiate their lives in the new environment. Not only does religion allow Filipinos to re-affirm and re-experience their connection with the sacred as understood in Philippine Catholicism but it also gives them a sense of community, a linkage to compatriots that allows them not only to have a feel of "being home" but also provides a support system that is important in the process of relocation and integration. We see here the intersection of a vertical connection to the sacred and a horizontal linkage to the people from home and country. As Filipinos assemble in their churches to worship God, they also establish linkages with compatriots and relive traditions of the homeland as they say some prayers and sing hymns in the language, and gather together for a fellowship meal afterwards. These church activities provide a space for social and cultural interactions and become a springboard for engagement in other spheres of life in the community. Joaquin Jay Gonzalez III, in his latest book, *Filipino American Faith in Action* (2009), elucidates the intersectionality of Filipino migration, civic engagement and religious institutions of the second largest Asian Americans and how faith foments integration in the social, economic, political and cultural spheres.

In pursuing our argument on gender and religion, we examine two distinct Filipino communities in North America mainly defined by their migration status: the immigrants in Philadelphia and the migrant workers in Alberta. By immigrants we refer to those granted entry as permanent residents while migrant workers are those with temporary residency status contingent upon contracted employment. Some migrant workers participate in immigration schemes like the Live-in Caregiver Program (LCP) in Canada with a path toward permanent residency. This chapter is divided into two sections: Filipino immigrants in Philadelphia and migrant workers in Alberta. In Philadelphia, we look at the roles of the pastors and Filipino members of the church; how church space becomes a place where community links are created and nurtured; the integrative function of Filipino Catholic rituals, and how these communities function in relation to members' adjustment to American life. Also, we examine whether traditional gender roles in the Philippine Catholic church change or are maintained in the Philadelphia setting. This study is based on materials at the Temple University archives, interviews and visits to St. Peter, St. Augustine and St. Thomas Aquinas churches in Philadelphia as well as participation in a number of Philippine Catholic rituals in these churches and meetings of Filipino charismatic groups in Philadelphia and in Washington. The study was supported by the Harvard University Pluralism Project. In Alberta, we present the use of religion in the lives of migrant workers in the settlement and integration into local communities. As the most visible global labor force, Filipino migrant workers in Canada find ways to make meanings of their marginality through religion and shared faith beliefs, demonstrating the usefulness of this seemingly unrecognized aspect of their lives in their transition from temporary to permanent residents. Data is based on interviews and focus-group discussions with thirty live-in caregivers between 2007 and 2008 through the support of the Prairie Metropolis Centre.

Filipino Immigration to the United States

Based on the last census in 2000 there were 1.8 million Filipinos in the United States (Azada 2002: 127). Filipino immigration to the United States in large numbers started in the early 1900s when the country was an American colony. Filipinos came to Hawaii as migrant workers in the sugar plantations (Takaki 1998) and from there, moved on to the west coast of the United States. There were others who came as government scholars called *pensionado* (because they received a stipend—*pension*), wives of American soldiers, or family members who had been petitioned by those who came to the United States earlier. It was, however, the 1965 *Immigration and Nationality Act* that brought thousands of Filipinos to the United States. Two major purposes of this Act were to relieve occupational shortages in the United States and to achieve family reunification. Most Filipinos came to the United States under the third preference (as professionals) but many others came under the family reunification provision of the law. Numerous medical professionals who had come earlier under the exchange visitors program opted to stay in the United States after their training and had their exchange visitor visas converted to immigrant visas. In addition, they, like other Filipinos who immigrated, started to petition their dependents or their parents to come under the family reunification provision. Parents then petitioned other children, who in turn petitioned their spouses and families. The tradition of helping family members and relatives now transcended international boundaries and went beyond the earlier practice of sending money to help family and relatives in the Philippines. This process of chain migration (Okamura 1998) continues to the present time.

The post 1965 immigration presents a very different picture from the early 1900s. The new immigrants are better educated—teachers, doctors, nurses, engineers, lawyers, scientists and others fitting the description of "professional, technical and kindred workers" indicated in the Immigration Act. Filipino women immigrants outnumber the men and they represent varied professions. In 2006, the ratio of Filipino immigrant women to men was three to two or 58.7 percent women and 41.3 percent men (Terrazas 2008). Filipino nurses are sought after in many American hospitals since 1965 (Choy 2003). Three out of ten Filipinos in New York, for example, work as nurses or in other health-related professions (Berger 2008).

Since the passage of the 1965 law, various other legislations were passed that either allowed or restricted immigration. The Immigration Act of 1990 allows the naturalization of surviving Philippine-born veterans of the United States Armed Forces in the Far East, Philippine Army, Philippine Scout Rangers and recognized guerilla units who served between September 1, 1939 and December 31, 1946 (Posadas 1999). Veterans' groups who lobbied for this provision argued that since President Roosevelt incorporated the Philippine army into the U.S. armed forces by Executive Order, Filipino veterans, therefore, were also entitled to citizenship and benefits. Thousands of qualified Filipino veterans started coming to the United States in the 1990s and were immediately sworn in as citizens. Their benefits are not the same as their American counterparts but are certainly better than their government pension in the Philippines. In addition, coming to the United States opened the possibility for veterans' children to immigrate to the United States under the family reunification category.

Immigration, however, is not just a matter of transporting bodies across boundaries. Immigrants bring their culture, their traditions and religion as they cross international borders. These are the things that sustain them but yet, they know, they would have to make adjustments and concessions if they have to survive the new environment.

Filipinos in Philadelphia

Establishing population figures for Filipinos in the Philadelphia region is fraught with difficulties. One reason is that the 2000 census allowed respondents to indicate more than one ethnic background (Philadelphia City 2000). Secondly, the number 4,012 in the category of "Filipino Alone" in Philadelphia does not give a complete picture because it excludes many undocumented Filipinos who, although "invisible" officially, are nevertheless very much involved in Filipino church activities in Philadelphia. In addition, many Filipinos of mixed parentage identify themselves officially as Americans but consider themselves Filipinos as they demonstrate their affinity for the culture, traditions and religions.

Many Filipinos who settled in Philadelphia after 1965 came from the medical profession—doctors, nurses and medical technicians who worked at Temple University, Hahneman, Einstein and University of Pennsylvania hospitals. Recruiters who came to the Philippines in the mid-1960s or had local representatives in various medical schools introduced Filipinos to Philadelphia hospitals. There are also dependents of United States Navy personnel who lived in South Philadelphia, close to the navy base. Most Filipinos in the United States Navy remained in the country after serving their terms, and Philadelphia, like other cities where there are navy bases, was a logical place to settle.

Creating the Filipino Church

Before Filipinos in Philadelphia were organized at St. Augustine Church and St. Peter Church, they attended services in their own parishes just like other American Catholics. However, their involvement was minimal—basically just going to church with a very small number of Filipinos performing roles of Eucharistic minister or membership in the choir. More than ten years after the 1965 Immigration Law, at a time when the migrants were already settled, Filipinos in the Philadelphia area felt the need for a "home church" and several Filipinos thought of St. Augustine Church which was facing declining membership in the 1980s.[2] Leaders of the Filipino community discussed the possibility of creating St. Augustine Church as a shrine for the image of the *Santo Niño* (Carvajal 1992) with the pastor at the time, Fr. Quinn. In January 1992, about 600 Filipinos brought a twelve-inch image of Santo Niño to St. Augustine Church. Made of Philippine mahogany, the image is a replica of the Santo Niño image brought by Magellan to the Philippine island of Cebu in the sixteenth century. The Santo Niño was enshrined in an alcove, below an oil painting of Our Lady of Counsel to the right of St. Augustine Church's main altar.

The fact that Santo Niño image was made in the Philippines and brought to the United States provides a symbolic linkage and continuity of the Santo Niño devotion across the seas. Thomas Tweed (1997) demonstrates this kind of linkage when the Lady of Exile was installed by Cubans in Miami. With the enshrinement of the Santo Niño in this colonial church that figured prominently in American history and which had been historically responsive to the needs of Catholic immigrants, St. Augustine Church had been reconfigured to become a Philippine church in America, a "home church away from home." In a way, this points to the emergence of a transnational religion (Levitt 2007) which, while Catholic and Christian, is also Filipino. Since there were still local parishioners attending St. Augustine Church, Fr. Quinn and representatives of the Filipino community agreed that only certain parts of the Mass would be celebrated in Tagalog, a major Philippine language. These include the Our Father prayer and some songs during the communion while the rest of the Mass would be in English.

Since the creation of St. Augustine Church as the national shrine for the Santo Niño, Filipino priests have helped in ministering to the Filipinos and serving as assistant pastors. Although Filipinos have good rapport with the local Augustinian pastors, having a Filipino priest in the community who is familiar with Filipino traditions and rituals contributes to the continuity of Philippine Catholicism in the American landscape. With the Filipino priest and a "home church," Filipinos re-enact the Philippine version of the Christmas story, the singing of the Passion of Christ during Holy Week, the *Flores de Mayo* (Flowers of May) in honor of the Virgin Mary, the *Santacruzan* (in honor of St. Helen) and, most in especially, the feast of the Santo Niño. They sing church songs in Tagalog, offer prayers and novenas, bring the image of Mary from one house to another where they say the rosary and then share food. These celebrations and rituals are performed to resemble, as close as possible, those that are held in the Philippines (Priest 2007). But, these activities, as Charles Hirschman notes, assume new meaning in the host country in the sense that they provide "an emotional connection especially when shared with others" (2004: 1211). Some of the rituals, like the reading of the passion story during Lent, are linked to immigration. Several families host it in their homes and at St. Augustine Church every year as a way of thanking God for His beneficence and for the success of their children in their careers and families. A Filipino couple made a vow to continue hosting the singing of the Passion story of Jesus as long as they could because their good life would not have been possible without the help of God.

Filipinos from the Delaware Valley come to St. Augustine Church for the eleven o'clock Mass on Sundays which is followed by a novena to Santo Niño and afterwards, a fellowship lunch catered by various Filipino organizations in the church social hall. The language spoken during these lunches is Tagalog, the food served is Filipino and while confined within the social hall of the church, it is like a weekly return to the culinary culture of the home country while reaffirming one's identity as Filipino and Catholic. Filipino children also learn traditional dances of the Philippines, thus making St. Augustine Church a place for the reproduction and perpetuation not only of Philippine Catholic rituals but Philippine culture as well. The interactions at St. Augustine Church also connects earlier Filipino immigrants with recent arrivals and provides a social network where advice on such issues as housing, employment and education of children, veteran's benefits and social security are given. At the fellowship lunches after Mass on Sundays, Filipinos bring flyers and information about Filipino businesses like real estate, travel agencies, car repairs, shipping boxes filled with various goods to the Philippines.

The rituals and celebrations at St. Augustine Church, St. Peter Church and St. Thomas Aquinas Church are overseen by Sister Loreto Mapa, a Filipino nun from the Assumption order who was appointed coordinator of the Filipino Apostolate of the Archdiocese of Philadelphia. In these churches, it is noticeable that although Filipino couples participate together and volunteer as *hermanas* (female sponsors) and *hermanos* (male sponsors) who contribute financially to the celebrations, fulfill various functions in the church as ushers, choir and committee members, it is the women who tend to be more visible than the men. At the choirs in these churches, three fourths are women and in the fellowship meals after Sunday services, most of those who bring food and help in serving are women. In the Philippines, this pattern is also noticeable although there is now a growing involvement of men in church activities and parish councils. Sister Loreto notes the strong sense of volunteerism in the community regardless of gender but adds that many Filipino women plan and organize activities then take on assignments and responsibilities that come with the activities willingly. As immigrant women themselves who were able to restart their lives and pursue careers in another country, without the usual support of domestic helpers that are common in the Philippines, they are confident and demonstrate a strong sense of commitment to their religion and the community.

Looking at the subjective meaning of Filipino women's participation in these activities, their visible yet supportive roles imply certain connections to the perceived expectations of women in the Catholic tradition. While many of the women actively involved in church-related activities have "made it" in Philadelphia, their positionality as women, as volunteers, and as Catholics circumscribe their role in it. As women in Catholic-inspired rituals and festivities, they form a huge group of devotees whose faith keeps the tradition alive in their adopted country. The experiences of migration and the challenges of settlement and adaptation enhance strong religiosity among Filipinos, more so among the women, who like their counterparts in the Philippines, are often the primary initiators of worship for the blessings received by the family. Following Regina Gagnier (1991: 8-9) on her notion of a subject, Filipino women's subjectivity is not only seen with her own self but also in terms of other Filipinos and the knowledge of tradition where their roles, albeit marginal, are central to the community.

In more ways than one, the Filipino community in Philadelphia reflects the Philippines of the immigrants' time, where remembered traditions and religious rituals play essential roles in forging a bond among community members and helping them negotiate their lives in Philadelphia. It is religion that brought Filipinos to St. Augustine Church and from there, they created social networks that assist them as they navigate their immigrant lives in the new country. In this situation, the church becomes a place where love of God, love of country and nostalgia converge and become a springboard for engagement in the larger Philadelphia community.

Filipino Migrant Workers in Canada

The Philippines is one of the top ten source countries of immigrants and migrant workers to Canada since the 1980s. The Filipinos are the third largest Asian community representing about 8 percent of the total ethnic population. They comprise the largest group of permanent and temporary migrants for the first time in 2007 with 19,064 immigrants and 15,254 migrant workers (*The Asian Pacific Post* 2009). As of December 2007, the stock estimate of Filipinos in Canada reached 462,935 (CFO). According to Citizenship and Immigration Canada (CIC 2008), the Philippines is the number one source of female migrant workers since 2003. Filipino women predominate in the Live-in Caregiver Program as temporary migrant workers with a compromised right to apply for permanent residency after serving twenty-four months of live-in work conditions since 1992. This particular class of migrant workers has typified gendered migration from the Philippines and constructs the image of Filipino women as nannies, domestic workers or caregivers of the sick and the elderly in Canada (Pratt 1997, 1999, 2005; Stasiulis and Bakan 2005).

With the expanded temporary foreign workers program and the different Provincial Nominee Programs (PNP) in Alberta and other provinces, the Philippines is fast becoming the main source of foreign migrant workers. The persistent labor shortages in the oil-rich province of Alberta prompted the aggressive promotion of PNP which resulted in a memorandum of understanding between the province and the Philippines' Department of Labor and Employment in 2008 (Uy 2008). Almost all sectors are eligible to hire foreign migrant workers; from the original base of temporary foreign workers program, the Live-in Caregiver Program and the Seasonal Agricultural Workers Program, to the Low-skilled Pilot Project for the retail, services and warehousing, construction, hospitality, and service industry sectors. Migrant work is highly embedded in the daily lives of many Albertans as they queue for their favorite coffee at Tim Hortons, grab a healthy sandwich at Subway, a sumptuous family dinner at Swiss Chalet, or stay at the welcoming Ramada, among other places. In 2008, Alberta is home to about 57,000 foreign migrant workers (Zabjek and Pratt 2009).

Based on the 2006 census there were 51,095 Filipinos in Alberta; 25,565 of these live in Calgary and 19,625 in Edmonton (Statistics Canada). While small in size compared to the 140,405 Filipinos in the Greater Toronto area alone in the province of Ontario, Alberta is distinct because it is widely known as a conservative province where religion is integral in socio-political life and formation (Manning 2005) and is the site of the so-called "Bible belt" in Canada (Goertz 1981). It is in Alberta where ties of the globalized economy (i.e., oil and gas industry) and migration of foreign workers connect and provide a case of how religion manifests in the process of integration into the community.

Under economic globalization and the ensuing demand for migrant workers in industrialized societies, religion has been identified as an important aspect in the lives of Filipinos migrant workers in Asia and Europe (Cruz 2006; Magat 2007; Baggio 2009; Nakonz and Wai Yan Shik 2009). Filipino migrant workers create spaces of belonging within limiting social structures and institutions in receiving countries. In Canada, they have identifiably forged with one of the core values of the country—Christianity—and utilize familiar settings of worship as a means to integrate into the community. In this section, we present the Filipino migrant workers, specifically the live-in caregivers, and the role of religion in their transition from temporary to permanent residents.

Religion and Settlement

Christianity is the dominant religion in Canada. Roman Catholics form the largest group with 12.8 million declared adherents or 43 percent of the total population followed by Protestants with 8.7 million or 29 percent (Statistics Canada, "Overview"). The trajectory of mostly Christian Filipino migrants to a predominantly Christian Canada show a facilitation of cultural ethos based on shared religious beliefs. Filipinos are the largest Christian-affiliated immigrant community from Asia in Canada; a consequence of its long historical connection with Christianized Spain and America. Today, while Christianity and other "conventional religion is undoubtedly in decline, and may indeed be in crisis" (O'Toole 2006: 18), the number of Christian, mainly Catholic, Filipinos in Canada is increasing. A Roman Catholic school principal in Mississauga conversed that the Filipino community fill the halls of the parish, introducing a new flair to the solemn service with livelier music. In rural communities in southern Alberta, church attendance of Filipinos is notable. The active involvement of many Filipinos in church-related activities injects a religious vitality which, according to Gonzalez III in his study in San Francisco Bay area, is the "second coming of Christianity" (2002: 19).

The ritualistic devotions to patron saints in selected months of the year in Canada coincide with the celebratory dates in the Philippines. For example, the feast of Our Lady of Peñafrancia is held on the third Saturday in September in the Bicol region in the Philippines and, during this day, Filipinos converge at the Annunciation of the Blessed Virgin Mary Church in Toronto (Mastromatteo 1996). Infusing their own brand of Catholicism in Canada or elsewhere has brought the so-called *Filipinization* of Christianity in North America (Gonzalez III 2002).

Although the labor deployment program brings much needed revenue to an ever failing Philippine economy since the 1970s, Filipino migrant workers who practice their faith in myriad ways such as attending Sunday Mass and devotional worship subtly embody the Christian mission of evangelization (Pantoja, Tira and Wan 2004). As the world's largest group of foreign migrant workers in over 160 countries and territories, Filipinos are considered as "God's secret weapon" by the Lausanne Committee for World Evangelization (2005: 45) facilitating the global spread of Christianity.

In Alberta and elsewhere, Filipino communities are diverse yet there seems to be a unified character of religiosity. They are visibly marked for continuing practices that define their spiritual and cultural traditions in Canada mediated by local churches. Roman Catholic churches are centers of Filipino social interaction outside the confines of their homes: a place to forge new relationships with other Filipinos in the community. Migrant workers, especially live-in caregivers often isolated from each other, find one sure way to meet Filipinos by going to church. The sense of community and imagined bonds of ethnic identity is enabled by a familiar setting.

Filipinos generally value community life (Burgonio-Watson 1997: 328). They recreate this collectivist social frame by building quasi-familial associations with other Filipinos they encountered first at churches in Canada. It becomes apparent that building a network of friends and associates emanate after a "theologizing experience" (Smith 1978: 1175) arising from migration.

It helps that Canada is a multicultural society where the principle of respect for cultural diversity, among others, is enshrined in policies like the Canadian Multiculturalism Act. Even more favorable to the settlement of Filipino migrant workers is the presence of established Christian churches in both urban and rural areas. Religion becomes the realm to nurture bonds within particular communities in the process of integration (Rodriguez 2004: 7-11). Because Filipinos have high levels of religious participation, Catholic churches in particular foster the spatial mechanism to "provide cultural continuity" (Jarvis et al. 2005) to recently arrived migrant workers. It is through religion that migrant workers find a sense of familiarity away from home. As echoed by a Filipino live-in caregiver in Alberta, "I will go crazy if I cannot go to church." Considering her full-time live-in work in a house located in a sprawling agricultural land, the church is the nearest public space to interact with people and potentially watch for other Filipinos in the pews. In many instances, employers of live-in caregivers who reside in the rural outskirts give them a ride to the church on Sundays.

Faith from the Margins

Live-in caregivers under the LCP are positioned marginally in Canadian society based on gender, race, citizenship status, and class (Stasiulis and Bakan 2005). In the absence of a national child-care policy, the LCP and the Filipino women who construct the phenotype of the "nanny" are the cheap and better alternative to institutional day-cares in chronic shortage of staff. As well, this class of migrant workers is the best option in providing care for the infirm and the elderly in the comfort of their homes. Foreign migrant workers are guaranteed the minimum wage with no effective means of protecting their rights and dignity as workers. Many suffer in silence and endure the abuse to meet the required months of live-in work as a step toward gaining permanent residency, and the eventual reunification with their families.

Amidst all the challenges in the lives of migrant workers, religion or spiritual beliefs and traditions are said to impact on the psychological well-being of different ethnic communities (Shimabukuro, Daniels and D'Andrea 1999). Filipino live-in caregivers find strong connection with familiar religious practices that contribute to their transition from temporary to permanent residents in Canada. In Alberta, there is a general understanding among the Filipino live-in caregivers in this study that the services provided by immigrant serving agencies do not meet their needs, or are unaware of their eligibility to access the programs and services for newcomers. Major settlement programs include language instruction, referrals, and employment preparation that do not meet the needs of many live-in caregivers. Foremost, all have been pre-qualified of their English language skills prior to migration and posses the necessary aptitude to negotiate public spaces. Being alone in a foreign land with families to think of in the Philippines, these settlement services are not considered significant in their lives at this stage of their migration. In most cases, religious groups, together with friends and families, have replaced the government-funded agencies in providing assistance to migrant workers (Bonifacio 2009).

An interesting case of how religion facilitates the transition of Filipino migrant workers as live-in caregivers in Alberta is their involvement with the Couples for Christ (CFC)[3] and *El Shaddai*.[4] With its permanent recognition from the Vatican and most of the dioceses in Canada, the CFC is quite active in fostering community building among Filipino immigrants, migrant workers and Canadians since 1993. Southern Alberta alone boasts of more than 300 members including a number of non-Filipino nationals. In one monthly assembly of the CFC held at the basement of the St. Basil's Catholic Church in Lethbridge, a Canadian couple shared their story of joining the Filipino-dominated CFC to continue their pastoral ministry as those organized by the parish failed to attract members in the community.

Filipinos engaged with the CFC meet in small groups in households every week where members share gospel readings, food, and information. Many live-in caregivers attend these sessions as a way to establish social networks and find meaning in their quotidian lives. The CFC, according to a Filipino live-in caregiver in Lethbridge, "help us adjust to the new environment by being there [for us] like chauffeuring, sharing, or giving of household appliances" (Bonifacio 2008). This is an important gesture that is reminiscent of the Filipino value of *kapwa* or "shared self" that has become important in their initial settlement in the community.

In the same manner, involvement with El Shaddai provides ease in resolving issues many live-in caregivers face. For example, a migrant worker in Calgary confides that members of El Shaddai "find ways to accommodate us, sometimes assisting us in looking for another employer because of abuse" (Bonifacio 2008). Many live-in caregivers rely on the goodness of other Filipinos to connect them with possible employers in the area. This act is critical as the change of employers require another work permit which takes a few months to process and, eventually, affects the period of complying with the requirements of LCP.

Women positioned as racialized migrant workers are steadfast in their goal to gain permanent residency. Their resilience to meet the daily challenges of live-in work is strengthened by their faith and belief in a better future in Canada. Since many of the Filipino live-in caregivers have previously worked in parts of Asia and the Middle East where the working conditions are, reportedly, far worse than in Canada (Thorold 2008), the two or three years of live-in work under the LCP is considered "bearable." This is consistent with the social conditioning of women in the Philippines to sacrifice for the welfare of the family. According to Jocelyn Eclarin Azada, "[i]ndividual needs are subordinated to the family's common good, and helping the family collectively is viewed as one's most primary responsibility" (2002: 127). In the Filipino religious psyche, *may awa ang Diyos* (God has mercy) is most invoked in the face of personal adversity, enabling the migrant worker to believe in the best days ahead.

Conclusion

Migration is a fact of life. The continuous flow of people leaving the Philippines each day, as well as those returning from work overseas, has shaped the lives of many Filipinos. North America is a favored destination of Filipino immigrants and migrant workers where community building is facilitated by shared religious practices and beliefs. Religion offers a common bond among Filipino immigrants in Philadelphia and migrant workers in Alberta. Filipino Catholics continue to practice rituals and activities that they are familiar with in their home country, and enriches the diversity of Catholicism in the United States. While gender roles in the Filipino Catholic churches in Philadelphia do not differ from those in the Philippines, women demonstrate strong commitment to their faith and community as a way of expressing gratitude for a perceived successful migration story. In Alberta, the Filipino live-in caregivers with temporary resident status make use of religion in coping with the difficulties of their peculiar work conditions. The Catholic churches serve as a venue to establish initial contacts with other Filipinos in the area. Established religious groups like CFC and El Shaddai demonstrate traditional Filipino values like *kapwa* to make a difference in the lives of migrant workers. The experiences of Filipinos we studied in Alberta and Philadelphia show that shared religious beliefs become the entrepoint of integrating into society, of finding ways to belong in lands they want to call their own.

Notes

1. The Philippines has elected two female presidents, Corazon Aquino and Gloria Macapagal Arroyo. Their rise to power was facilitated by their connection with men; a slain husband and former senator, Benigno "Ninoy" Aquino, and a former president, Diosdado Macapagal. In general, however, the level of Filipino women's political participation is about the same as women in Western Europe. See Linda K. Richter, "The Status of Women in the Philippines," *The Philippines Reader*, ed. David Schirmer and

Stephen Rosskamm Shalom (Boston: South End Press, 1987), 136. Economic globalization provides the impetus for overseas employment and contributes to the shift in gender roles and family dynamics. As more women leave the country as overseas Filipino workers (OFW), they become the primary breadwinners and, consequently, demonstrate care from a distance. It is also becoming a norm where both parents are OFWs deployed in different countries and, thus, form a transnational family. See the works of Rhacel Salazar Parreñas, *Servants of Globalization* (California: Stanford University Press, 2001) and *Children of Global Migration* (California: Stanford University Press, 2005).

2. St. Augustine's is a historic church, whose corner stone was laid in 1796 with President George Washington and Governor Thomas Mckean in attendance. Originally built to serve German and Irish immigrants, St. Augustine's was the largest church in Philadelphia at that time. Almost 200 years later, demographic changes in Philadelphia affected St. Augustine's parish so that by the late 1980s, it had become a struggling parish, with only about twenty-five parishioners coming to each of their Sunday Masses. See "First Augustinian Church," *Catholic Standard and Times*, September 29, 1967.

3. CFC is purely rooted in the Filipino tradition since 1981. It has branched into specific groups based on marital status and age such as the Kids for Christ, Youth for Christ, Singles for Christ as well as Handmaids for widows, single mothers, or women whose husbands are away or do not wish to join them in service; the Servants of the Lord comprising widowers or whose wives are away or do not wish to join them in communal gathering.

4. *El Shaddai* is a populist charismatic movement in the Philippines led by Brother Mike Velarde. It has a worldwide membership of eight to ten million. See Katharine L. Wiegele, *Investing in Miracles: El Shaddai and the Transformation of Popular Catholicism in the Philippines* (Honolulu: University of Hawaii Press, 2005); Phra Paisal Visalo, "The Dynamics of Religion in the Age of Globalization," in *The Asian Face of Globalization*, ed. Ricardo Abad (Tokyo: The Nippon Foundation, 2004).

Bibliography

Aguilar, Carmencita. "Women's Political Involvement in Historical Perspective." *LILA-Asia Pacific Women's Studies Journal* 2 (1992): 14-23.

Almirol, Edwin B. *Ethnic Identity and Social Negotiation: A Study of a Filipino Community in California.* New York: AMS Press, 1985.

Asis, Maruja B. "The Philippines' Culture of Migration." *Migration Information Source Country Profiles.* January 2006. http://www.migrationinformation.org/Profiles/displ ay.cfm?ID=364 (accessed April 21, 2009).

Azada, Jocelyn Eclarin. "Diaspora Economics: Filipino American Families and Globalization." Pp. 125-143 in *Gender, Ethnicity and Religion: Views from the Other Side*, edited by Rosemary Radford Ruether. Minneapolis: Fortress Press, 2002.

Baggio, Fabio, ed. *Faith on the Move: Toward a Theology of Migration in Asia.* Quezon City: Ateneo de Manila University Press, 2009.

BBC News. "Factfile: Roman Catholics around the World." April 1, 2005. http://news.bb c.co.uk/1/hi/world/4243727.stm (accessed April 29, 2009).

Berger, Joseph. "Filipino Nurses, Healers in Trouble," *The New York Times*, January 27, 2008. http://www.nytimes.com/2008/01/27/nyregion/nyregionspecial2/27Rnurses.h tml (accessed April 20, 2009).

Bonifacio, Glenda Lynna Anne Tibe. "I Care for You, Who Cares for Me? Transitional Services of Filipino Live-in Caregivers in Canada." *Asian Women: Gender Issues in International Migration* 24, no.1 (Spring 2008): 25-50.

————. "From Temporary Workers to Permanent Residents: Transitional Services for Filipino Live-in Caregivers in Alberta." *Our Diverse Cities* no. 6 (Spring 2009): 136-141.

Burgonio-Watson, Thelma B. "Filipino Spirituality: An Immigrant's Perspective." Pp. 324-332 in *Filipino Americans: Transformation and Identity*, edited by Maria P. P. Root. California: Sage, 1997.

Carvajal, Doreen. "How a Church Dying Slowly Found its New Life as a Shrine," *Philadelphia Inquirer*, February 12, 1992.

Choy, Catherine Ceniza. *Empire of Care: Nursing and Migration in Filipino American History.* Durham, NC: Duke University Press, 2003.

Citizenship and Immigration Canada. *Facts and Figures: Immigration Overview Permanent and Temporary Residents, 2007.* Ottawa, ON: Research and Evaluation Branch, CIC, 2008. http://www.cic.gc.ca/english/pdf/pub/facts2007.pdf (accessed April 27, 2009).

Commission on Filipinos Overseas. "Stock Estimate of Overseas Filipinos as of December 2007." http://www.cfo.gov.ph/Stock%202007.pdf (accessed April 25, 2009).

Constantino, Renato. "Identity and Consciousness: The Philippine Experience." *Journal of Contemporary Asia* 6, no. 1 (1976): 5-28.

Cruz, Gemma Tulud. "Faith on the Edge: Religion and Women in the Context of Migration." *Feminist Theology* 15, no. 1 (2006): 9-25.

"First Augustinian Church," *Catholic Standard and Times*, September 29, 1967.

Gagnier, Regina. *Subjectivities: A History of Self-Representation in Britain, 1832-1934.* New York: Oxford University Press, 1991.

Goertz, Donald Aaron. *The Development of a Bible Belt: The Socio-religious Interaction in Alberta Between 1928 and 1938.* Ottawa: National Library of Canada, 1981.

Gonzalez III, Joaquin Jay. "Transnationalization of Faith: The Americanization of Christianity in the Philippines and the Filipinization of Christianity in the United States." *Asia Pacific: Perspectives* 2, no. 1 (February 2002): 9-20.

————. *Filipino American Faith in Action: Immigration, Religion, and Civic Engagement.* New York and London: New York University Press, 2009.

Hirschman, Charles. "The Role of Religion in the Origins and Adaptation of Immigrant Groups in the United States." *The International Migration Review* 38, no. 3 (Fall 2004): 1206-1233.

Jarvis, G. Eric, Laurence J. Kirmayer, Morton Weinfeld and Jean-Claude Lasry. "Religious Practice and Psychological Distress: The Importance of Gender, Ethnicity and Immigrant Status." *Transcultural Psychiatry* 42, no. 4 (December 2005): 657-675.

Lausanne Committee for World Evangelization. "The New People Next Door." Lausanne Occasional Paper no. 55, 2005. http://www.lausanne.org/documents/2004forum/LO P55_IG26.pdf (accessed September 5, 2008).

Levitt, Peggy. *God Needs No Passport: Immigrants and the Changing American Religious Landscape.* New York: New Press, 2007.

Lott, Juanita Tamayo. "Migration of a Mentality: The Pilipino Community." *Social Casework* 57 (March 1976): 165-172.

Magat, Margaret. "Teachers and 'New Evangelizers' for their Faith: Filipina Domestic Workers at Work in Italy." *Paedogogica Historica* 43, no. 4 (August 2007): 603-624.

Mananzan, Mary John, ed. *Essays on Women.* Manila: The Institute of Women's Studies, 1987.

Manning, Preston. "Prairie Companions," *Maclean's,* July 1, 2005, 34-38.

Mastromatteo, Mike. "Devotion Remains Central to Filipino Faith Life," *Catholic Insight,* November 1, 1996. http://www.thefreelibrary.com/Devotion+remains+cent ral+to+Filipino+faith+life-a030185037. (accessed April 28, 2009).

Nakonz, Jonas and Angela Wai Yan Shik. "And All Your Problems are Gone: Religious Coping Strategies among Philippine Migrant Workers in Hong Kong." *Mental Health, Religion and Culture* 12, no. 1 (January 2009): 25-38.

Okamura, Jonathan Y. *Imagining the Filipino-American Diaspora: Transnational Relations, Identities and Communities.* New York: Garland Publishing, 1998.

O'Toole, Roger. "Religion in Canada: It's Development and Contemporary Situation." Pp. 7-21 in *Religion and Canadian Society: Traditions, Transitions, and Innovations,* edited by Lori G. Beaman. Toronto: Canadian Scholars' Press, 2006.

Pantoja, Luis Jr., Sadiri Joy Tira and Enoch Wan. *Scattered: The Filipino Global Presence.* Manila: Life Changing Publishing, 2004.

Parreñas, Rhacel Salazar. *Servants of Globalization: Women, Migration and Domestic Work.* California: Stanford University Press, 2001.

———. *Children of Global Migration: Transnational Families and Gendered Woes.* California: Stanford University Press, 2005.

Posadas, Barbara M. *The Filipino Americans.* California: Greenwood, 1999.

Pratt, Geraldine. "Stereotypes and Ambivalence: The Construction of Domestic Workers in Vancouver, British Columbia." *Gender, Place and Culture* 4, no. 2 (1997):159-178.

———. "From Registered Nurse to Registered Nanny: Discursive Geographies of Filipina Domestic Workers in Vancouver, B.C." *Economic Geography* 75, no. 3 (July 1999): 215-236.

———. "From Migrant to Immigrant: Domestic Workers Settle in Vancouver, Canada." Pp. 123-137 in *A Companion to Feminist Geography,* edited by Lise Nelson and Joni Seager. Oxford, UK: Blackwell, 2005.

Priest, Kersten Bayt. "New Immigrant Filipinos Bring Changes to their Parish." Pp. 243-258 in *This Side of Heaven: Race, Ethnicity and Christian Faith,* edited by Robert J. Priest and Alvaro L. Nieves. New York: Oxford University Press, 2007.

"Profile of General Demographic Characteristics: 2000." Philadelphia City, Pennsylvania, 2000. http://www.philaplanning.org/data/sf3profile.pdf (accessed March 10, 2009).

Richter, Linda K. "The Status of Women in the Philippines." Pp. 135-143 in *The Philippines Reader,* edited by David Schirmer and Stephen Rosskamm Shalom. Boston: South End Press, 1987.

Rodriguez, Gregory. "Tamed Spaces: How Religious Congregations Nurture Immigrant Assimilation in Southern California." Pp. 7-20 in *Immigrants, Religious Congregations, and the Civil Society,* edited by Gregory Rodriguez, Karen Speicher and James R. Wilburn. Malibu, CA: Davenport Institute, Pepperdine University

School of Public Policy, 2004. http://publicpolicy.pepperdine.edu/davenport-institute/reports/faith-public-policy/content/faith-public-policy-report.pdf (accessed December 15, 2008).

Rodriguez, Luz. "Patriarchy and Women's Subordination in the Philippines." *Review of Women's Studies* 1, no. 1 (1990): 15-25.

Root, Maria P. P., ed. *Filipino Americans: Transformation and Identity*. California, Sage, 1997.

Shimabukuro, Kathryn P., Judy Daniels and Michael D'Andrea. "Addressing Spiritual Issues from a Cultural Perspective: The Case of the Grieving Filipino Boy." *Journal of Multicultural Counseling and Development* 27, no. 4 (1999): 221-239.

Smith, Timothy. "Religion and Ethnicity in America." *The American Historical Review* 83 (1978): 1155-1185.

Sobritchea, Carolyn. "The American Colonial Education and its Impact on the Status of Filipino Women." Pp. 79-108 in *Women's Role in Philippine History*, edited by Proserpina Domingo Tapales. Quezon City: University Center for Women's Studies, University of the Philippines, 1996.

Stasiulis, Daiva K. and Abigail B. Bakan. *Negotiating Citizenship: Migrant Women in Canada and the Global System*. Toronto: University of Toronto Press, 2005.

Statistics Canada. *Ethnocultural Portrait of Canada: Visible Minority Groups*. http://www12.statcan.gc.ca/english/census06/data/highlights/ethnic/pages/Page.cfm?Lang=E&Geo=CMA&Code=48&Table=1&Data=Count&StartRec=1&Sort=2&Display=Page&CSDFilter=5000 (accessed April 20, 2009).

————. "Overview: Canada Still Predominantly Roman Catholic and Protestant." http://www12.statcan.ca/english/census01/products/analytic/companion/rel/canada.cfm#overview (accessed April 21, 2009).

Steinberg, David Joel. *The Philippines: A Singular and Plural Place*. New York: Basic Books, 2000.

Strobel, Leny Mendoza. "'Born-Again Filipino': Filipino American Identity and Asian Panethnicity." *Amerasia Journal* 22, no. 2 (1996): 31-53.

Takaki, Ronald. *Strangers from a Different Shore*. Boston: Little, Brown and Co., 1998.

Terrazas, Aaron. "Filipino Immigrants in the United States." *Migration Information Source*. September 2008. http://www.migrationinformation.org/USFocus/print.cfm?ID=694 (accessed February 5, 2009).

The Asian Pacific Post. "Filipinos are No. 1," January 8, 2009. http://www.asianpacificpost.com/portal2/c1ee8c421e892f19011eb8f2447200a5_Filipinos_are_No__1_.do.html (accessed April 28, 2009).

Thorold, Crispin. "Philippine Ban for Jordan 'Abuse,'" *BBC News*, January 24, 2008. http://news.bbc.co.uk/1/hi/world/middle_east/7207094.stm (accessed April 30, 2009).

Tweed, Thomas. *Our Lady of the Exile*. New York: Oxford University Press, 1997.

United Nations International Research and Training Institute for the Advancement of Women (UN Instraw). "The Feminization of Migration: Gender, Remittances and Development." Working Paper 1, 2007. http://www.un-instraw.org/en/grd/facts-and-figures/facts-and-figures-feminization.html (accessed April 26, 2009).

Uy, Veronica. "Alberta Opens Doors to OFWs," *Inquirer*, October 1, 2008. http://globalnation.inquirer.net/news/breakingnews/view/20081001-164013/Alberta-opens-doors-to-OFWs (accessed April 25, 2009).

Visalo, Phra Paisal. "The Dynamics of Religion in the Age of Globalization: Lessons from India, the Philippines, and Japan." Pp. 25-35 in *The Asian Face of Globalization*, edited by Ricardo G. Abad (Tokyo: The Nippon Foundation, 2004).

Wiegele, Katharine L. *Investing in Miracles: El Shaddai and the Transformation of Popular Catholicism in the Philippines*. Honolulu: University of Hawaii Press, 2005.

Zabjek, Alexandra and Sheila Pratt, "Scarce Jobs Ignite Debate over Alberta's 57,000 Temporary Foreign Workers," *Calgary Herald*, February 26, 2009. http://www.calg aryherald.com/opinion/reader-comments/Scarce+jobs+ignite+debate+over+Alberta+ temporary+foreign+workers/1331967/story.html (accessed April 26, 2009).

Chapter Sixteen

No Greater Law: Illegal Immigration and Faith-based Activism

Connie Oxford

Since the late 1990s the Sonora desert in southern Arizona has become the busiest corridor for illegal immigration into the United States (U.S.). Consequently, activism that facilitates and deters migration across the U.S.-Mexico border has surged. Many pro-immigrant groups working to help migrants today trace their grassroots lineage to the North American Sanctuary movement, an amalgamation of faith-based groups that provided refuge for Central Americans fleeing violence and war in the 1980s. Like their predecessors in the Sanctuary movement, many of these activists embrace the notion that humanitarian work serves a greater goal than the consequences of breaking laws that impede migrants' livelihood. This chapter addresses contemporary pro-immigrant activism in southern Arizona and the ways in which gender, the law, and faith-based ideology inform activists' understandings of why they work with illegal immigrants crossing the southern border.[1] I situate contemporary pro-immigrant faith-based activism in Arizona in the context of the North American Sanctuary movement and the militarization of the U.S.-Mexico border.

The North American Sanctuary Movement

In the early 1980s, civil unrest in many Central American nation-states, El Salvador in particular, reached a turning point. Widespread human rights abuses committed by governments of these nation-states left many citizens without any choice but to flee for their lives. In total, nearly two million Central Americans left their country during the 1980s (Castles and Miller 2003). Many critics of the Central American crisis identified U.S. foreign policy as one of the major causes of regime brutality because it provided economic and military support to the governments of El Salvador, Nicaragua, and Guatemala. Therefore, according to these critics, U.S. foreign policy makers were in part responsible for Central American migration to the United States (Tomsmo 1987).

While U.S.-based activists trace their involvement in the Sanctuary movement to a variety of incidents, four events serve as pivotal moments that turned many people in faith-based communities into activists (Cunningham 1995; Lorentzen 1991; Golden and McConnell 1986). These events are the assassination of Archbishop Oscar Romero in El Salvador in March 1980 (Nepstad 2002); the discovery of thirteen Salvadoran migrants found wandering near Aijo, Arizona in July 1980 (Davidson 1988); the murder of four Maryknoll nuns in El Salvador in December 1980 (Lorentzen 1991); and the Immigration and Naturalization Service's (INS) detainment of a Salvadoran hitchhiker that Jim Dudley picked up in May 1981 in Nogales, Arizona. These events made the Central American refugee crises real and provided personalized accounts of a mass tragedy (Nepstad 2002).

In most accounts of the Sanctuary movement, its origins in the U.S. are traced to two leaders: Reverend John Fife, the pastor of Tucson's Southside Presbyterian Church and Jim Corbett, a Quaker rancher living in southern Arizona (Corbett 1991; Crittenden 1988; Davidson 1988; Tomsmo 1987). Reverend Fife became involved when his church, Southside Presbyterian, volunteered to assist the survivors from the Aijo tragedy. In July 1980, thirteen Salvadorans were found lost in the Sonora desert. They had been abandoned by their smuggler and were near death. Some members of the group had been raped, beaten, and left for dead, while others had succumbed to the elements. Those who survived were placed into deportation proceedings by the INS. Reverend Fife's congregation posted bail for the survivors, provided them with housing, food, and clothes, and helped them apply for political asylum. On March 24, 1982, Southside Presbyterian was the first religious organization to publicly announce that it was a Sanctuary for Central American refugees.

Jim Corbett's entrée into the movement is traced to his involvement in assisting the hitchhiker that Jim Dudley picked up and who was later detained by INS. In May 1981, while Jim Dudley was on his way to visit fellow Quaker Jim Corbett, he offered a Salvadoran man a ride, unaware that he had fled for his life. The U.S. Border Patrol stopped Dudley and took the migrant into custody. Troubled by the turn of events, Dudley described what had happened to Jim and his wife, Pat Corbett. The next day, Jim Corbett attempted to locate the detained hitchhiker, and through his initial interactions with the INS, learned that unauthorized Salvadorans were overwhelmingly returned to El Salvador, even when they asked for asylum. Corbett reached out to his Quaker friends across the country asking them for donations for this migrant's bail as well as other detained migrants in financial need. Corbett's persistence in aiding Salvadoran asylum seekers propelled him into a leadership position in the movement.

One consequence of focusing on these two men as the central leaders of the Sanctuary Movement is that such an account underscores activists as white, male, and American (U.S.-based). Becky Thompson (2001) argues that while women, people of color, and Mexican and Central Americans were essential to this movement, their participation has often been erased. Without the help of the Mexican, Central American and U.S.-based Latino/a population, the U.S. role in the Sanctuary movement would not have been possible.

Sanctuary movement activists engaged in a range of activities that included smuggling refugees across the border through the desert, operating an underground railroad that moved refugees to safe houses across the U.S. and into Canada, and helping refugees negotiate the legal bureaucracy when applying for asylum. When members of churches, parishes, and synagogues tried to help Central American refugees gain political asylum they often encountered hostility from the U.S. government. INS viewed Central Americans as economic migrants looking for work rather than refugees fleeing persecution. This position was particularly problematic since Congress had recently passed the *Refugee Act* of 1980 that broadened the definition of persecution permitting refugees who sought asylum from non-communist countries into the United States. Over 440,000 Central Americans applied for asylum in the United States between 1984 and 1994 (Castles and Miller 2003). Between June 1983 and September 1986, only 528 or 2.6 percent of the 19,207 asylum applications from Salvadorans and fourteen or 1.8 percent of the 1,461 applications from Guatemalans were approved by the INS. These rates stand in stark contrast to the 60.4 percent of Iranians and 51 percent of Romanians who were approved for that same period (Crittenden 1988).

Although many accounts of the Sanctuary movement depict it as a men's movement (Corbett 1991; Davidson 1988; Tomsmo 1987; Loder 1986), women, too, were heavily involved (Lorentzen 1991). The sexual division of labor and the public/private dichotomy is useful for understanding women's activism and their exclusion from leadership roles. Much of the work done by Sanctuary movement activists was "women's work." Women performed private "domestic work" by providing clothing, food, and medical care for migrants. However, their activism was not exclusive to the private realm. Women engaged in dangerous forms of activism by escorting migrants across the border and through the desert to safety. In the public realm, women were often excluded from religious leadership roles, such as priests, pastors, and rabbis. Consequently, men emerged as the leaders of this movement.

Most studies of the Sanctuary movement culminate in the arrests and trials of activists in the United States. In January 1985, the U.S. Government issued a seventy-one count criminal indictment against leaders of the Sanctuary movement (Golden and McConnell 1986). In Tucson, six of the eleven activists who were charged were women (Davidson 1988). These arrests, in addition to the Central American peace agreements in 1987 and the American Baptist Church (ABC) settlement which allowed certain Central Americans to be eligible for asylum in 1991, marked the end of the North American Sanctuary movement (Rader 1999). Over the course of the 1980s, approximately 70,000 U.S. citizens were involved in this movement (Golden and McConnell 1986).

Militarization of the U.S.-Mexico Border

While the beginning of the 1990s ushered in the end of the Central American refugee crisis, a new migration flow across the U.S.-Mexico border had increased significantly by the end of the decade. Since the passage of the North American Free Trade Agreement (NAFTA) in 1994, the number of Mexicans crossing the border illegally has risen dramatically. Mexican nationals have historically comprised the greatest percentage of immigrants crossing the U.S.-Mexico border, even during the Central American refugee crises (Portes and Rumbault 2006). However, the total number of Mexicans crossing the border illegally waxed and waned over the twentieth century depending on U.S.-Mexico geopolitics. According to the Pew Hispanic Center, approximately 400,000 Mexicans entered the U.S. illegally between 1995 and 1999. This number rose to 485,000 between 2000 and 2004. These numbers have nearly doubled from the 1990-1994 period when the number of Mexican nationals entering the U.S. illegally was 260,000 (Passel 2005).

U.S.-based law makers and corporations that supported NAFTA argued that the proceeds gained by the Mexican government from the elimination of tariffs would be available for investment in Mexico. These investments were to be used to create jobs, build schools, and improve infrastructure. Instead, the Mexican government, the U.S. government, and U.S. corporations cooperated to build U.S.-owned factories in northern Mexico known as the *maquiladoras*. Employees in the maquiladoras earned as little as $5 per day, working as much as ten hours or more a day without benefits. These factories, along with agricultural trade provisions in the treaty, devastated the manufacturing and agricultural economy of Mexico. Consequently, Mexicans are left with few choices—eke out a subsistence living in towns where jobs are scarce, work for low wages in the maquiladoras, or risk crossing the border into the U.S. to find work (Nevins 2002). As demonstrated by the data gleaned from the Pew Hispanic Center report, many Mexicans chose to migrate to the U.S. in search of work.

Although NAFTA is, in part, responsible for creating the increased flow of Mexican migrants to the United States, militarization of the U.S.-Mexico border accounts for *where* these migrants cross. In the 1990s, the INS embarked on numerous campaigns to increase border security (Andreas 2000). Two operations in particular included building a wall along the border and increasing the presence of Border Patrol personnel. In 1993, Operation Hold the Line was the first of two militarized plans to stem illegal immigration in U.S. urban areas. Operation Hold the Line, renamed from its original title Operation Blockade, was Silvestre Reyes's, Chief of the El Paso Border Patrol Sector, solution to illegal immigrants coming across the Rio Grande into Texas (Bean et al. 1994). The second initiative, Operation Gatekeeper, took place in 1994 in San Diego, California. The operation was eventually extended from the Pacific Ocean to the San Ysidro border checkpoint covering the entirety of the state of California (Nevins 2002).

The logic behind these two operations was to enhance border security in areas that were geographically easier to cross. Immigration policy makers in the U.S. assumed that migrants would choose not to cross in areas where the terrain is more difficult to navigate and, therefore, these new border security strategies would decrease the flow of illegal immigrants across the U.S.-Mexico border.

On the contrary, these policies did not curb illegal immigration but instead funneled migrants into dangerous areas in rural parts of the desert. Migrants crossing through the rural areas of the desert face a journey where they are limited to the water, food, and supplies that they can carry with them. What few migrants know as they embark on this treacherous path is that it is impossible to carry enough water for their entire journey. Migrants face dehydration, starvation, heat exhaustion, and hypothermia, among other difficulties. The gravest of all consequences is, of course, death (Ramos 2005; Urrea 2004).

Women's Migration across the U.S.-Mexico Border

The geopolitics of the U.S.-Mexico border that include policy changes such as NAFTA and the militarization of the border explain general migration patterns. Yet, one crucial change in migration across the U.S.-Mexico border is the increase in female migrants. While there are no definitive data on the number of illegal border crossers, migration scholars attempt to capture the estimated number of undocumented migrants in the U.S. According to the Pew Hispanic Center, there were three million undocumented women between eighteen and thirty-nine years old, and 1.7 million undocumented children in the U.S. in March 2004 (Passel 2005). These approximately 3.5 million women and children comprise 51 percent of the undocumented population under the age of forty in the United States.

The rise in women's migration is a global phenomenon (Pessar and Mahler 2003). The increase in female border crossers from Mexico into the U.S. can be attributed overwhelmingly to the demand for low wage domestic work in the U.S., such as housekeeping and childcare (Hondagneu-Sotelo 2001; Hondagneu-Sotelo and Avila 1997) and family reunification with parents, spouses, and children (Hondagneu-Sotelo 2003). Women's migration within Mexico has increased as well. Currently, most workers in the maquiladoras are women who travel from central and southern Mexico to work in northern Mexico border towns. In the Juárez area, many women who work in these factories have disappeared as they travel between their homes and work making employment in the maquiladoras particularly dangerous (Segura and Zavella 2007).

Another indicator of the increase in women's migration across the U.S.-Mexico border is the death rate for female migrants. The death rate for female migrants crossing the border has increased significantly since 2000. According to the Pima County Medical Examiner, there were 125 deaths of unauthorized migrants between 1990 and 1999.[2] Of these 125 deaths, seventeen were women making them 13.6 percent of the total for that decade. Between 2000 and 2005, these numbers rose drastically when the total number of deaths jumped to 802. Of these 802 deaths, 181 or 22.6 percent were women. In half the time period of the ten years of documented data in the 1990s, the number of migrants dying in the desert increased seven times and the number of women who are dying while trying to cross increased eleven times during the first five years of the new millennium. Women currently comprise about a quarter of all migrant deaths in the Sonora desert (Rubio-Goldsmith et al. 2006).

The increase in women's migration also affects the number of children who cross and die in the desert. Prior to 1990, there were no deaths of migrant children reported by the Pima County Medical Examiner. There were five deaths of minor migrants reported between 1990 and 1999. This number increased to forty-two between 2000 and 2005. Again, similar to the increase in deaths for adult migrants, there was a dramatic increase in deaths of minor children migrating across the desert. In half the time period of the ten years of documented data in the 1990s, the number of minors dying in the desert increased nine times during the first five years of the new millennium.

These data show that more women and children are dying in the desert, in part because more women and children are embarking on this journey. The sexual division of labor may explain why adult female deaths and child deaths are linked. Children are more likely to be traveling with adult women than men because women tend to perform more childcare than men.[3] Another gendered dimension of migration includes the likelihood of death from exposure (e.g., heat, dehydration, and hypothermia). The Pima County Medical Examiner also found that women are nearly three times (2.87) more likely than men to die from exposure.

Women are also more likely than men to experience sexual assault by other migrants or smugglers while in the desert. Along some migrant trails are "rape trees," desert bushes adorned with women's underwear. These rape trees ostensibly are the site of sexual violence where the assailant placed his victim's underwear in the tree as a sign of his conquest. These trees signify sexual access to female migrants' bodies and instill fear in migrant women.[4] During my interview with a member of the *Coalición de Derechos Humanos*, I was told that many women traveling through the desert with their daughters cut their daughters' hair and dress them as boys as one tactic to thwart potential attacks.[5]

Another gendered phenomenon of migration is that female migrants are more likely than men to be forced into sexual slavery. One of the consequences of militarization of the border is that migrants are often forced to pay a coyote, or smuggler to guide them across the border because the journey is nearly impossible to make without knowledge of the desert terrain (Kyle and Koslowski 2001). Women are sometimes subject to forced prostitution when the responsible party does not pay the coyote, or smuggler's fee. In Arizona, migrants are often held in safe houses in Tucson or Phoenix until their families pay the coyotes.

Contemporary Faith-Based Activism
in Southern Arizona

Beginning in 2000, three faith-based groups formed in Tucson, Arizona in response to the militarization of the U.S.-Mexico border and its grave effects on migrants. These groups are Humane Borders, Samaritans, and No More Deaths.[6]

Although a variety of activists, including former Sanctuary Movement members, were responsible for initiating these groups, Reverend John Fife was a key figure in organizing these groups' response to the new border crisis (Moser 2003). Similar to the gendered demographics of the Sanctuary movement, the majority of the volunteers are women. Each group is connected to a church in Tucson: Humane Borders hold their meetings at The First Christian Church, Samaritans gather at Southside Presbyterian, and No More Deaths organize their training sessions at St. Mark's Presbyterian. However, unlike faith-based activism during the Sanctuary Movement where churches were the central organizing unit, these organizations operate independently of the churches which they use for meetings and other events.

All of these faith-based groups operate exclusively on volunteer labor. Volunteering with these groups is demanding because they patrol the desert daily. Like their Sanctuary Movement predecessors, these groups advocate policy changes that include the demilitarization of the border in addition to providing humanitarian aid to migrants in distress. The primary goal for each of these groups is to decrease the number of migrant deaths in the desert. Faith-based groups include immigrants (documented and undocumented) and people of color; however, the majority of members are white U.S. citizens.

Humane Borders

Founded on June 11, 2000, by Reverend Robin Hoover, Humane Borders operates approximately eighty-three water stations in the desert (Scharf 2006). The stations provide water for migrants or anyone else in distress in the desert. Each water station consists of two fifty-five gallon blue tanks with a thirty foot flag hoisted next to the tanks. The flag is positioned so that migrants may locate the tanks from a distance. Approximately 8,000 volunteers, including sixty-five truck drivers, operate the water tanks. Volunteers test the water, fill tanks, and pick up items left in the desert by migrants such as backpacks, clothes, and water bottles in the area daily.[7] The tanks are located on federal, state, city, and private land and the organization maintains permits for all tanks placed in the desert. During my visit to Humane Borders in June 2007, one of the tanks had recently been vandalized. Stenciled across the tank in Spanish was *Peligro! No Beba El Agua* ("Danger! Do not drink the water"). The tank was removed from the desert for cleaning. During a Humane Borders meeting I attended there was speculation that the vandal may have been a member of the Minutemen.[8]

In addition to maintaining water tanks, Humane Borders has distributed maps to potential border crossers in Mexico (Lange 2006; Martinez 2006). These maps explain the dangers of the desert including the warning "Don't pay the price!" referring to the harrowing journey that lies before them. The maps plot sites for the water tanks and show places that are particularly dangerous, and instruct border crossers to avoid those areas. The maps caused a huge outcry from anti-illegal immigration groups who accused Humane Borders of providing directions on how to enter the United States clandestinely. Members of anti-illegal immigration groups sent threatening phone calls and emails to Humane Borders regarding the maps. During my interview with Frank, a volunteer from Humane Borders, he responded to what he believed was an unfounded fear from anti-illegal groups that the maps were facilitating migrants unauthorized entry into the U.S. by stating that "it's not like it's a AAA map."[9] Criticism of Humane Borders' tactics is not limited to phone and email complaints. According to Frank, the organization has received threats of violence against its members and property from anonymous groups claiming they will shoot volunteers and blow up their church.

Samaritans

Samaritans Patrol, or Samaritans, was initiated on July 1, 2002. In 2005, a second Samaritans group was formed in Green Valley, Arizona. The mission of Samaritans is to provide water, food, and medical care to migrants in distress. Unlike Humane Borders that restricts its contact with migrants to those volunteers happen upon while servicing the water tanks, Samaritans takes a more active role in seeking migrants in need of help. They do so by forming patrols, a group of at least four volunteers that includes one Spanish speaker and one trained medical provider, who walk the migrant trails. Rose, a volunteer, describes how Samaritans "go to areas where we are reasonably certain there is a lot of traffic and we start calling out in Spanish: 'Do you need help? We are Samaritans. Do not be afraid. We have food, clothing, and medical supplies.'"[10] When volunteers encounter migrants in medical need they offer to call the U.S. Border Patrol only at the migrant's request.

The group also stops on highways and other roads when they notice that the Border Patrol, or its contractor, Wackenhut Services Inc., has apprehended migrants. Volunteers report mixed responses from Border Patrol and Wackenhut agents. According to Rose, "I have had border patrol agents ask me for help with migrants with bad feet. The ones with bad feet can't walk." The bad feet that Rose referred to are the blisters and sores that migrants get from walking thirty or more miles in the desert for sometimes over a week. Volunteers provide new socks and dress migrants' feet with bandages when necessary.

Samaritans also attend court hearings for migrants who have been detained through the Department of Homeland Security's (DHS) Operation Streamline program that was established in 2005 to expedite cases of illegal immigrants who are in deportation proceedings. Samaritans also receive requests to search for specific migrants. Through their transnational networks of activists in Mexico and Central America, family members in search of lost migrants contact Samaritans in hopes that volunteers will find their missing loved one while on patrol.

Unlike Humane Borders that uses a humanitarian name, Samaritans derives its name from the New Testament story of the Good Samaritan. Luke 10:25 describes how Jesus Christ replied to the question "Who is my neighbor?" through the parable of the Good Samaritan. Jesus described a man traveling from Jerusalem to Jericho who "fell among thieves, who stripped him of his raiment, and wounded him, and departed, leaving him half dead." Jesus continues the story by describing how a priest and a Levite passed the injured man without offering to help. Then a Samaritan passed who cared for the man's wounds, found him shelter at an inn, and offered money to the host for the cost of the injured man's care. After finishing the story, Jesus turns the question back to its originator and inquires: which of the following was the man's neighbor? The questioner replies that the neighbor is the one who showed mercy. Jesus instructs his listeners to go and do likewise.

Samaritans ground their activism in this Biblical command to show compassion to those in need. Moreover, their use of this story grounds their notion of "neighbor" in compassionate activism, not geographical proximity. The use of the term "neighbor" stands in stark contrast to the term "stranger" that was often used during the Sanctuary movement (Cunningham 1995; Bau 1985). Sanctuary movement activists capitalized on the Biblical command to provide refuge for strangers. Contemporary activists, however, situate their activism in redefining the notion of neighbor.

No More Deaths

No More Deaths started in April 2004. Like Samaritans, No More Deaths orchestrates desert patrols offering water, food, and medical care for those in need. In addition to organizing patrols, No More Deaths runs two other programs. The first program is a permanent camp on private property near Arivaca, approximately twenty miles north of the U.S.-Mexico border, named The Ark of the Covenant and was initiated in 2004. This camp serves as a base from which No More Deaths volunteers patrol migrant trails that are located on the property. Unlike Samaritan patrols that involve a group of volunteers meeting at a designated location, driving to an area to patrol, and then returning home later that evening, most No More Deaths patrols originate from the Ark of the Covenant camp. Volunteers stay for days or sometimes weeks at the camp providing food and equipment at their own expense.

No More Deaths runs a second program in coalition with other Mexican humanitarian groups: an aid station in Nogales on the Mexican side of the Mariposa port of entry that began offering services to migrants in 2006. Migrants who are deported from the U.S. in the Tucson sector are usually transported by the Border Patrol or Wackenhut to the Mariposa port of entry into Mexico. The Border Patrol or Wackenhut agents park the bus adjacent to a gate and open a side door so that deported migrants are forced to exit the bus on the Mexican side of the border. Migrants then walk alongside a gate into an area where they pass the aid station. Volunteers at the aid station provide water, food, and medical care for deported migrants. According to a No More Deaths volunteer, the aid station estimates it serves between 600 to 1,000 migrants per week. The majority of those deported are young men, although the number of women and children are increasing. The day that I visited the aid station one of the deported women was six months pregnant and another woman was experiencing heart palpitations from the drugs that a smuggler had given her.[11] Smugglers often require migrants to take stimulants in order to speed up their trek across the desert.

A central activity at the aid station is caring for migrants' feet. As mentioned earlier, migrants' feet become covered in blisters and sores from walking through the desert. For faith-based activists, bandaging migrants' feet takes on religious significance as well as the practical matter of helping someone who can no longer walk. During my visit to the aid station, one volunteer expressed his work with migrants in the context of the rite of foot washing similar to the way that Jesus Christ washed feet with his apostles during the last supper.

In July 2005, No More Deaths volunteers Shanti Sellz and Daniel Strauss received national news coverage when they were arrested for transporting illegal immigrants from the Ark of the Covenant. Sellz and Strauss were escorting three migrants who were vomiting, disoriented, and had blood in their stools to a medical facility when they were pulled over by the Arizona Border Patrol (Martinez 2005). They were charged with transporting illegal aliens and the migrants were placed into deportation proceedings. According to Section 274 8 U.S.C. 1324 of the U.S. Code, it is a felony to transport undocumented migrants. Their case was dismissed in September 2006. Like their Sanctuary Movement predecessors, border activists in the new millennium also face potential prison sentences for helping migrants in need of medical care. This incident sparked a new campaign for No More Deaths that now advocates the slogan "Humanitarian Aid Is Never a Crime," paralleling Holocaust survivor Elie Wiesel's plea that "No Human Being is Illegal" (Chmiel 2001).

Although these organizations operate independently of one another, there are a significant number of members who work among the groups. For example, when Sellz and Strauss were arrested after leaving No More Deaths' Ark of the Covenant camp, they were driving a vehicle owned by Samaritans. When I inquired why volunteers become involved in these groups activists would often give me personalized accounts of various tragedies in the desert. However, unlike during the Sanctuary movement when the stories that propelled faith-based communities into activism were widely-circulated events, the stories that contemporary groups linked their activism to, such as hearing about a migrant's death in a local paper, often never made national media coverage. Frank, a member of Humane Borders, described how each of these groups developed: "For each group it was a small number of people who kept asking 'what more can we do to keep people from dying'?" Each group is independent of the other, yet they all work toward the common goal of alleviating suffering for migrants in the desert.

Gender, Faith-Based Activism and the New Border Crisis

At least five shifts have taken place between the 1980 Central American refugee crises and the new millennium border tragedy. These shifts are the gendered dynamics of border crossers and border activists, migrants' motivation for leaving their country, the ways in which migrants experience violence and injury regarding movement across borders, volunteers' motivation for action, and the use of the terms "stranger" and "neighbor" to justify activism.

The greatest gendered change in the new border crisis is the increase of women who cross and die in the desert. One of the effects of the militarization of the U.S.-Mexico border is an increase in violence for female migrants. Female migrants are subject to sexual assault including rape and forced prostitution to pay their smugglers' fees. Another gendered phenomenon is the demographic of the volunteers and leaders of humanitarian groups. Like Sanctuary movement volunteers, the rank and file members of these organizations are mostly female. Yet, compared to the Sanctuary movement, women have taken on greater leadership roles in contemporary organizations. While the media continues to portray Revered John Fife and Reverend Robin Hoover as the leaders/founders of these organizations, it pays far more attention to the efforts of women in the pro-immigrant movement. This may be attributed to the increase in female leadership positions of organizations, such as *Coalición de Derechos Humanos* and Border Action Network.

The second difference is that migrants' motivation for crossing the U.S.-Mexico border has shifted from fleeing human rights abuses committed by their government to migrants leaving their countries in search of work. In the 1980s, INS refused many Central American applications for asylum on the grounds that the applicant was leaving for economic reasons rather than political. According to Citizen and Immigration Services (CIS) policies, Mexican migrants who come to the U.S. in search of work are ineligible to apply for asylum because lack of employment opportunities does not meet the criteria for fleeing persecution.[12] Sanctuary movement activists had a legitimate complaint against the U.S. government for denying Central Americans asylum. Current faith-based activists cannot rightfully argue that the U.S. government is applying its immigration laws unfairly because Mexican migrants are economic migrants, not refugees.

The third shift is how migrants experience violence and injury regarding movement across borders. In the 1980s, Central Americans were overwhelmingly tortured in their own country, causing them to flee. The location where the harm took place was outside of the United States. Currently, the harm overwhelmingly takes place on the U.S. side of the border. Pro-immigrant activists argue that the border is not a line between two countries, but instead a region that includes whole communities. Crossing the "line" that demarcates Mexico from the United States in southern Arizona is relatively easy compared to the journey from the U.S. side of the border to the migrants' destination. One shift from the 1980s to the present is that in the past the abuse was perpetrated by Central American governments which caused people to flee. Currently, the cause of most migrants' deaths is the act of migration itself.

The fourth variation between Sanctuary movement activists and contemporary faith-based activists is that pro-migrant advocates trace their involvement in these groups to a desire to change a generalized border crisis rather than publicized events like those that galvanized supporters of Central American refugees, such as the assassination of Archbishop Oscar Romero. The volunteers I interviewed often told personal accounts of why they entered this movement, such as how their religious beliefs regarding helping others mandated their activism. Members of faith-based groups overwhelmingly contextualize their motives by referencing the number of migrant deaths as the impetus to their activism—making the amalgamation of border fatalities rather than any one particular instance as the root cause of why they joined a faith-based group. Therefore, none of their stories were linked to an event that had received international or national attention such as those during the Sanctuary movement.

The last distinction is the use of the term "neighbor" rather than "stranger." During the Sanctuary movement, activists from many different faiths deployed the term stranger in order to justify their defiance of U.S. immigration laws that defined Central Americans as economic migrants rather than refugees. Contemporary faith-based activists rely on a transnational notion of neighbor that defines themselves as neighbors to migrants in need because of their plight rather than geographical location. According to this definition of neighbor, actions rather than physical proximity define social relationships.

The consequences of these shifts in migration patterns for contemporary faith-based activists is that their activism addresses gendered violence, the causes of migration which includes a critique of U.S. corporations and international treaties such as NAFTA, as well as the U.S.-backed militarization of the border, and nation-state responsibility for violence and injury that occurs within its borders.

Conclusion

This chapter contributes to the field of gender, religion, and migration studies because it examines the increase of women crossing the U.S.-Mexico border and the gendered character of faith-based responses to illegal immigration. I have provided a gendered analysis of border crossers, activists, and institutions, in addition to the ways in which gender structures the geopolitical climate that gives rise to illegal immigration at the U.S. southern border. This analysis shows how illegal immigration is deeply structured by gender, race, class, and nation. This intersectional approach to social life is useful as well for understanding the ways in which faith-based activists understand their responses to the new border crisis.

Faith-based groups are often the first point of contact with illegal immigrants crossing the Sonora desert. These groups are the initial site of integration for illegal immigrants rather than state agencies. Faith-based groups, therefore, stand in opposition to the nation-state regarding the facilitation and welcoming of illegal immigrants. Contemporary pro-immigrant faith-based activists in southern Arizona do much more than simply provide water and medical attention to migrants in the desert. They stand in opposition to the laws and policies of the U.S. government and practices of U.S. corporations that have created a catastrophe for migrants crossing the border. And they do so because their activism is driven by the belief that a greater commandment than U.S. immigration law requires human beings to act with compassion and mercy toward all human suffering.

Notes

1. This paper is part of a research project on responses to illegal immigration and border activism in the United States. I collected data through qualitative methods using in-depth interviews and participant observation of faith-based groups in Tucson, Arizona. Using a semi-structured interview guide, I interviewed members of three faith-based groups, Humane Borders, Samaritans, and No More Deaths, and two pro-immigrant groups, *Coalición de Derechos Humanos* (The Human Rights Coalition) and Border Action Network. I also participated in these groups' activities which include filling water tanks and bottles, walking migrant trails in search of those in distress, and caring for migrants who are deported at the Mexican border, as well as attending meetings and events sponsored by these organizations. All interviews and references to participant observation of these groups were conducted on June 11-22, 2007.

2. Pima County is one of four border counties in Arizona.

3. Some minors do travel alone. For example, Nazzario documents a young Honduran boy who crosses many borders in order to find his mother in the U.S. See Sandra Nazzario, *Enrique's Journey* (New York: Random House, 2006).

4. These rape trees do exist; I saw one on the migrant trails on private property in Arizona. However, there are no definitive sources that attribute bushes with women's underwear to sites of sexual violence. During my phone interview with a sexual assault counselor for immigrant women in Arizona on June 21, 2007, she told me that while none of her clients had described the trees, nearly all had confided at least one sexual assault during their passage across the border.

5. Interview was conducted on June 19, 2007.

6. There are numerous organizations in southern Arizona that work with migrants and border communities. I focus on these three because they are explicitly faith-based.

7. The language of belongings/trash is highly politicized at the border. Pro-immigrant groups such as those discussed in this chapter are critical of the term "trash" to describe the things that migrants discard in the desert. Anti-illegal immigrant groups refer to these items as trash.

8. The organization they referred to is the Minutemen Civil Defense Corp (MCDC), an anti-illegal immigration group that operates border patrols on private property in southern Arizona and alerts the U.S. Border Patrol when they encounter migrants. This meeting occurred on June 13, 2007.

9. All interviewee names are pseudonyms. Interview was conducted on June 19, 2007.

10. Interview was conducted on June 11, 2007.

11. I observed this on June 12, 2007. All references to the No More Deaths Aid Station occurred on this date.

12. Some Mexicans are eligible for asylum such as those who claim persecution because of domestic violence or sexual orientation. In May 2008, Mexican law enforcement personnel applied for asylum because they were targeted by the drug cartels. See James McKinley Jr., "Mexico: Police Chiefs Seek Asylum," *The New York Times*, May 15, 2008, 11.

Bibliography

Andreas, Peter. *Border Games: Policing the U.S.-Mexico Divide*. Ithaca, NY: Cornell University Press, 2000.

Bau, Ignatius. *This Ground is Holy: Church Sanctuary and Central American Refugees*. New York: Paulist Press, 1985.

Bean, Frank, Roland Chanove, Robert Cushing, Rodolfo de la Garza, Gary Freeman, Charles Haynes and David Spener. *Illegal Mexican Migration and The United States/Mexico Border: The Effects of Operation Hold-the-Line on ElPaso/Juarez*. Washington, DC: U.S. Commission on Immigration Reform, 1994.

Castles, Stephen and Mark J. Miller. *The Age of Migration: International Population Movements in the Modern World,* 3rd ed. New York: Guilford Press, 2003.

Chmiel, Mark. *Elie Wiesel and the Politics of Moral Leadership*. Philadelphia, PA: Temple University Press, 2001.

Corbett, Jim. *Goatwalking*. New York: Viking, 1991.

Crittenden, Ann. *Sanctuary: A Story of American Conscience and the Law in Collision*. New York: Weidenfeld and Nicolson, 1988.

Cunningham, Hilary. *God and Caesar at the Rio Grande: Sanctuary and the Politics of Religion*. Minneapolis: University of Minnesota Press, 1995.

Davidson, Miriam. *Convictions of the Heart: Jim Corbett and the Sanctuary Movement*. Tucson: University of Arizona Press, 1988.

Golden, Renny and Michael McConnell. *Sanctuary: The New Underground Railroad*. Maryknoll, NY: Underground Books, 1986.

Hondagneu-Sotelo, Pierrette, ed. *Gender and U.S. Immigration: Contemporary Trends*. Berkeley: University of California Press, 2003.

———. *Domestica: Immigrant Workers Cleaning and Caring in the Shadows of Affluence,* 2nd ed. University of California Press, 2001.

Hondagneu-Sotelo, Pierette and Ernestine Avila. "I'm Here, But I'm There: The Meanings of Transnational Motherhood." *Gender and Society* 11, no. 5 (1997): 548-571.

Kyle, David and Rey Koslowski, eds. *Global Human Smuggling: Comparative Perspectives*. Baltimore, Maryland: Johns Hopkins University Press, 2001.

Lange, Jason. "Rights Groups Distribute Maps for Mexicans Crossing into Arizona," *National Catholic Reporter*, February 17, 2006, 8.

Loder, Ted. *No One But Us: Personal Reflections on Public Sanctuary by an Offspring of Jacob*. San Diego, CA: Lura Media, 1986.

Lorentzen, Robin. *Women in the Sanctuary Movement*. Philadelphia: Temple University Press, 1991.

Martinez, Demetria. "Maps for Migrants are Placed on Hold," *National Catholic Reporter*, April 26, 2006, 16.

———. "College Students Prosecuted for Assisting in Desert," *National Catholic Reporter*, September 2, 2005, 19.

McKinley, James C. Jr. "Mexico: Police Chiefs Seek Asylum," *The New York Times*, May 15, 2008, 11.

Moser, Bob. "Samaritans in the Desert," *The Nation*, May 26, 2003, 13-18.

Nazzario, Sandra. *Enrique's Journey.* New York: Random House, 2006.

Nepstad, Sharon Erikson. "Creating Transnational Solidarity: The Use of Narrative in the U.S.-Central America Peace Movement." Pp. 133-149 in *Globalization and Resistance: Transnational Dimensions of Social Movements*, edited by Jackie Smith and Hank Johnston. Lanham, MD: Rowman & Littlefield, 2002.

Nevins, Joseph. *Operation Gatekeeper: The Rise of the "Illegal Alien" and the Remaking of the U.S.-Mexico Boundary.* New York: Routledge, 2002.

Passel, Jeffrey S. *Estimates of the Size and Characteristics of the Undocumented Population.* Washington DC: The Pew Hispanic Center, 2005.

Pessar, Patricia R. and Sarah J. Mahler. "Transnational Migration: Bringing Gender In." *International Migration Review* 37, no. 3 (October 2003): 812-846.

Portes, Alejandro and Rubén G. Rumbault. *Immigrant America: A Portrait.* Berkeley: University of California Press, 2006.

Rader, Victoria. "Refugees at Risk: The Sanctuary Movement and Its Aftermath." Pp. 325-345 in *Illegal Immigration in America: A Reference Handbook*, edited by David W. Haines and Karen E. Rosenblum. Westport: CT: Greenwood Press, 1999.

Ramos, Jorge. *Dying to Cross: The Worst Immigration Tragedy in American History.* New York: Rayo, 2005.

Rubio-Goldsmith, Raquel, M. Melissa McCormick, Daniel Martinez, Inez Magdalena Duarte. "The "Funnel Effect" and Recovered Bodies of Unauthorized Migrants Processed by the Pima County Office of the Medical Examiner, 1990- 2005." Binational Migration Institute, University of Arizona, October 2006. http://immigration.server263.com/images/File/brief/Full %20BMI%20Report.pdf (accessed December 12, 2008).

Scharf, Daniel A. "For Humane Borders: Two Decades of Death and Illegal Activity in the Sonoran Desert." *Case Western Reserve Journal of International Law* 38, no. 1 (2006): 141-172.

Segura, Denise A. and Patricia Zavella, eds. *Women and Migration in the U.S.-Mexico Borderlands: A Reader.* Durham, NC: Duke University Press, 2007.

Thompson, Becky. *A Promise and a Way of Life: White Antiracist Activism.* Minneapolis: University of Minnesota Press, 2001.

Tomsmo, Robert. *The American Sanctuary Movement.* Austin: Texas Monthly Press, 1987.

Urrea, Luis Alberto. *The Devil's Highway: A True Story.* New York: Little Brown, 2004.

Contributors

Vivienne SM. Angeles teaches Dynamics of Religion and courses on Islam at La Salle University in Philadelphia. She holds a PhD in Religious Studies, major in Islamic Studies from Temple University. She is an affiliate of the Harvard University Pluralism Project and has published on Muslim movements and Muslim women in the Philippines and Southeast Asia. Her current research is on visual expressions of Islam in the Philippines and Malaysia. She received a Lindback Minority Faculty research grant in 2004 and a Fulbright research and lecture grant to Malaysia in 2007. She was president of the American Council for the Study of Islamic Societies in 2006-2008.

Michiel Baas commenced in the doctoral (masters) Program in Cultural Anthropology and Non-western Sociology at the University of Amsterdam in 2000. He conducted a research among the IT professionals of Bangalore, India for his MA thesis and graduated cum laude in December 2003. He was a PhD candidate at the Amsterdam School for Social Science Research from 2004-2008. His dissertation is entitled *Imagined Mobility: Migration and Transnationalism among Indian Students in Australia* and has published papers on the topic since then. He is the Branch Office Coordinator of the International Institute for Asian Studies in Amsterdam.

Synnøve Bendixsen is a lecturer in Social Anthropology at the University of Kurdistan-Hewler. Her PhD thesis focused on the religious identity of young female Muslims in Berlin at the European Ethnology, Humboldt University (Berlin) and social anthropology at Ecole des Hautes Etudes en Sciences Sociales (Paris). She was a DFG-Fellow at the Transatlantisches Graduiertenkolleg Berlin–New York, based at the Center for Metropolitan Studies (Berlin) from 2005 to 2007. She has been a visiting scholar at the Department of Sociology of New York University and was a consultant for the Section of International Migration and Multicultural Policies of UNESCO (Paris). She specialized in the field of migration at the Institute des Sciences Sociales in Paris after completing her Master's of Science at the London School of Economics and Social Science (UK) in 2001. Some of her works on Muslim women were published in *Informationen zur modernen Stadtgeschichte* (2007), *Islamisches Gemeindeleben in Berlin* (2006), *Berliner Blätter* (2005), and the *Journal of Policy Analysis and Management* (2003).

Krystyna M. Błeszyńska is a professor at the University of Life Sciences, Warsaw. She was born and raised in Poland, and currently divides her time between Warsaw and San Francisco. She received her PhD and postdoctoral degree (habilitation) from Warsaw University and served as an Associate Professor at the School of Education, Warsaw University. She was a Visiting Professor and researcher at various universities in United States and Europe; adviser and reviewer for Polish and foreign governmental and non-governmental organizations; and a board member of the International Association for

Intercultural Education. She received fellowships and research grants from Kosciuszko Foundation, Soros Foundation, and Warsaw University. She was the founder and the first director of the first counseling and training center for immigrants and refugees in Poland. Her research interests relate to psychology and sociology of migrations, diverse societies, immigrants and refugees, transnational communities, ethnic enclaves and inner cities, intergroup relations, intercultural education and counseling.

Glenda Tibe Bonifacio is an Assistant Professor in Women's Studies at the University of Lethbridge, Canada. She completed her PhD from the School of History and Politics at the University of Wollongong, Australia; her BA in Social Science (Political Science) and MA in Asian Studies from the University of the Philippines where she taught for several years prior to migrating to Australia and then Canada. Some of her works on Filipino women and migration have been published in the *Asian and Pacific Migration Journal, Review of Women's Studies*, and *Asian Women*; book chapters in *Doing Democracy: Striving for Political Literacy and Social Justice* (2008) and *Resistance and Revolution: Philippine Archipelago in Arms* (2002). Her current research project centers on migration, identity and community of Filipino women in Canada.

Cristina Maria de Castro is a postdoctoral fellow and collaborator professor at the Universidade Federal de São Carlos (UFSCar) in Brazil. She teaches Sociology of Religion at the Postgraduate Program in Sociology in UFSCar where she obtained her PhD in 2007. Her research focuses on the production of Islamic knowledge and its practice in Brazil in cooperation with the International Institute for the Study of Islam in the Modern World (ISIM) based in Leiden, The Netherlands, from 2007 to 2008. She was a visiting researcher at ISIM in 2005 and 2007 under the supervision of Prof. Abdulkader Tayob and Prof. Martin van Bruinessen, respectively. In the same week of her thesis defense, she was accepted to a very competitive program for new PhDs in one of the most renowned research institutions in Brazil, the Brazilian Centre for Analysis and Planning (CEBRAP). Some of her forthcoming works on Muslims in Brazil are included in *The Sociology of Islam and Muslim Societies: Secularism, Economy and Politics* and *Review Hommes et Migrations*.

Wafa Chafic is a registered psychologist, and a PhD candidate at the University of Technology Sydney (UTS) where she also teaches in the Faculty of Arts and Social Sciences. Her research examines the social construction of the masculine "other" in Australian society. She has worked for many years in the south western region of Sydney as counselor, teacher, or caseworker for people from disadvantaged backgrounds and "at-risk" youth. Her recent project includes a research report on recently arrived Muslim men to the Auburn Migrant Resource Centre in 2008. In 2007, she evaluated the efficacy of a vocational education and training program for young Australians of Arabic background at TAFE NSW. She was honorary consultant to the Multiculturalism and the Law review conducted by the Australian Law Reform Commission, a member of the Gulf

Crisis Special Reference Group, and was appointed to the inaugural NSW Advisory Council on Migrant Settlement in 1992.

Hugo Córdova Quero is a visiting researcher at the Ibero-American Institute at Sophia University in Tokyo, Japan; and adjunct faculty at Starr King School for the Ministry, Graduate Theological Union at Berkeley, California. He holds a Master in Divinity from Instituto Superior Evangélico de Estudios Teológicos (ISDET University) in Buenos Aires, Argentina, an MA in Queer Theology and (post) Colonial Studies (2003), and PhD in Interdisciplinary Studies in Religion and Ethnic Studies (2009) both from the Graduate Theological Union at Berkeley. He was professor of Ecumenism at Santa María de Guadalupe Seminary (Roman Catholic Church) in Buenos Aires, and coordinator of EDUCAB (Educación Abierta), the Department of Education by Extension at ISEDET University, and visiting scholar at the Institute for Advanced Study in Asian Cultures and Theologies (IASACT), Chung Chi College at the Chinese University of Hong Kong. His most recent research examines the experiences of queer migrants in and from Asia as well as the intersection of gender and issues of migration among Latina/o migrants in Japan.

Gemma Tulud Cruz is Visiting Assistant Professor in the Program in Catholic Studies at DePaul University in Chicago, Illinois. She holds a PhD in Intercultural Theology from Radboud Universiteit Nijmegen in The Netherlands. Migration, particularly its intersection with gender and religion, is her ongoing research interest. Her essay, "One Bread, One Body, One People: The Challenges of Migration to Theological Reflection" was awarded the Best Academic Essay in Theology by the Catholic Theological Society of America in 2005. Her recent publications include "Christendom on the Move: The Case of the Filipina Domestic Workers in Hong Kong," in *Global Christianity: Contested Claims* and "Between Identity and Security: Migration in the Context of Globalization" in *Theological Studies*. She has served as a consultant, paper presenter, and moderator in various conferences in Asia, Europe, and the United States.

Gertrud Hüwelmeier is an anthropologist and senior researcher at Humboldt University Berlin. She has worked on religion, gender and transnationalism for many years and conducted fieldwork among Catholic sisters in Europe, the United States and India. She is the current director of a research project on "Transnational Networks, Religion and New Migration," focusing on Vietnamese and Ghanaian migrants. She has forthcoming articles on "Spirits in the Market Place—Transnational Networks of Vietnamese Migrants in Berlin" in *Transnational Ties: Cities, Identities, and Migrations*, "Women's Congregations as Transnational Networks of Social Security" in *Social Security in Religious Networks: Changes in Meanings, Contents and Functions*, and "Global Sisterhood: Transnational Perspectives on Gender and Religion" in *Untangling Modernities: Gendering Religion and Politics*.

Helene Pristed Nielsen is a postdoctoral fellow at Aalborg University Denmark. Graduating from Aarhus University in 2002 with a humanities degree in English and philosophy, her interest in political philosophy and sociology has given inspiration for research projects on the intersections between humanities and social science. Specializing in democracy and minority participation, she has previously published on the inclusion of indigenous minorities in Australia and New Zealand as well as participation of immigrant minorities in Denmark. Her doctoral thesis is entitled *Deliberative Democracy and Minority Inclusion in Australia and New Zealand* with data collected during stays as visiting researcher at Murdoch University, Western Australia and The Stout Research Centre at Victoria University, New Zealand in 2004. Her recent publications include "Education, Democracy and Minority Inclusion" in *Journal of New Zealand Studies* (2007), and "Multicultural Feminism in Denmark and Norway?" with Cecilie Thun, University of Oslo in *Kvinder, Køn og Forskning* (forthcoming). She is involved in the large scale European research project, "EUROSPHERE—Diversity and the European Public Sphere, Towards a Citizens' Europe," 2007-2012.

Lilian Odera is a licensed clinical psychologist at the Counseling and Psychological Services Center at Florida International University in Miami, Florida. She completed her doctoral work in the Clinical Psychology Program at the University of Michigan at Ann Arbor, and postdoctoral residency at Florida International University. She is involved in teaching, clinical activities, diversity outreach events, multicultural seminars, and immigration research. Her research interests include immigrant health with a focus on the acculturative processes, stressors, and health outcomes among non-American Black immigrants in the United States; the role of social support, spirituality, religiosity, and religious coping strategies in the cultural adjustment of immigrants in the United States; the mental health of ethnic minority college students and how they navigate cultural stressors; the help-seeking behaviors of individuals from ethnic minority groups' experience of trauma and how they express psychological distress.

Abolade Ezekiel Olagoke is a native of Nigeria currently residing in the United States. He finished his doctoral degree at the Iliff School of Theology in Religion and Social Change, University of Denver. At present, he is an Assistant Professor of Sociology at Waynesburg University in Pennsylvania. Previously, he was a Visiting Assistant Professor of Sociology at Taylor University, IN, and until August of 2008, an adjunct Professor of Sociology at Arapahoe Community College in Littleton, Colorado. He participated in three summer programs at Oxford and Cambridge University on Religion and the Public Sphere; Life and works of C.S. Lewis, and Religion and Violence—Rene Girard's Mimetic Theory. He is deeply involved in the dynamics of religion and the public sphere especially after September 11, 2001. Some of his works were published in *Religion, Culture, Curriculum and Diversity in 21st Century*

America (2007) and *The Language of Diversity: Restoration Toward Peace and Unity* (2008).

Connie Oxford is an Assistant Professor of Women's Studies at the State University of New York, Plattsburgh. She received a PhD in Sociology and doctoral Women's Studies certificate from the University of Pittsburgh in 2006. She is working on a manuscript entitled *Fleeing Gendered Harm: Seeking Asylum in America.* Among her publications are "Protectors and Victims in the Gender Regime of Asylum," *National Women's Studies Association Journal,* and two book chapters, "Acts of Resistance in Asylum Seekers' Persecution Narratives," in *Immigrant Rights in the Shadows of United States Citizenship,* and "Changing The Research Question: Lessons from Qualitative Research," in *Research Methods Choices in Interdisciplinary Contexts.* She also has a forthcoming book chapter "Gendered Suspects: Immigration Practices after 9/11," in *The Politics of Populations.* Her most recent research project is a study of the anti-illegal immigration movement and right-wing activism in the United States. She is a fellow at the Institute for Ethics in Public Life at the State University of New York, Plattsburgh.

Patricia Ruiz-Navarro is a PhD candidate in the Social Psychology program at the Graduate Center, City University of New York (CUNY). Currently, her research interests include the study of gender and immigration, transnationalism, and immigrants' lives and identities. She graduated from the Universidad de las Americas in Puebla, Mexico with a degree in psychology. She was granted a Fullbright scholarship to study for an MA in Psychology at the New School for Social Research in New York. She worked at the International Center for Migration, Ethnicity and Citizenship (ICMEC), and collaborated on a multiyear project about religious incorporation of multi-cultural immigrant groups in New York, funded by the Pew Charitable Trust. Her dissertation explores how personal, social, economic and institutional factors influence migrant mothers' orientation to homeland with a grant from a Mellon Dissertation Fellowship in 2009.

Sonia Ben Soltane is a PhD candidate in Urbanism and Space Renovation at the Institut d'Urbanisme et d'Aménagement Régional of Aix-en-Provence (Université Paul Cézanne). Her thesis presents a study of North African female immigrants' urban practices and citizenship in Marseille. She holds a bachelor's degree in Private Judicial Law (1999) from Faculté de Droit et des Sciences Politiques de Tunis (Tunisia); a master's degree in Urbanism and Space Renovation at ENAU (Ecole Nationale d'Architecture et d'Urbanisme, de Tunis) with high honors in 2004. She also completed a master's degree in Legal Theory and Philosophy with honors at the Université de Droit d'Économie et des Sciences d'Aix-Marseille III in 2003. She is a researcher at CIRTA, University Paul Cézanne Aix-Marseille III and collaborated with some projects like the Empowerment and Migration group. She is also a member of Les Femmes et la Ville at Marseille.

Jamel Stambouli is a PhD candidate in Human and Economical Geography at the Université Paris Ouest Nanterre La Défense. He received a BS in Management at the Faculté des Sciences Economiques et de Gestion de Tunis in 1999. He completed an MA in Urban and Regional Planning at Institut d'Urbanisme et d'Aménagement Régional d'Aix en Provence in 2004. His interests center on international trade, migration, ethnic business and religion.

Marek Szopski is an adjunct faculty at the English Institute of Warsaw University. He collaborates with the Intercultural Psychology Institute of the Warsaw School of Social Psychology, ASU in North Carolina and Notre Dame University, Indiana. He obtained an MA from the Warsaw University, and PhD at the Notre Dame University, USA. His research interests include social theory, sociology of intercultural relations, sociology of culture and intercultural communication, theory of translation and intercultural education. He is the coordinator of the Center for Refugees and Immigrants funded by the European Union, and founder of Multi-Culti partnership. In 2005, he published a Polish handbook of Intercultural Communication. He is a member of the Polish-American advisory group at Warsaw University. He is also a translator, a publicist and commentator.

Index

Abesamis, Marilen, 20
Abu-Lughod, Janet, 238
acculturation, 6, 187, 191, 195, 200-
    211; American, 205, 208, 212;
    among Kenyans, 11; and gender,
    211; and transnationalism, 207,
    210; and women, 201; bicultural,
    212, 210; scales of, 201
adaptation, 6, 187
Afonja, Simi, 220-221
Africa, 115-116, 126
Ahmad, Kasem, 137
Alberta, 264-268
Al-Hilali, Sheikh, Mufti of Australia,
    57, 67n4
Allah, 98
Al-Mizani, Hamza, 164n32
Al Qaradawi, 103, 110n20
Al Qaeda, 2
Althus-Reid, Marcella, 45-46
Ami, Hiroko, 44
Andersen, Jørgen Gaul, 134
Andreassen, Rikke, 134
anti-racism, practice of, 65
Antone, Hope, 19-20
Antorcha Guadalupana, 241-243, 246,
    248
Appadurai, Arjun, 3, 5
Arab, 173
Argentina, 169
Arizona, 275
Asad, Talal, 4, 99
Asia, 1, 10, 18, 47, 115, 126, 264
Asian Migrant Coordinating Body
    (AMCB), 21
Asis, Maruja, 257
assimilation, 7, 188, 200, 251
Associación Tepeyac, 240-248
atheism, 222
Auburn Migrant Resource Center, 55
Australia: and belonging, 61-63, 87;
    citizenship, 55-57; Cronulla Riot,
    57, 63, 67n5; Department of
    Immigration and Multicultural
    Affairs (DMIA), 78; education in,
    73, 76, 79-80, 87-88, 90n2; Gang
    Rapes, 57, 67n1, 63; Indian
    community in, 82-83, 85; Indian

students in, 71-75, 77-80, 82-84,
    86-88; media, 63; Migration
    Occupation in Demand (MODL),
    78; migration to, 77, 84; Muslims
    in, 55-67, 72; permanent residency
    in, 71-72, 78-80, 85, 87-88, 90n8;
    student loans, 74; Tampa incident,
    57, 67n2; values, 58-59; White
    Australia policy, 82
Awe, Bolanle, 220
Azada, Jocelyn Eclarin, 268

Baas, Michiel, 10, 71, 80, 82
Baduel, Pierre Robert, 150
Batnitzky, Adin Keryn, 76-77
Baumann, Martin, 1, 6, 107, 117
Bautista, Tina, 25
Begag, Azouz, 161
Benavides, Gustavo, 240
Bendixen, Synnøve, 10, 101, 103-104
Berry, John, 200
Bergeaud-Blackler, Florence, 155-156
Bessis, Sophie, 153-154, 164
Bible, 25, 32, 115, 121-123, 185, 222,
    226-227, 232n1, 233n3, 262, 282-
    283
Bhabha, Homi, 102, 110n17
Bonifacio, Glenda, 267
Boucher, Anna, 75
Boukhobza, Noria, 162n15, 164n28
Bourdie, Pierre, 148, 161n5
Bracke, Sarah, 111n28
brain drain, 17-18
Brazil: Christians in, 168; immigrants
    in, 167-170; Indian Gujarati in,
    174; Islamic Center of Campinas,
    173-175; Islamic Youth League in,
    168, 170-173; Japanese in, 38;
    labor recruitment, 169; Lebanese
    merchants, 169-170; Lebanese
    Muslims in, 170-173; Lebanese
    women in, 169; Libyans in, 174;
    migration to, 179n4; military
    dictatorship in, 38; Mozambicans
    in, 174; Muslims in, 167-179;
    South Africans in, 173; State
    University of Campinas (Unicamp)
    in, 173-174, 179n6; Syrian-

297

Breinigsville, PA USA
20 April 2010

236485BV00004B/2/P